The Life of Henry Morley, LL.D., Professor of the English Language and Literature at University College, London

4/

4/

THE LIFE

OF

HENRY MORLEY, LL.D.

Henry Morley

THE LIFE

OF

HENRY MORLEY, LL.D.

Professor of the English Language and Literature
at University College, London.

BY

HENRY SHAEN SOLLY, M.A.

EDWARD ARNOLD
37 BEDFORD STREET, LONDON
1898

THE LIFE

OF

HENRY MORLEY, LL.D.

Professor of the English Language and Literature
at University College, London

BY

HENRY SHAEN SOLLY, M.A.

EDWARD ARNOLD
37 BEDFORD STREET, LONDON
1898

DEDICATED

TO

MY WIFE,

IN MEMORY OF

OUR LOVE AND ADMIRATION

FOR

HER FATHER.

PREFACE

—◦◦◦—

IN the autumn of 1894 the executors of the late Henry
Morley placed in my hands all the family papers which
were thought to be of biographical interest. Examination
of these proved that it would be possible to tell the story
of his early life in his own words, and with sufficient detail
to exhibit the development of his mind and character.
To have fully carried out this plan would, however, have
required two substantial volumes instead of one, and much
compression has been exercised in the first part of the
book. But all his letters have been carefully read, and,
as far as possible, they have been left to convey their own
message.

For the second part I have had to gather materials from
many sources, and thanks are due to Professors Arber
and Moyse, to the Rev. H. E. Dowson and the Rev.
L. P. Jacks, to Miss Day, Miss Buckland, Miss Shipley,
and Miss Morison, to Mr. B. P. Neuman, Dr. James
Gairdner, Mr. H. R. Fox Bourne, Mr. E. W. B. Nicholson,
Dr. H. Bond, Mr. T. Gregory Foster, and others, for the
contributions they have made to these pages.   Their
testimony includes some record of the impression made

by the oral teaching to which Professor Morley devoted so much of his time and strength.

With regard to his own writings, they remain to speak for themselves, and finally attain their rightful place, whatever that may be, in our English literature. I have tried to bear in mind his conviction that a book is part of the man who writes it, and that to understand the book we should know the man.

The Life furnishes a remarkable record of work accomplished. It also tells a tale of incompleteness and hopes unfulfilled. Its chief worth will probably be found in its testimony to the brave, loving spirit in which so many high aims were sought and so much faithful service rendered.

BRIDPORT,
    February, 1898.

TABLE OF CONTENTS

PART I.

LEARNING LESSONS.

CHAPTER I.

GENEALOGICAL.

CHAPTER II.

FRAGMENTS OF AUTOBIOGRAPHY, 1822—1832.

CHAPTER III.

NEUWIED, 1833—1835.

CHAPTER IV.

FROM SCHOOL TO COLLEGE, 1835—1842.

THE LIFE OF HENRY MORLEY

PART I.

LEARNING LESSONS.

CHAPTER I.

GENEALOGICAL.

HENRY MORLEY was born September 15, 1822. His ancestry may be traced back without difficulty for several generations, after which there is a probable connection with the Morleys of Halnaker, Sussex.

His father was Henry Morley, born at Lichfield, September 19, 1793; died December 29, 1877.

His father was William, born September 12, 1754, at Stoke Aubernon, Surrey; died January 1, 1810; married January 29, 1788, Alice Abbott, of Canterbury, who died October 4, 1851. He had an elder brother, Robert, born October 11, 1748, died September 26, 1807, who had a daughter, Anne. This Anne Morley married a Mr. Kendall, and was in 1838 a widow living at Lisson Grove, London; of her more anon.

His father was Robert, born 1720, at Haslemere, Surrey; died September 26, 1807, and buried at Farnham. He married February 2, 1747, Ann, daughter of Benjamin Kemp, a blacksmith, of Midhurst. This Robert was the seventh child of a family of nine, his eldest brother being William. He was first a schoolmaster at Haslemere, afterwards wharfinger at Stoke Aubernon, then land steward to Mr. Richardson, Molland House, Hants, and finally a schoolmaster again at Farnham.

His father was William, baptized December 25, 1690, at Haslemere, and buried there September 4, 1748. He was married at Rogate, on October 13, 1710, to Mary Urry, of East Harting. He was a glover and ' britches' maker, Haslemere being at that time noted for its leather industries, and supporting several tanneries. He was also parish clerk, being appointed to the office when only fifteen years old, probably on account of the excellence of his handwriting. He used the blank pages of one of the registers as a memorandum-book, making entries concerning the domestic arrangements of his dog and other live stock, also of a bill against William Figg, who, besides owing for gloves and buckskin 'britches,' is charged two shillings for two years' ' clark's waiges,' probably his rateable contribution.

His father and mother were William and Ann Morley, who are the first to appear at Haslemere. Where they came from is not clear, but they had connections at Singleton, between Midhurst and Chichester. He was a land surveyor, and came to Haslemere to look after the interests of the Mores of Loseley, lords of the manor. The borough then returned two members to Parliament, and a sharp look-out was kept as to boundaries.

There are extant some good maps of the borough by William Morley, senior and junior, from 1720 to 1758, also a land surveyor's rule which belonged to them.

The next question is: Was this William Morley one of the Morleys of Halnaker, Sussex? There is no absolute proof of this, but there is a curious bit of evidence in its favour. The Halnaker estates having passed by will into the hands of Sir Thomas Dyke Acland, Bart., were

by him sold to the Duke of Richmond in 1765 for £48,000.
Now, an agent of the Duke of Richmond paid £20 to the
Mrs. Kendall mentioned above in return for her renouncing
all claim to these estates. She was certainly the heir of
the Robert Morley born 1720; and if his elder brothers
and sisters left no descendants, she might well be the heir
of our earliest William Morley; and possibly there may
be an interesting romance dealing with disinheritance and
other freaks of fortune, which some future biographer may
disinter. The family tradition gives a descent from a
brother of the Sir William Morley who is buried in
Boxgrove Church, near Chichester.

The Manor of Halnaker was granted by Henry I. to
Ralph de Haia. It passed by marriage to Roger de
St. John, and thence to the wife of Sir Thomas West,
who rebuilt the house in the reign of Henry VIII. He
filled the windows with armorial glass, and had the arms
of the West family and those of their relatives extensively
carved on the wainscoting. Halnaker fell as Goodwood
rose : it was turned into tenements for cottagers, and was
finally destroyed by fire; but remains of the glass and
wood carvings are to be found in Chichester houses.

In Queen Elizabeth's time the manor had become
vested in the Crown, and by her it was granted to Sir
John Morley, Knight, of Saxham, Suffolk, at an annual
rent of £66 4s. 6d. His grandson was the above-named
Sir William Morley, who died in 1701. He was a man of
considerable eminence, and his virtues are handsomely
commemorated on a marble tablet in the church. His
descendants died out, and the property then passed to
his sister's great-grandson, Sir Thomas Dyke Acland.

The Morleys played a part of some political importance
during the reigns of Elizabeth and the earlier Stuarts.
In 1592 Herbert Morley was elected M.P. for New
Shoreham; in 1597 and 1601 John Morley for the same
borough. In 1614 Sir John Morley, Knight, was elected

for New Shoreham and Robert Morley for Bramber, the elections being repeated in 1620. In 1623 Robert is re-elected for Bramber, and in 1628 he is elected for New Shoreham. During the Civil War there is a Colonel Herbert Morley, who took the side of the Parliament, and in 1644 joined Sir William Waller in the siege of Arundel, and was one of the judges who condemned Charles I. to death, whilst Sir William Morley was a stanch Royalist, and after the Restoration added considerably to the family estates.

The name Morley is in the roll of Battle Abbey, and there is a manor Morleia in Domesday Book; it is in the parish of Shermanbury, Sussex, six miles from Steyning.

The Morley arms are: Sable, three leopards' faces, or, jessant, a fleur-de-lys, argent.

This chapter may be concluded with a poem found in Professor Morley's handwriting among his papers, and not, I believe, published elsewhere:

'The Earth's our ancestor; from dust the grass;
    From herbs the herds; and from them both the man:
Fixed Earth feeds moving earth, until it pass,
    Dust to the dust, and end where it began.

'Earth, grass, ox, man, behold our pedigree.
    Restored to earth, the meditative brain
Takes other shape; perchance, in bud or tree,
    Earth that was part of Newton lives again.

'Children of earth, we love the parent soil:
    But whence the touch that breeds another love?
In the clay lump there lies the pregnant oil
    That gives no light till kindled from above.

'God, whom our fathers reverenced, and we
    Seek as the Source of all abiding strength,
Thou art All Truth, and Thou hast made man free
    To question, and to find All Truth at length.

'By many paths we travel, and we seek
  To serve Thee, and to tread the upward way :
When, in each track, with willing steps though weak,
  We falter, guide us, that we may not stray.

'Dear earth of England, which has clothed the minds
  Of English searchers for the way of life,
Land that we love, the happy land that binds
  Us man to man in brotherhood of strife

'For truth and right, and the fulfilled design
  Of our Creator ; and thou, English Soul,
One in the strength of all the souls that shine
  In English annals, and with wise control

'Seek to subdue the wrong, maintain the right ;
  Breed through all time high shapers of mankind,
Till all be good in the Creator's sight,
  And God's fair earth be temple of His mind.'

CHAPTER II.

FRAGMENTS OF AUTOBIOGRAPHY, 1822—1832.

SOON after he was engaged to be married, in 1843, Henry
Morley wrote a sketch of his own life down to that year.
He describes three periods, the first of which is mainly
occupied with his early experiences of English schools.
In 1848, just before he gave up the practice of medicine
for teaching, he wrote out the account of this first period
at much greater length, heading it 'Vita Mea,' and
probably intending it to be the first chapter of an autobiography. This intention, however, if it ever existed,
remained unfulfilled, and we have his own account of himself in any detail and as a connected narrative only down
to the time when his age was ten years and nine months.

In 1891, after he had retired to Carisbrooke, he wrote
with great care a paper which he called 'Some Memories,'
and this he prefixed as an introduction to a volume in
which he republished a number of his early writings.*
This paper should be read by everyone interested in his
life. No doubt it contains all that he himself wished to
tell the world about his career, its special object being to
link together two portions of his life and work, which he
felt needed some such connection. As he himself abandoned the idea of a fuller autobiography, it would not be

* 'Early Papers and Some Memories.' Routledge, London.

fair to print ' Vita Mea ' as it stands, though extracts may be made from its pages.

He passes some remarks upon his ancestry. He believed in the connection with the Sussex family, he noted the Midhurst blacksmith, and he dwelt with some satisfaction on his middle-class position, his nearest relatives being for the most part engaged in various branches of trade. His father was a surgeon, living, in 1822, at 100, Hatton Garden, which was the Harley Street of the period. Probably the house was unhealthy, for when his mother, aged twenty-seven, died of a mysterious throat disease, which would doubtless now be recognised as diphtheria, the father was too ill with typhoid fever to be told of her death. Some years after this we learn that frequent days of severe headache compelled him to reduce his practice. So he sold that part of his practice which lay on the north of the Thames, and removed to 2, Harleyford Place, Kennington, retaining his patients only on the Surrey side. The change, however, did not cure the headaches; and in 1843, having inherited a little property from his great-aunt, Mrs. Lefford, of Midhurst, he retired there, and ceased to practise his profession except gratuitously for the benefit of his poorer neighbours. Here his health was completely restored, and he lived to the age of eighty-five. He was a man of strong character and high principle, with a lively humour, and great power of making the best of everything. He also wished to make the best of every person, and it was one of his rules, which he frequently enforced on others, never to say anything to the disadvantage of anyone else. He suffered much in his last illness, but in the intervals of pain was ever ready with a joke—altogether a man to be admired, and sometimes to be feared.

In 1813 Henry Morley senior married Ann Jane Hicks, by whom he had two sons, the elder, Joseph, born 1816, the younger, Henry, born 1822. She died December 29,

1824, when their younger son was little more than two years old. What he felt respecting her may now be told in his own words, and the following sections from 'Vita Mea' will speak for themselves:

In the fulness of possession, those who have mothers can scarcely understand the fountain of love which flows instinctively from child to parent. One of the most powerful emotions throughout my life has been affection—the deepest affection—towards her whom I do not remember to have ever seen. I was worn as a closed bud upon her bosom, but it is from heaven that she is looking for the blossom. It is a source of happy feeling when I reflect that, unremembered though the time is, it was from her lips that my first utterances were learned, that she first told me of a God, that she lived until I could put my arms around her neck, kiss her, and call her mother with a childish understanding. Since that time, I think there is no day throughout which she has been absent from my thoughts. Among the most vivid of the images of my childhood present to me now are those in which I see myself sitting alone and peering up into the stars, with pleasant tears and a full, softened heart, thinking of her, as of a kindred angel.

One of my childish amusements was the reverse of this. I used to lie in the sunlight prostrate among the grass, and, shading my sight with both hands, look down among the blades. A thousand visions in a day my fancy could create out of the glimmer among grass-roots and bits of stick entangled in them. If they stirred, I had an event represented; if they were still, an object.

So distinct were these visions, and so powerfully were they impressed upon me, that many of them I can still remember—some of them I can now almost re-create before my eyes. In these scenes I often looked upon my mother. One object, which I remember now with great distinctness, was a white tomb, with her figure, white and glimmering, upon it. At one period of my very early childhood, this exploration in the grass constituted my chief amusement, and no enthusiast of larger years could have believed more firmly in the truth and importance of his own delusion. I had no consciousness of the working of my own fancy in the matter.

Once, when on a visit in the country, I persuaded a playfellow to join my sport—or, rather, share in my discoveries.

He was content to see whatever I saw, and our last vision before dinner was this: two angels, each carrying a heart, and both hovering over the mouth of a deep pit. At dinner-time the family were curious to know what pleasure we had discovered in lying for a whole morning upon our stomachs almost in one place in the meadow. We were bribed with a penny to reveal our mystery. The temptation was great, but our virtue was greater. We preserved our mystery uncommunicated. The first vision after dinner was this: the two angels with the hearts flying away from the black pit. Which I expounded thus: we had been in great danger through that temptation of the penny which impended, but had come forth triumphant. . . .

I remember living at a preparatory school in the Clapham Road, kept by two ladies—Mrs. and Miss Matthews—who have been, so long as I remember anything, friends of our family, regarded with feelings of the kindest intimacy. By them I was treated as a pet, and have been told since that I used to be very good and quiet, with a taste for making heaps of dust, and denominating them gunpowder stores. But I vividly remember being naughty, when on one occasion I spent a whole morning vainly endeavouring to master that complex legend of days and months,

> ' Thirty days hath September,
> April, June, and November,'

and I don't know it now. . . . Whatever does not interest me I cannot coerce myself to bear in mind; and the great part of human learning being put in a most uninteresting form, there was a great deal of instruction wasted upon me. The knowledge acquired up to this date forms in some manner a single mass, of which I can scarcely refer an item to the source from which it was originally derived; and after a wide extent of reading, I can scarcely quote a line of poetry from any author without the book to save me from a blunder. From this statement let me except Satan's address to the sun in ' Paradise Lost,' which has done me most excellent service. At a grammar-school where we were required to learn a piece of English poetry every week of our own selection, I never failed to make my appearance with,

> ' O thou that with surpassing glory crowned
> Look'st from thy sole dominion,'

as often as I fancied it safe. That was my sole dominion, and
as the master and myself were near on a par in point of
memory, I taxed it with impunity. This speech, then, I
repeated so often that I am not likely ever to forget it wholly.

Another reminiscence of my residence with Mrs. and Miss
Matthews is the pleasure I took in scrambling about, with all
the dignity of freedom, to see how my companions made pot-
hooks and hangers. I did not write. But there was arithmetic,
and complex accounts were balanced with cherry-stones (oh
that they could be so balanced now !), and there were the dinner
and the pudding, the long board and trestles for tea, and the
treacle, of which I fear I had too large a share; and there
were the prayers, when we all knelt round the little table, and
repeated the Lord's Prayer and evening hymn, not wasted
upon our childish hearts.

> ' Teach me to live that I may dread
> The grave as little as my bed '

were lines which made a powerful impression. Arithmetic
always came before prayers, and I rarely hear the evening
hymn now without going back in memory to the cherry-stones
and to a happy thought of childhood. The grave was a pleasant
thought to me then, and so—not through discontent or moody
sentimentalism—but so, since such my nature is, it always has
been. I remember being kindly nursed while at this place
with measles, and allowed to jump out of bed to see a balloon.
Of my little companions I remember nothing but that there
were no quarrels among us.

And now for a home recollection, every circumstance of
which stands in the sharpest outline, marked out and complete
among the fragments of the past. We were in the front-
parlour at Hatton Garden, near a window—I remember which
—at breakfast. My grandmother—whom I very dearly loved,
and who had kept house for my father since my mother died—
my grandmother and my father were at a table—I could place
the chairs as they were then placed—and I was on the seat of
one of those amputative machines, a child's chair screwed aloft
on a child's table; but my little table was before me with my
breakfast on it. ' Will you take that cup of tea up to the old
woman ?' said my father.

My ears were open. 'What old woman?' 'Your new
mamma,' said my father; 'will you go and see her ?'

Up to that moment I had been wholly ignorant of any pending change, and my intense astonishment fixed the whole scene, upon my memory. So I went up with the tea to kiss my new mamma, with the one sentiment of wonder. I knew her before as a teacher in the family of an uncle, and had been astonished to see how much she boxed one of my cousin's ears. That cousin was a plague, however, it is to be owned, with a kind heart and tremendous spirits then. He was a playfellow of mine, a little my senior, and more than proportionately rough. . . .

My first reading involved the whole circle of fairy tales with which nurseries in those days were freely permitted to have acquaintance. A great folio of ' Paradise Lost,' in which the devil is represented stirring up a ground of bodies with a three-pronged fork—a favourite picture—was often examined, and a folio of Foxe's ' Book of Martyrs,' full of great pictures of flames and stakes, and men being stung by wasps, etc., was industriously thumbed and studied. I read the greater part of it, and knew all the pictures as familiar friends. Miss Edgeworth's tales I read, and liked them, as every child must; but they were not after my whole heart. The ' Seven Champions of Christendom '—that was my encyclopædia of entertainment.

I remember that ' my new mamma ' taught me the Catechism and some of the Church prayers. My father always influenced me by his example towards a strong reverence for religious thoughts, and his incessant love and never-clouded kindness towards his own and all other children had a great influence for good.

He was of a joyous, gentle temper, too kind to bear the thought of giving pain, simple and unworldly. At that time he often had sick headaches, and even then I remember that he would have me in his bedroom, and patiently assist me in mastering some lesson, rather than think that I was labouring alone.

I have a brother, six years my senior. Throughout our childhood we had a father who watched for us with the most devoted care. Every evening, whatever may have been his own day's task, he would share ours—join in our school lessons, and lighten all the toil of our preparation for the morrow. . . .

To return to my books and amusements. My first and chief toy was a sword and belt, in which I looked upon myself as an eighth champion of Christendom. . . . When past sword-bearing—at about eight or nine years old—I set up a theatre, with scenery and characters for two plays, ' Black-eyed Susan,' and ' Timour the Tartar.' It was a very good little toy theatre, with foot-lamps, abundant slides—on which to introduce my pasteboard *personæ*—bell, curtain, etc. When I knew my plays by heart, and got quite tired of representing them, I took to combining my stock, and acting plays of my own, impromptu, and doubtless edifying. The scenery accorded with my taste, and may perhaps have helped to form it. There was a gorgeous Oriental tournament, and a gloomy cavern, with the moon shining through its entrance, a strong castle, a wood, a rural cottage, all of which could answer a great many imaginative purposes.

, Reading and amusing myself thus, I was at the same time a perfect visionary. Night after night, when my candle was removed; my bedroom became filled with strange shapes, which crowded around me while I was broad awake. Monkeys sat upon my counterpane, parrots hung against the wall, elephants loomed indistinctly in the doorway ; the room would be sometimes crowded with animals, and to this zoological recreation I did not, after a time, much object. I never spoke of it. Two only of these visions were told. Once an apprentice of my father's, who was always very kind to me, and near whose room my bedroom was, took me in his arms to a cupboard, and said he would give me to the rats. It was in a game of ours that he used of a morning to throw me across the room (not a very large one) upon my bed, and during this sport he made his threat, when I had in some way offended him. From that period for the succeeding fortnight, after my candle had been removed, the cupboard door appeared to fly open, a rat seemed to scamper across and shake my chair with leaping on it. At the end of a fortnight I told my trouble, but not its origin, was told it was fancy, and in due time the fancy ceased.

The other vision was in the street one evening. I looked up and saw in the sky a flaming sword, of the pattern usually ascribed to avenging angels—something between a sword and a corkscrew. It was of large size, distinct and fiery. The clouds were arranged around, so that it appeared in the sky through a break distinctly oval. I can remember it clearly as

I·write. No real vision could be more distinct. It may have been suggested to me by excitement then existing on the subject of cholera, for I think it must have been at about the period of its visit that I had this day-dream. I pointed it out to the servant who was with me, and she pretended to see it— did see it, as I thought. It appeared in a part of the sky behind me as we were walking, and we stood in the road with our eyes upwards. People passed and repassed as usual, which surprised me; but two or three looked with us, attracted by our gazing. It was an illusion of my brain, undoubtedly, but wonderfully distinct and lasting. . . . Its position was fixed. If I turned away I did not see it, and I stared up at it for a long time without seeing any diminution of its brightness or change in its form. . . .

My night-dreams were, of course, during this period very vivid. At one time I stood with my father in the centre of a vast hall, the lofty ceiling almost concealed in gloom, the walls so distant as to be removed from sight. I heard the tread of an armed knight upon the marble pavement towards us, and saw my father murdered. At another time, after a sermon one Christmas Day upon the Last Judgment, that day was present to me in a dream, whose details remain indelibly fixed upon my mind.

I stood before the splendour of the throne in heaven; angels ascended and descended upon beams of light. The evil stood on one side upon a black thunder-cloud, the good upon a cloud interwoven with light, and I alone upon a third small cloud, unjudged.

There was music in heaven, and angels descended around me, and placed me upon a seat among them.

He goes on to describe a habit he also had of talking in his sleep, and the alarming consequences which this once nearly produced. Mrs. Lefford, of Midhurst, was his father's great-aunt. She had some property to leave, and, being dissatisfied with the marriage of her elder brother Robert, she sent off her two other brothers, James and Charles, to London, to hunt up Henry Morley senior, and when they had found him practising there as a surgeon, she adopted him as her heir. The old lady demanded ·much deference from all who had 'expectations,' and one night, when little Henry was on a visit to her house, she came to give him a kiss in bed, and found him with his eyes shut. But he began speaking to her, and answered her questions so pertinently, and also so impertinently, that she believed he must be awake, and it was with great difficulty that he could clear himself the next morning, and make it plain that, though he had conversed with her, he was really fast asleep, and unconscious of committing any sin.

Another frequent consequence of the state of my imagination in these years was the fancying of sounds. I used not only to see, but to hear things that were not. At home I have at all times been called Hal, in a dear familiar voice, and the call of 'Hal!' has very often fetched me from one part of the house to another, when there was no one who required my presence; sometimes it would be inconveniently repeated, and bewilder me a little. It is true that in the illusion of the rat I heard the cupboard door fly open, and heard the rat scamper, as perfectly as though those events had really taken place; but in general it is to be remarked that there was not in deceptions on the ear the same *vraisemblance* as when the eye saw images.

About the call of 'Hal!' there was always a spectralness which did not accompany illusions of the other sense—a vague awe came with it, even when its repetition made me think it real; and I fancy that this awe—a feeling allied to the terror of nightmare—always accompanies false hearing.

It is not a month since I heard, during two minutes, perhaps, a connected conversation in my bedroom, when I was quite awake and had been reading letters. A great sense of alarm accompanied it.

Another peculiarity of my childhood, allied to these, was a remarkable power of half-abstraction. On one occasion I remember that I walked to school in this unconscious state, without missing my way, and went through a great part of the morning's routine, until in the middle of a class—perhaps spurred by some question—I woke up as out of sleep, and was completely unable to remember anything either of having left home, or of what I had done since I arrived at school, although I must have read books, have answered questions, and possibly said lessons through. In such a case, if no one observed my

look of momentary amazement on recovering myself, I never
told how I had been wool-gathering. I never got any consola-
tion for such intelligence on the few occasions when I did
volunteer it, and so I kept my dreamland to myself. Such
thoughts and feelings children dread to communicate, except-
ing to a mother. The tenderest father in the world is unable
to give the woman's sympathy which is the one balsam for a
child's sick mind.

The religious impressions which I received during these
years of childhood may be readily understood. A heaven of
glory and a hell of groans were vivid in my imagination. I
remember well our pew at St. Andrew's, Holborn, in the front
of the gallery, above the clock, and never shall forget the
painted window. That was exactly opposite our seat, and I
doubt whether anything else at church attracted much of my
attention. It contains a large and somewhat grotesque picture
of the Resurrection, and Sunday after Sunday I used to marvel
over the angel's wings. One wing had the appearance of a
scythe for want of plumage; that was the part of the picture
which every week excited my attention and provoked innumer-
able speculations. My feelings upon religious subjects were
very deep, but almost wholly pictorial—assisted by frequent
visions, ' interpositions,' and so forth.

A daughter was born within a year of my father's second
marriage, the only fruit of that union. Polly was her household name, and I used to delight, as she grew able to attend, to
paint to her in some deserted room the crowns of heaven and
the terrors of hell, until we joined in resolves to be good, and
never to do those things at which God would be angry. My
ideas were so far spiritual that I remember being on one occasion very much disturbed because my pupil could conceive
nothing beyond a real golden crown covered with diamonds.

' Vita Mea' then proceeds to narrate an incident which
affected the boy a good deal. Polly was one day directed
to say something which seemed to involve an untruth. She
refused, and, when asked her reason for refusal, said that
she would not get God's reward, but would be sent to
hell; upon which she was asked who put that nonsense into her head. Unfortunately, there was no wise
correction of the crude theology of her tutor, but only

a scolding, which left the impression that all the efforts he had been making for her soul's welfare were lost, and a very painful impression this was, especially when confirmed by some further childish incidents of a similar kind.

My religion in those days was what the Germans call 'Schwarmerei.' In all troubles I prayed to God as though He were present, asking for signs often of His will, and then receiving as from Him, with perfect trust, such indications as I had fixed upon. It was the religion of an excited brain, yet without terror, for I felt God to be my Friend and Adviser, rather than my Judge. With all my imaginations, I was never timid—accustomed to go about in the dark, night never had any terrors. I always loved churchyards as pleasant places. In the first days of childhood I was mild, quiet, and happy—happiest when most quiet and most full of dreamy fancies.

There were now circumstances connected with the home-life which made his father wish the boy, young as he was, to be sent to a boarding-school. From this arose experiences in England and in Germany, which had a most important influence on his subsequent career. He tells the first·part of the story at some length in ' Vita Mea.' It is also referred to in ' Early Papers.'*

My first experience of school, after leaving my kind friends the Matthews, was at Stony Stratford. There was a stony playground there of pebble pavement, upon which it was not pleasant to tumble down, and it was a rough place altogether. The master was a Mr. K., the father of an apprentice—a most amiable young man—who about that time was bound to my father. Mr. K. was a white-headed gentleman, of whom I remember nothing but mildness; of his school I remember only cruelty and vice. The boys were too many for his care, perhaps—there were a large number—the ushers were bad-hearted men, and the system of fagging was triumphant. ' Fagging,' at any time, is an insult to reason ; but at a public school it has redeeming traits, at a private school it has none. It is a hell, in which the fiends are children.

---

* See p. 25; also p. 207 *et seq.*

It was my good fortune to be a fag, and not a master—
thanks to my extreme youth—and so I was spared the lesson
in tyranny. I had no power to abuse. My brother was with
me, six years older than myself, but he was a master, and had
not strength to resist the universal spirit. So in this school,
to which I must have gone at the age of six or seven, I suffered
silently. I know that I was there in the year 1829, from this
circumstance: I vividly recollect seeing the chief usher print
his initials with ink upon a desk, with the date—' J. P. 1829.'
A boy, ignorant of the fact, happened to put his arm upon the
inscription while it was wet, smeared it, and was mercilessly
flogged.

My memory of the chief usher is very distinct. He was an
ingenious man. On one occasion he delighted the school by
fastening six boys abreast with their heads under his desk,
and flogging them all together with a postilion whip, which he
used always in preference to a cane. One poor fellow had the
property of leaping to a great height when he was flogged;
very often of an evening the boys would gather round the
stove, exulting, while the usher laid the whip upon him mercilessly—for amusement. This spirit was soon communicated.
Every master had a collection of 'tommies'—instruments
which inflict far more torture than a mere cane—and punishing
his fag was a great part of his daily recreation, having the
advantage also of being a recreation in which he was privileged to indulge during school hours. In play-time fags were
tied upon the floor and suffered 'tommy' for their masters'
exercise.

In the night I slept with my master, and my duty was to go
to the bottom of the bed and coil around his toes after the
manner of an animated hot-water bottle, having previously
warmed myself by a compulsory fight with another little boy,
who was my quiet friend. His Christian name was Septimus.
We being little and quiet, and fond of each other, it was great
fun to the other inhabitants of the room in which we slept to
compel us to engage in battle, ready to spur us on with ' tommy '
if we did not seem to be in earnest.

I will not write down all the repulsive scenes and all the
miseries which crowd into my memory as I think over the
days spent at Stratford. I remained at that school eighteen
months, not daring, when I came home for the holidays, to
utter a word of complaint, because complaining would involve

2

my brother, whom I loved; at the end of eighteen months, however, my bodily condition caused my father to suspect the truth, and I was, of course, then taken away. At Stratford I had been exposed to a corrupting influence, and did not come out whole. While there I preserved my childish character, and felt the acutest pain at all the cruel deeds I saw. A French usher died, and the boys kicked the turf from his grave maliciously. The witnessing of this act, and of daily kindred actions, kept me constantly in strong emotion. My own bodily sufferings I became used to.

But in some measure my heart was hardened. At the next school—a Mr. Paglar's, at Putney or Chelsea—I was no longer a quiet, dreamy child—there was a ' devil ' put into me. Released from ' tommy,' cane had no terrors, and I set myself at once in opposition. It must have been, I think, chiefly my own fault that, after one quarter's stay, I made such complaints during the Easter holidays as caused my father to remove me from that school in anger. I may have had cause for complaint, but I am sure I also gave it. All my memories of myself during these three months are little to my credit. When the master put into our ground to dry a sofa which had been cleaned, within a day or two after my arrival, I thought myself a hero for daring to jump upon it with my dirty boots. When I was flogged, I tried to perpetrate some kick worth boasting of. When a task was set to be written on my slate as punishment, I was proud of my spirit in taking up nothing but a rude caricature, with ' Paglar ' written under it, for his approval; and when my patch of garden was taken away in punishment for that last offence, I could not sufficiently express my gratitude. Systematically averse to hard dumplings, I threw them underneath the dinner-table. In short, I considered the schoolmaster my natural antagonist. With the boys I was on friendly terms. Living at that time nearer home, and supplied with unusual bounty—in consideration of my former tribulations, it may be—I distributed the whole of each parcel directly it arrived. There was goodwill for everyone except the master and his wife, whom I believed to be laughing when the boys were flogged. I did not understand her actions: she covered her mouth with her handkerchief to hide some emotion, and I had been so used to seeing laughter over suffering, that I gave her credit for nothing better. . . .

My father, after I left Putney, did not try another boarding-school. I remained at home, and went as a day scholar to Dr. Worthington, then living in Chapel Street, Bedford Square.

Dr. Worthington was a patient of my father's, a man highly educated, and attached to literary pursuits. Here I began to learn. At Stratford my lessons had been only in reading, writing, and arithmetic. At Putney I suppose I never attended to any lessons. The groundwork of a liberal education was now laid by Dr. Worthington, and at home my father assisted. . . .

At Dr. Worthington's we had weekly recitations of poetry, and also got up the whole of ' Julius Cæsar.' Robert Carr' [a schoolfellow] made a good plump Mark Antony, and when he was absent from rehearsal, I could spout the most important speeches for him, having abundant leisure, for my own duty was no more than to enact Lucius. Antony, however, was my more ambitious love; and I teased them pretty often of an evening in the parlour at home by mounting on a chair and letting them know that I had ' come to bury Cæsar.'

I have pleasant school memories connected with Chapel Street. Our teacher was a scholar and a gentleman whose spirit spread through the community. The meannesses common to the private school were wholly absent, and when the spirit of war possessed a couple, and a fight sometimes arose, the duel was allowed, honourably performed, received in satisfaction, and the quarrel ended. I was a small being then, accustomed to travel to school in a camlet cloak, of ample skirt, but somewhat too stiff of material to allow of its hanging as a classic drapery. Dr. Worthington, encountering me in the passage as I arrived one morning, compared me to a ' hog in armour,' which saying seized my fancy, and remains well remembered. I must have made good progress at this school, for I certainly did not remain in it longer than a year—if I remained so long—before I was again sent into the country to a boarding-school, and found myself at once within three or four places of its head-boy, though I was then not much more than nine years of age. When I left I was nine months older than ten, and I remained at that school during three half-years.

This school was at Chichester. It contained about fifty boys, under the care of a Mr. W. . . .

At Chichester I was in the vicinity of friends. Within a

stone's-throw of the school lived a Mrs. Jaques, with her son, a gentleman both deaf and lame from childhood upwards. . . .

The boarders of the school were all of them farmers' sons, with the exception of one native of Chichester, who, with me, constituted a town faction of two, against the country faction of about eight-and-forty, or less.   It was a tolerably large school at that time, but I am not sure about the number of us. S., the Cicestrian, was driven into close association with me by the fact that he was a town boy, but I never felt in my heart much admiration for him—there was a smallness in his character which I felt as a trouble; but he was the only boy with whom I had a sympathy of any description, so that I was in duty bound to make him my school friend.

At Stratford I had lost all sense of fear in school matters, and I suppose my heroism must have savoured of the ridiculous when 'the country' was in arms, and I entrenched myself with S. in a circle of stones, ready to fight all who should step over.   This was one feud.   But there was another.

My brother had been at the same school before me.   Older than I, of great physical strength, he had ruled over the school somewhat tyrannically—had imported some rough Stratford customs—and left behind him a large unpaid debt of vengeance. Upon his departure I arrived, and when Mr. W., introducing me to the school, said, ' You remember Joseph Morley; this is his younger brother,' the desire arose straightway in every breast to punch my head on the first opportunity.   I was little, and looked not a Hercules; but now it was lucky for me that I had been to Stratford, too.   When we were left to ourselves, I was surrounded with statements of the grudges left by Master Joe, and ' Won't we pay you for 'em !' was the general cry.   There was not much chivalry about these rustic youths, but I had read ' The Seven Champions,' been to Stratford, and profited by Dr. Worthington's instruction, so that it soon was made clear to them that I not only sat above them in the schoolroom, but that there were not more than four or five of them whom I could not thrash.   Of those four or five, one would, when it so pleased him to pay an instalment to the memory of Brother Joe, summon me to fight him, which I accordingly would do, and manage to make his refreshment too stimulating to be pleasant, unless indulged in with a due regard to moderation.   I never sought a fight, and never feared one.   I remember, after perseverance in a fair ring, driving out of the ground, amid shouts of triumph, a great fellow of twice my height. I was not strong, but I was never beaten. Caring nothing for raps, I kept at work until my opponent either confessed himself conquered, or, being unconquerable, wearied of exercise; and as boys, even if mean-spirited, honour the brave, I was sufficiently in good esteem.

Moreover, there was another quality which raised me to importance—my faculty of sending them to sleep with a good story. Only part of them slept in my room, and my crude inventions were, to their crude tastes, sufficiently delightful.

Those who did not sleep in our room would pin me in the playground by day, and coax for a tale, or threaten war 'if it were not forthcoming. There was no squeamish taste to please in myself or my hearers, and I was glad to weave, as they to hear, my stock of knights, dragons, castles, forests, fairies, and so forth, into combinations perpetually new. Schoolboys generally 'tell stories' to each other in the bed-room, and even at Stratford I had burned in emulation, and longed to be allowed to contribute. Only once they suffered me, and I distinctly remember how, elated with the honour, I began—scorning even then to draw upon the story-books—with, 'Once upon a time there was a parrot,' and I was going on to say, 'in a great wood,' when a shout of derision stopped my mouth for aye.

In later years derision has silenced me with the same instantaneous effect, for (to jump over a long space of time) when I began my course as medical student, and at the same time joined the Students' Medical Debating Society, at the very first debate (on Instinct) I rose to contribute some anecdotes. The then senior member mentioned them presently with a slighting derision, and I was abashed. Without the slightest anger or ill-will, I abided tacitly by the first sneer, and never ventured another observation. Through four sessions I was reproached as a silent member. I read papers which were respected when my turn came, but never spoke in their defence, except to answer questions; and when in the last session I became secretary and senior myself, and it was my duty, according to immemorial custom, to lead and encourage the debates, I never spoke a syllable. I was active in the society's affairs, filled it with new members; but, while I had an influential voice at other of our public gatherings, I never

found my voice again in that society. However, to go back
to childhood.

It was at Chichester that my invention first began to run an
applauded course. My theatre previously had caused me to
invent dramas, and sometimes to attempt to write them. Of
these writings I now remember one line alone, which is impressed upon me by the fact of my having been specially
interrupted after it was written. It seems I was dealing in
wholesale personification, for somebody was invoking thus:
'Envy, Envy, Envy, rise!' and Envy was going to rise, up a
trap-door.

At Chichester the tale-telling business soon became my
monopoly. My ultimate ambition at this time, and until
I reached fifteen, was for professional excellence. I always
knew myself intended for 'a doctor,' and inside my desk at
Stratford, almost as soon as I could write, the inscription ran,
'Sir Henry Morley, M.D., Physician Extraordinary' (which
I thought meant something more than ordinary) 'to the King.'
In that channel my ambition ran until I was about fifteen
years old, and then the master faculty which had possessed
me through life with unrecognised despotism began to play
the tyrant.

There was another circumstance also connected with my
social condition at Mr. W.'s. The sons of Sussex farmers,
who made up the school, were not characterized by a very
refined sense of honour. Mean actions committed and concealed not seldom brought the whole school into disgrace
through the offence of one member. Whenever the offence
was one which I could reasonably take credit for, I always
claimed to be the sinner. Perfectly hardened against fear of
punishment, and philosophically reflecting that, whether
punished with the school or for the school, punishment was
equally sure, for the real offender never had honour enough
to speak, I was willing to earn popularity among the boys at
the expense of the good opinion of the master.

Thus, one morning it was found that the bedroom mattresses
had been cut and injured; the offender was not to be discovered, and all the school was to be kept in until he confessed.
Whereupon, 'Please, sir, I pretended to do it,' which phrase,
born of a qualm of conscience, was, as I meant it to be, considered as a timid admission. I was flogged, and there the
matter ended.

I remember also a somewhat kindred incident. These farmers' sons clipped the King's English sadly—they abounded in provincialisms. To cure this, Mr. W. devised a scheme. A large piece of wood was suspended around the neck of the first person who spoke bad English in the morning. He was to wear it until he detected the same fault in someone else, to whom he was to pass it, to be worn on the same terms, and whoever wore it at the end of the day was troubled with a heavy task. After a little time, our indignation against the log rose to a great height. The incumbrance in playing, the publicity in walking out, were quite intolerable. I, being a Londoner, was free from all chance of wearing the machine, unless I took it wilfully, for I was not accustomed to bad grammar. Not to make invidious distinctions, however, I took care to change my style of speech, and share the dangers of the rest.

At length, when the nuisance began to cry for a reform, I undertook to effect one. With that end in view, I arranged that the wood should come to me invariably as the last possessor, and I invariably threw it away. When the inquiry came in the evening, 'Who had the wood last?' the answer was ready, 'I had, sir.' 'Bring it to me.' 'Please, sir, I've thrown it away.' Great scold. Punishment. Next day a new log. Evening scene repeated. Again a new log. Again the same fate attended it. Indignation, cane, task, another new log, but smaller in size—a saving in the expense of wood. That was an inch gained. But the smaller wood went the way of the larger. I was in for a contest, and perfectly ready to give up my playhours to tasks, and my body to any punishment a master could inflict—since that has very safe limits—if only I could win the point; and I did win it. The unpopular burden was removed. Such services were received by our community and soon forgotten: evil services did not so easily step out of mind. Boys are like men in that matter.

There was at the school a boy from Bognor, a great coward, and a most incorrigible tell-tale. So great was the general persecution of this poor fellow, that he was obliged to roam in playhours up and down a little passage, guarded from the playground by a wicket, in a space tabooed to all the others, and not to be entered except under fearful penalties. At night he slept, for safety, in a garret by himself. Protected thus against any instalments of hatred, he had his arrears paid off in the lump. Whenever Mr. W.'s family spent the evening from home, the whole establishment adjourned to his room armed with bolsters, braces, and the like extemporaneous weapons. A shower of blows fell upon his bed, inflicting in the general rush more terror than pain, for he was allowed the benefit of his bedclothes, except when he had recently committed any very atrocious offence; and that business transacted, we scampered back to our own rooms again, where the servants sometimes provided us with a festival of ' French toast' and beer.

There is enough here of Chichester to illustrate the history of my mind. I still had my imaginative religion, but of religious ordinances I only remember being bothered to learn the Collect on a Sunday. Although I know Chichester well, I do not remember even to what church we went, so little was I interested in the services of religion; only I know that at one school (it must have been Stratford) I sat in a large square pew of worm-eaten oak, and the boys amused themselves in the season with catching flies and poking them head foremost into the worm-holes.

Visits to kind uncles and aunts in the holidays; juvenile courtships of one small cousin in the country, and then of another in town; reading ' Pilgrim's Progress,' Byron's ' Poems,' Scott's novels, and all Shakespeare's plays; pitying the ducks killed for dinner, and being unable to eat them in consequence; rambles over the Sussex Downs—so passed the time till he was nearly eleven years old, and so ends ' Vita Mea.'

CHAPTER III.

NEUWIED, 1833—1835.

IN the summer of 1833, when Henry Morley was aged ten years and three-quarters, an event occurred which had a most important influence on his whole life. This was his being sent to the school kept by the Moravian Brethren at Neuwied, on the Rhine. We will first learn what he felt about it ten years later, when he wrote the earliest of the autobiographical sketches mentioned in the last chapter.

I would to God that toil and trouble had not changed my heart from the simple, earnest thing it was ten years ago! One would have thought my early education tended little to develop cheerfulness or kindly sentiment. And yet, though my quick feelings were wounded almost every hour, I had as much of happiness as of tears. To have buffeted so sharply even in the first years of my passage through the world made me more earnest in my sentiments, and the more careless of those petty troubles that annoy a schoolboy. I was enthusiastic, and in some respects a dreamer. Close addiction to the reading of Byron, whom I knew at that time better, and read more than any poet else, had destroyed in some degree the healthy tone of my imagination. Even before this time I had made a few attempts at poetry myself. What they were like it would be amusing now to see. Byron, Shakespeare, and Scott's novels were, I think, at this period—eleven years—my only reading.

Distinctly do I remember that, to me, all-important day when my education in Germany was agreed upon. I was sitting in my father's little study, reading ‘ The Pirate,’ with both elbows on the table, and my head resting on my hands, absorbed in Minna and Brenda, when my father entered and asked me suddenly whether I would return to Mr. W.'s at Chichester (the holidays were nearly over) or go to school in Germany. Never was a novel-reader so thoroughly wakened up from his reveries. Up rose into my head knights and castles and woods and peasants, foreign people, foreign scenes —there was not a thought that could have given me at that time more delight. My decision was given in an instant, and I started off within three weeks. · My father grieved much when we parted ; but as for me, I was too full of the pleasant prospects in my fancy to feel anything but delight and pleasure. The state of my mind at this time I should not have remembered to be as it was had I not seen frequently of late, and read, for the pleasure of old memories, the letters that I wrote from Neuwied. I take shame to myself that I am become so changed as to have blushed for their childlike affectionate simplicity. I held it my duty to tell every thought, every little thought of conscious pride, or fear, or sorrow—they were such childish thoughts ; to read them afterwards, even as the mood may be, I must either laugh at them or cry.

The two years spent at Neuwied were (till now) the happiest portion of my·life. A universal favourite, entirely free from care, in a school where quarrels were unknown, the masters were called Brothers, and all was canopied over with a veil of the tenderest and kindliest religion, I spent my time laughing and loving everybody. I was noted as the merriest little scamp of them all ; and, for the first time, I had here a friend.

He was a pale, sickly boy, a dreamer of fancies like myself. He had been born amid luxury, and the roughness even of a school like that was almost more than he could bear. He had little sympathy with the other boys, and was not greatly in their favour. They did not understand his quiet, gentle temper ; being better born than most of them, his dreamy reserve was looked upon as pride, and few could make allowance for the delicacy of his health. His name was Rudolf von Gross.

For studies I learned at Neuwied the German language, and unlearned everything else; for although when I went there I carried with me a good stock of Latin and Greek, with other school delights, it was all to be learned over again another way. And that plan, when I came back, had all to be undone again ; so that in fact these two years brought me to worse than a standstill in those matters.

But to the impressions made upon me in that quiet, happy place I owe nearly every feeling of the few that have remained as treasures from the wreck of childhood. And to the language that I then acquired my mind is indebted for such power as it has ; my tone and taste is modelled from the German literature, which I have since studied with devotion, and in which I am perhaps more versed than even in my own.

Meanwhile, my imaginative propensities, which had from the first gradually been increasing (and which I trace the rather because I know that they will grow some day into the staple of my life), became at Neuwied still more apparent. I and my friend Gross used to tell our own stories to each other as we walked, set ourselves apparently impracticable tasks, and then tax the invention of each other to overcome them, wrote verses on all kinds of subjects, received homage and flattery to our hearts' content, and were admitted by the boys, and masters too, as the poets to our little circle.

I remember once having written a tale in my copy-book instead of the Latin exercise for which it was intended—I was rattle-brained enough for anything. It was before I had acquired the language of the place, and so the tale was writ in English. Being detected in the contumacious act, I was pre-pared to suffer accordingly—but quite the contrary. The master understood English, and read my tale instead of the exercise. So soon as the school hours were over, he called the boys to silence, and sat him down and translated it to them —with improvements, I have no doubt, of his own, or I should not have got quite so much credit by the matter. The by no means critical boys thought it something tremendously first-rate.

When I had not been at Neuwied two years, my brother came to see me. The sight of a relative made me long to be with my family again. After he had left I grew homesick, wrote dolefully miserable letters, and in consequence returned back shortly afterwards.

With all my rattle, my early education must have given me a certain degree of sobriety, for I was trusted both to go to Neuwied, young as I was, and to return thence, entirely by myself. It must have been rather queer in the first case to see a fat little dot of eleven years old, not able to talk anything but English, trotting over the strange towns, seeing the sights, going to hotels, hunting among the packets, taking places like a grave old gentleman. Well, well, I gained considerably by it, so I do not care who laughs at me.

There are other sources from which it is possible to supplement these early recollections. In December, 1884, Mr. Edwin R. Ransome, of Rushmere Cottage, Wandsworth Common, wrote to Professor Morley:

Probably you may feel a little surprised at my addressing you after a lapse of forty-nine years, but a little explanation may possibly be the means of bringing up pleasurable recollections of boyhood. Some time last summer I learnt for the first time that there was a Society of Old Neuwieders, and as they were about to have a meeting and social tea at the Star and Garter, Richmond, I presented myself, and was gladly welcomed. . . . I produced my Stammbuch, amongst which is a leaflet with the following:

'Lebe heiter, lebe froh
Stets in dulce jubilo.

'Zur erinnerung an deinem Freunde
'H. Morley aus London.'

I was then told, for the first time, that this must have been written by you, and the wish was expressed that you would join the society. . . . Amongst my 'Recollections of Neuwied,' I find I have made the following entry: 'Henry Morley, from London, a cheerful sort of boy, with curly brown hair—a nice sort of fellow.'

This letter led to Professor Morley at once joining the society, and taking great interest in its proceedings. He regularly attended its annual conversazione while he lived in London, and acted from 1886 till his death as editor of the society's magazine, *The Old Neuwieder*. He thus begins the preface to No. 2, July, 1886:

The Old Neuwieder who signs his name here as 'Editor' has this only to say for himself: that more than fifty years have gone by since he left the Neuwied School, and that his love for it and gratitude to it have grown clearer instead of dimmer in the course of time. He cannot think the school away out of his life.

It lived in his memory as the one school where childhood was not robbed of any of its joys or of any of its innocence. For No. 12 of the magazine, June, 1891, he wrote a short article on ' Moravian Schools,' from which the following are extracts :

There are, I believe, not more than 115,000 members of the Moravian Church, the *Unitas Fratrum*, in all this living world. They are brother Christians who do not seek to make proselytes to this or that form of Church government or doctrinal belief, but uniting themselves with a broad catholic sympathy to all Christians who put their hearts into the service of their Master, they act according to the spirit of Christ's own prayer that they all may be one, even as their Father is one. The bond of union is the Christian life, of which the chief marks are faith, patience, and love. By this they become powerful for good in their relations with children, and they are able to bring Christ into the homes of the untaught tribes among whom they are, of all missionaries, the most quietly successful.

He speaks of some of their missions

among snows of the North, or fever-smitten coasts under a burning sun ; in corners of the world where men might lie forgotten, with their best life unrevealed, the Moravian brethren settle, and bring with them the magic power of their gentle, patient fellowship in a love that looks up to the Source of love, and seeks no glory but that of God.

In Christian lands the Moravians are missionaries through their schools :

The design of these schools, as of the missions, was from the first, is, and always will be, to help unobtrusively in spreading through the world the peace of God. Their power over young minds is exercised almost insensibly by bringing them into habitual contact with a life that is the happier for being spent in the service of God, and shaped, as far as human frailties make it possible, in simple accordance with Christ's teaching. Love that has saving power for the old has it in tenfold measure for the young. Cant—that is to say, the phrase without the feeling of religion—drives child and man into the desert. But a child's heart set among strangers who become as brothers and sisters by the quiet force of a human love that is bound inseparably to the love of God; who do not speak bitterly, or jangle, or boast themselves; whose yea and nay are always truth; whose motives are always kind; who are slow to think evil of anyone; and in whose thoughts and customs the prevailing feature is a childlike innocence—a child's heart set in a little world so fashioned, may well grow into a man's heart that will help a little towards bettering the fashion of the larger world.

I do not think that in the present day we depend only on the Moravians for such schools as these. But the Moravians alone, I think, have made this element in their teaching a first consideration—their reason, in fact, for being teachers—while I know no other Christian community as uniformly true to the larger catholic spirit that seeks to draw Christians of all forms of doctrine to fellowship in the one life that can unite them in a helpful brotherhood. They demonstrate religion in their daily ways; have it, and do not cant about it. Only they have not the false shame that substitutes in daily speech the lower for the higher aim.

This is the witness borne by Professor Morley, nearly sixty years later, to the debt he owed to the school at Neuwied. Those two years furnished him with experiences which determined his career. From 1835 to 1848 we shall find him being trained for and practising a profession which was not his true vocation. That he had the courage to throw it up and start afresh under circumstances of extraordinary difficulty, and that he at once began to succeed in life when he began to be a teacher, is mainly due to the contrast between Neuwied and the schools to which he had been previously sent in England. In 'Some Memories'* he refers to the events already recorded here, and adds: 'From all these experiences there sprang one of the deep roots of that opinion as to

* 'Early Papers and Some Memories.' Routledge, 1891.

the right way of teaching, which I now resolved to carry into practice and to live or die by.'

This same volume republishes two papers, one entitled 'Ten Years Old,' the other, 'Brother Mieth and his Brothers,' which were originally written for *Household Words*, in 1854, describing at some length the journey to Neuwied and the life at the school. As they have been several times reprinted, and are readily accessible, I have not quoted from them here. The first is in the writer's happiest vein, and gives a vivid picture of a somewhat adventurous journey for a boy not yet eleven years old. His father saw him through the really difficult part of it —the London streets; from St. Katherine's Docks to Rotterdam was all plain sailing, and any boy could find his way up the Rhine. His difficulties began when it appeared that there were in Rotterdam seventeen gentlemen of the same name as that of the agent to whom he had been given a letter of introduction, without further address. But all difficulties were finally overcome; he met a kind friend on the Rhine steamboat, a Mr. Tombleson, who was taking sketches for a book upon Rhine scenery. After a journey which did him unmixed good, he arrived safe at Neuwied, to be at once welcomed and begin his 'new birth.'

The other paper gives many interesting details of the school life, the recollections of the concrete facts which were generalized in later reminiscences. He speaks of what he was when he went :

I had learnt to be reckless about blows, to regard a big boy or a schoolmaster as a natural enemy, and to feel proud because there were few others so prompt to defy or insult the teacher, or to bite him when he plied the stick.

At Neuwied corporal punishment was unknown, and very slight penalties sufficed for the maintenance of discipline when so much was done to make the boys happy, and therefore good. Henry Morley was cured of a ten-

dency to romance, to tell imaginary stories about himself
and his home as though they were true, simply by finding
the kind Brother to whom these stories were told ready
to believe them to be true. He had been a missionary
in strange lands, he had seen strange things, he professed
his belief in all that the boy told him, and the boy soon
became ashamed of imposing upon this gentle credulity,
especially as ample opportunity was afforded his imagination in the legitimate field of avowed invention. This
cultivation of the imagination played an important part
in the school training, and the legends of the Rhine
furnished many a subject for dramatic play or narrative.
The most powerful impression of all came through the
hand of Death.   More than one of the Brothers at
Neuwied were missionaries who had sacrificed their
health in some trying station abroad, and came to give
their last months of life to the service of the school.
Tablets to their memory adorned the walls of the playground, and recalled the affection with which they had
been regarded by their scholars.   No more striking contrast could be than between this feeling and that of the
English boys who had kicked the turf from the grave
of the dead French usher.   Brother Mieth, yet a young
man, died at this time, and every event connected with
his illness, his last gifts of remembrance, and his simple,
almost happy funeral, struck deep roots in the boy's
mind.   There is much else narrated of a bright and
cheerful character.   Birthday festivals were regularly
kept ; the great Christmas festival was a most joyous
time ; so, too, was the happy summer excursion, where
the only hardship was that on one night out of six they
had to sleep at a hotel on feather beds instead of on
straw in a barn.

One more feature may be noticed.   When Henry
Morley went to Neuwied, his Shakespeare was taken from
him, to be restored only when he left.   Dramatic authors

were forbidden fruit to the Moravian Brethren. He grew up to expound Shakespeare as the lay Bible of the English nation, and to draw from these plays the three great lessons which he made the rule of conduct of his own life, ' Love God, love your neighbour, do your work.' He received much from the Moravians, but his was far too large a nature to be bound by their limitations; he could go on to find good in all things.

This chapter may conclude with a sonnet which he wrote for *The Old Neuwieder Magazine.* It is called ' A Christmas Wish ':

> The Peace of God was in the gentle smile
> Of men who lived as Brothers with the Child,
> Being themselves child-hearted. Undefiled
> And unacquainted with the touch of guile,
> United brethren, vowed to God erewhile
> Where they made God their Shelter, made the wild
> A garden ; where ice-bar on ice-bar piled
> Kept man from man, or in some sunburnt isle
> Where the Soul's Frost, with harder severance,
> Kept man the thrall of man, their touch of love
> Gave life to love. Brothers, we children, too,
> Whose hearts your hearts taught :—' May each year advance
> Your work,' we pray, ' with blessings from above
> Large as the measure of all the good you do.'

CHAPTER IV.

FROM SCHOOL TO COLLEGE, 1835-1842.

WHEN Henry Morley returned from Neuwied he was nearly thirteen, and his education was continued with a view to his following his father's profession. The question whether this was what he was best fitted for seems never to have been considered. In 'Some Memories '* he says:

The most loving pains were taken to bend the twig as it was meant to grow. When I was taught, as a boy, drawing and painting, it was stipulated that skulls and bones, painted by me from Nature, should have their turn among the charcoal heads and sunset cottages. . . . When I went to a country town for schoolboy holidays, I was made free of the infirmary, and was allowed, as a young dog of the regiment, to look on at the practice of the surgeons and physicians.

But though he had no distaste, he had no liking for this training, and the following account which, in 1843, he gives of these years is significant of much that follows :

When I returned home from Neuwied, æt. twelve and a half, I went to the Proprietary School at Stockwell. When I left, I held the second place in the school, and imagine it might with ease have been first had the idea of competition ever entered into my head. The headmaster constantly complained that I was indolent, and I as constantly went on in my own way.

---

* P. 10.

My good master (he was a nice fellow) judged me rightly; I am indolent, and I feel it as a fault I cannot conquer even now. . . . In those places where to be first is to be where anyone might be that chose, I never cared farther than to maintain a respectable position. If I sank to mediocrity my pride was stung, and I would work just sufficiently to keep somewhere near the best, and there my care was ended. But where distinction is to be earned in fields that others cannot, or that otherwise they dare not tread, there I am by no means indolent, there I can put forth my energy, and by that means have been always able to maintain a character satisfying to my pride (and I am very, very proud), quite independent of all other people. . . .

It was from about my fourteenth year that my turn of mind strongly developed itself in the propensity to scribble. I began to write the most execrable verses with incessant diligence. Commenced a play—a tragedy, forsooth—'Aristomenes' . . . and very fine I thought it. Towards the latter end of my period at school, and while I was in the highest form, my literary vigour developed itself in a most alarming manner. I started a school newspaper, a burlesque of the common daily journals, a sort of medium in the shape of leading articles, advertisements, etc., for squibbing and quizzing things in general connected with the school establishment. Being particularly personal, this production, which appeared twice weekly, became soon popular beyond my utmost expectations —nay, so successful that an opposition paper soon arose, and the fun became doubled. Then I worked away at my publishing in forms of every sort—sent round comic tales in weekly parts, wrote an antiquarian treatise upon a shabby cap pertaining to the rival editor—and, urged on by applause, wasted in such nonsense all my school hours, and spent odd moments in bed, or walking to and fro from school, over the necessary dull routine of lessons. At the same time also, at the recommendation of Dr. Forbes, I had commenced the translation of a German work on anatomy, and while my school hours were spent in writing things of the lightest, my home hours were devoted to translating a thing of the driest. I did not understand a word of anatomy, but my father put my translation into a medical and proper shape, so I translated on with patient drudgery, and actually completed about eight hundred pages,

3—2

when the publisher who had engaged to take them became bankrupt (lucky 'twas no later, or it would have been laid on to me), and though the work was consigned to his successor, I was thoroughly tired of the job, and so it rested. Mechanical task-work as this was, I have been gainer by it; I have learned perseverance, acquired so first the habit of spending day by day without weariness my pen in hand, and gained a studious turn of mind. This I have preserved, and though my studies have assumed a somewhat out-of-the-way direction, for the last five or six years of my life not many days have been spent otherwise than in closely studying at something. Neither do I think that I have paid much attention to subjects that had not intrinsic worth.

All this, then, I put down to the tutorship of Krause's 'Anatomy,' and am particularly grateful to Herr Krause accordingly.

At sixteen I was transferred to King's College, where I continued about two years in the department of general literature, still acting on my own principle to do just enough that I might have a place that I could hold without blushing, and make sufficient progress to give pleasure to my father. Beyond that point I gave the freest license to my natural indolence—missed lectures day after day for no other reason than that they were dry. Literally *wasted my time.* Not the less that at that time a great part of it was spent in writing the huge heap of stupidity, with its one or two good bits, which I considered a pattern of romance, under the name of 'Ellerton Castle.' I was working, too, at all sorts of other things—all trash—but I suppose they had the same effect as school exercises that teach one to get better as one goes on.

*　　　*　　　*　　　*　　　*

There are a few other stories of his schoolboy days. He was in the habit of paying Sunday visits to an uncle, who regularly read a Sunday newspaper, with frequent ejaculations of 'Bless my soul!' The boy determined his uncle should have something to read more worthy of these manifestations of astonishment, and sent to the paper an invented account of some marvellous performances of 'Spring-heeled Jack,' who was then frightening everybody with feats of highway robbery. This account was duly inserted in the newspaper, and its reading aloud caused much gratification.

At the house of another relative, his host, apologizing for the smallness of a dish of turnips, remarked that ' turnips were scarce.' On leaving, he went to all the greengrocers in the neighbourhood—tradition says twenty —and at each bought and paid for one pennyworth of turnips, desiring them to be sent to the address he gave. . During the whole of the next day turnips continued to arrive there at frequent intervals.

The charge of being indolent may seem strange to those who remember the enormous capacity for work developed in later days, but Professor Morley always maintained that his natural inclinations were indolent. He enjoyed relaxation, and could never have become a mere machine for turning out work. Undoubtedly, from the age of fifteen the love of literature became the master passion. He looked to medicine for a livelihood, and it was many years before he dreamed of the possibility of earning a livelihood in any other way. Moreover, he was by no means unsuccessful, either as a medical student or a young practitioner. If he had ever become a specialist, it would probably have been in connection with mental diseases. Among his own ancestors he found what he called ' a trace of insanity,' though others, perhaps, would have been content to call it 'a nasty temper.' In his correspondence he several times alludes to the fact with a seriousness which shows how he regarded it as a warning for himself. The vividness of his childish illusions, and the vigorous creativeness of his imagination in after-days, indicate at once a real danger and a source of literary power. Had he led an ill-regulated life, instead of one of absolute temperance and purity, the consequences might soon have been serious ; but he passed scatheless through the temptations that beset the path of a medical student, and by the exercise of strong common-sense he escaped all danger, and developed a quickness of fancy that was to serve him in good stead. One night, when he had been working late, he looked up from the table where he was writing and saw a white lady seated in a chair at the other end. Without hesitation he got up, walked round the table, and seated himself in the chair which contained his spectral *vis-à-vis*. Under this treatment the white lady disappeared. She returned no more, and the story may be taken to illustrate the life passage from a morbid to a healthy imagination.

His own experience gave him in after-years a singular power in dealing with cases of incipient insanity. It is remarkable how many people, knowing him as a kind friend, came to consult him on such subjects; and, while never assuming professional responsibility, he gave advice and explained principles of treatment which were often found of the greatest value.

His regular medical studies at King's College began in 1838, and he matriculated at the University of London the following year. He studied geology under John Phillips, and diligently attended the botany lectures of David Don. He says :

Visible interest in the class of botany, and unfailing attendance at the herborizing expeditions, deluded Professor Don one year into the supposition that I was his best man. It was not possible without rudeness to stay away from the examination, but there was one unobtrusive student in the class who had worked harder and knew more than any of us. When we were in the examination-room, and were left now and then to ourselves, with freedom for talk, that student referred frankly to two questions on mosses and seaweeds for which he was not prepared, and said he could not answer them. I could, but did not; so the right man had the prize, and the favourite came in second.*

He obtained the first prize in T. Rymer Jones's class on Comparative Anatomy and Zoology in 1840. He

* 'Some Memories,' p. 18.

attended three courses of Descriptive and Surgical Anatomy, and dissècted under R. Partridge. He had two courses on Surgery by W. Fergusson, and three courses of Experimental Chemistry in the Laboratory under W. Allen Miller. He was appointed, after an examination, Dr. George Budd's clinical clerk for the in-patients at the hospital on August 25, 1842.

He was honorary secretary to the College Medical and Scientific Society during the session 1842-43, and was afterwards elected an honorary member of the society. He took no degree, but in October, 1843, was enrolled as a free member of the Society of Apothecaries, having previously obtained a license to pràctise medicine in any part of England and Wales.

This is a creditable, but by no means distinguished, college career; his real interest, as he has already told us, lay in other pursuits, in the tragedies, novels, poems, and essays, of which many specimens are still extant in MS.

For the King's College Literary and Scientific Society he wrote an essay on 'The Comparative Excellence of Ancient and Modern Literature,' and one on 'Spectral Impressions.' For the Medical Society he wrote an introductory address, and essays on 'The Colours of Flowers,' on 'Spontaneous Combustion,' and one, with considerable pains, on 'Minute Diagnosis of Diseases of the Brain.'

But there were not in existence sufficient societies to occupy his literary ambition, and, with two college chums, he founded the Owl Club. These were Christopher Wharton Mann, of King's, and Charles H. Hitchings, of St. Bartholomew's.

We three medical students formed a small confederation of rhymers for common enjoyment of the poets, and for freest criticism of one another. We called ourselves the Owl Club; one was Ulula, one was Aziola, and I was Screech. We were ready to admit more birds into the nest if we had found them. We met daily as friends, once a week as the club, when each read what he supposed to be the best piece of work done by him since the last meeting. Upon each Owl's work there was the frankest criticism from the other two. When any paper came up to the Owls' standard of excellence, it was stamped with the great seal of the club, that represented an owl flying, with the Athenian proverb for success, Γλαὺξ ἵπταται.*

This club made its appearance in public by starting the *King's College Magazine*, which found a publisher in William Houlston. It ran a course of monthly numbers from July, 1841, to December, 1842, and now binds up into two fair-sized volumes. Henry Morley's principal contributions to it are ' Ellerton Castle,' translations from Lessing and Novalis, and a good deal of original verse.

One of the papers which obtained the seal of the club was called ' The Dream of the Lilybell.' It was written in 1841, and reappears among the ' Early Papers.' This is a love poem, and he speaks of it in a letter he wrote while at college.

The ' Lilybell ' was called a dream because it was made Canto II. of a poem in which a lady went to sleep in her garden in Canto I., at evening time, and, by request of the poet (who wanted her to love him), all his friends, the flowers, sent her dreams. Four dreams were intended to embrace the several phases of love, and the current of the dreamer's thoughts was intended to be followed in the regular chain, showing how each dream became suggested, predisposed in this by the scent of a lilybell.

Of course, when he was writing it, the young poet was thinking of one particular lady. His nature craved for love, and contained a great wealth of love that was ready to flow forth in an abundant stream of pure unselfish affection. He was for a short time engaged to one of his cousins, but this was broken off; and after one or two brief flutters in other directions, his heart found

* ' Some Memories,' p. 14.

the mate to whom it rendered a lifelong devotion ; and
on each side love and faithfulness triumphed over difficulties that might well have daunted hearts less faithful
and loving.

His friend at Chichester, C. A. Jaques, introduced him
to a Mr. Adames, a leading citizen engaged there in business, and a strong Liberal politician. Mr. Adames took
his young friend over to Newport, Isle of Wight, about
1841, and introduced Henry Morley to the family of
Mr. Joseph Sayer, his brother-in-law. Mr. Sayer's second
daughter, Mary Anne, was a bright-eyed, attractive, intellectual, well-read girl, not so handsome as the cousin just
mentioned, but with a mind that had been fashioned in
heaven to be the corresponding helpmeet to his own. So
during the next two years, whenever his heart was feeling
desolate, his thoughts would keep going back to the girl
he had met at Newport, and had counted as a friend ever
since. It is no wonder he hesitated before asking her
to become his wife. His parents were strict Church
people, and the Sayers were Unitarians. Moreover, Mr.
Morley was a surgeon, and Mr. Sayer was a draper. The
son knew what family opposition there would be on his
own side, though perhaps he was hardly prepared for the
family pride which aroused at one time at least equal
opposition on the other side. But the young people
knew their own minds, and were quietly determined to
carry through what they felt was their own affair. They
became engaged, at first secretly. Henry Morley was
naturally anxious that his father should see something
of the girl he loved, and know more of her than the two
facts of the heresy and the shop, before the parents'
consent was asked to the engagement. He hoped to be
able to arrange for her to meet his family, and felt sure
the engagement would then soon be recognised.

The engagement lasted from the summer of 1843 to
the spring of 1852. These nine years are the stormy

period of Henry Morley's life. He met with altogether unlooked-for difficulties, partly through his own fault, much more through the evil in other men, and the bad advice given him by his own friends. He became involved in lawsuits and loaded with debt, from which he found no possibility of honourable escape (he did not count bankruptcy honourable), until he had thrown up his profession and made an entirely fresh start as a teacher and a writer. The whole story of this period is told minutely in the letters he poured forth to the girl who was waiting for him at Newport, and who had her own family difficulties to encounter, and much home opposition to bear during these long years of hope deferred. A large number of these letters have been preserved, and it has been one of the privileges of my life to read them. They tell a tale full of interest; it is a romance of true love running its troubled course, and ending, like an old-fashioned novel, with marriage and happiness ever after.

But they show more than this. They tell the story of *the making of the man.* He himself knew what he had won during these years of storm and strain. His religious faith was infinitely deepened and strengthened. He found how all things could be made to work together for good. He passed through the fiery furnace, and nothing after this could ever make him doubt God's love and goodness. Those who gave him their love and reverence in after-years, and found his words to them so helpful in their difficulties, as well as all who have found the true soul of the man in the religion of the writer, will be glad to trace some of the steps by which this spiritual experience was won.

The series of letters to Miss Sayer begins on July 6, 1843, and there are several written while he was still at college, during that July and the following August.

In the second of these (July 11) he says something of

his plans.   He is now living in lodgings with his friend
Mann, at 63, Hatton Garden.   On September 14 he
expected to leave, having obtained his license to practise,
by passing the examination at the Apothecaries' Hall, and
to settle in some other part of London, taking his degree
and becoming Dr. Morley a twelvemonth later, and he
thinks it may be prudent for them to wait still another
' year before marriage.

The conclusion of this letter refers to an important
subject, which he treats with characteristic earnestness:

One point more remains to be spoken of : the difference in
creed.

On this he writes at considerable length, expressing his
conviction that 'there is not much difference between our
views when they are rightly compared and comprehended.'
He proposes that they shall set apart special letters
for theological discussion.   He wrote the first of what
was intended to be a series of such epistles.   It is an
earnest plea for the acceptance in faith of mysteries
which we cannot understand.   Miss Sayer read it, as he
hoped she would, one Sunday morning, sitting alone on
the seashore at Sandown.   But she was not convinced,
and sent him a spirited reply in defence of human reason,
with several quotations from Dr. Channing.   Her lover
felt somewhat discouraged, and thought it would be
better to defer the discussion till they were man and
wife.   Before that time came, however, his own creed
was greatly changed, and his wish was fulfilled, though
not quite in the way he expected, 'that hearts in sympathy
together should utter in every point to God the self-same
prayer.'

Writing on July 28, he relates the following :

A scene that occurred the night after I first wrote to you
has taken such a strong hold of my memory that it keeps
rising, sometimes so distinctly that it makes my eyes water

over again, and yet it is nothing but a common everyday
occurrence; perhaps not a week passes but I see two or three
more worthy of remembrance, and yet take no note of them.
I think I told you that it was upon that evening Mann went
into the country.   I rode with him to the railway terminus (he
didn't know what was in my head, though), and when he left
me, there I was in Bishopsgate Street—a sadly remote region—
lonely and dreary and anxious, the evening before me, and what
could I do?   Of course I went in search of music, and started
off in a bus, hoping to be in time for a good bit of ' Tancredi.'
Habitually deficient in the talent of ' having my eyes about
me,' and then, my dearest Mag, of course more so than ever,
I became suddenly conscious that the unhappy bus-driver had
conveyed me to the still more out-of-the-way regions at the top
of Tottenham Court Road.   He might as well have driven me
to Barbary.   I got out directly, but ' the thing ' was too far
gone.   There was no chance of getting near music; indeed, I
was farther from it now than ever.   So I had no help for it,
and went into a little neighbouring theatre, to see if I could
pluck up spirit sufficient to have a laugh over a melodrama.

I don't know whether you have any experience of the mood
I was then in—it is no very uncommon one with me—fearfully
earnest, stern.   I went to the part of the theatre which I knew
to be the least·frequented, consequently the part I always
patronize at minor theatres.   It is a part belonging to the
boxes, placed above them, next the ceiling, and divided only
by a partition from the gallery—they call it ' the slips.'   Of
course they must be empty generally, because for those who
go to ' see the performances ' it is precisely the worst place in
the house—perched directly over the stage, level with the gods,
and costs the same price as the boxes.

I prefer to go there, because at such a place I do *not* go to
see the performances, but find more amusement in the audience
(which is by far the best seen from that point), where I, or I
and Mann—for, except on such extraordinary occasions, I don't
go alone—can sit in reserve and make our observations upon
things in general in perfect peace and quiet.

When I went in, there was a donkey of a man pretending to
amuse the audience by sitting nearly an hour upon the stage
and telling anecdotes.   That was a terrible deal to be put up
with, considering my humour.   At length the melodrama began.

Outrageous beyond the common order, for it was considered a
good melodrama, and now and then (in its most striking and
pathetic points) positively did succeed in getting a good laugh
out of my dumps. It was, of course, full of the unhealthy
stage sentiment, especially full of those fine things about the
depth of woman's love, the honour and respect to woman due,
which were received always with vociferous approbation, and
upon which the scene I want to tell you (but I don't think I
ever shall get to it) is a painful commentary. It was in the
middle of an ' interesting situation ' in this style, when some
hoarse woman was talking heroism about the Lord knows
what, and the whole house was breathless with attention, that
there arose what is called ' a row among the gods,' which
increased until the stage business was stopped for a few
minutes before order could be re-established. From my situation I looked down into the gallery, and I could see what the
row was. A widow woman, dressed in the garb of the most
decent poverty, but pale, and ill, and thin, was endeavouring
to lead her son out of temptation. He was a great fellow of
about eighteen, without his jacket, with his shirt-sleeves tucked
up his arms—the picture of a reprobate. He had been disturbed at an interesting point. His mother, as she said (for I
was able to hear every word that passed), had missed him in
the afternoon, and had spent her evening, that she very, very
ill could spare, in searching for him. *Here* she had at length
found him. They were struggling when the row began—she,
that is, was endeavouring to lead him away, and he resisting.
She held his wrist, not in anger—there was not the faintest
trace of vulgar passion in her look and tone, but, oh! such
sorrow, such a heart-broken face, dear Mag, beneath that
widow's cap. Then the boy struck her, and shook her off with
violence—struck her off several times. Dear Mag, I felt as if
each blow were on my heart ; and the poor woman looked so
deeply grieved, and yet no word of anger. ' What ! strike
your mother !' that was all she said. ' Oh, naughty boy !'
Poor soul ! she could not form a harsher phrase than that—
and I thought perhaps because he was her only son. Some in
the gallery cried ' Shame !' and the poor widow recognised a
face she knew, an honest workman's face, in all that crowd of
ugliness. ' Help me, Mr. ——,' she cried—' help me to take
him away from here. *He is my boy !*' Oh, there was so much

agony and so much of the tender mother's love in those few words, that I turned away at them, and cried most bitterly. The boy grew more angry, and again struck her; but I know not well what followed; there was more struggling, then there were two loud piercing shrieks. I looked; he had either thrown her down, or they had fallen, for they were both upon the ground, and she had fainted. This is the scene, Mag, that has since been constantly in my mind, and often makes me cry like a great fool (I have cried again while I wrote it); it has made so deep an impression that it never can be erased from my mind. It will for ever be associated with that funny time of the suspense that you so pleasantly did put an end to.

The next letter, August 1, opens with exultation over a proposal that Miss Sayer should come to London and teach in Miss Corner's school, Portland Place. The lovers would be able to meet one another 'naturally'; if people suspected, no harm in that; his half-sister Polly was at the school; there would be just the opportunities he desired for his own family to become better acquainted with Miss Sayer before the engagement was announced to them. It mentions an unexpected call at his lodgings from his father and stepmother, who very nearly discovered a pile of love-letters which would have prematurely revealed the secret.

Here also is a characteristic episode from the life of a senior medical student, left during the vacation in charge of many patients, and also deeply in love :

Yesterday morning, at seven of the clock, a stern summoner broke my rest and departed. I rose and dressed. ' I'll fortify myself with breakfast ere I start.' I sat down, had just commenced—the stern summoner reappeared in breathless haste. ' I'll be back to breakfast!' I exclaimed in desperation, and rushed forth. At 9 a.m., seated by the bedside of my patient, I revolved in thought. ' The post is now in Hatton Garden. I am an hungered for breakfast and Mag's letter. I can return within an hour—surely for that space they can spare me.' I made known my thoughts; they opposed; I was determined, expostulated, encouraged, and ran off. Post was not in. For twenty minutes love and conscience struggled in my buzzum. Conscience triumphed. I set forth on' my return—beheld the red coat of the postman halfway down the street, approaching with him the stern summoner. He was inexorable—dared not wait ; with unwilling haste I followed in his path. The' red coat paused. I rushed after him suddenly across the road. He had dived into an office, and was lost. I returned, resumed my path. The postman reappeared ; again I darted after him, ascertained that he possessed a letter, which he would not give me in the street ; rushed home to wait for him, leaving the stern summoner in the middle of the road, gazing with speechless astonishment on my eccentric and unprofessional performances. I got at last your letter, and, having thrust it into my pocket, galloped off like a mad bull through Holborn, the stern summoner following with ' a stitch in his side ' (most naturally, since he was a tailor), arrived in a little time and a perspiration at my deserted post, and, having performed expected duties, sat down by the bedside to read your letter.

Having posted this letter, he begins another the same evening, containing more about the arrangement with Miss Corner, and all that this may lead to. ' I want to hear the result of your negotiations with Miss Corner ; like the little boys, " Please may I begin to make castles ?" is always in my head.' And so it was all through his life ; never was there a man with a stronger tendency to build castles. Some of them became substantial edifices, enduring monuments of solid, honest, skilful hard work, but that was not to be just yet.

He had a very tender feeling towards dumb animals, and once gave himself a bad headache by going without his dinner to feed a hungry dog which promptly adopted him as her master. This, too, is his judgment on cats:

You must know I hold an opinion about cats which causes me to think in no complimentary terms of every man (not woman) who don't like them. I look on them as the most perfect four-legged personifications of feminine grace, to treat which otherwise than with complete respect would not be manly. This is not so out-of-the-way an opinion as you may think it at first sight. I do think it a real and positive test. Indeed, I once broached it to a cat-hater of my acquaintance, who was so smitten in conscience with the truth of the remark, that he has never dared to speak irreverently of a cat since.

The next letter describes a meeting of the Owl Club, held the previous evening. There was first the usual devotion to poetry, after which came the following reaction.

Now, dearest Mag, if you had seen the Owls last night after their meeting, what a laugh you would have had at their expense!

But I'll tell you their proceedings. You must know that after their fortnightly meetings, the evening being spoiled, and the Owls not yet domestic animals, it is generally the plan to go out somewhere together for amusement. Last night our deliberations as to where we should go were peculiarly intricate. Nothing could be thought of that would suit us. For three-quarters of an hour we were in active consultation—Aziola walking up and down, Ulula divided between sitting on the chair and upon Screech's stomach, for Screech was extended on the floor. That posture being favourable to thought, Screech got an idea. 'Let us buy,' he said, 'a few grains of veratrine, go to the slips of the Queen's Theatre, and make the actors sneeze in all their speeches.' The idea was hailed with enthusiasm. Veratrine, you must know, dear Mag, is the active principle of hellebore, and a very active principle it is, its principal property being that if a particle thereof floating in the air come into contact with a mortal nose, it immediately provokes a violent, incessant sneezing. The Queen's Theatre is the little place at which the incident occurred of which I told you, and the slips therein (above the stage) as I before described. We discovered there were two melodramas, the first being 'Alonzo the Brave and the Fair Imogen,' which fond lovers we desired should sneeze out their affection for each other. Imogen is a ghost, too, and a *sneezing ghost* we thought would be immense! Lo and behold, then, in those lofty slips, the powder among them, Aziola, Ulula, and Screech. It was at first proposed to try the effect of our practice on the pit, and Aziola dusted a little down. No effect. A little more. It didn't at all answer. Aziola seemed afraid of being seen. Screech took the paper. ' You don't dose them

enough!' But at the words there arose in the gallery a sound
as if everybody had suddenly acquired a horrid cold. Sneeze
thundered after sneeze in every form of melody and all varieties
of intonation—masculine, feminine, and juvenile. The powder
was too light to fall. It had dispersed, and floated at the top
of the theatre, where, of course, it made its attack upon the
gods alone. Screech, however, was not to be satisfied unless
he could disturb the stage. Planting himself over the trum-
peter, he hoped to make him sneeze into his trumpet, and
threw over for that purpose an efficient dose. Sapiently poking
his head over then, for the purpose of watching its effect, he
fell into his own snare, and began himself 'tishooing' for ten
minutes without ceasing. For the rest of the evening Screech
appeared to have a worse cold than anybody; but in a short
time the whole theatre was taken bad.' Ulula then took the
powder under his direction, and by the time he had used it all,
sympathized with Screech; they wandered about arm-in-arm
and sneezed together. All this time we had been dancing
about the theatre in all directions; now, however, going into
the boxes, we placed ourselves in the front row of the dress-
circle, sneezing like judges, with our ears wide open in intense
enjoyment. The effect was little on Aziola: he did not handle
the veratrine so rudely. Ulula and I were really very bad.
The chief fun, indeed, consists in our having so completely
victimized *ourselves*. Not a particle disturbed the actors. We
might have known it could not had we considered. There is
always a sharp draught *from* the stage, which, of course, blew
it all among the audience. Of course we used a very little
only, for a large dose would have produced danger.

On our return, having escorted Aziola to his own abode,
Ulula, feeling his nose very sore from sneezing, and his eyes
smarting and his lips (in all which Screech did too well
sympathize), proceeded to inquire into the properties of
veratrine, and what it was, and so on. The result was, he
seriously believed that he was poisoned. I tried in vain to get
rid of the fancy. Well, Mag, and what do you think was his
most sage and medical treatment of his case? Don't scold *me*
for not physicking myself properly. Hark to poor Ulula's
account of himself, given this morning: 'I left you when you
would not come with me to supper, and devoured a plate of
alamode beef, a large quantity of salad to cool my mouth, and

4

drank a quantity of beer. Then I thought it was a narcotic
poison, and therefore' (this was serious) 'felt afraid to go to
sleep, as I knew that it was dangerous to sleep when one was
poisoned with narcotics. I was the more afraid because I felt
so drowsy' (no wonder, considering how late it was!). 'So, I
walked about in the park till four o'clock (! ! !) to keep myself
awake; then I went home, and, being hungry, had another
supper. At six o'clock this morning, finally, I went to bed!'
There's a doctor for you, Mag! I think that is the best part
of the fun—Ulula so seriously fancying himself poisoned, and
his scientific treatment. Certainly, if the most sapient Owls
see any joke in their proceedings, 'tis entirely at the expense of
one another. With poetic justice their offence recoiled upon
themselves. My nose was sore when I woke, and Ulula
sneezed all the morning. Can you fancy, Mag, three steady,
'poetical young gentlemen' making themselves so perfectly
and thoroughly ridiculous?

On August 5 he hears that it is definitely settled that
Miss Sayer is to come to Miss Corner's, and gives full
vent to his rapture over the prospect. He has a plan for
meeting her at the station which is not approved. Probably, too, there were some remarks on the episode at
the theatre which call forth a very true and thoughtful
rejoinder, dated August 7 :

I think, dear love, that I must borrow your most philosophic
pen, for I am in a moralizing vein. First, you shall have a
little sermon responsive to your scolding of this morning, which
you founded on my most romantic notion of our gossiping
together previously to your deposition at Miss Corner's. It does
not require one quarter of a minute's consideration to coincide
with you upon the absurdity of the matter. My sermon, however, proposes to exhibit that it was not a thing to scold, but
laugh at. Do not—the sermon thus begins—mistake conventional for moral laws, nor assign to both a similar importance :
the one expedient alone, the other just. To break the one is
folly, and deserves to be laughed at. To break the other is
sin, and deserves to be condemned. Now, in the notion, my
dearest Mag, which is the subject of this little sermon, I think
if you sent inquiries round into each corner of that, to me,

invaluable little heart of yours, none of them would be able to tell you in reply the name of any rule of virtue or morality which the said notion is so wicked as to oppose. That it outrages the most fundamental doctrines of society, I readily admit. That to society, and us as members of it, those doctrines in the present state of human nature are indispensable I have no will to deny. It is by these that we maintain our stand among each other, by which alone our bodily eye can judge. Yet, while we respect them, we must not forget that as the moral law is far above, this, the more tangible, yet lies beneath us. We look *down* upon this one, as the ground on which we plant our steps; but we gaze *upward* to the other, as into the depths of the bright heaven we revere. To hide before the sight of Heaven is sin; to seek to jump away from off the ground is folly. To this folly I own a childish predilection. I know not whether it be the vanity of eccentricity, or if it be in the constitution of my mind, that I am constantly offending against all these wholesome laws of conventional restraint. That many of them are absurd is true; these I take pleasure in upsetting. But there are many absolutely necessary, and, as in the present case, I fear I am not free from many an impulse that would lead me to break these as well. I am afraid, spite of your scolding, Mouse, that I cannot say, ' I won't do so no more.' I will not wilfully offend, but I may darkly prophesy recurrence of the crime, nevertheless. To keep pure the moral law, we have a ' conscience ' planted in our breasts, that takes upon itself the task of prompting us. Conventional laws have not a whit of this self-acting power—they are acquired by practice; and, alas! I practise them but seldom! Well, love, 'twill be a little business for you to help me. Hitherto I have but lived by impulse, trusting to God that He, in His mercy for a child, would mould my heart so that its impulses led not to sin. I do respect these impulses, dear Mag, and if you love me, so ought you to do, since one of them brought you and me together. . . .

If I have been deeply moved, if I have been wounded in some cherished feeling, the wound being such as shall provoke thoughts that exalt the mind, I am most keenly sensitive, but inevitably then reaction follows, and I sink into the child awhile. So, on the other hand, if I seek to acquire for a time a poetical tone of mind, it is no trivial means of attaining the object to reduce the mind, by effort, to its simplest point; pressed thus as a spring, the moment that this restraint has been removed, it shoots at once up to its highest point, and vibrates there. This is no peculiarity; I believe it to be in minds of a certain character invariably the fact, although the pride of wisdom prevents it from being a fact invariably recorded. So you must not cross my childish freaks, nor pity and despise, but *understand* them. Time has been that I and Mann have rolled and practised summersets together on the carpet; played for an hour at marbles, simply with a marble each, to strike each other's marble and a third—cheating and laughing—childishly eager to strike oftenest—our knees upon the floor. 'A fool' himself, or one that knew us not, would say that we were silly; we, however, neither feel nor do we own a degradation.

This quotation, like most of the others given from these student days, indicates a striking feature in a character which expanded and deepened with advancing years, but lost little or nothing of its early tendencies and capacities. Naturally, it was only Professor Morley's intimate friends who knew how intensely fond he was of sheer nonsense, but they know well how keen was his delight down, we may say, to the time of his wife's death, in childish fun, defying propriety that is merely conventional, and in general outrages upon the dignified side of human nature. A special verb, 'to toodle,' had to be invented to describe this utter abandonment to joking, and the throwing off of all the restraints which generally control sensible people. But without any sense of restraint, all this nonsense was controlled by perfect allegiance to purity. No man ever heard him make a coarse jest. What he enjoyed was the sort of fun which delights a child. Equally characteristic was his reverence for all else that really deserves reverence. He never laughed at aught that could be conscientious conviction. Seldom, if ever, was his humour sarcastic. Once there may have been a slight tendency to this, but it was burnt out of

him in the trial that was to come, which left him very
tender-hearted, full of kindly feeling, and very slow to
think evil.

There are many other references to the Owl Club
in these college ‘letters, and he speaks of it in ‘ Some
Memories’ in a way that shows the affection and gratitude with which he remembered its meetings. It keenly
stimulated his poetic and critical powers, and the nonsense was not allowed to interfere with its real object.
He says: ‘ We choose to make game out of ourselves in
order to remove the sense of absurdity that would otherwise annoy us in pursuing gravely the business of a
complex association with only three real members.’ He
thought it might ‘ some day become a very powerful
society’; but it may safely be said that its permanent
influence on literature was limited to the culture of his
own mind.

Literary projects, not his medical degree, fill his head.

You shall help me learn Italian. That's my next leisure
task, for I hope to be able to read Tasso and Dante by this
time next year. There's only Spanish then among the
requisites. Calderon, Cervantes, Lope de Vega, and the
ballads *must* be read. Camoens I must be content with in
translation.

Before finally leaving King's College, he succeeded in
carrying his point in a matter on which he had set his
heart. The Medical Society offered a ten-guinea prize
for the best essay on some appointed subject. Mr. Morley
proposed that the subject should ‘ be left to the option
of each competitor under stringent regulations that made
originality, and a valuable obscure subject, *sine quâ non*.’
He also succeeded in persuading the society not to confine the competition to its own members, but to throw
it ‘ open to the men of every class that had but wits to
try for it.’

Two more letters remain belonging to this period.

One is later than September 14, but is simply dated 'Chichester, Tuesday morning,' and begins :

MY DEAR FATHER,

I have just received a letter from Miss Sayer acquainting me with certain steps that you have taken, which I do sincerely and confidently trust your heart will not suffer you to insist upon when you are made more fully acquainted with the whole circumstances.

The propitious moment for telling his father of his engagement with Miss Sayer had never come, and the father had made the discovery for himself, and, as the son had expected, strongly opposed the union. The letter is a beautiful earnest appeal, relating very fully various early experiences through which he had passed, and showing how absolutely his mind was now made up, how for the first time he loved with his whole heart, and could henceforth never change. His father's objections are combated with much filial and tender reverence, but, for the time, evidently without success. The other letter is dated October 30, 1843, and is the rough draft of a letter from London to his father on the same subject, especially begging him to withdraw the objection he had made to his son's seeing Miss Sayer at Miss Corner's school. It is a letter again showing the fixity of his determination, and soon after this the father's objection seems to have been withdrawn, and the lovers were allowed to see one another again, to go out together on Sunday, and to look forward to a Christmas together in the Isle of Wight.

CHAPTER V.

DUNSTER, 1843.

HENRY MORLEY would have had a simple and easy entrance into the medical profession if he could have succeeded his father in the South London practice. But his father's headaches had followed him to Kennington, and made him anxious to retire from practice and live in the country. The legacy he received from Mrs. Lefford made this possible, but did not afford him power to do much more to help his son forward in life. Towards the end of 1843, therefore, the son was looking out for an opening on his own account. He made one or two attempts to get an assistantship in London, but older men were preferred, and he soon resolved to seek his fortune where his services were really wanted. He thus speaks of the introduction to his five years of medical practice:

They began most happily. A year was to be spent in continuance of study, and seeing work as assistant to a medical practitioner. I was one of forty or fifty who answered an advertisement from Dunster, in Somersetshire.

The advertiser—odd name now for a kind friend who brought much happiness into my life!—replied, asking me to meet him half-way at a hotel in Bristol. We met, and the result was that I began work under easy conditions. 'Can you ride?' had been one question. 'I rode once on a donkey, and came off; once on a horse' (it was my father's gig-horse), 'and stuck on. I can try to stick on.' There were some miles of a poor-law district to look after, up and down stony lanes upon hill-sides, as well as along good highroads. My employer was a man of independent means who had the happiest of tempers. He paid me liberally; I lodged next door. He and his wife had no children, and I was treated as if I had been their son. There was no picnic or dinner-party from which I was left out. The wicked old bent towards books of the poets seemed here to strengthen friendships and make life the happier. I did stick on the horses, oftener than not. My employer had seven in his stable, and had a theory that every gentleman ought to be able to break in his own horses. At first a groom was sent with me to show the way from place to place, and give some lessons in the art of riding. I went over a horse's head only four times in the ten months at Dunster. After the first three months of those ten, parish work was given up. Then there was much leisure for a busy idleness. So came the temptation to make a little volume, of which the first pages were printed in 1844, with a coloured illustration on its paper cover, as No. 1 of the *New Phantasus*. Tieck's *Phantasus* was the old one then in mind. . . . The piece in the Appendix to this volume called 'Our Lady's Miracle' was written at Dunster. It was planned as an introduction to a series of incidents show-ing the force of gentleness; but the framework was too fanci-ful, the first incident (not here reprinted) was a failure, and no more was written.*

There is little to add to this picture of his happy start at the beautiful old town, with its grand castle and quaint market-house.

On January 1, 1844, he left Midhurst for London, saw his lately-married brother there, spent the evening at the opera with Mann, and returned with him to sleep. 'We amused ourselves playing the fool; I was a bear, and broke by token the little trestle-bed I slept upon. We were very mad that night, and the next morning off I started to Dunster.'

His employer was Dr. Abraham, whose name is still well remembered there, and who for a long series of years

* 'Some Memories,' p. 19.

had a succession of young men, generally for a twelvemonth at a time, as his assistants. Henry Morley must
have been a pleasant addition to the summer picnics and
the parties.

By the autumn he was planning a further move. Dr.
Abraham would willingly have kept him longer, but had
not sufficient work to occupy his time; and, however
great his interest in his little volume of verse, Henry
Morley meant to succeed in his profession. He looked
out for a partnership, and on September 18 writes to
describe one which he may have at Madeley, Shropshire, with a Mr. G., who asserted his practice to be
worth £700 a year, and capable of being easily raised to
£1,200. For a half-share in this he required £500, with
a further payment of £600 if he should altogether retire
at the end of seven years.

Considerable caution was exercised over this Madeley
partnership. His old teacher, Dr. George Budd, writes:

> I think you are quite right to get into partnership if you can
> obtain a good one. When a man starts on his bottom, what-
> ever his merits, he generally has to wait two or three years
> before he gets his salt, and during this time spends money
> enough in living to have bought him a partnership which
> would at once have made him independent. I think, too, that
> a country district, well peopled and wealthy, offers as many
> advantages for practice as a provincial town. Medical men—
> all but those in commanding practice—are more respected, and
> hold a better social position, in the country than in towns.
> Before you make any bargain with Mr. G., you will, of course,
> learn all you can of his temper and character. Much of your
> comfort in partnership will depend on this. You will take
> care to satisfy yourself that the practice is as good as he
> represents it to be."

Excellent advice, but, alas! not easy to follow.

The idea of a partnership was also approved by his
uncle, William Hicks, a successful man of business, who
had been first junior and then senior partner for many

years in his firm, and who expressed his willingness to
help in certain pecuniary arrangements required for meeting the charges. His father, on October 3 and 4, writes
two letters about a possible partnership with a Midhurst
doctor, but on October 6 he writes again, agreeing that
the Madeley offer is much the better of the two. One of
the oldest members of the Apothecaries' Hall, who knew
both Mr. and Mrs. G., wrote of them in highly favourable
terms. So Henry Morley went to Madeley to look at
things with his own eyes, and have a personal interview
with Mr. G. His father either went with him or joined
him there. Neither of them detected anything wrong
in the statements made to them, though they found Mr.
G.'s books kept in such a way that several hours' work
would have been required before the extent of his practice
could have been accurately verified, and this they did not
undertake, partly because they felt that they had only
Mr. G.'s word for the respectability of patients and
the value of each name. They liked what they saw of
Mr. G., and no one breathed a hint to them to raise
suspicion in .regard to those all-important points : his
temper and character. So the father entered into an
agreement with the landlord of the house which his son
was to occupy, and the two left the place with the matter
practically decided. A deed of partnership was drawn up,
and duly considered by Mr. Hicks' lawyer, who suggested
certain alterations in connection with the eventual retirement of Mr. G. The father and the uncle were not quite
satisfied, and wished for further delay ; but Henry Morley,
feeling that the point in dispute was one not worth discussing, signed the deed on the day originally appointed.

What made it possible for him to do this was a legacy
under the marriage settlements of his father and mother
of £223, to which he was entitled on attaining the age of
twenty-four. There was also a sum of £93 paid to him
when twenty-one, and certain accrued interest which his

father, who was authorized to use it for his education, had preferred to add to the capital. Henry Morley would not be twenty-four years of age till September, 1846, but by insuring his life, and by the help of his uncle, he secured the immediate benefit of these sums. £300 was paid to Mr. G., bills were given him for the remaining £200, and a sum of £150 was provided to start furnishing and housekeeping.

The ten months at Dunster were worth much to him. It was a 'season of refreshing' between two periods of excitement and storm. Writing early in 1845, and looking back on the past year, he says :

The peace of Dunster wiped away every old trace of turmoil. Surrounded by kindness—uninterrupted kindness—met with pleasant looks by everyone I saw, my heart was sensibly refreshed, sore places healed, and my temper at the year's end is certainly improved. With the temper I had a year ago I should have been at war now in all directions, whereas I have now established friendly relations everywhere.

He was indeed soon to meet with treatment which would try his temper to the uttermost.

CHAPTER VI.

MADELEY, 1844—1848.

HENRY MORLEY was anxious to begin work at Madeley on November 1, 1844, and on that day, or soon after, he took up his residence in Mr. G.'s house till he should secure possession of one to be vacated by another surgeon, a Mr. Good, who was leaving Madeley for Warwick. A series of letters to Miss Sayer describe in great detail the house which he hoped would soon be her home as well as his. He bought some of Mr. Good's furniture; he packed and swept, and urged on the whitewasher and paper-hanger to do a better day's work than the man had ever done in his life before. He sketched a bird's-eye view of the house and garden, and a plan showing their situation in the village. A little later he sends plans of the rooms, showing the position of the furniture, and how they two would sit and work. He enters into all particulars with a true lover's confidence that every word he writes will be equally interesting to his sweetheart. These letters, telling 'all about everything,' run sometimes to six quarto pages, written all over and then crossed; luckily, his handwriting, when he had a good quill pen, was exquisitely neat and clear.

On December 14 he begins a long letter:

Saturday night, 10 *o'clock.*

At home . . . for the first time in my life, sitting in slippers and dressing-gown in my own house, by my own fireside.

And such a pretty house ! and such a comfortable fireside, too ! Thank God ! He blesses us abundantly. . . . You'll bless this room, I hope, thousands of times—put your feet beside mine on this very rug.

And so the letter runs on, all description and anticipation.

It would have been 'love in a cottage' if his dreams had come true. The house is still standing in much the same condition as it existed then, and is now tenanted by the mistress of the National School. There is a porch over the front-door, a neat little entrance-hall, right and left are two sitting-rooms about eight feet high and fifteen feet square, with good kitchen premises behind. Upstairs is about the same amount of accommodation. The garden is large, and the orchard and field, with a two-stalled stable and chaise-house, ran the rent up to £37.

In the garden he notes a bed of violets, and the first of the letters from Madeley contains a new pet name for Miss Sayer, Violet, which had originated out of some verses written at Dunster. This has since become common as a woman's name, but it was certainly not common, perhaps it was unknown, when the memories of those days caused the father and mother to choose it for their eldest daughter.

A letter written early in January, 1845, contains a characteristic picture of himself. He had a little leisure on the Sunday, and used it to potter round his property with just the same pleasure that he enjoyed doing the same so many years later at Carisbrooke :

And how have I spent my day ? Throughout this afternoon and evening, my own heart, thinking of you. Thinking of you, dear, directly after dinner I took my stick and called Fanny [his dog]—it was a pleasant afternoon of sun and cloud—and so we rambled through the fields beside our house—through that gate, you know (*vide* pictur'), we come at once into field-paths, and the first field is my own—and as we returned I walked all

round the field, examining its points for good and bad, and
deciding that a frolic of hay-making couldn't ever be perpetrated
there, because it has a wide path through it, and is overlooked
by the rising ground of the neighbouring churchyard. Then
out of the field I came in half a minute to our home, and
passed by the side-entrance to the orchard; explored the
garden, the summer-house, the orchard, settling what wanted
to be done; examining the dog-kennel, the pig-sty, the hedges,
fences, and all; then going into the surgery and seeing therein
much cosiness 'when Mr. G. was gone'—a distant thought
for the present; then scraping my shoes and coming into the
house, and looking at my pretty library—pretty, but not yet
what it is to be.

And then his thoughts wander along the familiar
channel of the joy it will be to have her there, and he
proposes a wedding tour which shall include Dunster.

In some of these letters he enters minutely into plans
and calculations. He expects the partnership to last
five or six years, and that then he shall go on by himself,
and certainly do well, having heard some encouraging
statements about the success of a doctor who lived at
Broseley, just the other side of the Severn. Such were
his hopes; nor were they unreasonable. He was only
twenty-two, an age when many of his medical contem-
poraries had been still hearing lectures, while he had
made a start which should give him a thoroughly satisfactory position before he was thirty.

Intermingled with these professional forecasts comes
the mention of his ambition to be a poet. The scheme
for the publication of successive parts of the *New
Phantasus* had been dropped, and he meant soon to issue
a little volume of poetry. He writes :

Nothing can be done in a day, nothing without perseverance.
That my poetry is not calculated to make an impression, I
know very well. You know, I don't imagine it first-rate, and
don't think either, dear, that I am incapable of wandering out
of my quiet world of flowers and books, etc. It was the plan I

had before me to complete one book in this style—which, if not perfect, is at any rate tolerably original—and then forsake it for more earnest themes. Don't you know, sweetheart, that the muse *matures with life ;* youth plays, manhood works with a purpose. My first scheme was, you know, to use *Dims de Castro* for my next imaginative work—a tragedy—but I think otherwise. What I shall do I know not, but of this rest certain, that my truest guide is my own consciousness of power, that has grown with me from childhood. My imagination gained distinction at school, at college, among its equals there, and why cannot it maintain the same post among its same equals when I and they are men in the world ? I know that ' reason why not ' might be shown in the distractions, etc., of society, as contrasted with the little world of youth ; but there is, for all that, the same comparative power. And do you not know that there is no aim which perseverance and energy cannot attain ? To fight on in the face of every discourage-ment, conscious of strength for the battle, that is to win certain victory. ' Hopeful Eagle.' Yes, dear, I acknowledge no power which can prevent the acquisition of my wish in this respect but death or my own inaction. At the same time my opinion of the merits of this my first book—shortly to appear —is lower perhaps than yours. For the future, it may be possible—there are vague notions often in my head to that effect—to strike out a new path entirely. At present, actual life demands my attention, and thus you see, love, that I don't, as people fear, leave my bread to find its own way to my mouth, and forget duty over pleasure.

One or two more extracts may be given to show what his hopes were for their home-life. Here is a letter written on Sunday evening, January 19 :

DEAREST VIOLET,
I have been sitting in church following my own thoughts of Love and Death and Heaven till my eyes watered, and now I'm back in my snuggery, thinking of Love and Life and Earth. I scarcely dare, sometimes, Marianne, to think of the bliss in store for us. It seems something so unusual, so difficult to realize without trembling lest death or change of any sort save change of heart (for that change cannot be) should intervene to dash aside our cup of sweetness. Yet we shall

taste this cup. I think it is God's will to place it in our hands and bless us. Oh, dearest spirit, do not let us ever forget what we owe to Him. Let us join our souls in love of our dear Heavenly Father, who bestows already joys upon us far—very far—beyond our deserts. May neither of us ever beckon the other aside from the path of God. Singly, the world might tempt us, but together we shall be strong, and, being stronger, shall have less excuse for sin, for want of forbearance and love and charity to our companions. We must keep apart from sordid thoughts, hold loving ward over each other's hearts and lips. We can watch each other's hearts, for in our love they will be open ; there will be no cloud, no obscurity, between us. Our two hearts we will make into one, our thoughts shall run together in one channel, and our love shall never be stained— though we may live on into the twentieth century—not once, dear—no, not once—with an unkindness. And now, my one dearest companion, let us fancy our companionship in life visibly and matrimonially established. Let us fancy Marianne Morley mistress in the Madeley cottage, and Henry Morley master ; and let us draw some true pictures, for we have facts now, thank God, to deal with. We know our lot in life, so far at least, and need no draughts upon the fancy.

Family prayers play an important part in his antici- pation of the beginning and ending of each day :

Then Mary and Ben will come, and we four shall sit together in a semicircle round the fire, and thank God together for our household peace and happiness. That is soon done, but it leaves its impression through the day. I see it does so here, and feel it in myself. The memory of our household prayer often acts as a check upon me when I might become angry, or do or say something in unchristian spirit. Then we shall breakfast together, and make known to each other our plans and·hopes and arrangements for the day, or discuss them, being already known. Formal visiting won't occupy much time, but you can have more rational and pleasant morning calls among those I recommend to your care of the sick poor. *You,* dearest, shall have patients to see. Why not ? Wherever she can do good—without the appearance of ostentation—my wife shall move as a good angel of charity and love. It is right that a well-ordered household should set apart something—

permitted by its means—for the poor. You will enjoy the sweet consciousness of having all around the little circle of our dwelling many hearts that you have eased, many that love you. How shall we spend our evenings? The curtains will be drawn by five o'clock, and the cloth laid on the green table (the open card table, you know), and the lamp lighted, and then we shall sit *tête-à-tête* to dinner, and after dinner we shall sit before the fire for half an hour in quiet, happy conversation. That will be the time when we may love to recur to our past, to Miss Corner's, the Brixton chapel, or to Mr. Cleeves—farther back—or to Chichester, or to any of the numberless adventures and trials of our love.

And so runs on the anticipation of evenings devoted to reading aloud, listening to her singing, and sometimes to working separately, but never too much absorbed in work to be unconscious of the happiness afforded by her presence, or to be unable to chatter with her. He always had, in later life, a wonderful power of not letting little interruptions interfere with the current of his deeper thought. He seldom required to be alone when he was writing a book, and would be refreshed, not hindered, by an occasional break off to discharge some impulse of domestic interest or affection.

This, love, is our winter scheme. And summer—summer will be quite different, but not less happy. Madeley in summer becomes quite another place out of doors—all beauty and romance in its vicinity. Hills, woods, waters, ruins, views, the Wrekin, our garden and orchard, our summer-house with jessamine and roses and ivy over its walls, our field and our hay-making, and our joyous hearts. Ah, what a happy future is before us, love! and, ah, how very quickly it's approaching! I've been here three months already—January is flying. When we may marry, we can't say quite determinately, but every day is a firm step, and every month a stride. We shan't be more than a year—in fact, may make next Christmas the object of our view. I'm almost sure I shall be able to marry you about that time—and here's one month nearly gone towards it.

5

A little later comes a letter which contains the following:

You say my tale of 'Home' reads like a description in fairyland. I am sure, dear, it feels to me imbued with more than fairy happiness. I wish, dear Violet, that many who think they have a home to live in could just sit in my heart sometimes of an evening, and then see whether they can't reform their own firesides. Your Eagle don't understand, dear Magpie, why he should confine the blissful ideal to verses, and make no effort at its realization. Very well. Now, love, let us look into the theory of the matter. What *are* homes ? Every man makes his own a mirror of his inward heart. There he casts aside reserve and formality, and follows the bent of his spirit unreproved. A clockwork man will have a clockwork home; a selfish man will have a selfish household; a passionate man will live in a house of strife; an 'uncomfortable' man (like Mr. G.) will live in an uncomfortable home. Now, which makes a man most fit for the discharge of his worldly duties— intervals of rest and peace, or intervals of meanness, selfishness, anger, or discomfort ? Yet these last you would class as working households, and doubt the worldly advantage of the other. Sweetheart, even business men are none the worse for unbending; they *must* unbend, and the best way to do so is by *pure* enjoyment. We strive and battle in the world, dear love, until our very hearts ache oftentimes. Woe to us if we have the worldly strife also in our homes ! No, Violet, home should be our sanctuary, and we should keep it pure and holy. When we pass its threshold we should shake the figurative dust from our feet, suffer our excited feelings to sink to peace under its influence, and all our holier thoughts to have sole sway. So we go forth into the world again refreshed as out of a bath, and so God and love are preserved in our hearts. *By a pure home only* can we hope, through every trial, to preserve them. Sweetheart (you, of course, the first element in the assertion), there is nothing holier on earth than a man's home. Every unkind word, every evil passion, should be banished from it as far as it is possible among erring creatures so to do. A good home, too, is a light in the world; its lesson rarely fails to creep into the hearts of all who frequent it. A bad home is a curse among society. This you admit, doubtless. You question only how far can this be carried out. *As far as our will and exertion* is able to conduct us, as far as our hearts are able to instruct us. In us, dear, the will and example need not be deficient. If we have children, they depend on us, and I for one don't fear on *their* account. The servants form the difficulty. We must select well, and on somewhat different grounds from those usually followed—think most of the moral character, and less of culinary or stable education, in those we admit under our roof. We shall, at all events, *start well.* I can desire no improvement in either Mary or Ben. Ben you may consider a fixture. Mary will some day get married, but that will be some time after you come, and then we surely can find a successor amiable and trustworthy. The domestic economy will be under your direction, and oh, dearest wife! when you have been a week among us you will be full of our peace, and need no arguments to convince you whether this ' fairy tale ' be solid possibility or no. No, you won't be here an hour without feeling that after all your worry you have come to peace at last. Love, I will eat you, if you don't meet with immediate sympathy and ' radiant welcome ' from Mary and Ben and Fanny. I won't answer for the cat, because she's old, and does nothing but sleep. Do you think, dear, that what they may gain in affection they lose in respect? Dearest, it is not respect that springs of fear. I like to compare Mr. G.'s things with mine—they show the working of contrasted principles. Mr. G.'s servants do not keep in their places at all ; mine never take an unbecoming liberty, although they have full freedom. Why is that ? Because mine is the better way of winning their respect. I keep myself, as far as I can, undegraded in their eyes ; never call on them to tell a falsehood or to perform a mean service ; avoid, so far as I can, saying and doing unworthy things before them. Prayers, too (oh, their value is incalculable ! I feel already that they are the foundation to a rightly-managed home)—these and Scripture teach us all our relative duties, constantly remind us of what is required at our hands. They feel *why* they are treated kindly, and what is expected of them in return ; we don't misunderstand each other. Every bird likes his own nest, and so, dear, I don't think there'll be a home in the country to beat our Madeley cottage when you come to it. Already it has the peace, and when the love comes also—ah, then indeed !

5—2

These letters reveal the religious spirit which was always one of his most marked characteristics, showing itself in many different ways. When his 'Book of Prayers' did not contain one sufficiently appropriate, as, for instance, for the last day in the old year, he wrote one himself. He carefully selected passages to read from Scripture, his favourite book being the Gospel of St. John. The following, too, is characteristic. New schools had been opened at Madeley, and a sermon on the occasion was preached by a Mr. Hill, of Birmingham.

He preached—not extempore, to my joy—one of the finest, most eloquent and touching sermons I have heard, one of the boldest, too, for he came here among the miners and read an unflinching lesson to the ironworkers. . . . Fearless and true to his duty, a man of the highest talent, writes a first-rate sermon, and delivers it in first-rate style.

Mr. Morley seldom liked extempore preaching, never extempore prayers. From his cottage he could see the spire of Madeley Church, celebrated in connection with the ministry of 'Fletcher of Madeley'; and in the church, close to the steps of that marvellous erection, its combined reading desk and pulpit—not to be ascended without some gymnastic ability—is the little front-pew which was regularly occupied on Sundays by Henry Morley. Of Miss Sayer's Unitarianism he writes :

that your creed, if ever it was, is now no source of discomfort to me. . . . We have a world of holy sympathies together, and this difference is one of opinion only upon what I by no means consider an essential.

During the three months at Madeley with which we have so far been dealing, he much enjoyed riding a horse, 'the best I have ever ridden,' which he had bought under the name of Lord Walnut, and promptly rechristened Peter. The last ride we hear of was along the beautiful road to Shrewsbury. The town itself he did not much admire, and coming back Peter fell lame. The lameness proved incurable, and the horse, which someone shortly before had valued at £100, had to be sold for £5. He could never afford to buy another, and henceforth all his rounds were done on foot.

The first premonitions of trouble with his partner came early after his move to Madeley, and on December 1 he warns Miss Sayer that she will often hear him grumbling at Mr. G. He tells her facts the meaning of which she, with quick woman's wit, understood long before he did himself, so that his letters are full of passages to reassure her that ' Madeley is ours,' and that success will come in spite of personal unpleasantness between the partners. At first he writes that he and Mr. G.

have a true and grounded respect for, and confidence in, each other, although possessing traits of character that must and will often conflict. . . . You call me too trustful of good in others. I don't know, but when I see it, I don't withhold belief in it, or poison my own enjoyment of it with suspicion. And, my own Violet, who has deceived me? What have I lost by always trusting? *Nothing*. And have gained how much!

This quotation affords good evidence of the spirit in which Henry Morley entered upon his partnership. What is really wonderful is that his subsequent experience did not alter his disposition. He never did withhold belief in the good which he thought he saw in others, or poison his enjoyment of it with suspicion. But he was soon forced to alter his estimate of Mr. G.'s character. Mr. Morley could not respect a man who starved his dogs, horribly neglected his own horses, and then was always wanting to borrow Peter, and who in small pecuniary matters soon showed a despicable meanness. But he tried very hard to establish working relations with Mr. G., summoned all his patience when the latter told stupid long stories, and learned to keep his own temper as well as to assert his dignity when treated with positive rudeness. He also says he learnt the importance of ' giving way upon trifles,' a lesson which developed into a life-long habit. Mr. G. was a most extraordinary partner. As soon as the Goods went off to .Warwick, within a week of Mr. Morley's arrival, Mr. G. borrowed Peter and went off after them. They were in great trouble, and Mr. G. stopped away, helping them to settle their affairs, and posing as their benevolent friend (really he had been guilty of gross dishonesty towards them), and did not return home till Christmas. Meanwhile Mr. Morley sat in the surgery waiting for patients, and went out to meet such calls as came, and little by little began to show people that he could cure his patients quickly and with much less medicine than they had been in the habit of having from Mr. G. Of course, he ascribed the badness of the practice to Mr. G.'s absence, and his own want of proper introduction to the neighbourhood. But when Mr. G. did at length return, a new discovery was made, viz., that the practice was good only in Mr. G.'s absence, and simply could not be worked up in conjunction with him.

For another two months Mr. Morley considered it his duty, 'having made his bed, to lie upon it.' At length a letter from Mr. G., who was then in London engaged in a lawsuit, showed him the necessity of a separation for the sake of his own character. It was a letter requesting him to report a private conversation which he had had with the man with whom Mr. G. was carrying on the lawsuit. Mr. Morley replied :

DEAR SIR,
   Of course you have anticipated my answer to your note. When even Law does not use the words of a sixty-times convicted felon without warning him of her intent before he speaks, can you suppose I would so deeply stain my honour as a gentleman as to comply with that which you suggest ? Assuredly I

will not. I hope ere you receive this that you will already
have lost sight of a notion so manifestly wrong. Practice has
kept me very busy of late.

I am, dear sir,
Yours truly,
HENRY MORLEY.

Mr. Morley now consulted a solicitor, and by his advice
secured Mr. G.'s day-book and ledger, and had them
examined by an accountant, with this result: 'The
practice, stated to be worth £700 a year, was found to be
worth only £290, allowing everything to be charged at
the full price and every bill paid, which is so very far
from being the case that I do not think the receipts
actually reached £150, if they came up to £100.' The
total sum received by Mr. Morley during his four months
of partnership, which included the period of Christmas
bills, was £3 10s. There was abundant evidence of fraud;
but a Chancery suit would have cost £250, and not saved
the payment of the bills for £200 to complete the premium
of £500. A miserable time followed. Mr. G. was at
first frightened, but an injudicious friend consulted by
Mr. Morley senior wrote a letter which betrayed weakness, and Mr. G. then blustered and threatened. He
was the victim, and 'no money could compensate him
for having introduced such an abandoned character to his
house and to his patients.' Finally, Mr. Morley resolved
to go his own way and simply ignore the deed of partnership. Before long he received full legal as well as moral
justification in so doing, as another lawsuit decided that
Mr. G. was *not legally qualified to practise,* and consequently could not sell anything to a partner.

Mr. G. was a man with a mania for litigation, and at
the time when Mr. Morley came to Madeley was hopelessly in debt through unsuccessful lawsuits. His victim's
purchase-money averted his fall for a time; but in the
course of the next year another £700 went in legal costs.

Having got all he could out of Henry Morley, his next object was to drive him away and sell the partnership to a fresh victim.   This he tried to do by

circulating slander through a very ignorant and scandal-loving population.   For one week it was village talk that I had been seen drunk ; next week there was a deceased patient of mine, whom I had poisoned with an overdose of laudanum.   Anonymous letters were sent to me, or addressed to those who showed themselves to have some care about me.   Vagrants were sent to sing insolent ballads, tallying with the last libel—that they might wound the fame, perhaps, of others with my own— beneath my window.   Scandal so foul as some of that which spread can hardly be conceived by those who have not lived where ignorance and immorality abound.   I knew the fountain of it all.   Nothing on earth but my dog saw that I ever suffered.   Whatever scandal came to me, I put aside with the invariable answer to the questioner : ' You know whence the report came ; it is for you to believe it or not, as you please.'

The above is an extract from a paper called ' Pulling Through,' which Henry Morley wrote for *All the Year Round* in 1857, as well as one entitled ' Buying a Practice.'   Both papers are reprinted.*   In 'Pulling Through' he is young Pawley, and Mr. G. is Dr. Hawley.   The story tallies closely with a long account which he wrote of the whole business, in December, 1845, to Mr. Sayer. Here he made a brave attempt to put the matter in the most favourable light, for the sake of the girl at Newport. But the experience of the first months was very bitter, and there is autobiography in the account young Pawley gives of

the little study into which I had crammed my books, and in which on many a lonely evening, after the day's calm endeavour, I had sobbed over poor Deborah's desponding letters. Then my one friend, the dog, in tribulation over my distress, would seize my arm between his paws, and leap up with a

---

* ' Early Papers,' pp. 271-295.

distressed whine to lick his master's face. No matter. I had set every nerve for the contest.

Financial difficulties, too, soon began to grow. But as the blood rises when the tempest beats upon the face, and all the limbs grow vigorous when buffeting the wind, so flute-playing Tom Pawley was made, earlier than happens to beginners in all cases, something of a man through troubles. He saw no way out of his wood but a quiet marching steadily in one direction. He went into no by-path of false pretences, never denied access to a dun, nor cheated a creditor with more than fair expressions of hopes, not in all seasons to be fulfilled. He found that the world was composed mainly of good fellows, glad enough to be generous and trustful with beginners who do not fear work, and who are open in their dealings.

But Mr. G. was to succeed once more at Madeley after his old fashion.

Then it happened that, one evening when I was at tea, a middle-aged gentleman knocked at my door. I rang immediately for another cup and saucer when I knew his errand.

'I am told, sir,' he said, 'that you were Dr. Hawley's partner.'

'I was so,' I replied, 'by a deed that is not acted on.'

'I have been advised to come and speak to you. I have just bought a partnership with Dr. Hawley. Some doubt has arisen in my mind. Things have been said to me——'

This gentleman had been a ship surgeon. He had earned money enough in Australia to buy a practice in England, where there was a sweetheart he longed to marry. Hawley had found him. All his money was in Hawley's pocket.

'Can I make a practice here?' he asked.

'That,' I said, 'is what I am now doing.'

'Hawley told me you were a young simpleton, an interloper in the place, starving upon a hundred pounds a year.'

'I earn three hundred, but starve upon that. Through Dr. Hawley I am much oppressed with debt, and lose much that I earn in lawyer's costs, forced on me by impatient creditors. I shall succeed in the end. There may be room for both of us.'

'Ah no !' my friend sighed ; 'I must go to sea again. The long hope of my life is at an end.'

He went away from Beetleborough. He gave his last kiss to his sweetheart, and departed.

So Henry Morley wrote in 1859, feeling bound to do all he could to expose such villainy, and warn the credulous of their danger.

In 'Buying a Partnership' he narrates the fate of some of his fellow-students. But Mr. G.'s Madeley career was drawing to an end. In 1847 he finally disappeared from the scene. His last appearance in another quarter is thus described in 'Some Memories ':

I thought sometimes then, and am sure now, that my partner was insane. A few years after the battle was over, when I was prospering as journalist in London, I saw my old tormentor in the dock of the Mansion House Police Court, charged with fraud as a trustee. The last I heard of him was that he had been convicted and sentenced. But a man cannot be sane who wastes abilities that, as in this case, would have made life easily and largely prosperous, in seeking feverish excitement from the failures or successes of ingenious strokes of fraud, and gambles constantly in litigation.*

Henry Morley senior was, of course, terribly disappointed at what had occurred, and he was vexed that his son would not declare himself bankrupt, and come to Midhurst to try a fresh start there. But finding his son's mind made up both to pay his debts and to 'stick on' at Madeley, he did all in his power to render this possible; in July, 1845, he raised £250 for him, and by August 12, 1846, had advanced £450, probably quite as much as he could afford.

Other friends and well-to-do relatives declined to help the young surgeon in his troubles, evidently regarding him now as an 'ugly duckling,' and being annoyed at his

* P. 21.

refusal to clear himself by bankruptcy. In later life Professor Morley never uttered a word of reproach against those who might have given him aid in the hour of sorest need; but he had a keen sense of what was not done when the service would have been . invaluable, and the memory influenced his own conduct in a very characteristic way; He tried to help all his young friends at the start, and many know how much he did for them at the beginning of their career. His time and his money alike were freely given in the way that he had once wished others would act towards him.

During the early months of 1845 his cares were lightened by the printing of the little volume entitled ' The Dream of the Lilybell,' tastily bound in cream and gold, named after the principal poem it contained, but including several other poems, ' The Star in the Brook,' ' Our Lady's Miracle ' (written at Dunster), and ' Dwarf Edward ' ; also the tales ' Lisette ' and ' Liebesthal,' and some shorter pieces both in prose and verse, with translations of the ' Hymns to Night' from the German of Novalis, and of Jean Paul's ' Death of an Angel.' The little volume was favourably reviewed in the press, the *Athenæum* finding in it ' delicacy and tact of execution, both in verse and prose, frequently rising into tenderness and beauty,' and calling it ' the production of an elegant and educated mind.' It is ' affectionately dedicated to C. Wharton Mann, Esq., the author's friend and fellow-rhymer.'

The ' Dream of the Lilybell ' and ' Our Lady's Miracle ' are reprinted in ' Early Papers,' and there also will be found ' Nemophil,' with the date 1847. But it was begun two years earlier, as its author writes about it in a letter to Miss Sayer, dated Sunday night, October 19, 1845. This is a love-letter pure and simple, telling no news, too sacred for transcription, but proving, if any proof were needed, how strong were the cords which held the lovers together during the troubles of this year. Towards its close he says:

Apropos of weakness, you speak doubtingly, whether it be weak or right to continue love towards an unworthy object. That is the very theme of ' Nemophil.' I picture her sacrificing all for the beloved, in the bitterest hour of his unworthiness utterly forgetful of herself, following his path with her blessing. And then, when he is lost, not weakly yielding to either sorrow or temptation, she remembers the love she gave, and is happiest in the hope that he, though distant, lives blessed elsewhere. Now and then a few sad visions rise, but she is true and good and firm. She lives to God, cheerful and unrepining, though alone in the wide world, seeking to do good around her with a strength unshaken by the sharpest trials, till Death comes in her old age to summon her to heaven. Nemophil is my incarnate love ideal. When love has once been given, the giver may be content. In life or death his heart contains a holy thing; but it is so only, and he loves only, when he is prepared to stake all possible allurements of the world upon the single venture. *Love* given cannot be recalled. Its course is in the hands of God.

We may now return to his medical practice, and summarize all that need be said about it for the next three years during which he continued to be a village doctor. About the end of 1845 a son of Mr. and Mrs. Sayer, Frederick William, came to stay with him at Madeley, and it was soon decided that the lad should be apprenticed to his future brother-in-law instead of being placed in his father's business. This brought great happiness to all concerned, and the admirable early training which Frederick Sayer must have received is shown by his distinguished career afterwards at University College, London. In a letter dated November 9, 1845, Mr. Morley speaks of Mr. G.'s rage at his being elected surgeon to the Foresters' club, instead of Mr. G., and the vilification which began as soon as he was away, and which took the form of insinuation that he was not legally qualified. This gave Mr. Morley a good opportunity of printing and circulating copies of his college testimonials and certificates.

Some account of the contest for this appointment to the Foresters may be found in a paper, ' The 'Club Surgeon,' reprinted from *Household Words*, among ' Early Papers.* Here Mr. G. is Parkinson, but the likeness is not close, and it was the teetotalers who were Mr. G.'s special supporters. The picture he gives, however, of his installation was a lively memory of what really happened, and the following passage expressed his real feeling :

The great majority of working men are from their hearts truly courteous and polite. I wish to say something about this. I began practice as assistant in a purely agricultural district, employed by a practitioner of ample independent means. From the first day that I went there, very young and utterly unknown, every cottager touched his hat to me. Strangers who came on a visit to the place, if they wore good clothes, were greeted invariably with touched hats, bows, and curtseys. That is not courtesy ; it is a mark of a degraded state of feeling. When I first went among the colliers, I got no signs of recognition until I had earned them. Better wages and a little more to think about have made our workmen in the North more independent than the Southern agriculturist ; but it is precisely because they are less servile that they are able to be more really courteous. Now that I have made my way here, and am prosperous, many hat-touchings do indeed greet me—when, for example, walking against the stream, I meet our congregation coming out of church. But these greetings express a genuine respect. I have joined broken bones for the greeters, I have watched by their sick children, I have brought health to their wives, often receiving, and I may venture to say contented by, these kind looks, for my main remuneration.

He soon had abundance of work among poor patients. New iron furnaces at Madeley were started in 1845, and for some years after that the place grew fast, and it was impossible to get a house without securing it before it was built. There was constant work, with wages at

* Pp. 260-272.

3s. 6d. a day. But there were comparatively few residents with larger incomes than this, and it was the tradition of the neighbourhood that doctors for well-to-do patients must live at Broseley, some two or three miles off, beyond Ironbridge. Such traditions exercise considerable influence in determining the choice of a doctor. Here is his summary of his experience, from 'Some Memories':

Of patients there came plenty who had pockets as empty as my own. There was a dispensary which gave 'notes' to the sick poor for attendance by any medical man in the district to whom they chose to take them. We all received them, and were paid by the dispensary at the rate of 5s. a note, which covered the whole treatment of a case, unless it extended beyond six weeks, when a new note was required. My dispensary notes brought £60 a year for a great deal of work that sat heavily upon the drug bill. There were sick-clubs, in which every member paid 4s. a year for free treatment of those who might fall ill. I assisted at the births of four hundred children, of whose parents only a dozen or two could pay more than the usual fee of half a guinea. There was a large surgery in the garden 'at the back of the house, where thirty or forty poor people usually sat round the walls to be attended to before I had my breakfast. Work of this kind was so plentiful that at one time there was a current fable in the parish that I had not been to bed for a fortnight.*

Further details may be picked from the paper on 'The Club Surgeon':

At that time, after receiving patients in the surgery, and visiting in busy seasons as many as ninety sick people at their own homes, very often there were only three or four doubtfully profitable private entries for the day-book in the evening, and my poor heart rejoiced at any midnight knocking that might bid me give up my night's rest for a half-guinea fee. . . . If two urgent calls were simultaneous—as they would be sometimes—there was a certainty of getting heartily abused by

---

* Pp. 21, 22.

somebody, and a chance, perhaps, of having one's professional and moral character be-argued in a court of law.

Then he speaks of the unremunerated work among the poor, and its reward :

Though among ignorant patients many things occur to vex him, he bears with them patiently, and if he comes with a sound heart to his work, he acquires faith in the poor.

' Love has he found in huts, where poor men lie.'

They become warm friends to him, and become lusty trumpeters, to spread abroad the fame of skill that he has been glad to exercise among them.

Here, too, is a bit of experience :

The drug bill of a young country surgeon who has parish work and clubs, with very little private practice, easily reaches £50 a year ; and if he has no friend from whom to borrow instruments [his father had given him all his own] the cost of them is serious. He must be prepared to meet every emergency, and to perform any operation. . . . In the first quarter of my attendance on the Ancient Woodmen, I spent all the quarter's money profit on an instrument required for the performance on a club member of an operation not likely to be called for half a dozen times in a long course of practice. I had a broken leg two or three miles away in one direction, and a fever case requiring for some time daily attention two or three miles off in another.

All had to be done on foot. A letter tells how Fred had come in with him from the ' long round ' tired, but how he had himself two more rounds to make before night.

The paper gives a vivacious account of the annual dinner of the Foresters, to which he was bound to go because he had been accused of pride. He had an opportunity of observing the wonderful appetites of the colliers ; ducks were simply chopped into two helpings, and when he removed the shoulder from the quarter of lamb which

he had to carve, a plate was at once advanced with, 'I'll
take that, if you please.' His character was satisfactorily
restored by his presence at this dinner, and the speech he
then made. He hit upon an ingenious device to meet
another difficulty :

Already the growth of private practice had been seriously
retarded by my unprofessional conduct in not wearing a beaver
hat. Subject to much physical fatigue, and liable to headache,
I had found beavers a source of torment, and wore, therefore,
in spite of much scandal, a light fur cap in winter, and in
summer a straw hat, using Leghorn in deference to public
notions of respectability. The want of a black hat retarded
the growth of my private practice very seriously. A very
lady-like individual, wife of a small grocer—Mrs. Evans—
frequently declared that ' she had heard me to be clever, and
would have sent for me in her late illness, but she could not
think of having a doctor come to her house in a cap ; it was so
very unusual.' As I really could not give in on the hat question,
it was a lucky day for me when I afterwards bethought myself
of making up for the loose style of dress upon my head by
being very stiff about the neck. I took to the wearing of
white neckcloths with the happiest effect. Everybody thought
of the Church. · I looked so good and correct in a clean white
neckcloth that I drew a tooth from Mrs. Evans in the second
week of it.

There is an interesting portrait, here reproduced, of the
young doctor, looking very ' good and correct ' in his
neckcloth, done while he was at Madeley ; but, still, even
such respectability round the throat could not make up
for everything else. He did not live at Broseley, he did
not keep a horse, he did not wear a hat. No wonder he
did not make a fortune.

He did succeed at length in making a paying practice,
something which he could sell to a successor, and out of
which his successor, who was certainly not more clever
or popular than himself, soon drew an income, I believe,
of more than £500 a year; but he never made this for
himself, and he never could save anything considerable

HENRY MORLEY. AGED 25.

To face p. 80.

towards paying off his load of debt. Those who knew him later will understand how impossible it was for him at any time to ' squeeze the poor ;' and, without a certain amount of squeezing, patients are slow to pay even what they can afford out of earnings at the rate of three and sixpence a day. An old ledger for 1847, with a very small proportion of its entries marked as *paid*, is sadly suggestive. He never knew what his income would be, and such un- certainty made it doubly difficult for him to save. He charged for attendance a guinea for six to ten visits, according to the circumstances of the patient, and gave medicines and a good deal besides gratis. Fred Sayer, writing to his sister on January 12, 1848, while 'the doctor' was posting his books in the same room, expresses himself very frankly.

One thing I'm very glad to see, *i.e.*, he is beginning to get sensible in the matter of making out bills. Don't say I said so ; I guess he's touchy in such matters. Contact with this exquisite sample of the world is rubbing off his romantic notions. . . . He had a too romantic faith in the honest payingness of human nature, and valued—or, rather, under- valued—his own services by an internal instead of an external standard ; but he is coming round, and puts down figures with a great show of resolution, which carried throughout would be A1. In fact, I guess he was not cut out for a money world. After all, it's astonishing what an extraordinary thing this money is. An individual is, oh, so fond of you!—such an earnest, disinterested friend ! (stop ! the Doctor ejaculates, ' Oh, I'm blowed if I won't teach that woman a lesson !') Touch his pocket, and ah ! I shall be all the wiser, I fancy, for the Doctor's experience.

He had to pay interest on borrowed money, and a heavy premium for life insurance. Legal costs and lawyers' bills swelled the amount of indebtedness which, I suspect, went on increasing most of the time he was at Madeley. During the year 1848 he made up his mind that nothing short of a revolution affecting his life, as political events

6

were affecting European dynasties, could lift him out of this miserable financial impotence with its stern barrier to his marriage.

Before, however, we enter upon the story of the great change, we must note two literary efforts which belong to the life at Madeley. His practice there was not always as engrossing as during the notorious fortnight, and perhaps Fred Sayer relieved him of some of the drudgery. At any rate, he found time, in 1847, to write two 'Tracts upon Health for Cottage Circulation.' The first was on ' Health Preservation,' the second on ' Interrupted Health and Sick-room Duties.' They were published by Charles Edmunds, 154, Strand, London, and afterwards sold for the Health of Towns Association, by Henry Renshaw, 356, Strand. The former tract is reprinted entire, the latter in part, among ' Early Papers.'* They will repay perusal at the present day, but the remarkable thing about them is that they should have been written in 1847 by a young country doctor struggling to make a practice. Very much later than this the idea has prevailed that it is hardly fair to expect a doctor to do anything to prevent people from getting ill; and the whole movement for modern sanitation, so far as it has been promoted by men earning their living by their medical practice, is one of the noblest and most disinterested efforts of our times. We do well to do honour to its pioneers. Henry Morley was not the first to call attention to the value of hygiene; the movement originated with statesmen, the physicians of London hospitals, Fellows of the Royal Society, enlightened clergymen, and leading Government officials. The Marquis of Normanby delivered an important speech in the House of Lords on July 21, 1844, and this was followed by a meeting in Exeter Hall on December 11. The Health of Towns Association was then formed, and published speeches and addresses and reports by

* Pp. 360-384.

various eminent men, including a speech by Viscount
Morpeth in the House of Commons on March 30, 1847,
on moving for leave to bring in a Bill for improving the
Health of Towns in England. At the bottom of the list
of the association's publications, June 1, 1847, comes a
heading: 'Other Cheap Literature approved by the
Association'; but the sole entry under this heading is,
'Tracts upon Health for Cottage Circulation. By Henry
Morley. Price 6d.'

He had not sought the aid of the association to publish
his work, but issued it independently; and then they had
found him, and, equally clearly, had found no other man
in a similar position doing work which they could recommend. *The London Medical Gazette,* October, 1847, very
favourably reviews the tracts.

In November, 1847, Dr. Sutherland and Dr. Hector
Gavin began editing a *Journal of Public Health and
Monthly Record of Sanitary Improvement.* To this Mr.
Morley was invited to contribute. He sent them some
papers, though nothing of importance till 1849, but two
years before this he had drawn from his practice in the
homes of the poor the experience which at length opened
to him a way to win the attention of the larger world.

He was, however, not yet off with his old love, Poetry.
As we saw, he was writing in 1847 a poem, 'Nemophil,'
intended to exhibit the perfection of true love; and in
December, 1848, John Chapman published for him a small
quarto volume of verse, tastefully bound, like its predecessor, in cream and gold, entitled 'Sunrise in Italy,
etc.: Reveries.'

In 'Some Memories,'* he writes:

The movements of that year in Europe had also set me
rhyming. Pius IX. had begun his Papacy with indications of
a policy of liberal reform that raised hope in the hopeful, a

---

* P. 27.

hope soon to be destroyed. He had taken some bold steps
towards the education of his people. For a year or. two it
seemed to many that a new sun rose for the Italians, bringing
a new day.

The poem tells of a husband and father released from
imprisonment on the accession of Pius IX., and touches
on such topics as : A Plea for Religious Tolerance ; A
Vindication of Shelley; The Progress of the Human
Race.   Part II., deals with the establishment of Liberty
of Thought under Pius IX., Part III. with his decree
for the establishment of schools throughout his dominion,
and the question, 'How to Educate the Children of the
Poor.' The poem concludes with an excursus, of which
the following is the Argument, interesting to us as
indicating the ideas which were this year taking stronger
and stronger hold over the writer's mind :

Principles of ·education—The child is a child of God, not of
the devil—Its innate capacities—Natural education provided
in the events of life—The false principles on which schools are
generally conducted have bred contempt of the profession of
teacher—In what way to guard the unfolding of an infant's
mind : love, imagination, reason—The mind must be at no
period coerced, but assisted in developing its faculties according to their own healthy proportions—The duties of the parent
—When the child should cease to be educated at home—The
girl, never—The boy. Course of study—The importance of
natural science as a foundation—History—Languages—They
tend to enlarge the spirit—Knowledge deepens the trust of
man in God—Return to the subject of the poem—Unexpected
awakening of thought in Europe.

Part of ' Sunrise in Italy ' is reprinted in ' Early Papers,'*
and also ' Nemophil,' but not ' Alethê,' which is a poem
containing some vigorous passages contrasting Truth and
Force, as the following extract will show :

* Pp. 330, 345.

XL.

Whose poet art thou ? Doth thy song pursue
    The path of armies, like some barrack trull,
Counting the terrible above the true,
    Butchery charming, but the Bible dull ;
The close allegiance unto Heaven due
    Paid to the Hero whose utensil-skull—
Like the grim goblet in the feasts of yore—
Its measure filled, most blood of foes will pour ?

XLI.

Or doth it lick beneath a lady's feet
    The soil, and, like the Lurley-spirit, sing
Strains which delight her ear with soft entreat,
    But foul disdain upon her nature fling ;
Float poison odours, dangerously sweet,
    Soft on the breath, within the breast to sting ;
Pour through her heart in languishing desire
A smoke which suffocates its vestal fire ?

XLII.

Or doth thy song delight to sing of wine,
    Of revels in the thought-destroying flood ;
Sing that God's image is the most divine
    With fish-like eyes, moist, in a maudling mood,
Or roaring frail affection, line by line
    In bully ballads, basely understood,
While Reason reeleth, poisoned, on her throne—
She falls—hell rises—makes her realm its own.

XLIII.

If thus to false excitement thou shalt give
    The labour which God lent thee for the Just,—
Servant of Dynamis, when he doth strive,
    Forgetful of Alethê, in the lust
Of his unaided power to arrive
    More quickly at his end,—into the dust
With his, thy toil will drop, thy gains decay,
Until Alethê guide thee on the way.

In a review of this volume the *Athenæum* says :

This poet has ambition, and has on a former occasion received a cordial welcome from us. . . . A spirit so disposed to contemplation cannot sing in vain; and though somewhat fantastical in his mode of treatment, there are such marks of meditation, such proofs of a love of truth, and such signs of sympathy with the highest hopes of man, in Mr. Morley's present volume, as entitle it to the attention of the poetic reader.'

The *British Quarterly Review* says :

' The general remarks on education contain no little sound truth beautifully expressed. His plea for religious toleration contains many powerful passages.'

Besides writing poetry he also read much, especially Spenser's ' Faerie Queene,' respecting the interpretation of which he wrote some notes for the *Athenæum*. He also scribbled some verses in a friend's album, which indicate a sadly different appreciation of Madeley from the raptures on its beauty which he had poured out four years previously.

MADELEY.

Madeley is bounded by coal-dust below,
    Above it the sky is besmoked,
Due north are black pits, and due south if you go,
    At Blest's Hill you'll expect to be choked.

Oh, come to the West, then—the beautiful West !
    Ah, now don't ! If you're wise keep away ;
Over pit-fields and brick-fields the walk's not the best,
    Performed over coal, mud, and clay.

Now, be candid. Well, then, we'll confess that due East
    By the Severn's a beautiful spot,
Where the boards on the trees grin like bones at a feast :
    'ALL TRESPASSERS PUNISHED—DOGS SHOT.'

Moreover, close Eastward there lies the canal,
  Evil neighbour to men's habitations,
Yellow and dirty and misty and al-
  So source of all bad exhalations.

To cleanness in Madeley, the only sure path,
  At its East end, its West end, its North, or its South,
Is for ever and ever to sit in a bath
  And never to open one's mouth.

EUPHEMIA MARIA WIGGENSON.

January 14, 1848.

CHAPTER VII.

MADELEY TO MANCHESTER, 1848—1849.

THE letters to Miss Sayer during the greater part of the residence at Madeley were destroyed, so that we experience a blank similar to the effect produced by the fall of the curtain between successive acts of a drama. Instead of hearing from his own words all that he is doing, and much of what he is thinking, from day to day, we have to conjecture and reconstruct from scattered sources and allusions in later correspondence. One of the important changes in his life occurred while the curtain is down. He abandoned his earlier theology and became a Unitarian. By what process this conversion was effected we do not know, but we know that he reckoned it as among the blessings arising out of his Madeley troubles, that he emerged from them holding the same faith as that of his future wife. Channing became to him one of God's true prophets, and henceforth he attended Unitarian places of worship; indeed, he was once invited to become a Unitarian preacher. But he was no sectarian or theological controversialist. Later in his life there was but one religious name by which he would describe himself, let others call him what they would: it was the name Christian.

The curtain rises again on October 12, 1848, and henceforward the series of letters is tolerably complete till it reaches its natural termination with the marriage in 1852. The situation at the beginning of this period may be briefly described.   He had now two pupils in his house, a young Mr. Wakefield as well as Fred Sayer.   He earned enough to live on, but not to pay off his debts ; and the work was so laborious in proportion to the pay, that there was little chance of increasing the income to any considerable extent. Indeed, one has only to go and look at Madeley, Salop, to feel how impossible it must have been for a young doctor there to do more than his daily routine of small duties, useful and honourable, but leading to nothing larger. The feeling of being imprisoned in that village, of finding it impossible to use and develop faculties where they were weighed down by wretched memories, sordid cares, and narrow limitations, must have grown on him more and more.   He had some kind friends at Madeley, but no intellectual intercourse.   There was certainly one happy picnic to the Wrekin, but none of the advantages of town life.   For the stimulus only to be afforded by meeting minds like his own he began imperatively to crave.   He felt he must leave Madeley.

Two courses were open : There was a medical partnership, and a jog-trot country doctor's life possible at Midhurst.   Family help would provide this for him, if he would first declare himself bankrupt.   This condition he now refused as resolutely as in the spring of 1845. On the other hand, he was beginning to know where his real strength lay.   Here are his own words from 'Some Memories ':*

A bold change of front seemed to be necessary.   Then for the first time came the thought that, if a change was to be made, it might be well to strike at once into a new path and cease from the practice of medicine.   Its right practice requires

---

* P. 24.

the sole and whole devotion of a life, and conscience told me this had not been given. Was there an alternative?

Up to that time, and at that time, there was no thought of literature as a profession. It was a source of intense private enjoyment, of pure recreation, though it set me working, as most people usually do work hard at pleasures. But there were two subjects, Public Health and Education, in which I took deep interest, and at which I could work zealously. Sanitary science was beginning then to win some public recognition. There was a large new duty to be done by a new army of workers. Could they live by doing it? If so, there would be transfer of services in the same army from one active regiment into another; there would still be direct use for the past course of special training, and the change of work would be only from curative to preventive medicine. I took counsel with friendly pioneers who were then spending energies in London for the advance of sanitary reform. They agreed in telling me that movements needing Government support were being strangled with red tape, and that there was little chance of any living to be earned by the most energetic work in that direction. There remained, though it meant quitting the profession for which I had been trained from a child, one other way of life into which I could put zealously all powers that I had, while in aid of it no kind of study could be useless. Why not endeavour to work out in real life my ideal of a teacher's calling, put entire trust in the truth of my convictions, and resolve to act on them as faithfully as faulty human nature would allow?

Then the ' Memories '* tell the story with which we are already familiar, of his own school experiences, and readers should turn to the book to see how closely his mind connected the contrast between English schools and the one at Neuwied with his determination to carry out his own principles of education in England. How desperate was the struggle in which he resolved to engage will appear as we follow its course. He says:

My resolution was to go into a large town—not London, where one would be lost, but any other town with room in it

* P. 25.

for growth of success, and where there was a chance of getting the first necessary foothold. I had faith enough in my ideal to be sure of success if I could once show it, however imperfectly, in practice. Having made a choice upon that principle, I went to Manchester, although I knew nobody there.

He had, however, some introductions there, partly through his own published writings, and partly through the Rev. Edmund Kell, Unitarian minister at Newport, Isle of Wight, who tried to help him to become a successor to Dr. J. R. Beard, Unitarian minister at Manchester, who was desirous of relinquishing an undenominational school, which he had been carrying on there for some years. A little pecuniary assistance would now have enabled Mr. Morley to purchase this. He came to London and saw his rich uncle, but reports:

Uncle William was minded to do nothing. Was kind in speech, but would hear nothing of Madeley, because I had been obstinate. Well, I was obstinate at twenty-two, and he is obstinate at seventy; knowing him also to be obstinate, and not being *compelled* to ask assistance, I did not trouble him with any solicitation, but made my talk more general.

On October 20 he gives this account of his Manchester scheme:

I walked last night to Wolverhampton—off to Manchester— saw Dr. Beard—looked over the house—saw the school at work—shared the school dinner—discussed all details—result on both sides *most satisfactory*. . . . The only business now is to find security for the [annual] payment of the £50 out of our earnings. . . .

I have no time for thinking, and am tired—for I walked all over Manchester—saw all that I could after leaving Dr. Beard, and came home the same night, walking again (being poor) from Wolverhampton—not tired in body, but wanting sleep— my eyes shut as I walked along, and when I arrived at five this morning and found some victuals I fell asleep over my eating. Bad correspondent, therefore, is your Henry for to-day. God bless us, love.

Ever your own.

Of course, if we conclude this, we must marry at Midsummer.

Dr. Beard's school had been thoroughly successful, and had begun to fall off only in the last year, partly through a death from typhus fever, so that if Mr. Morley had been able to carry out this plan, he would probably have made it succeed. The day he returned, tired as he was with a fifty-mile walk and two nights out of bed, he wrote a full account to his father of all he had seen and done in Manchester. This crossed a letter from his father, written chiefly in reference to his avowal of Unitarianism, warning him 'from the paths of hell, gray hairs, sorrow, fearful errors.' His brother, too, wrote to him, begging him to stop going to the devil. His father had known of his change of views for about a year, and this outbreak was occasioned by the son's proposal to take over an un-sectarian school with more or less of a Unitarian con-nection; and a very natural objection to this on the part of a strong Churchman augmented the regret with which he saw his son ready to abandon a profession which the father profoundly honoured, and throw away a special training which, at real personal sacrifice, he had secured for his son. No help could be expected from Midhurst. On October 29 Mr. Morley writes that his father will do nothing, and that by the same post he is declining Dr. Beard's offer. He now means to go to Manchester, and make his own way there, begin by advertising for day pupils, live very cheaply, and take boarders later as occasion serves.

'*I only want to begin* in order to prosper rapidly in this line. . . . I feel happy and strong in a good resolve, so aid me in it, darling Violet, and fear for nothing.'

He arranged to sell his practice to a Mr. Peirce, who was invited to come and stay some time in the house, and make himself thoroughly acquainted with what he pro-posed to buy.

A letter written on October 30 gives an interesting

touch. Cholera had reached Madeley, and Mr. Peirce was taking over most of the practice.

I have been with him to see his cholera patient. Cholera must have a hard fight before it can kill a collier—I believe our Noah will float through the dangers. I found the house in enormous tribulation, and left it quieted with hope. Peirce don't quite like my way of looking on the best side of a case— says it is more risk in case of death, and less credit in case of recovery. I doubt his philosophy even in that interested point of view. How welcome are the visits of the doctor when, by the light of his knowledge, he is ready to dispel the darkness of all vague alarm, when he brings into the faces around the sick-bed a cheerful, hopeful look! he comes into the dull chamber like a sunbeam, and how welcome does *his* face become! Nothing is easier than to leave impression enough of danger for all purposes of truth and professional credit, but I doubt the value of credit bought by over-rating danger, making a fuss over cases, as Peirce seems apt to do.

Dr. Beard was genuinely anxious to have Mr. Morley for his successor, and in response to a letter from Mr. Sayer proposed fresh arrangements, which were nearly concluded, much to the satisfaction of Mrs. Sayer, who now regarded it as certain that her daughter would be married the following midsummer. But a curious trifle upset the negotiations. The house at Madeley was not comfortable, with its various inmates, and alterations going on to suit the convenience of Mr. Peirce. Fred wrote home dolefully—he had also some sentimental troubles in connection with leaving Madeley—and Mrs. Sayer took alarm and offence, ordered her boy home, and refused to further countenance the Manchester scheme. To Mr. Morley this decision was a real relief. He felt, rightly or wrongly, that his past misfortunes and em- barrassments were largely due to the mistaken advice of ' older and wiser ' people, and to the conditions which had turned their pecuniary aid into millstones of indebted- ness. He wanted no more help from friends in this new venture, and he started off to see what he could arrange in Manchester for himself. He determined to take a house, and furnish in it at first only a single room, for all expense now meant more debt. After much hunting about, he decided on 88, George Street, Manchester, and writes full particulars about the situation and its advantages. Every detail is again described, for now this was to be the home which he hoped would soon be ready to welcome its mistress.

Meanwhile, Miss Sayer had been staying for some time on a visit at Hornsey, and serious trouble was brewing for her on her return to Newport. Mrs. Sayer was a dauntless woman, and had stern notions of discipline. Let an instance be told to illustrate her character. Some of my readers may have known the late Robert Pinnock, J.P., and will remember the honour in which he was held for very many years among his fellow-citizens at Newport. I have not forgotten the twinkle in his eye with which he told me this story. He began life as an apprentice in Mr. Sayer's business. He lived in the house. One of Mrs. Sayer's rules was that boots were not to be taken upstairs, and finding a pair in his bedroom, she promptly threw them out of the window. The boots were missed, but sought in vain. After three days, they were discovered in the back-garden, a good deal spoiled, and discipline after this was duly maintained.

Mrs. Sayer had good reason for feeling dissatisfied about her daughter's engagement. It had lasted five years, and there now seemed less prospect of marriage than ever. She resolved it should be broken off. So just before her daughter's return, she forced the lock of her box, secured a quantity of love letters, which she burnt, and a volume of poetry ('Lilybell'), which, with a few other things, she did up in a packet and sent off to Madeley, with some very bitter words, ending thus: 'My first opinion of you was the correct one, and I hope we shall never meet again.' Mr. Morley's reply was charac-. teristic:

Madeley, Shropshire,
November 26, 1848.

MY DEAR MRS. SAYER,

I received your packet, informing me that you have been guilty of opening your daughter's private drawers during her absence, and destroying part of her correspondence. I hope you will have many years to live, and know that before you have lived through one of them you will feel heartily ashamed of yourself; if not, you have less generosity and good feeling than I have been accustomed to give you credit for. With kind regards to all,

Yours very truly,
HENRY MORLEY.

This, then, explains the loss of so many letters previous to the end of 1848. It would have been hardly worth mentioning, if it were not necessary to show what these young people had to encounter, and especially necessary for the understanding of Mrs. Morley's own character in after-years. No girl could go through the experience she now had without its leaving its mark. There was a certain shell which had to be penetrated before her real kindness and goodness of heart were discovered; and she had a nervous dread of change, so intense as sometimes to make her ill when any new departure from the old ways had to be considered. This disposition greatly influenced and limited the possibilities of her married life, full and happy as it was. Something may safely be ascribed to the fortunes of her long engagement. To Mr. Morley the troubles may have brought only good—that was his own conviction—he was out in the world battling to overcome them. She had only to stop at home, bearing much, and waiting till he won success. When the saddest day he had ever known entered into his life, and the companionship of forty years was interrupted by her death, there was one remembrance, one thought, perpetually in his

mind, and breaking forth into utterance from his lips.
This was her faithfulness; it was, indeed, her grand
characteristic, showing itself in unfaltering attachment
to every old friend, and a clinging affection to old ways.
This spirit of fidelity had its source in her inmost nature;
if it also hindered the realization of important plans, it
should be remembered how it stood the strain of her nine
years' engagement.

What were the lovers now to do? They were not
going to abandon their plighted troth, they were not going
to give up their correspondence; but how was it to be
safely carried on? More than one scheme was devised
after the first resolve to have no secrecy had led to the
confiscation of more letters. Finally, a friend was found
in Newport, to whom Mr. Morley addressed his letters,
and who placed a cotton reel in the window facing the
street whenever such a missive had been received, and
was awaiting its rightful owner.

A large number of these letters have been preserved in
their original envelopes, and from these envelopes the
address has been carefully cut in order that no discovery
of it might involve the friend in trouble. Many of the
letters thus received deal with a situation into which it is
not needful to enter further in detail. They help us to
understand how a girl, who had such a lover, could remain
faithful to him, in spite of all opposition and discourage-
ment; but, for the most part, they must be 'taken as
read.' Here is one which deals with matters of more
public interest. With regard to it, and to many others
which will follow asserting confidence in his own capacity
and at length telling of some actual achievements, it is
imperative to remember the circumstances under which
they were written, viz., by a man whom all his friends
refused to help because they deemed him so foolish and
incapable, solely for the girl who had to sit, and bear, and
wait, at Newport. Another fact, which we may find diffi-

cult to understand at the present day, is the low estimation
in which all teachers were held at this time. They were
mostly incompetent, miserably paid, and socially despised.
One trifling example of this may be mentioned. As a
surgeon, Henry Morley had always been addressed as
'Esq.;' as a teacher, letters to him were as invariably
addressed 'Mr.,' and this as a matter of course, after he
had established a flourishing school at Liscard, and was
mixing on an equal footing with the most cultivated
minds in Liverpool. But this is to anticipate. Here
is the letter, which belongs to the period when all was
promise, not performance.

Madeley, Shropshire,
Monday night, November 27, 1848.

MY DARLING LOVE,

To-morrow I shall hear from you touching your home
condition, so, then, I will say nothing of all that to-night. It
seems that we must make up our minds to fight at Manchester
quite unassisted, and opposed by a few adverse circumstances.
Very well. Those are not bad conditions of success. I have
strength in abundance, some experience in life by this time,
and am not to be dashed by any fear or stopped by any
obstacle. I follow my path—obey the dictates of my nature
against whatever bugbears may be put across my way to turn
me into the way of other people. I follow an inward light, and
I can see my way when to others all may appear darkness.
Nor is this fallacious; the light *within us* seldom leads our feet
astray. I have—you must make up your mind to that, darling
—great difficulties to conquer before I can *begin*. Do not be
alarmed if our start look very boggling and inauspicious, if we
have much that looks dispiriting during the next few months.
The beginning is the entire battle, and we must fight it fearlessly; let us *begin*, and I have not an instant's doubt about
the rest. There are many things I can't do, but teaching is a
thing I *can* do, and can do right well. I do not in that aim at
mere bread, as I have done in medicine; I seek and expect
nothing under a success the most distinguished to crown our
labours. Many things that I must teach I must first learn—in
knowledge I have much yet to gain; but the *how* to use my

knowledge, how to teach to a good purpose, that is a talent
hitherto hidden, but which all my studies, all my changes of
character have added to, and which it remains only to show
that I possess. *Nous verrons.*

In Madeley I have done what I said I would do; I have made
the practice that I said I would make, and sold it: (1) because
friends and lawyers nullified all exertion, and made getting out
of debt almost a hopeless business; (2) because my character
is unsuited for a district in which it is necessary to be stern,
and to use legal compulsion as a matter of course, before I can
get anything like all the wages of my labour; (3) because, if I
got all the wages, I am old enough now, I believe, to put my
labour to a better hire; (4) because I do not and cannot shine
in my profession, nor practise well enough for my own con-
tentment, and therefore think it wiser to abandon a path upon
which I was started by others, and in which I never felt any
pleasure or satisfaction, and turn into the road which I am by
nature fitted best to walk on. As a teacher I shall at once
charge high prices, and that will be against my rapid progress
in the outset; but I *must* have to work for people who can pay
me without needing to be asked and urged for money long
overdue, and, moreover, I do not mean to rate myself at the
value of small-beer any longer. I claim the first rank as a
teacher, and, as my reputation and connection grow, I shall
not seek a large school, but increase my charges as much as
by experiment it shall be found possible to raise them. No
money is too much for *real education* of a child, and I expect to
acquire a reputation which will enable me to command a very
handsome price for my tuition. This I shall do, not from
covetousness, you may be sure, but partly because it is my
due, partly because I am too proud to stand upon a level with
the half-educated crowd of 'schoolmasters,' and desire to
vindicate the honour of my calling.

Before, however, he could begin at Manchester, he had
to get clear of Madeley. He does not always do himself
justice in 'Some Memories,' and there is one passage*where
the impression he conveys is worth correcting. He writes:

Of course, when it was known that I was going, and a
successor was being brought into the practice, I could go only

* P. 27.

by leaving behind me all I had except my clothes, and about twenty books from the lost roomful.

This suggests a very different flight from what actually took place. On December 1 he writes that he has every prospect of paying off all his Madeley debts before leaving:

I have cleared off £160 this week, and been saddled with another £25 for law. Oh, law ! law ! how it has burnt holes · in my pocket !

A little later he tells Fred that he has paid £57 of debt with £77 of bills due to him, and hopes to settle all at about the same rate, and adds that he has just put thirty-seven debtors in the County Court: As usual, however, he was too sanguine in his estimate, and some of the debts at Madeley had to be left unpaid for a time. Mr. Morley had sold his furniture to Mr. Peirce. His books were all packed in boxes to go with him to Manchester. He had previously offered to sell them for the benefit of his creditors, but the offer had been declined. Suddenly there was a change of policy, partly due to a misunderstanding about his leaving; and these boxes, containing also papers valuable only to himself, and many of Fred's books, were seized on Christmas Day by the Sheriff's officer, and transported to Shrewsbury to be sold there. This was the action of one single creditor, and was most unpopular at Madeley. The very partner of this creditor told me how strongly he had objected to the proceeding, how the universal feeling throughout the village was pity for Mr. Morley as the victim of Mr. G., with admiration for the plucky manner in which he was fighting his battle and endeavouring to pay all in turn what was due to them. Indeed, it would have been too absurd for the Madeley tradesmen to have taken any other view, seeing it was Mr. Morley's determination to avoid bankruptcy that caused all his embarrassments. But it

7—2

was possible for a single selfish creditor to seize the books which Mr. Morley had meant to take to Manchester, and so anticipate his fair turn for payment. The other creditors had not now to wait very much longer. Henry Morley knew what was coming to pass, and proved himself a true prophet, though, like many another true prophet, he was not quite right in all his details. He expected difficulties for three months at Manchester, and then he knew he should succeed. On December 14, 1848, he writes:

I was not born to sink, I promise you, run down as you will delusive hopes. Is it not the hopeful spirit which wins the day at last? Is it not the endeavour never to be discouraged which attains its end? I aim at more than mediocrity, hate the middle places in the world. There's a good time coming, love, and there's a noble struggle. Present happiness, that is, good conscience and mutual love: why may we not be happy now? Future bliss together, is it not worth any probation? A present in this world, a future in this world, a name to descend to my children's children, honoured in the world, a future in heaven. Love, we aim at much, and we have much to labour for. Is it not worth severer labour than men give for a plethoric competence and drowsy partner? Be happy, dear. Take half my blanket of enthusiasm to warm yourself. I am not in the wrong about the future; it is worth our toils. Let us be true and keep each other good, as far as earth will let us; then we shall have God's blessing, and the desire of our hearts will be fulfilled. Pooh! Why, if all life here is privation, what of that? It is but a cloud in the bright boundless heaven of eternity for which our souls and our loves were made. Be brave, dear, and say Pooh! to sorrow. There's no such thing apart from sin.

In that mood he left Madeley for Manchester.

88, George Street,
Manchester.

Come, there's sense in the sound of that. Now, God preserve us! This is the 28th December, Thursday evening, nine o'clock. I am sitting in our dining-room that is to be, surrounded by straw and mess; sitting on my portmanteau for a chair, and writing on the top of a big packing-case, with sixpennyworth of biscuits and a bottle of raisin wine—my lunch, dinner, and supper. Oh, Manchester! appreciate my worth and mend my breeches! I am a ragged being, positively without a coat to my back, and with 7s. 6d. in my pocket, much of which will be spent to-morrow upon soap and scrubbing. You shall be with me before this day twelve-months. I am not in the least taken aback. But directly things are straight and my way here clear, I must have you, dear love. I am too clumsy a great deal at house-keeping. For example, two men came to clean my windows to-day when I expected only one, and for an afternoon's work I suspect that they 'did' me in charging 2s. 6d. apiece. A sweep applied for the chimneys, but I put him off till Monday, and in the interval must find out what he ought to charge. I left my affairs at Madeley in good order enough. There is a balance there still very decidedly in my favour, but it has been lessened so much and in such a way that I have had a decided sickener. On the other hand, I came away loaded with kindness and good wishes. Ah, I see, I must sleep, though I intended to spend the night in writing. I was an ass not to get in some coals. It is too chilly for me, specially as I *have* already got a cold. I'll try what I can do in the little dressing-room rolled up in blankets.

Monday, January 1, 1849.

A happy new year to us, darling! All goes on *very* well. Things look blooming. Lots of introductions promised; only I can't get on with the house very well, because Manchester folks are seeing the old year out and the new in.

He had the following school prospectus printed at once:

MR. MORLEY'S SCHOOL,

88, George Street, Manchester,

Will be ready for the reception of Day Pupils on and after Monday, January 8.

The Plan of Education will differ very much from that which is in common use. The pupils will meet in a pleasant library, from which all the restraints and discomforts of school will be, as far as possible, excluded.

The course of instruction will comprise, in addition to the usual elements of a Commercial Education, French and German. Pains will be taken to give life to the study of the Ancient Classics. The structure of the English Language, its Literature, and the art of English Composition, will be taught somewhat more elaborately than is usual. A large portion of practical scientific knowledge, the first principles of useful and ornamental Arts, with outlines of the most important branches of Natural Philosophy and Science, will also be included in the ordinary course of study.

No attempt will be made, by a system of class teaching, to compel quick and slow thinkers to an uneasy uniformity of progress. Each boy will be guided separately in the pursuit of knowledge, and such classes only will be permitted as must arise inevitably, in consequence of their obvious advantage and convenience. By the adoption of this system it is made unnecessary that there should be fixed half-yearly vacations. The school will be closed only for a fortnight in the summer, and at Christmas for the same length of time, additional holidays being taken or not taken by each boy at the discretion of his friends.

The TERMS will be Half a Guinea for a week's attendance at the school. Pupils are allowed to enter upon trial for a single week, and they are at liberty to cease attendance without previous notice. There is no extra charge, except for cost of books and school materials.

The HOURS OF INSTRUCTION will be: In the morning from nine o'clock until twelve, and in the afternoon (except on Wednesday and Saturday) from two until half-past four. Accommodation and dinner will be provided, at the charge of a shilling a day, for pupils who do not return home between twelve and two o'clock.

MR. MORLEY PROPOSES ALSO TO ESTABLISH

A LABORATORY

FOR PRACTICAL INSTRUCTION IN THE ELEMENTS OF CHEMISTRY,

so soon as twelve gentlemen shall have signified their intention to make use of it. A Course of Demonstrations will then be commenced and continued every Wednesday and Saturday afternoon, from two until four o'clock, during a twelvemonth.

This course, therefore, will comprise a hundred demonstrations, each of them being two hours in duration. The first eighty will be spent in obtaining a complete experimental knowledge of the principles of Chemistry; the last twenty will be devoted to a study of its practical application to the Arts.

Gentlemen will not be admitted as students in the Laboratory under sixteen years of age.

The FEE FOR THE YEAR is Twenty Guineas, half being paid on entrance, and the remainder at the conclusion of the course. Apparatus and materials will be supplied free of cost.

A READING-ROOM containing the most valuable recent works on Chemistry will be prepared, and to this room gentlemen who have entered to the Laboratory course will be admitted daily at all reasonable hours for the purpose of study.

Lastly, it is Mr. Morley's intention to commence a series of

WEDNESDAY EVENING LECTURES,

upon any interesting topics in the range of Literature and Science.

These Lectures will be delivered every Wednesday evening at seven o'clock at the house, 88, George Street.

Tickets for the course during one year, or for fifty Lectures, price 10s. 6d., will be supplied only upon personal application.

The FIRST LECTURE, on The Crust of the Globe, will be delivered at seven o'clock on the evening of Wednesday, January 17; to this all parties will be admitted gratuitously who shall have signified their intention of being present on or before the previous day. The probable subjects of some early ectures are subjoined, as the best means of explaining the nature of the intended course: (1) The Crust of the Globe; (2) The World of Plants; (3) The World of Animals; (4) The Human Body; (5) The Human Mind; (6) Critical Analysis of Spenser's 'Faerie Queene'; (7) National Mythologies; (8) The Races of Man; (9) Parallel Histories of English, French and German Poetry; (10) Great Wars of the Ancients; (11) Sanitary Law.

Mr. Morley is a member of the Medical Profession, who from choice devotes himself to Teaching.

Some points in it were adversely criticised by Miss Sayer, so he defends them on January 8, 1849. He had already absolute confidence in his capacity to give lectures. He felt sure that people would come and hear them, and, liking them, would then send him pupils. He had brought his servant, Lizzy, with him from Madeley, feeling that one who had known him there would do better than a new one from Manchester, who would have her first experience of 'the master' under trying conditions. He also meant to keep Fred.

Now for Fred, I judge by his letter that he is ready now to come to me, but I cannot for a few days write with truth that I am ready to receive him. A portmanteau, two boxes, and a packing-case are not sufficient furniture. Lizzy sits on portmanteau, I on box, which is giving way under me. We eat and write on the packing-case. I sleep *in* it, with my head on a clothes bag, and my feet upon the kitchen hearth. Lizzy sleeps on the 'Library' floor, and I have made over to her all our stock of bedclothes. I lie down just as I am. All this is highly entertaining, but if I have the packing-case and Lizzy the bedclothes, there would be nothing for Fred but under the sink, or in the parlour grate. This is the force of circumstances, but circumstances will be conquered presently, and then (in a week if he pleases) Fred can make a triumphal entry into Manchester, and find here tolerable comfort.

Dear love, I am pleased that you have discovered the nature of Fred's mind. Whatever he may have learned from me, there is much which it would be well for me if I could acquire from him. There is nobody whose judgment is so useful to me as his is. I often consult him, often yield to his advice. His power of intellect is very great—decidedly greater than my own. He has not those qualities which make a poet of me, but he has a strength of judgment, a memory, and a clearness of comprehension far beyond the average. His nature is highly intellectual; he has great gifts intrusted to him, and after having so long watched with delight the development of his power, it would be more than vexatious to see his rich blossoms of promise crushed and smothered in an uncongenial London shop. No, love, I must not part with Fred. It's a glorious privilege to aid a mind like his in its advancement. It will be a bright item in my last account if I can claim part in the advancement of one soul. I can in Fred's, but I shall lose my claim if I suffer his progress to be checked. No, he must come back to me, and cultivate his mind in freedom, if he desires it. He is to consult no wish or interest of mine. But if he wishes to dwell still with me, he shall do so. I dare say we can manage it peacefully enough, but if needful, and if he desires it, I will claim him and keep him, as I have a right to do against all adverse title. He has been made over to me *for four years more* to come, to maintain and instruct. Then he will be his own master : until then, wherever I am he may be ; whatever I have, he may have part in, only I am bound to educate him as a surgeon. That was my compact, and I believe that it is not only right, but to his best interests that he should adhere to the design of practising his profession as well as of acquiring it. If Fred will resolve—as he is fully com-petent—to aim at nothing less than the *first* rank in his pro-fession, there is a splendid opening for him here.

He had also written to Fred Sayer :

January 5, 1849.

MY DEAR FRED,

I am not sorry you went home, neither need you be ; you have tried your strength ; you have taught Polly to regard you in a new and higher light than memory of you more as a child could furnish ; you have increased the force of your hold upon my respect, and partly by the void I feel in your absence from this household, partly by your conduct in the household at home, have caused me to be more conscious of the amount of strong regard which has grown up insensibly between us. Never be tired of trouble, it is but the shadow of a cloud ; the cloud passes and the shadow with it, but it is not for nothing that they have existed. Trouble is a good thing, I am sure of it. You and Polly might have had no trouble but for me ; my heart is doubtful whether you have not both been better off, even for that very trouble's sake. My troubles, I know, spring much from my own nature; but they are created chiefly by antagonism, as you see now at home, as I have felt always in my home, trouble arose because other people strove to compel me into their ways, instead of aiding me in mine. I do right in following my nature and seeking to put my talents to that use or those uses for which God seems to have adapted them. If the beaten path were a very valley of diamonds, and the path to which Nature urges led to manifest certain and con-

stant trouble, still it would most unquestionably be the duty of
every man to meet his trouble, ' take up his cross,' and follow
Christ by following the road upon which he feels most able to
be useful to his race, and a good steward of the gifts of God.
Moreover, in the light of an eternal day, how small a cloud is
the very darkest storm which can overshadow but a single
period of some sixty years—the body's lifetime.   Ah ! but you
may well say I am out of the pale of practice in regard to what
I preach.   Your sister's love makes it ridiculous for me to talk
of earthly sorrow.   God knows the future ; but I know enough
to know that we are already in enjoyment of an endless charm
against the heartache.   Polly's heart and mine have room for
you, dear Fred, but I wish you the possession of a true love
for yourself in whom you may rest as utterly satisfied as I do
in my good little missis.   For her comfort I do desire a little
earthly sunshine, otherwise I really do think that I have no
special predilection for either adverse or prosperous breezes—
what God sends, my sails are spread for ; whither His breath
directs, I seek to travel.   Now about your coming here.   I
think it may be managed peacefully ; we must endeavour to
continue so upon all accounts,

A reconciliation had been effected with Midhurst, which
meant much to his happiness, but nothing to his pocket.
Not so with Newport.   He had now a letter from Mr.
Sayer beginning, ' Mr. Morley, Sir,' which he says he
answered with some spirit, and then burned what he had
written.   This was a favourite practice of his about this
time, and until it became unnecessary for him to ease his
feelings by writing what he knew he should not send.   To
Mr. Sayer's daughter he continues to pour out encouragement to meet the criticisms which were continually being
dinned into her ears.

It is most true that, had I been a jog-trot person—a respectable, ordinary member of society—I might have settled down
at Madeley without *much* trouble, or somewhere else, in cosy
mediocrity, obscure and happy.   I grant that ; but my case is
different, dear love : you have linked yourself to one who aims
at more, and therefore suffers more in the attainment of his
object.   Were I a mere desponding, useless ' poet,' you might

despond about our future, love; but in my unabated energy
of purpose, my determination to be cowed by no rebuff, you
ought to see a character, with all its defects, able to win its
object in the world.   I seek to be more than an eater, drinker,
sleeper, and transacter of pecuniary affairs in this world, as you
know.   Those who seek to attain more than usual must pay
more than the usual price.   Moreover, love, I am not eaten
up with a mere literary ambition.   I have chosen a path which
offers to me henceforth a purely intellectual life, and I desire
to cultivate my mind to the utmost of my power, and to use it
in doing the utmost spiritual good of which I am capable.   I
shall not be disappointed if I live, die, and remain obscure
(although I don't expect to do so).   So long as I feel that I
am doing all I can do, I am happy, and having done that I
am quite content.   Would it have been more fit and right for
me to continue in the life I led at Madeley, in duties for which
I was but barely fit, barred from occupations more congenial
to my intellect, or have I done well, visionary though I be, to
come into a large and active town full of opinions congenial
to my own, ready to appreciate an active, scheming intelligence,
there use my knowledge in supplying real local wants as an
instructor, planning for myself boldly a busy, intellectual course,
and entering without fear into the lists against the few first
difficulties peculiar to my change?   I spent my youth in
discipline at Madeley.   Madeley had the raw years in which I
was fit for no task like the present.   I am now barely ripe for
them, and I am ready.   The lectures will make me known
sufficiently to support in due time the foundation of my school.
I shall, of course, here cultivate society, and take care to avoid
looking like a fool, as I make in this way new friends; it is the
most natural thing I can do to invite them to a lecture, and as,
fortunately, *now* my character is closely suited to my occupation, the more I become known, the more I must prosper.
Without the lectures, as I think it rude to come the philosopher
in company, I should make friends, and win goodwill, perhaps,
but I should be very slow in winning pupils.

On January 16 he gives Fred some account of the
lecture he was to deliver the following evening.   He had
been to one or two parties at Miss Walker's, had made
jokes as in his old college days, and found that what the

Madeleyites thought eccentric Manchester people could appreciate.

Miss Walker has been exerting herself like a brick to fetch up a party to my lecture; she will come with her own household, and one or two gentlemen will be present, I believe, but some who would, I am sure, have liked to come are unavoidably pre-engaged. However, I shall have an audience, tiny, but respectable; and I am much out if my lecture won't take Miss Walker's fancy. I could not help making it of a religious tone; the subject made that inevitable. Geology nowadays is much more interesting than it was when I used to study it at college. And whom are we to thank for that? That very jolly and truly philosophically scientific cock Professor Owen, the action of whose acute mind upon fossil bits of bone has given life and vigour to what was before little better than a dictionary science. Owen is a man naturally gifted with qualities which are required, over and above study, to shape out a perfect man of science. Try and be here, Fred, by the beginning of next week; our physical discomforts you are wise enough to stand now, and you will here find mentally quite a calm. Polly scolds me for laughing; but it *is* ludicrous, this present turning in my life. I think I see good fortune 'round the corner'; but there is a strange enjoyment in my present life—not only a liberty to read books, but *a duty* to do what was before a pleasure, which folks grudged me. I rejoice in the prospect of a life of uninterrupted study, gained upon the condition that I earn my bread and fulfil my use in the community by teaching what I learn. Jenny Lind in 'Elijah,' February 6—won't I be there! I'll sell my boots to buy a ticket.

In a letter of January 19, 1849, he gives full particulars of his furnishing. It all relates to the one room which was to be school-room, reception-room, lecture hall, and everything else, and where he lay on the floor at night with a dictionary for his pillow. This room he made to look comfortable and in good taste with a handsome carpet, large table, and cedar-wood chairs. Then he alludes to the lecture given two days before, the first he ever delivered:

I did not break down in my lecture—have one or two arts
to acquire before I can avoid being a little wearisome, I fear ;
but, in the matter of delivery, during all the first half I found
myself more capable than I expected ; afterwards I felt un-
certain whether my details were not often tedious, and that
rather interfered with me, headache and all. However, I
think, when I have had some little practice, that it will be in
my power to deliver lectures really well.

A wakeful night suggested to him another way of spending his time while waiting for pupils. This was to write
a comic poem dealing with St. George and the Dragon.

So, you see, here's room for some nice banter (in Spenserian
stanza) upon English bigotry, and for the setting up of ' my
idol '—Liberty of Thought. Liberty of Thought, no doubt ;
but I want people trained to think freely.

He wrote this poem, calling it ' St. George of Cappadocia,' giving a good deal of truth and some capital
satire with much quaint nonsense. He hoped this would
sell, and bring at least £5 into his purse, which would
have been £1 a day for the time he spent over its twelve
hundred lines. But the MS. remains unpublished. He
had not yet found his market.

A letter written on February 1 relates two important
facts. Fred had arrived the previous Monday evening.
He had run away from home. Various letters had passed
about his indentures and apprenticeship, and Mr. Morley
was determined to keep the lad, at any rate, till he could
find a way of securing him a better medical education.

He had been anxious that so bright an intellectual
genius should not be confined to a draper's shop, even
though that might have meant succeeding his father in
the best business in the Isle of Wight, and becoming a
rich man. Mr. Sayer, after some natural reluctance, had
consented to the apprenticeship, and now was sorely
puzzled to know what to do. At length he sent Fred to
London to a place where he thought his medical educa-

tion might be finished without much expense. Fred had many times told his father that he would rejoin Mr. Morley, and after a night in London he took the train, third class, thirteen hours, to Manchester, 'in the course of which I much lament to say I spent one shilling in grub, but it was so cold and *slow*.' At last he reached Manchester, found his way to George Street, 'and my troubles were so far over.'

Fred came to Manchester to share the accommodation of this house with one room furnished as a school-room. 'There was no regular succession of meals, but the occasional sale of one of the score of books, or of a personal trinket, found all the food that was necessary.' For the time it lasted all this was capital fun; but what had happened did not make things any pleasanter at Newport, where Miss Sayer no longer had her brother's countenance and sympathy.

The other fact was an introduction to Mr. Gaskell. Mr. Morley says:

In the pulpit he struck me by his intellectual style of preaching. So, as I am quite sure he is the best adviser I can meet with here, and I think the most desirable acquaintance, I broke the ice in matter of calling, by being the first to call, and left a card at his door yesterday. The same evening there came down to me a friendly invitation to a party at his house to-night—not formal and stiff in manner, but brief, free and friendly. So I was right in my interpretation of his manner; it was just what mine would be under similar circumstances. Mrs. Gaskell is the author of 'Mary Barton, a Tale of Manchester Life,' out not long since, and a good novel, *on dit*, so I suppose she and her husband go shares in intelligence. My paletot is sad wear for evening parties. I *must* get a dress coat next week; meanwhile I don't care much for the breach of etiquette, as you may fancy. Fred will study, I trust, always with me. He is now plunging into Latin. Dear love, I hope they will relent, and cease to plague you so much with all these manufactured miseries. We may open a shop for our friends as 'Agents for all kinds of Unhappiness. Troubles provided

on the shortest notice. Comforts extracted. All emotions
produced in this shop warranted to be quite free from pleasure.'
Ah, Browne is lecturing just now on insanity ; I offered to be
exhibited as an illustration to his class at the moderate figure
of ten and sixpence a day, but couldn't get him to accept.
If he had we should have begun to earn, should we not ? Ah,
again. No jesting matter. No, love. I beg your pardon,
but I feel so little *real* concern, that I don't mind so much as
you do. Now, dear, it is dark, and I must have tea, get clean,
and go to Mr. Gaskell.

This new acquaintance was an important stepping-
stone in his career. His 'Sunrise in Italy' had shown
his mental power, and explained many of his ideas
on education. Despite deficiencies in the matter of
clothes (he tells us there were reasons why he should
have been sorry to take off his paletot in company), his
personal appearance at evening parties always won him
friends, and none were so friendly or so helpful as Mr.
and Mrs. Gaskell.

He had before this taken a sitting at Cross Street
Chapel, Manchester, where the ministers were the Rev.
John Robberds and the Rev. William Gaskell. He used
to tell a story of how these two gentlemen formally called
upon him, wearing their ministerial gowns and bands,
and how he supposed this to be the proper thing for a
first call among the Manchester Unitarians. His memory
can hardly have deceived him in regard to the fact, but I
can find no trace of any such custom, nor had Mr. Gaskell
any remembrance of the incident. He and Mr. Robberds
must have called going or returning from some public
function, for which they wore their robes of office.

On February 6 he writes an account of an evening
spent at Mr. Gaskell's house. He met there Miss
Geraldine Jewsbury, who had lately witnessed the revolu-
tionary scenes in Paris in the company of Emerson, and
had much to say on the subject. The whole 'evening
was, oh, so different from a Madeley gathering! In-

tellectual conversation with rather an over tendency to
" hero-worship." ' The next day he called on Mr. Gaskell,
and had further talk about his prospects, with the result
that he determined to try to get pupils for private tuition,
and issued a prospectus accordingly.   He hoped for ladies
who had lately left school, and wished to carry on their
education.   This would not pay till he could form classes,
but might help him to make a start.   No other pupils
had been heard of.   But he had been to the oratorio.

There were three thousand five hundred present at ' Elijah '
on Tuesday to hear Jenny Lind.   There is merely one slip of
gallery round the walls, so you may guess the Free Trade Hall
is pretty big.   The oratorio was given as a spec. by a member
of our congregation—a tailor named Peacock, who is fond of
music and of enterprise.

On February 13 it is the old tale that he has to report
—no pupils yet—but he is not discouraged :

I battle on, and battling on is battling up.   I know, love,
what I seek—more than the bread which perishes ; mine cannot
be a calm, monotonous career : from point to point we battle.
Thank God for these early toils and struggles—we shall yet,
dear love, yes, we shall live to that—but the struggling is not
over yet.

On February 19 he reports that Lizzy, the servant
from Madeley, is wishing to return home, so he and Fred
are going to do the housework between them, for he will
not admit a new Manchester servant to be witness of
their contrivances.   He writes most cheerfully about this
coming change; the only trouble is the question about
answering the front-door.   Miss Sayer had written to
him lovingly contrasting his troubles with the comfort of
her home, and he replies :

Alas! I know how different it is in truth, and for truth's sake
you must put away the illusion.   My material inconveniences
are just nothing at all compared to the wounds of the spirit
which you have daily to suffer.   To me it is simply a joke to

be just now so very poor. I know that I have youth, energy,
and talents, and my attention is pleasantly engaged in the
excitement of a wrestle with the world ; how different a trial is
it passively to suffer pain from those who ought to dispense
peace and pleasure daily ! I have a full attention, and a merry
tranquil home which shuts the door on discontent ; your home
is the greatest torment that a soul like yours can suffer. You
have been as good and self-forgetful as an angel, my dear
Marianne, but I have seen it all—at any rate, I have seen enough
to make you like an angel in my eyes.

Then he goes on to urge her to the one thing that he
thinks deficient—to *rest* in God, to do one's best, to work
one's hardest, and then not to worry, but to trust. He
quotes the text, 'Thou wilt keep him in perfect peace
whose mind is stayed on Thee,' and asks :

Do you find that rest difficult to attain ? Yet it is worth
seeking. Why should a pure heart like yours, my Violet, deny
itself a just reward ? . . . All that man needs he has *within*
him. Then, you should do all that is possible to fix within
your soul a real impression about time and *eternity*, realize by
all means in your power the infinity through which we are
born to exist, and, finally, above all, study the deep, pure calm-
ness which is in all the words of Jesus. His words still the
troubled heart and strengthen the will to serve Him all the
time. If you like, I will send you a list of the most tranquilizing
passages of Scripture, or, rather, those which dwell most powerfully upon *me* when I read them, and you can read them, too.
God loves you tenderly, my Violet : what should you fear, then?
You and I, dear, look at the same religion with equal earnestness, but dwell upon it constitutionally, perhaps, in different
aspects. Much that engages your attention does not engage
mine enough ; much that I fix my eyes upon has not sufficiently
attracted yours. We must, therefore, as God means we should,
be aids to one another.

The letter concludes with an account of the scandalous
way in which many of his Madeley debtors were refusing
to pay what they owed :

Indulging a few whom I know to have a right to kind consideration, I have put the others in a list and written over it

8

that every sum therein not paid within a month will be then sued for in the County Court, and they are to be told verbally what I quite mean, that I will not after that consider anything but the necessity of having what is my due. None of my charges are oppressive or beyond their compass, and I will enforce a payment if need be to the utmost. People who prevent me from paying my own way in peace by their own dishonesty are at the same time scandalous enough to invent tales to my discredit ; not content with picking my pocket, they must lay hands upon my reputation also—murder as well as rob. These are the folks upon whom I have been spending thought and toil, and towards whom I have been exercising so much forbearance as not a few times to have borne a trouble or a pressing want rather than suffer any claim of mine to pinch or annoy them.

Doubtless this is no uncommon experience with doctors who practise among the comparatively poor, but the circumstances of the case made it particularly bitter just now to Mr. Morley.

On the same date, February 19, Fred writes to his sister, exulting in the splendid libraries open to him in Manchester at the Mechanics' Institute, the Portico, and the College. He is reading hard. He is also very glad to have made the acquaintance of Travers Madge. Then he gives one reason why he ran away to Manchester. The household in London where his father wished to place him he found to be neither pure-minded nor high-minded.

I dreaded the influences I might meet with elsewhere. I do esteem myself especially fortunate in being in constant intercourse with one so pure as Mr. M., for, really, medical students are as a class dreadfully depraved.

Here's another touch of the life to which he has fled :

My washerwoman washes most beautifully, but charges very much ; so I'll just wash my socks, handkerchiefs, and nightshirts myself. I can do so well enough.

This letter he encloses to one of his brothers, and asks him to forward it.

I'm afraid to address it myself, lest they should open it, for they opened one letter from Mr. M. to me. That was the thing that sealed my determination.

His P.S. is:

They say they'll gie me nor money nor clothes. Can't help that, must sell my teeth and whiskers.

There is truth in the saying, 'Darkest before dawn.' On February 25 Mr. Morley gives full particulars of how he managed the housework without a servant. That same evening he is able to add the most important piece of news which he had had to tell since he came to Manchester:

Evening. Love, I told you my friends here were good friends. Mr. Gaskell came to me after chapel this evening to know whether I would be disposed to accept an offer which implied leaving Manchester. It appears that on the Mersey, near Liverpool, there is a gentleman with three or four young sons, who wants to bring a teacher into the place, and will do his best to make it worth the while of a good teacher to come, by getting friends to join him and forming a class of about ten, perhaps, to start with. Out of that it would be easy enough to form a school. Mr. Gaskell will write to-morrow. He asked me what inducement I should think sufficient—whether a hundred pounds a year to start with would make it worth my while to go. I said it would. So matters stand. I think the place is Liscard. If I do leave Manchester for this opening, you will not of course consider that we have lost time here. I have made kind friends, and it could only have been by coming as I did to a great town like this that I was able to put myself in the way of progress. I do not in the least doubt my ability to make way *here*, but, of course, for a bird in hand I would leave off beating the bush.

Liverpool is not *much* smaller than Manchester, and there I am not friendless. Moreover if I *do* get eight or ten pupils as a start, anywhere among people who have acquaintances at hand, I'm safe enough to prosper.

He begins his next letter on Friday, March 2. He is posting only once a week now, because the friend who receives the letters at Newport has been joked by the postman about having got a lover, and it is feared that more frequent missives might lead to discovery.

At this time Dr. Hodgson was living in Manchester, keeping a large boys' school, and he invited Mr. Morley to supper to meet some literary friends.

The company consisted of Dr. Hodgson, who is undoubtedly a well-read and clever man; Mr. Noble, the surgeon, who writes phrenological treatises; Mr. Morell, who writes philosophy; Mr. Lewes, who writes novels, philosophy, and history; Mr. Charles Swain, who writes poetry; somebody else who writes sermons; George Dawson, who lectures with vast success; Mrs. Gaskell, who wrote ' Mary Barton'; Mrs. Morell; and Mrs. Somebody else—I forget her name, a very agreeable and well-informed woman. I came in when they had sat down to supper, and took my place next said Mrs. Somebody, to whom I began to talk, and she was as ready as I to dispense with introduction, so we got on tremendously about St. Paul, about Diogenes, and about Nineveh. It was a third-class literary party, but there was a much more entertaining and sprightly flow of conversation than one gets outside literary circles. I did not notice at the time, but remembered afterwards with satisfaction, that we all had water at supper— no beer, no wine or spirits afterwards; after supper we adjourned into the drawing-room, made a large semicircle round the fire, and began to amuse each other. Mrs. Gaskell quietly knitted, as her way is. Dr. Hodgson is a good hand at a joke; Mr. Lewes being quick-witted in his small way, his good opinion of himself made him the more unreserved, and perhaps more agreeable. He had acquired a notion of telling character by the formation of the hand, according to rules learned in France, and it was said he had told characters with remarkable success. I, being the greatest stranger to him, was his best example; then he started off accordingly upon my right hand with much laughter, for everything he said I declared to be the complete opposite of the truth. I did not like children— was unused to bodily exertion, etc. At last he gave up in despair; then it occurred to me that, as the form of muscles

was his usual test, my right hand might mislead him, and I
told him that perhaps my two hands differed, one side of my
body being slightly palsied, so he felt both hands, and immediately cried out. Others felt the two, and I felt, and it was
obvious that there is a very great difference, the muscles of
my right hand being much weaker, softer, and more wasted.
So he started afresh, and entering upon topics which he could
not have gathered from his former suggestions, the tables were
turned: I confessed freely some most strikingly correct defini-
tions. In fact, except that he attributes to me ' order,' his
character was, *so far as* it went, minutely accurate. I think,
too, that his system is quite a fair and rational one. I *can see*
why each point should be chosen as it is, and where he failed
is just where I *do not* see that there is any rational connection.
Order is marked by the development of the finger knuckles,
and I really don't see how they can have anything to do with
it. He said that in poetry my tendency was to enjoy elegance
of form ; that I had not so much taste for the dramatic or for
displays of passion ; that in music I should prefer composers
like Beethoven, and prefer music of a thoughtful cast ; that in
religion I had a tendency to encourage boldness of speculation,
but was not content with only speculating ; that I thought
much before I acted, and was very positive in my opinions,
dogmatical, but not lastingly persistent in them ; that I had
weak animal passions. Now, on the whole, and so far as it
goes, this is a fair specimen out of my character, and upon
these points he had no previous means of forming an opinion,
as we had not long come from the supper-room in which, beyond
a general remark or two, my conversation had been wholly with
the lady next me. Mr. Noble struck me as an intellectual man,
and if I remain in Manchester I shall cultivate his acquaintance.
He saw me yesterday at the Portico, and came and shook hands
very cordially ; I did not at first know him again. Dr. Hodgson
I thought clever, and the maker of very good jokes—much
above the average. George Dawson pleased me by the possession of much quiet power, but there is evidently no element of
greatness in him—less sensuous and more plainly religious, he
is a man who would be delightful as an associate ; as it is, he
is no more than a person who possesses great power of conveying entertainment—great vivacity of intellect and readiness of
speech. The other gentleman was snuffed out by a cold,

looked ridiculously woe-begone, and threatened himself two
days of bed. The three ladies were all lady-like, unaffected,
and agreeable. Mrs. Hodgson is from home in ill-health. I
might have gone yesterday to a mesmeric séance at Mr. Braid's,
but did not wish to do so, as I knew that I should not be able
to express any honest acquiescence in the wonder of the case.
If Mr. Noble were not blinded by phrenology, he would regard
it just as I do : utterly worthless as a marvel, acquainting us
with no more than was known to the first medical man probably after he had visited his first female patient. I was too
polite to contradict the faith of the other gentlemen, and
thought I had better not go and mar their sport by a sceptical
visage in the room ; the easy faith with which a willing believer
swallows inferences without making the most obvious preparation for them is very amusing. After the séance I saw Mr.
Noble, and asked him one or two natural questions on the
case, after he had told me how perfectly satisfactory it was,
whereupon I found that he had not made any professional
inquiries. There were ladies present which prevented him,
but he has seen the girl before. He shuts his eyes to the
obvious, natural circumstances of the case, in order that he
may not be disturbed in the enjoyment of a visionary wonder.
By-the-by, no wonder Mr. Noble is a phrenologist; he has a
noble forehead. It is to his credit that phrenology be true.
Now, I don't say that in depreciation of phrenology, for do we
not love naturally more or less whatever indirectly and with
sufficient delicacy flatters us? I am sure, for my own part, if I
count others base, it is because I feel base myself in the matter.
Phrenology assigns to me a large development of 'ideality,'
and 'being as how' I think myself a poet, that assignment
often seems to me as a bribe to believe in bump philosophy.
Talking of poetry, I wrote some stanzas of Polycarp; polished,
repolished, and discarded them after all as a failure; consequence was, more cogitation on the matter, and this morning I
was made happy before chapel with a delightful idea; and now
I know how to dress Mr. Polycarp and dish him up in a style
after my own heart. I think the nature of the design will
ensure my successful execution, and hope to make a sweet
little book. So that was another of the pleasant things which
have occurred to-day. Also, Mr. Gaskell preached this evening
such a thoroughly good sermon on the duty of seeing the bright

side of everything, and trusting completely in God's providence, that Fred wants to have it to copy. Mr. Gaskell's sermons do one good. They are very practical always, and he takes always the highest and the noblest ground, and has such a firm, manly, Christian love, that it is impossible to be inattentive, impossible, I think, to go away unimproved, unstrengthened.

He afterwards formed a much higher opinion of George Henry Lewes, and mentions it as one of the advantages of his residence in Manchester that he there began his acquaintance with him. Simultaneously with the prospect of Liscard, he had the offer of some private pupils in Manchester, but on March 6 he continues :

There is little doubt that I shall elect to go to Liscard, because the school is my object, and not private teaching. My terms I have left to the experience of Mr. Gaskell, but I shall be very much surprised if he calls £10 a year a fit remuneration to receive from day pupils. If it *be* a fit remuneration, I shall submit, but at the same time feel somewhat insulted in my vocation. Cheap schooling I dislike exceedingly as a matter of principle for people who can afford to pay a proper price, and most certainly I shall not attempt to establish a cheap school. When I receive boarders, I shall require a becoming equivalent for my services, you may depend upon it. A school with no end of boys to be herded and stalled, and my own profits to be scraped off their bread-and-butter, is in no way at all within my speculation. My whole heart is in the occupation, and both in tone of thought and qualities of mind I have, as I think you will find, the fitness to become a *first-rate* teacher; so I shall object to beggarly dole, if only for the honour of my office. You very evidently do not know how special a power I possess of establishing myself in the goodwill of children, how easy a sway they give me—for a simple reason, because I appreciate and love them heartily. Love will be all my discipline, in the old sense of the word. It will be a labour to my own heart to restrain even the slightest expressions of anger. All faults I shall reason with, *never* severely, but strive to put a double kindness into all warnings against what is wrong. You smile incredulous, think this an ideal state—of course, I shall be liable to slip—but, on the whole, I can promise you pretty confidently that you will find in a school of

mine prompter and heartier young students than the old
humbug of ' school-keeping ' could ever furnish. I will not be
feared, but I will be loved and respected, and on that score
you will find me able to get every word and look obeyed. I
hope to give a living interest and a significance to all the paths
of study, and get the boys infected with my own zeal—a very
easy matter when one knows the way to a child's heart and is
able to supply its cravings. Ah, love, you don't half know the
force of the instincts by which I am driven to turn schoolmaster! One thing I may tell you, however: I shall lay at
the outset and throughout enormous stress upon truth; it is
transgressed against miserably in almost every school, and the
want of it would poison my whole plan. I shall explain to
each boy when he comes the system upon which we are to
work briefly, but clearly enough to show him what I need, and
shall exact a promise of perfect truthfulness in all school relations. We must all trust each other, and if any boy cannot
maintain a strictly truthful character, I shall dismiss him altogether from the school. I do not fear any difficulty in that
respect so long as I remove all *inducement* to insincerity. Con-
current with my duties I hope to write a daily record of them,
so far as they concern the school, a complete history of my
school-keeping, in the hope that it may—some day after I am
dead, perhaps, and when my name has influence—live as an
undeniable proof of the correctness of my system and create
imitators. I am sure, if I live, of leaving my name honoured
as a poet; I am *as* sure of my power as a teacher among children.
If you find that I cannot guide them by the light of the strong
love I bear them, you may then fairly tell me that my poet's
hope is falsehood. I will sit down cheerfully and acknowledge
myself misled by vanity into undue pretensions. But I have
not a trace of doubt about either matter. In both cases I
know my path.

It is curious to note here how his faith was justified
rather than his definite hopes. He has left a name as a
writer, but not specially as a poet ; and while he was perfectly successful in his plans for teaching young children,
we shall see that he deliberately came to prefer to be a
teacher to those of riper years.

He was now writing for the *Journal of Public Health* two papers on ' Education : a Sanitary Measure.'

' The letter continues, March 6, with the following account of the one country excursion he took from Manchester :

This morning was very fine—a lovely spring day—so I determined on fresh air, and no mistake. It took *such a while* to get clear of Manchester, but I saw the outline of hills on the horizon, and was determined, wherever they might be, to mount them ; so I went through Ashton-under-Lyne and Staleybridge, finally crowning my walk with a real scene of hill and dale.   Climbing the tallest of some fine hills covered with heather at the top, let my hair fly on a beautiful bustling soft west wind on Wild· Bank Hill, and something Clough, and something Moor—verily, I forget their names ; made remarks to myself, geological, botanical, and economic—the last suggested by the busy-looking prospect ; lay down on the deliciously soft elastic heather, with my face turned up to the blue sky, seeing nothing of earth at all, and feeling nothing on that easy couch. I thought of you a bit, but on the whole I thought of nothing—speculated on the soft outline of the clouds, and felt the luxury of Nature.   Then I came down the hill with a scamper, and walked home through town and country in a pleasant reverie, stopping to note all that caught my attention —various odds and ends ; arrived home happy at seven p.m., having eaten nothing; and was not even hungry, nor tired.   I suppose I made my ramble about twenty miles. As I came into Manchester, the factories were lighted up, and one large one struck me especially.   I counted how many windows there were—light shining through all—upon one face ; there were one hundred and sixty. Only think ! On the way home I called at the Portico to see where I had been upon the county ·maps, looked at the day's news, came home, had some food, played housemaid, finished my article, and here I am, so bright and well after my escape into the distant land where grass is and trees vegetate, that I shall be trotting off again ere long to seek an exploration in some new direction.

After this a letter must be lost, but we can supply its place from ' Some Memories '*:

· * P. 28.

In a month or two this trial was over. I was asked whether it mattered to me if my experiment were tried in Liverpool instead of Manchester. Then the clouds broke, the sun shone, and the tide that was at the lowest began flowing in. For want of money to spend upon railway-fares, I walked from Manchester to Liverpool, fell among friends, and walked back from Liverpool to Manchester with my best hopes fulfilled. Walking was easier at six-and-twenty than it is at sixty-nine.

There, is, however, one more letter from Manchester:

Monday, March 18, 1849.

My Darling,

I leave Manchester to-morrow. Have been in a fidget of suspense, and therefore did not tease you by writing until all was settled. Everything is as we could desire, and my Manchester friends are full of congratulation on my success being quicker and more substantial than might have been supposed. There is an old chap—'stubbly-head'—to talk over, which will be easy, and then I begin with nine pupils certain at £16 a year over nine years, and something less for those which be younger. If I can begin next Monday, I may win another pupil or two at Easter. Is it not odd? This, you know, was my ideal—a school by the seashore—which I gave up as impracticable. How things consent for good! A stock of pupils and such powerful friends are a fortunate turn-up at the end of our three months' patience. So the world rolls. *Now*, love, I feel as if I were going into my proper element. You shall see what you shall see. Were it not for a legacy due to the past, our future would be wholly tumbled up in musk and roses. Fondly, and for ever and ever,

Your own,

Persevere, and you must succeed.

CHAPTER VIII.

LISCARD, 1849—1851. STARTING THE SCHOOL.

ONE of the leading merchants of Liverpool at this time
was Charles Holland, who lived in a pleasantly-situated
house called Liscard Vale, near New Brighton. He was
married to a sister of the Rev. William Gaskell, and it
was this connection which helped Mr. Morley to the
start he had vainly sought in Manchester. Mr. and Mrs.
Holland wished to give their children a good school
education, at the same time keeping them under home
influences; hence their desire to import a schoolmaster
who could live near Liscard Vale, and to induce some of
their neighbours to join with them in placing children
under his care. When Mr. Morley walked over to Liverpool, he did indeed, to use his own expression, 'fall among
friends.'

Of course he had to tell Miss Sayer all about everything, and though some of his letters have been lost, we
soon have enough to tell their tale very fully. Unfortunately for peace with Newport, the parents there had
no means of knowing that this new venture would prove
prosperous. It involved fresh expense; it promised but a
very small income; no wonder they were obdurate, and
there were threats of enforcing claims which would have
meant ruin.

A letter which Mr. Morley wrote now to Mr. Sayer is

worth giving as an illustration of the experience in which
the writer acquired his wonderful power in later years of
pouring oil on troubled waters. Those who profited by
his wise and gentle counsel, when he was a well-known
teacher in London, little guessed through what bitter
trouble he had learned how to say just the right thing,
and, still more, how not to say the wrong thing. The
lesson was learned in those days when he was hardly
judged by his future father- and mother-in-law, and had to
think in defending himself of how every word would affect
the happiness of his future wife.

> 2, Marine Terrace,
> Liscard, near Liverpool,
> *April* 14, 1849.

MY DEAR SIR,

In consequence of what I have just heard from Marianne,
I at once send you my address.   Whatever may be your cause
of offence as against me, I entertain none against you ; and it is
only because you have repelled my confidence, not because I
have willingly withheld it, that you are in any degree ignorant
of my affairs.   If I despised a man, I would not quarrel with
him ; it is still less likely, therefore, that I should quarrel with
you, whom I still respect.   If you write to me, I will answer
you frankly ; if you write angrily, I will not answer you so.
You have been, and will again be, a kind friend ; as such, and
as Marianne's father, I always shall consider you.

I came hither from Manchester by invitation on the part
of Liverpool merchants, who offered, if I would come, to
guarantee me a minimum of income during the first year
(£100).   I have commenced under active patronage with pupils
which will yield me more than the sum guaranteed ; my plan
of teaching has given complete satisfaction, and rumours of
new pupils surround me now.   My supporters, and those who
talk of supporting me, are all among the wealthy class, and I
have now a clearer and calmer prospect in life than I ever yet
had.   My heart is in my task completely ; I delight in my
scholars, and my scholars delight in their school.   Had I
remained in Manchester, friends had arisen around me there
through whom I was beginning to form a profitable connection.

Your daughter deserves a happiness which she cannot have while your anxieties so very much increase her trouble. Be satisfied with having ascertained that between her and me there is a strength of union which it quite passes your ability to break. . . .

With kind regards to all, and the sincere assurance that I am quarrelling with none,

I am,

Yours very truly.

HENRY MORLEY.

Marine Terrace was a newly-built row of houses about half-way between Egremont Ferry and New Brighton. It is still standing, very little altered, save that the surrounding land is now all covered with houses. In 1881 Professor Morley came to stay with my wife and myself in Liverpool, and we three made a pilgrimage to Liscard. We found the house empty, and were able to go all over it. That day he told us more of his early life than he had ever told anyone by word of mouth, and the recollections roused so vividly, and our keen interest in them, helped to induce him afterwards to write ' Some Memories.'

Mr. Morley's letters from Liscard are full of the joy with which he undertakes his teaching :

Prosperity seems knocking at our door—no unnatural result of my following my real vocation. I do dare now to revive many an image that I had timidly repressed lest it might overcome my courage when the fight was hard. And I will whisper in your ear, dear, that I think there is not much more fighting to be done; but if there be, why, then we must do it. . . . I will win all my aim, if God so please. I don't doubt of my ability. I will win you, and peace, and love, and prosperity, in this world, and cultivate my talents, too ; I will do all I can do. We will smile at our past struggles in a placid old age, perhaps.

And then he adds much more, contrasting his own happiness with her troubles :

The sitting alone, exposed to daily, almost hourly, bitterness, from sources that should yield sweet water only. . . . It would have maddened me to bear what you bear.. . . . Go on yet but a little while, and we will atone for all the past by sharing a household of love with one another.

On Sunday, April 22, he has leisure to write some account of his new establishment:

Mrs. Pipchin—I mean Miss S., our housekeeper—has arrived, dear love, last night.   Age, nearly fifty; stature, small; aspect, shrivelled; tongue, long and loosely hung.   I think she will be a very useful faithful help to us on the whole.   More expensive than a common servant, as she will require occasional help, but likely to devote herself to my interests, and able to comprehend those very little comforts which common servants are too rough to think about, and the absence of which has been a daily tax upon my toleration.   So much for that.   Last night also my schoolroom tables arrived, and so to-morrow we begin with the room as I had planned it, which will cause a great increase of comfort and decrease of labour to myself. The schoolroom looks very pretty and cheerful.   It is a tolerably well-proportioned room, light, with an elegant white paper (the house being new, I had the control of the papering to my own taste), a large window looking out upon the sands, the sea-shipping, and Liverpool opposite, looking exceedingly pretty of an evening towards sunset.   There is a little green terrace before the houses — between them and the sand — so that our street-door is considerably higher than the sea; probably that is why we were named Marine Terrace (a name I hate as in Cockney taste, and give my address always with a feeling of humiliation).

Then follows an elaborate description of the schoolroom, in which everything was as light and cheerful as possible, with chairs, not benches, for the children as well as for the master.   After a happy week of teaching he writes again in a very cheerful tone, and describes a regular routine.   He had a mixed school, with more girls than boys, and had to teach children who varied considerably in age, in previous acquirements, and in quickness of apprehension.   School hours were from nine to twelve, and from two to five; and his plan was to break up each of these periods of three hours with two intervals for seven or eight minutes' recreation, when the children, and sometimes their teacher with them, could run and tumble about on the sands just in front of the house. When at work he expected and secured close attention. In the morning a good deal of time was devoted to the English language. ' The details of grammar we are going through in scientific fashion (not *à la* Lindley Murray) . . . The sources of the language, and all the leading facts in philology concerning it,' were fully explained. ' Then the girls write, the boys work at Latin with me, I labouring to substitute everywhere thoughts for mere technicalities as we toil over the grammar.' In arithmetic, De Morgan's thoughtful book was the foundation of their study. In the afternoon the first hour was devoted to what he called Nature, *i.e.*, to a study for which we have since adopted the word ' physiography.' He started with the creation of worlds, and poured forth day after day a great wealth of interesting facts of natural science and natural history. Then came a lesson on the history of man. This he began with Nineveh and Babylon, and came on through the early story of Ethiopia and Egypt, with something about India and China, then on to the Medes and Persians, and so to the history of Greece and Rome. These history lessons were very popular. At first they must have been somewhat slight and rapid, but soon we find him devoting a good deal of time to studying large works, such as Champollion and the works of Sir William Jones in six quarto volumes, with a view to giving his children a complete history of mankind in a three years' course. This idea developed into the design of writing a Universal History. Such a work, suitable for young students, was much wanted in 1849. The day's tuition was often finished by his reading to his children a piece of good literature, serious or comic, prose or poetry, often dramatic. He says:

Shakespeare is a poet for childhood, youth, maturity, old age; each assimilates and enjoys after its own fashion. This universality is one of the miracles of Shakespeare. Of course, children are not critical hearers, but they are true enjoyers. *It requires no taste* to enjoy Shakespeare. People without a spark of poetic sympathy can hug him to their bosom; the most ideality-mad enthusiast can worship no higher divinity. The children laugh and pity by turns over ' King Lear'; that is enough for me. I don't mean to neglect the cultivation of the fancy in my management of little hearts and brains.

Again he writes :

Just now I am teaching them at odd times to go through with free voice and action a comic scene in the ' Midsummer Night's Dream,' which delights them greatly.

One of his elder pupils speaks of his method of teaching as closely resembling that in use in the High Schools to which she has been able to send her own daughters, schools which, it need hardly be said, were non-existent when she was herself a child. The principle consists in the teacher thoroughly mastering a subject, and then giving oral instruction upon it, lecturing, in fact, upon the subject in a style suited to children. With a good teacher there is far less danger of this leading to mere cram than when the pupils are set to study class-books. When children and teacher are alike quick-witted, such oral teaching, with the frequent use of question and answer, means true education. His two youngest pupils were Walter and Arthur Holland. They afterwards went on to public school life, and were found fully as well prepared for it as their companions, so that the teaching they now received must have been thorough as well as wide in its range.

The reader who is interested in Henry Morley's methods and principles of education should now turn to a paper entitled ' School-keeping,' which he wrote for *Household Words*, and which will be found reprinted in 'Early Papers.'*

* P. 296 *et seq.*

Here, too, will be found much biographical matter. The most striking and original feature is that which relates to punishments. In many respects, modern education has come up to the level on which he established his school half a century ago; but there are very few teachers even now who may not learn something from the success which attended the application of his theory of punishment. He refused to administer corporal chastisement in any form, knowing the tendency of the cane to make liars. He would not keep a pupil who, after a first warning, told a second untruth. This only happened once with a lad who came to him at the age of fifteen, spoiled by long previous mismanagement, and left him in less than three months. For such a case, he admits, different treatment is required. For his other scholars, a plan which succeeded admirably was a simple system of gaining marks, which only meant gaining credit—he did not believe in competition for prizes—by good conduct, and losing the same by inattention or misconduct. One other punishment remained in reserve, only once actually inflicted; ever afterwards the mere threat of it evoked such memories that nothing more was needed, and this was—let the reader be prepared to shudder—this was, *to stop lessons.* Here the paper on ‘School-keeping’ relates literal fact. The freezing of a pond one winter caused such excitement that once, for a short time, Mr. Morley had to stop teaching, and the children to put aside their books, ‘and the school looked like a dismal waxwork exhibition until the prohibition was withdrawn.’ This desperate remedy evidently succeeded because Mr. Morley made his teaching so interesting. He pours out all his scorn on ‘punishments which consist in the transformation of the school-room to a prison, or in treating studies and school-books as if they were racks and thumbscrews.’ That is not the way to make children love learning—to keep them in after school-hours, and give them something to learn as

9

a penalty. He intended that his children should like to
come to school, and should enjoy learning, and in this he
was entirely successful.

The details of a system of mutual examination will also
be found in the same paper. This was started towards
the close of his residence at Liscard, and proved in his
hands an admirable method of stimulating his scholars'
interest in their studies. Indeed, so good were the
children's memories, and so eager were they to put difficult questions, that these examinations were often a severe
test of the teacher's thorough mastery of the subject.

This will suffice to show the kind of work Mr. Morley
was now doing in his school. It left him no time for
letter-writing between Monday morning and Friday evening. But every week, generally on the Sunday, he wrote
a long epistle to Miss Sayer, and these letters, fresh from
his work, help us to feel the pulsations of sympathy with
the child's heart which made his labour so successful.
He had other matters, too, to write about, not all equally
pleasant; but troubles, taken as he took them, become
the steps leading to higher and fuller life. On Sunday,
May 20, he wrote one of the most beautiful of many love-
letters. It is too sacred for quotation, too private and
personal, save in a few lines. He had been dwelling on
the thought of how their trials had brought out their love
for one another, and how, especially, he had learned to
know her love and faithfulness as he never could have
known it if all had prospered as had first been hoped.
He utters some true words about the change for the better
effected in his own character, and adds a prophecy about
their old age, which was fulfilled to the very letter. And
then out of the very depths of his soul come these words:

Do you remember how even at Dunster I used to feel, and
more afterwards, that I had some task to perform in life; that
I knew this, but did not know what paths I had to tread, and
did not try to make paths, but trusted that if God intended me

to serve Him in some way then unforeseen, He would guide my feet aright? I had only to obey, and follow the guidance of my conscience from day to day. Have I not sometimes expressed to you my vague forebodings of an unknown future? It was at all times evident that the profession for which I was educated was not my destined field of action. But, love, you know I did not leave it wilfully. God *did* guide; through many trials I have been prepared for my true calling; without a motion forward upon my part, I have been led by events into the proper field. One by one my fetters have fallen, and now do you not see how noble is the path which lies before me? From many trammels I have freed myself, and am pledged to labour on behalf of intellectual liberty. I speak to you, Violet, as to my own soul. You have been my guide-star sent by God, and you have led me away from many frivolous and vain flirtations with my talent, made me earnest, energetic on a worthier course. Now I feel, love, for what use I was born a poet. Do not fear. I am not gone astray, nor following vain gods. Only a poet can be indeed a teacher; shall I be a teacher and regret all that I have myself had to learn? I teach children, because I have deep love for them, and know no nobler task.

On June 17 he writes that his school holidays for three weeks are beginning, and he can look back with much satisfaction on his first quarter, especially as he has heard of new pupils coming when he reopens. Here is a further touch which adds to the picture of these days:

The ascendancy I have gained over my pupils is even *beyond* my calculation, and it is most completely separate from fear. If I for any reason call a Baines in as he passes by, he runs up laughing and looking pleased. If I go into their house, they at once surround me. Directly I appear at one end of the Hollands' walk, the children begin to shout 'Mr. Morley!' and when they are all at school, and go out for what little Watty calls 'Recraha-ay-shun,' if I play with them, as I some-times do, instead of being a restraint to them, they consider it joyously as a great occasion of good fun; they often try to tempt me to run after them, and begin a game of romps. Truly, it would shock a grave schoolmaster of the old school to see me dance like a wild Indian, roll on the floor or in the sand,

9—2

make such a child of myself. How can I do that and sustain authority? Authority—perhaps I have none. But I am equally earnest in teaching as in play, and so I get by a natural impulse all that authority might otherwise demand. There is one thing, too: I do not expect too much, I let them be children. For example, I do not scold when I see fairy tales in the place of study, only of course I sometimes take them away; but when I saw that such books were sometimes concealed under a Latin grammar, or hidden in a lap, I told one of the children good-naturedly that the attempt at concealment looked like falsehood, that it was a form of untruth (our one sin, you know). That was a new view of matters, so he said, 'Is it? Then I won't do it any more;' and since that time there has been no book read in a sly way by any of them; the interloper, when he comes, lies boldly on the table until I see it and shut it up. I told them that I did not consider it an offence to read any book of their own in school-time openly, subject, of course, to the chance of my shutting it up. These fairy tales, too, educate, and when they are brought out they are generally the substitution of an interested and occupied, for a listless and unoccupied, state of mind.

Then he refers to his lessons on geology, a subject beginning to attract much attention at this time. The Dean of York had lately promulgated a 'new system,' containing sundry absurdities, which the Liscard scholars were quickly able to detect. Of course, this raised the question of the authority of Scripture, and Mr. Morley soon determined to deal with it before the children in a thoroughly straightforward manner.

One thing, by-the-by, I have done, upon second thoughts, which at first I intended not to do. I was tired of hopping round the vulgar literal reading of the Cosmos in Moses. It perpetually stands in the way of science, and, if not set in its proper light, will always worry us and cramp our movements. Now, a dignitary of the English Church has lately propounded a liberal interpretation of those matters, so I took shelter behind him. Pointed out the evidently legendary character of the history of Moses down to the Deluge, and the source of the legends, all of which I had weeks ago read to them out of

Indian mythology. I had also twenty times before pointed out how there arose, now here, now there, the legends of a universal deluge, so it was easy to explain that of Noah. I showed them why it is *impossible* that a universal deluge can have occurred for the last many, many ages at the very least; pointed out how ill the interests of religion were served by misinterpreting the sacred books into antagonism with human knowledge; showed how little it was true that science led to irreligion; how infinitely grand and Godlike—truly followed out by us—the works of Nature are; how immeasurably the true Cosmos is more worthy of a Divine being than that which is misinterpreted by theologians of a past day from Moses. I had previously taught them the absurd disputes which had distinguished the last century or two, based on the misuse of Scripture, and so, I believe, the religious principle is strengthened, and not weakened, by the removal of this stumbling-block. I taught thus, not as a sectarian, what educated men of every sect are only beginning nowadays to coincide in. The truth was too like truth not to be received instantly as a thing of course, and forty parson-power now will never make my pupils believe in a real talking serpent or a universal flood. I have ridiculed nothing, you may be sure, but they *know* better. They might learn to suspect the Bible if they found in it views certainly erroneous, and were told to receive them literally as the inspired Word of God. Every day of my teaching points to a wise Creator, but a superstition (not a point of doctrine) which contracts the mind I have felt it to be my duty to remove. I had, by-the-by, from them some puzzling questions about Noah's ark. Their last teacher had told the Baineses that Noah lived on grass. Because I knew that Charley had been long puzzled in his own mind on the subject of why God sends people trouble, I took occasion on the text of earthquakes and their attendant horrors, when we were describing them, to point out how pain and sorrow were reconciled with the Divine goodness and the high destiny of man. They saw it clearly, and echoed the question of the disciples, How is it with the rich and fortunate of this world? Then they informed me that, since trouble was good, I ought to be obliged to them for being inattentive, if that ever troubled me. I know that the removal of these childish difficulties strengthens the heart very much. Such little aids slip in occasionally, without seeming to be intended, often enough to keep alive the consciousness that the works of which I tell them are the works of God.

The letter winds up, after receiving one from Miss Sayer, with further reference to the home troubles at Newport, and with a proposal, made in all seriousness and earnestness, that they should marry at once. The burning of his letters, and the whole position since then assumed by Mr. and Mrs. Sayer, deprived them, he considered, of all moral claim to obedience. But Miss Sayer replied, ' No '; and so they waited another three years, till they saw their way clear to the payment of the last farthing of debt. Four days of his holidays he now spent on a walking tour in North Wales, planning a new poem.

We may add a little more about those early days of school-keeping.

Here is an instance of his method of dealing with his pupils. One of the youngest boys was passionate, and one of the elders had been fond of putting him in a passion. It was suggested to him that the elder boy should be held up to scorn for teasing a little boy. But he says:

No scorn is allowed among us. *I never appeal to a low feeling.* The next morning I began a conversation, perfectly kind. The children, who had ever amused themselves with putting Atty in a passion, freely and unasked confessed to their doings. I simply guided the conversation, and they said among each other how he was generous, and bore no malice. One owed him a penny, one an orange—all appeared in his debt. He is a generous little chap, but very hot. Then I pointed out how each of us had some failing, how essential it was to make allowances for a defect when discovered, and take care not to touch each other on sore places, etc. I need not retail all the bearings of the matter. I put it as a matter of Christianity in all manner of lights; let them discuss and say what they could on the other side ; they said nothing ungenerous, were very candid. Presently after came recreation, and Tolly, instead of playing, spent his time (unasked) in looking for the plaything he had thrown away. In the afternoon Atty came, and it was restored to him. He took it with no very good grace, and Tolly bore that gently, and none the less endeavoured in boyish style, that was amusing to watch, to be kind to Atty and repair his error. There has been no attempt to tease him since. Even to-day, when Atty came, Tolly had brought an orange for him, and I feel morally sure that the old offence will never again revive. Had I been angry, or turned Tolly into derision, he would have felt wounded, and given me a sullen submission, have felt ill-will towards the cause of his disgrace. Now he feels not disgrace, but a pure conviction that what he did was wrong, and therefore he has left off doing it ; that what he now does is right, and that he chooses right because he desires to be a Christian. Now I've diarized. Except that, as I've no time for reading fairy tales to tell the children, and it is part of my plan to tell them, I've been driven to rely upon my own invention. The last thing before we part, during the twenty minutes before five o'clock, you will be generally right in picturing me seated in the chimney corner, telling outrageous marvels to my childish circle. I start a new tale on Monday, and make it last the week; and as I know their tastes, I find that my own inventions amuse the children more than if I get them out of memory of print.

This last-mentioned incident shows the origin of the ' Fairy Tales,' of which he afterwards published so charming a volume.

He gives a lively account of a Christmas party at the parents, of some of his scholars :

Evening. Dear love, I'm home and tired. Certainly I managed pretty well for the evening, considering the state of my feelings in the morning. There was a large party of children, three or four gentlemen, and five, or six, or seven, or eight ladies. First we had riddles round the fire before tea ; then I had sundry romps with detachments of children, which completely defaced all appearance of clean linen and tidiness from my person. Then we had a game with a trencher, which was injudiciously selected, gave no room for fun ; then country dances, which I hinted objections to, but, finding them desired by the seniors, converted them into a romp. Then there was

a plot at the other end of the room for acting charades, and I
was requested to act an old nurse with a tremendous baby;
the word was cof-fee. The baby had a cough; the doctor was
to see it, and receive his fee; nurse, baby, mother, and doctor
were the characters. I was dressed by the ladies in a servant's
gown, with a mob cap, apron, shawl, etc., and played the
nurse in broadest farce; being too well familiar with old
women's ways of talking to the doctor, and being able to
assume an old woman's voice, I made my nurse very ridiculous. Our play was performed almost in dumb show; we
couldn't be heard for laughter. When we had done, I found
a lady in the 'dressing-room' who had laughed herself into a
fainting state. Then the charades were set aside, and it was
voted that we should make fun simply. Next time I was to
be an Irishwoman, and the doctor an Irishman, and we were
to dance a burlesque jig. The doctor, who as doctor had not
had much room for fun, made an exceedingly good Irishman
with a shillalah, and we capered about till we were tired, and
did many absurdities. Then I was to be 'Molly,' a farcical
servant wench, and the Irishman was turned into the dress of
a fine lady. He did the fine lady, and looked it well; and in
the person of Molly I quarrelled with all the company, gave
my mistress warning, scolded, gave myself airs, did courting
with a gentleman who wasn't acting, etc. Molly played her
play, and my fellow-labourer then converted himself into a
sailor, with a blue jacket and straw hat, while I covered my
face with pipe-clay, and dressed up as a ghost. The hornpipe
done, the ghost came and did things by no means solemn.
After being a silly ghost, there remained a final joke with the
pipe-clay. But for you, I should have kissed all the ladies and
pipe-clayed their faces; but you know I never kiss lips, even
in jest, so I, as ghost, must kneel and kiss each lady's hand,
rubbing off upon each a due proportion of the pipe-clay. In
that operation I got a great scratch on my hand with a pin or
bracelet. Then I went and was obliged to go through an
elaborate wash, and restore tidiness. Hunt the slipper was in
progress among the children; then we had a song or two, and
then a supper. I had much carving, and among other things
a fillet of veal, adorned with laurel leaves stuck in *by pins*.
Before a servant warned me of the pins, I had myself
swallowed one, thinking at the time it must be some small

bone or bit of bone. I hope it won't stick anywhere. After supper we had some songs, and a young lady's health having been drunk after she had sung a song, I was called upon merrily to return thanks; she is an unmarried young lady, who begins to think it time she was engaged. I returned burlesque thanks, with pretended confusion and modesty, and so on. Then we went upstairs, and we seniors danced, but my dancing was burlesque, for the children were there, and finally I came away thoroughly tired. I was overwhelmed with thanks and compliments for my displays of histrionic genius; the servants were fetched up to see the fun from the landing. Well, and now my loins ache with so much gymnastics, and I'd better go to bed, seeing that last night I had little sleep.

Fortunately, the pin did no harm, and on December 17 the school broke up for the Christmas holidays. On that day he writes :

It is now evening. When I had finished tea, there was a ring at the bell, and a great clatter upstairs, and all my children appeared with a little letter, and their names affixed, expressing their respect and affection, and begging me to accept a little token thereof. A pretty drawing-room ink-stand and glass was then produced by one; another produced an attendant blotting-case, which they had fitted up with every writing material they could imagine—paper, envelopes, sealing-wax, penholders—and then in the third place there was a case of pens. I could not say much to them; then they all came and shook hands and went away. I sat staring at the inkstand, and was just going to cry, when Mrs. S. came, and began commonplace, weighing the glass, and saying it was a good one, telling me I had got a blotting-case, etc.; and I had not much to say, but as she was a fixture, I took a candle, and went into my bedroom, and there had my cry, and was very grateful to God, and prayed that I might be a teacher worthy of the love the children have for me.

Many matters of general interest are touched on in his letters during 1849, but space can be found only for a few which are connected with the current of his life. He is afflicted by a bore : 'The very refinement of a bore is a person whom you can't dislike, despise, shake off, cut; whom you must respect, whom you cannot with a good conscience disoblige in anything. Is it not a shame that bores should come clothed like angels?' All through life he was very successful in concealing symptoms of boredom, but few men felt it more quickly or keenly, particularly if the bore was loquacious. He reads Froude's 'Nemesis of Faith,' and thinks it shows a very sickly state of mind. 'In Shelley's doubts and mystifications you could see a spirit loving the true God, and hating His fictitious image.' He has long theological letters from his brother Joseph, which he answers at first; but his dislike of all controversy, especially theological, was great. Sometimes his letters are very lively, *e.g.*, when he is describing a dilatory postman, or the efforts made by a family who lodged next door to make his acquaintance; often they are deeply religious, looking forward to an eternity of wedded love, in comparison with which the sufferings of this present time are as nothing, and revelling in the delight of reading Channing. He has a plan for a new poem, 'The Hermit's Toy,' which should show a man cut off from the world, but longing to get back and take part in its real struggles and interests. He himself now followed the fortunes of Hungary with profound interest, and, had he been free, would probably have been off to fight for Kossuth. He also plans a great prose work, a 'History of Man,' telling the whole story of human progress, and not exclusively devoted to wars and dynasties. He thought much about this book, and believed that undertaking it would finally fix his lot in life. Of course the grand project was never realized. Very soon it was indefinitely postponed, but the remembrance of what he once planned influenced his determination to begin his 'English Writers,' and to make that solid contribution to the history of literature the *magnum opus* of his life. There was both inflexibility and versatility in his purpose. He was always ready to change a plan the moment he saw a better way of doing what he wanted to do, but no man was more tenacious of real aims.

Fred Sayer went to Madeley for a summer holiday, and returned with the news that Mr. Peirce was making an income of over £700 a year, so he had no reason to be dissatisfied with his bargain. In the autumn Fred was sent to University College, London, where he had a most distinguished career as a medical student. To Mr. Morley it was a great disappointment that he was not sent to King's, where he could have given Fred many useful introductions. But he gives Fred information about second-hand bookstalls, showing a knowledge of London almost as ' exclusive and peculiar ' as Sam Weller's.

Some of his letters this autumn show serious mental strain. One afternoon, when he had been greatly worried, he saw a ' spectral illusion.' He says little about it, and did the most sensible thing he could—went and spent the evening with the Hollands. But symptoms recurred which he knew were warnings. He was what he called ' nervous,' but he knew that a much more serious name might be given to his mental condition. He had always to guard against a tendency of blood to the brain. This summer he had one bathe in the sea, but it made him feel ill for four days by causing a rush of blood to the head. Hard walking, such as he undertook in North Wales, or on another occasion, when he started at 10 a.m., and returned home the next morning at 6 a.m. with a young companion who ' wanted something to brag about,' made him feel better and clearer in mind for many days after. His keen poetic fancy, his powerful constructive imagination, everything which contributed to the mental strength he had shown, and was yet to show, was now leading him perilously near to serious illness. It was, of course, worry, not work, which caused the danger. Impelled by an imperative instinct, which told him that he had a work to do in the world, he had been driven into courses which his family and many friends regarded as eccentric, irreligious, some said dishonourable. To Mr. Sayer, a highly respected and prosperous man of business, prompt payment of pecuniary obligation seemed the first duty of life. He would probably have preferred a bankruptcy, duly conducted according to legal forms, to the course Mr. Morley was taking. There was a great deal to be said against such a course, and whatever could be said was said—at Newport. Even Fred Sayer, now at home, seems to have wavered for a while in his allegiance. The money Mr. Morley was earning from his school, after six months' trial, just enabled him to pay his way, including interest and life insurance premium, but no more. If he died, his insurance policies would have paid his debts; but he was as yet earning no income which could be applied to reduce his indebtedness.

There was absolutely no one but Miss Sayer who in the least understood his aims and his motives. He had been far too proud to explain himself to anyone else, supposing anyone else had cared to listen. Certainly it was her fidelity which saved him from a serious illness, and the probable break-down of all his mental powers. The materials for a tragedy were not distant. An inward necessity, acting like a Greek fate, had forced him into a situation which love rendered intolerable, because it brought constant suffering on one whom he longed to shield from every harm. But Christian love and faithfulness are stronger than Greek fate, and under God they wrought redemption.

On September 14 he is able to write that he is much better, that a week's holiday begins that day, and that he means to take some long walks. He goes on :

I cannot help these fits, you know, darling; from my way of speaking of insanity, you think it a constant painful thought to me. It is a constant thought, but not a painful one. I know my tendency, and that these nervous fits are warnings; *while* nervous, I am, of course, painfully conscious, but otherwise it is merely a wholesome remembrance of a matter of fact. I know that certain precautions ought to form part of my daily life, and that with them, and the rest upon your bosom, I am safe. The excitement of the mind remains, then, only in the degree useful to me; it is that which enables me to be quickwitted and imaginative.

He adds in this letter some strong opinions about the interference of third parties between lovers who have shown to one another the depths of their hearts, and have therefore a knowledge of one another that no one else possesses: 'The partial judgment of love is in effect the *truest.*' It was not easy for his friends to judge him rightly. There was a fresh difficulty with a lawyer, and his father recommended him to take a tutorship in Australia—salary £80 a year for three years—and brother Joseph wrote kindly offering all assistance if Henry would join him in the wholesale pickle trade. Miss Sayer's constancy was unshaken, but her hope was low. She had sent him a present of a pair of gloves, and when he wrote saying he would put them by to 'wear when we are married,' she replied asking if he thought people wore gloves in heaven. In Liverpool he was beginning to find appreciative friends, and in February, 1850, was elected member of a Natural History Society, whose meetings he much enjoyed. He also joined the larger Literary and Philosophical Society, where he thought the social chat generally the best part of the evening.

With all his activity, he still thought himself indolent, and that he ought to devote some time to teaching poor children in connection with the Liverpool Domestic Mission. He made one or two attempts to see the Rev. Francis Bishop, minister to the poor, and never abandoned the idea till his time was completely absorbed in the way described in the next chapter. He wrote a powerful letter to the *Examiner* about public executions at the same time as Charles Dickens wrote on the same subject to the *Times*. His sympathies, too, were deeply stirred in connection with the imprisonment of juvenile offenders, and the mixing them up with hardened criminals, for no greater crime than selling oranges on a Sunday.

New scholars came slowly, but early in 1850 a lady asked him to give her lessons in French and Italian. He did not say that he knew Italian, but that he thought he could teach it, and he promptly set to work to learn it. About this time he reports a dinner-party, to which he went in his paletot, and says how the man-servant in the hall had offered to take his coat. It had not mattered, because he knew when he came away that the wearer of the paletot had made a good impression; but he got a dress-coat for another dinner-party to which he was invited a few days later, and was glad he had it then, for the company talked scandal, and he felt 'shut up.' At another time, writing to Miss Sayer, he says:

You and I, as lovers all our days, may talk to each other as to our own hearts. I grumble at sundry folks to you, but in the world I do abhor and avoid such conversation. You and I can grumble and retain abundance of kindness for the folks we grumble at, and we can recant between ourselves when we find we have blundered. But to the world what we say is carved in stone sternly and rigidly, and the company will never assemble again to hear our recantation. So, then, the secret treasures of our neighbour are not a justifiable subject of everyday talk. When such topics are broached, we must oppose favourable to unfavourable words, or else be silent.

It is quite true that his letters contain much sharp criticism which would interest modern readers; but, in accordance with his own principle, it is thought right to exclude such matter from this book. The following passage, however, is an admirable illustration of the aggravation he could feel (and pour out to Miss Sayer, but to her alone) while acting in the kindest possible manner, and really feeling genuine respect towards the source of his annoyance:

Mrs. S., love, you will have seen, I was not cross with outwardly, and brought her home from Liverpool a lot of news and talk. It serves me right for feeling so impatient at her, that you should compare her to yourself. She is decidedly thirty years your senior—probably much more. She is supernaturally thin, and so unpleasant an object that I rarely dare to look at her. Her temper stands on three legs, her ailments are many and obtrusive, and her conversation never yet contained a sentence which it did not require an effort of patience in me to bear with inward fortitude. She talks the baldest commonplaces, and flatters clumsily by far too much. Those are her qualifications as a companion. Remember what I said about the two sides of a question. On the whole, I have respect and sympathy for Mrs. S. It is as a companion that she is least to be admired, but I don't think I have shown much of the impatience that her ways have made me feel. I consider it my duty to her to be as careful for her comfort as she is for my well-being. I shut my eyes to skim milk, and accept as unconquerable her argument for taking to herself the cream (that she does not take sugar). I consent daily, or 'jointly,' to the device by which she gets the outside slice of all roast meat. I don't oppose her argument that small coal is best for a small parlour grate, and large lumps are adapted for a large grate in the kitchen. I eat my dinner on holidays almost directly after breakfast, because she 'likes to get it over.' I take her weakness of body into due consideration, and indulge her to the utmost of my power. She sits with me of evenings, and every now and then I stop to joke and keep her spirits up ; I carry her bits of fun at odd times in the day, and show little attentions enough to satisfy my conscience. It's all kindness and goodwill between us, only she does now and then give one's patience a tremendous wrench. She is attached to me, and knows how to keep house—is an invaluable aid. It's quite invigorating to contemplate my house expenses, and see how different accounts look under the frugal management of Mrs. S. compared with the old waste under ordinary servants. I am naughty for *feeling* cross with her ever, but I am tolerably clever, when I do feel so, at not showing it.

On December 22, 1849, he went to Midhurst with his brother Joseph and his wife, and spent a week there, keeping them merry with his fun at some effort to himself, and surprising them by not looking thin and pale, but stout and rosy. Liscard sea-air and teaching were improving his health. He returned to London on the 29th, and spent some time seeing relatives, renewing and re-kindling friendly feelings. He went every day to sit for an hour with his grandmother Morley, for whom he always had great affection and admiration. There were the Manns and other college friends to look up, and there was enough mud and fog to make him think he preferred Liscard to London. But nothing made up for not going to Newport, and he came back to Liverpool determined to go there at midsummer, whatever might happen.

CHAPTER IX.

LISCARD: THE OPENING FOR JOURNALISM.

THE summer of 1849 brought to England a visitation of cholera. The deaths in London alone from this epidemic, between June 17 and October 2, amounted to over 13,000. Mr. Morley thought he had some symptoms of an attack, and took a pill of opium with remarkable consequences. But, in order not to ascribe undue importance to a trivial incident, we must remember how he had taken deep interest in the question of public health for several years ; how he had published two tracts on the subject ; and how, at the request of the editor, Dr. Gavin, he had already contributed three or four papers to the *Journal of Public Health*. So the musket was loaded, and the pill of opium pulled the trigger.

On August 5 he writes :

I took my dose of opium, wrote two or three letters, and then, under the influence of the opium, wrote an article for the *Journal of Public Health* in no time—one of four or five intended to point out how we mismanage ourselves in our homes ; the private errors of the middle and wealthy classes in affairs of domestic health.

To give spirit I have put it in the form of inverted instructions, ' How to Make Home Unhealthy '; with greater spirit, however, that plan gives it the appearance of a sustained sarcasm ; it is very unsparing against the errors of society, which are more influenced by satire than by sober advice. Fred calls it 'grim.' You know how I like to fire shot into

the army of conventional ideas. I do feel 'fee-fa-fo-fum.'
The conventionalists give no quarter to me when I use my independent judgment and do not act with them; they stigmatize
eccentricity. So I feel no mercy towards them. Every darling
prejudice that is a misbegotten son of civilization I delight in
battering and knocking on the head. So far good—copied,
sealed up, and done with.

These papers met with immediate and widespread
appreciation. On September 8 he reports that the *Times*
has copied from the *Journal of Public Health* his paper on
'How to Make an Unhealthy Bedroom.' This example
was speedily followed by the *Examiner*, and by other
journals all over the country. His next paper was called
'Two Ways of Making a Bad Dinner,' which was also
widely copied by the London and provincial press. He
then wrote and sent to the *Journal of Public Health* two
more papers—one on graveyards, called 'A Londoner's
Garden,' and one on balls, entitled 'Spending a Very
Pleasant Evening.' But before they could appear, the
Journal of Public Health itself ceased to be, and his series,
begun so favourably, came to a sudden and premature
conclusion.

He thought for a long while about the best thing to
do under these circumstances, and ultimately arrived at
a fateful decision. On the occasion of the pilgrimage
already referred to,* he took us up into the room overlook-
ing the Mersey, which had been his bedroom, and told us
it was there that he had one night determined on the step
which brought him all his prosperity. He had long had
a great admiration for the *Examiner* and its editor, John
Forster, and he now wrote to him this letter:

Liscard, Cheshire,
March 25, 1850.

SIR,

In the last two numbers of the *Journal of Public Health*,
published at the conclusion of last year, I commenced an

---

* P. 125.

intended series of papers entitled ' How to Make Home Unhealthy,' wherein it was my object to inculcate practical sanitary truths to the best of my ability in an amusing form. New arrangements connected with the Health of Towns Association caused their journal to be discontinued ; there was a design to re-establish it as a private enterprise, with benefit of capital, under the former editor, who has been at great trouble to obtain the requisite support, but that design has dwindled into a hope, and it has become doubtful whether a journal can be established exclusively devoted to the subject of public health, without an amount of speculation that there is no one willing to undertake.

Since, therefore, there is no sanitary journal, it has occurred to me to ask you whether you would think it inconsistent with your own relations to the public to allow the series, ' How to Make Home Unhealthy,' to be completed by an occasional or weekly paper in your columns ; you did transfer to the *Examiner* each of the papers already published, or the greater part of them. If you permit me to contribute the rest of the set directly to your paper, where it might class under sanitary intelligence, be kind enough to let me know, and I shall supply them gladly. I enclose Nos. 1 and 2, as you may very possibly have forgotten what they were ; 3 and 4 have been for some months in the hands of Dr. Gavin, but I will ask him for them, and forward them to you if you think worth while.

I need not say that I received no payment from the *Journal of Public Health*, and that I desire none for sanitary writing.

I am an old subscriber to your paper, and that implies,

Yours with respect,

HENRY MORLEY.

To the Editor of the *Examiner*.

P.S.—I write with my full name in good faith, but otherwise am, if you please, only H. M.

He received the following reply :

5, Wellington Street,
March 26, 1850.

The Editor of the *Examiner* presents his compliments to Mr. Morley, and, thanking him very much for his obliging offer, assures him of the great pleasure with which he will avail him-

self of it. He remembers perfectly with what satisfaction he
read the papers at the time of their appearance, and believes
that much good may be done by their continuance. But perhaps Mr. Morley will not think it necessary to begin them at
' No. 3,' as a broken series, but will so adapt those in Dr.
Gavin's hands as to make them the first and second of a new
series. He again thanks Mr. Morley for his polite note.

He writes about this to Miss Sayer very soberly for one
whose nature was so sanguine, but he immediately set to
work to make the most of the opportunity.

When the *Examiner's* note came, methought I must let them
see we are not slow coaches, and so resolved to write an introduction and a new first paper the same evening, and send by
the succeeding post, perhaps to be in time for this week's
paper. Now, I had no idea in my head, and furthermore had
a French lesson to give in the evening, so that it was nearly
ten before I could begin. I thought then, ' As there is no green
tea, and the paper *shall* be written, if it is to be good I had
better meet the emergency with a bit of opium ;' and so I took
a pill, which enabled me to sit up until past two thoroughly
wakeful, and I wrote a general introduction to the series,
together with some ' Hints to Hang up in the Nursery,' now
on the road to London. The two next papers I have but to
write to Dr. Gavin for, and as I cannot be again called upon to
get two papers out of my brains after 10 p.m. without previous
reflection, you need not fear that I shall use artificial excitement. To produce a weekly sanitary satire will not add greatly
to my labours, and by keeping a week or so ahead of publication, I may always write at leisure. I intend to take great
pains, and *do my best.*

He strictly kept to this determination not to resort to
opium for intellectual stimulus. The two pills had done
the work required of them, and only once after this, under
special stress, did he ever take another.

His promptitude was rewarded, for in Saturday's
Examiner (March 30) his paper appeared as a leader, the
editor making a slight alteration in order more completely
to adopt as his own the views in the paper. Mr. Morley

had made a point of asking Mr. Forster to alter anything he
desired, remembering from his own experience, as an editor
of *King's College Magazine*, what trouble had been given by
contributors who were touchy in this respect. For many
years after this, and in relation to his books as well as to
journalistic articles, he was extremely glad to have the aid
of John Forster's criticisms, deeming it a wholesome corrective to his own style, which he knew to be too much
moulded on German models.

On Friday, April 5, came another letter from the
Examiner office, enclosing a request from Charles Dickens
that he would write on sanitary matters in *Household
Words*.

More compliment. If we begin so, how shall we stop?
Well, I must put my knuckles into my brains and root about.
That's a fact. I don't care very much for *Household Words*,
but this will lead to my making Dickens' acquaintance, and as
I respect his labours heartily, I shall be glad of that.

He has a good look at *Household Words*, likes an article,
evidently by Dickens, on 'Valentine's Day at the Post-
Office,' does not care for much else, but makes up his
mind what is the kind of thing to write for that journal,
and is glad to have a second pulpit from which to preach
'health' to the people.

On April 7 he writes his first article for *Household Words*
on City abuses, entitling it 'Wild Sports in the City.' He
dwells in a letter on his admiration for Dickens, believing
that he will take a place in literature next to Fielding.

But he has not a sound literary taste; his own genius, brilliant as it is, appears often in a dress which shows that he has
more heart and wit than critical refinement. So I much doubt
whether he is the right man to edit a journal of literary mark,
though it would be full of warm and humane sympathies, and
contain first-rate writing from his own pen. *Nous verrons.* I
shall be heartily rejoiced if my fear prove unfounded.

For *Household Words* he then writes a second paper on the water-supply to the poor, calling it 'The Great Unwashed.' He knew it to be a good paper, but after writing, he rejected it, because its satire was too personal. It was highly characteristic of Miss Sayer, with her absolute straightforwardness and transparency, that she much disliked these satirical writings, and he has to think over earnestly with himself what are the limits within which satire may be legitimately used. He says to her :

I am not cynical, you know. I wish I had never been asked to write for *Household Words*. Dickens' journal does not seem my element . . . the readers are an undiscriminating mass to whom I'm not accustomed to imagine myself speaking. I wrote my tracts imagining a cottage audience, and poetry I write for cultivated tastes; in the *Journal of Public Health* I had a sanitary assembly to speak to, in the *Examiner* I speak to people who are clever, liberal-minded, and love wit. *Household Words* has an audience which I cannot write for naturally.

This is interesting as showing difficulties which he did not finally overcome for nearly twelve months, during which he was diligently learning what to do and how to do it. Here is what he says to Fred about this time :

Polly thinks my papers 'harum-scarum,' but I am glad she is so sober, earnest, and so cold to satire. Would that all people were so! It would be a holy world if men had but to be told their duties in an earnest voice, and then to do them; but since human nature is not so, and needs to be teased, laughed at, and humoured into the right way, so be it. Having satiric talent, it is my *duty* to employ it, but I do not hold it in much honour. It refreshes me to feel that Polly is pure earnestness, and loveth not the harum-scarum reasoning which cheats the world. Amen.

To Miss Sayer he writes :

As for sanitary satire, you must be content with it. The world is not made up of people like you, who would gladly be told of their duties plainly, and then strive to do them. Nobody would thank me for a series of 'observations on the present

state of civilized society in its bearings upon public health ';
they would go to sleep over my sermon.   I have no right, as I
do in poetry, to say I will seek to please a highly cultivated
few.   In this case it is the most thoughtless whose attention is
most wanted.   Witty satire and a laughing style arrest attention.   Bodily health is not a tender point of conscience; satire,
on neglect of it, can give no pain, but it can stir up to quiet
self-accusation. . . .   The jokes and anecdotes pin down the
topics in the memory, besides acting as a bait to people to read
on.   I could not well make a better use of the satiric power I
possess, and *not to use* a talent given me by Nature or by God
is wrong.   Not to *misuse* it, you shall help me, darling, to have
care.

The same letter, April 13, tells of what he proposes to
do for *Household Words* :

When I was in Liverpool to-day, I bought half a pound of
green tea for private use, and ' got an idea ' of a series for
Dickens.   When I came home in the afternoon, I got some
green tea made, and wrote off with perfect facility a brilliant
paper.   So easily—no erasure, no correction needed; and I
think it will be just what Dickens wants of me.   I write as a
gossipy old lady with conceits and prejudices, giving *my* views
of things, characteristic and laughable, but so put as to inculcate sanitary truths.   It's the same upside-down style as in
the *Examiner*, but treats of different topics, and puts them in
queer, crotchety points of view, so that there's not the slightest
identity of plan.   Writing as an old woman, there will be no
polished composition wanted—only a quizzical slip-slop.   Not
writing in my own person again, there will be less direct satire
—it will not be so stern; and my plan will never entail upon
me the working-out of a subject in a paper.   I have only to
string together the most striking odds and ends that occur to
me bearing on sanitary discipline, interweaving the old woman
among all.   So it is a series that, if Dickens like the notion, I
can carry on easily together with the *Examiner* articles, and
make both good.

It may well be asked how he found time for journalistic
work in addition to teaching in his school, and reading
the large books which he required to study in order to

teach history and science as he knew they should be taught. The answer is that he sat up at night, and wrote when the house was quiet. Now begins systematic overwork. He knew, and said in an earlier letter, that he ought to have eight hours' sleep, but henceforth this amount was most exceptional. On Monday night, April 22, he finishes his *Examiner* paper at half-past two, and thinks he had better go to bed. On May 8 he confesses that half-past two had been his bedtime for the past week, and when he is coming to Newport at midsummer, he sends a warning that he is not looking very well, as he had been trespassing so much on proper sleep. But so it continued with little intermission till he left London in 1889. For many years his splendid constitution stood the strain ; but at length symptoms of a disease, the result of overtaxing the brain, began to appear, and though this was resisted for twenty years, it eventually proved fatal, and brought his career to a close earlier than Nature had intended.

All this, however, is in the future. At present the chief result of sitting up late appeared to be that the children generally found him finishing breakfast when they arrived at nine o'clock, and were pelted with any lumps of sugar that remained in the bowl. His ' Introduction ' and ' Nursery ' papers were extensively copied from the *Examiner* by the *Times* and other journals, and Forster wrote to him in a way which showed how satisfactory was the impression he had made. He hopes this will soon lead to his earning money by writing.

I must do my best now to turn all things into bread. And I'm conscientious, too. I will not for money fritter my time with novel-writing, though that would earn easy certain money. It is not, perhaps, conscientiousness so much as pride. The future volumes—' Works '—I keep in mind, and try to publish nothing that will not bear reading by posterity. . . . Not that these papers *by themselves* are worth remembrance, but they are a fit portion of the edifice which you shall live to see me rear.

Then he adds much more about his hopes and resolutions, and the good done to him by the Madeley troubles,
and about how much better a husband he will consequently
be. All things working together for good to those who
love God—that is a thought henceforward never far away
from his mind.

On April 27 he begins his letter, ' I am very happy ; I
have tasted a new pleasure '—the reward of preparing
himself to teach Italian. He can now read Italian poetry
by himself, and greatly enjoy it. He had, indeed, a
remarkable gift for quickly picking up a working knowledge of a language, and guessing its idioms by instinct,
and for his subsequent studies in literature he was seldom
dependent on translations. These studies took him into
such by-paths as Icelandic and Mœso-Gothic, where he
rapidly learned what he needed to know. In Anglo-
Saxon, of course, he became a good scholar. Miss Sayer
had remonstrated on the subject of the green tea, but this
was one of the few points connected with meals where he
clung to his own opinion. In this letter he defends himself
vigorously, and carries the war into the enemies' country
in the matter of drinking tea too hot. He never would
be persuaded that green tea was unwholesome, and to the
end of his life a little of it had always to be mixed with
the rest in the teapot to suit his liking. A day or two
later he learns what is news to him—that Dickens pays
liberally for contributions inserted in *Household Words;*
and he begins to hope that this connection, too, will prove
profitable. So far his articles, asked for and sent a month
ago, have none of them appeared.

In his next letter, however, begun May 8, he announces
that he has heard from *Household Words,* and that his
' old lady' will make her bow to the public next week.
This duly came about, and he cuts out the paper, and
sends it to Newport. It is lively reading, but it was
rather mutilated at the office, and it is not up to the best

he could do. So he sent *Household Words* his 'Adventures
in Skitzland,'* one of the most original and striking of his
fairy tales. It is a story which always captivates a child's
imagination, and sets many children digging deep pits in
the garden, and otherwise working out its leading ideas.
It was at once inserted, and liberally paid for, and henceforth, though his articles are frequently altered, communications from *Household .Words* generally contain a.
' cry for more.'

But he felt most at home writing for the *Examiner*,
and what he says here about Forster will be read with
interest :

I know well enough the value of my style to the *Examiner ;*
it is precisely the right market for it to be taken to—terse,
polished, educated style with a quick fancy, store of illustration, vein of fun, and earnestness at heart, must make me worth
their money ; but I want judgment, deference to prejudice,
am even fond of outraging predilections that I feel no reason
to respect, therefore I don't feel safe without a censor. . . .

Forster is a first-rate man, generous and high-minded ; I
know him by what he has written. His ' Life of Goldsmith '
is perfection of its kind—wise, charitable, thoughtful, written
in vigorous and manly English. When my life is written
after I am dead (as it will be, trust me, sweetheart), may I
get such a biographer, not to slur over my faults and weaknesses, but to meet them fairly, and present them in their just
relation to the entire character. It needs philosophy and
manliness to understand us poets. Hem ! Never mind. I
know I do not speak in vanity. By-the-by, love, my spring
poem blossomed late. I always get one into my head when
the spring comes. I suppose the *Examiner* papers occupied
my ground, but the idea is out now at length ; it came quite
spontaneously in. chapel on Sunday night, and it will do. Not
very, but moderately long ; in my old style of blank verse

---

* He had had this by him for some time. Now he began
to find a legitimate use for early compositions, and felt, he tells
us, like a schoolboy munching in public the apples which he
had previously hidden, and enjoyed only in surreptitious bites.

interspersed with rhyme, and long enough, probably, to be itself a book, called ' Dead to the World '—the moral of my rejected ' Hermit's Toy '—differently evolved. I think that it is likely to be a great advance upon my former doings in that line. I hope so, for I must improve for the next twenty years—must go on growing.

That poem proved an unbuilt castle, probably from want of leisure. As soon as he had finished his series of articles for the *Examiner*, Forster wrote suggesting their republication in book form, and offering to find a publisher and make all arrangements—an offer which was gratefully accepted. Mr. Morley could now point to undeniable progress. Since Christmas he had increased his school, and largely increased the circle of his friends. He had completed his series of papers in the *Examiner*, and arranged for their republication. Without asking, he had been enrolled among the writers for *Household Words*. He thinks he may soon add by writing £100 a year to the £200 he earns from his school. He has had a meeting of the Natural History Society at his own house, made his schoolroom look very pretty for it, had 'his children' there to look through the microscopes, and their parents to take part in the evening's proceedings. He has been working hard at history, for the story of the whole world to the birth of Christ had to be told before the midsummer holidays began. Now he is full of plans for these holidays. There are lawyers to see in London, but the most important thing there is to be an interview with Mr. Forster, and future arrangements in regard to the *Examiner*, to which he is continuing to send, gratis, a weekly article. Miss Sayer did not like everything in these articles, and her criticisms draw from him a valuable expression of one of his lifelong convictions. It was not only lovers who could help one another, he knew, by being contrasts. He rejoiced in all the natural variety there is in human minds, and believed this variety to be the divinely appointed means for securing progress in truth and righteousness.

Of course, dear girl, you find plenty of antagonism in my writing; it would be odd if you didn't. We are contrasts—it is a bond of love that we are contrasts—in our outward character, and when I write of outward things in a terse way, too forcible for your gentleness, you naturally feel a porcupine. Believe me, dear, that instead of fretting about such antagonisms, we may fight and love each other over them quite fearlessly. Dissimilarity of crust is essential to two genuine lovers. Only there must be unity of soul—and that we have—under the peel of each of us, our hearts throb both as one. Your comments on the red-faced gentleman and the bird came from your heart to mine, and made me feel how inexpressibly—in our two souls—we are like-minded. A thousand times I have felt that as thoroughly; that is what assures me that we love for ever. Difference of outward way, of mere acquired knowledge, bodily habit or infirmity, give all the tender human hopes and fears and doubts and perturbations; but there is no discord between soul and soul. Just take now, for example, this 'bustle' question. In the first place, trot up and down my mind in order to see what an exceedingly small part of it my profanity on that point makes; then I think you will acknowledge that the thing attacked is absurd, but sanctioned by custom. Then comes our antagonism: you respect custom, I don't; you by association and the nature of your home have been educated into an exaggerated, somewhat false idea of delicacy. I by association and the nature of my home have been educated into an exaggerated and somewhat false taste for outraging over-propriety. So I get as often to be less than proper as you get to be more than proper; mine is the best fault for a man, yours for a woman. You scold me, and I scold you; perhaps we do something to mend each other—nay, I am sure we do. Each of us used to be worse. . . . I have been lately reading Goldsmith's life, and with deep interest. I think I've told you that a place in literature something like that which Goldsmith has is what I fancy my labour may attain—a kindly honourable place, but not among the grandees of the world. In reading Goldsmith's life I was struck, and you would be more struck, with the similarity of his character to mine. Our lives and labours differ, of course, but our hearts and minds and weaknesses are in a close resemblance. Yet I have maintained a worldly fight better than Goldsmith would have done, have a certain prospect of respectability and comfort—of a regular calling and a home—through *you*. Your love supported me, your counsel instructed me; for your sake I have persevered and studied to correct my faults, and I felt clearly when I read that life that mine would have been like it had I not been held up by the love of you. Goldsmith had no Violet, and had I had no Violet I should not have cared to fight so hard at Madeley for my home, and when lost should not have now been here; my mind would then not have been chastened by your holy influences, my aspirations would have been all different. I should have gone to London, should have lived and starved upon my talents, should have made a name, and felt in doing so as Goldsmith felt, and as I do now feel over multitudes of books, and so on, that good folks applaud, ' Why, I can do better than that myself.' I should have been envious when I saw men, less clever, better fed by the product of their wits. I should have lived a genius, and died in debt. Now, darling, you have trained me for much more regular campaign. I can afford to know myself a jewel not yet worn, and see people delighting in paste brilliants very cheerfully. My time is sure; the interval now is not wasted. As a teacher I am doing the most good that my mind is capable of doing. I am schooling myself, and becoming every year more and more able to build safely the structure of a lasting fame, and meanwhile my pen is not idle. And I am in a house, and have a respectable working connection, a good character, an income yielding even a little bit of surplus already towards payment of my debts, and giving a sure prospect of increase. Well. Every bit of this I owe wholly to *you*. God bless you, dear, and teach me to love you as I ought.

On June 20 he writes that the holidays are begun, that the trains are so arranged that it is impossible to get farther than Birmingham third-class in one day, so he means to come up by night, and have an extra day in London. Chapman and Hall undertake to publish the little book, for which they want him to write a few notes.

Then he replies to some remarks in her letter which had answered his last, and what he says is useful to remind us how entirely he kept his consciousness of growing strength for the one who had a right to read his whole heart:

Hem! your lecturer who says that genius is not conscious of itself is a great blunderer. No man but a blockhead thinks *while he is writing*, ' Now I am writing cleverly,' and when he has written, only a vain man gloats over his own performance. But to have genius and not to know it argues an amount of blindness of which no man of any note in history, to my knowledge, was ever guilty. It is *impossible* not to know it. Goldsmith used to go to see a play, and was laughed at for saying simply on that and a hundred things, ' I could do better myself.' But it was inevitable thought, and Dr. Johnson truly said to him, ' We all think that, but we do not say it.' I ' do not say it,' save to you, where my heart has a right to speak aloud, though I know it, and I am not vain in knowing it. It delights me to admire men who can do what I cannot do; I prefer looking up to looking down. I can look up like a little child to those who are my betters, love; you don't yet know quite all about me, if you are not sure of that. So I look up with a fond reverence to you, and count myself as little worthy of your love; so I look up to Channing; so I feel our Mr. Thom to be my superior in goodness and in wisdom. So I look up to men of learning, and feel the littleness of my small store compared to theirs; so I look up to masters in the art of poetry, and feel that I am of a like but lower nature. Genius is not vain, but it is often proud; ignore itself it cannot.

The following Tuesday he arrived at Newport, and while there of course letters cease between him and Miss Sayer. But there is a letter from Fred, who was in London, to his sister, written on Sunday, June 23, telling her what to expect:

Tuesday, about 4 p.m., expect a genelman wot can't abide you. He isn't going to give the paternals any warning of the approaching shock to their nervous systems, but is coming down upon them in this wise: He'll open the hall door and deposit his carpick bagge in ye hall and march straightways into the parlour, where, if he finds the dragon who guards you,

you lovely golden apple, why, he'll assault her straight, like another George of Cappadocia—I mean Hercules—only not with carnal weapons, which is fistes—unless druff to it—but with words of truth and conciliation. Poor Polly, won't she listen for the opening doors as the hour draws on ! . . . Ain't my sympathies a-getting ready their wings against Tuesday afternoon ! . . . Polly, I'm aghast at the idea of a man's tackling *my mammy* in that manner. . . . When you hear the door open and signs of his arrival, you are to make a descent into the parlour. We decided that 'twould be better not to give any notice to the powers that *would* be, lest they should take measures, provide a stock of constables in cupboards or bully you, and so on. Be of good cheer, the Dr. will soon soap over .the mammy, and then you'll have a happy time of it, which, moreover, you richly deserve.

In reply to this, there is a joint epistle written by them both on June 28. Mr. Morley, on arriving, found more difficulties than he expected, though not more, Miss Sayer adds, than were *to be* expected. So he retreated to the Bugle Hotel, and we must imagine the siege carried on from there. Before long, however, the garrison capitulated: Mr. Morley's strong personal influence prevailed, and from this time forth the greatest trouble of the two lovers was over. They write to Fred a very happy letter, and they had a good time together till July 11, when Mr. Morley went to London. That evening he dined with Forster, and went with him to the opera, where they heard Lablache, Carlotta Grisi, and Pasta in ' Tempesta.' He says, ' Lablache's acting and singing in Caliban very fine, like Sontag.' The following Sunday morning he breakfasted with Forster, who renewed a promise of a paid engagement as a leader-writer for the *Examiner*. Forster was buying the paper from Fonblanque ; the old staff were to go on for another six weeks ; and then he hoped to be able to pay for the articles which he was glad to have from Mr. Morley. He at once offered Mr. Morley orders for operas and theatres, and this was the beginning of a good deal of theatre-going.

I did enjoy the music; heard the 'Prophète,' Meyerbeer's new opera—a glorious treat to me—and saw the great Rachel in 'Andromaque' at the French plays. Oh! A first-rate actress is far greater than a first-rate actor; because it is more natural in woman to display the passions, and because a woman's voice has greater flexibility of tone. Rachel's voice is most exquisitely flexible; every shade of passion or feeling she can express by its tones as if it were some divine instrument of music (so it is) such as God only could have made so perfect. Her action is no less expressive: her person has dignity; her face handsome, with a tragic severity of expression in the mouth. Hermione, in 'Andromaque,' is her best character. I never knew what acting could be till I saw her. Where Pyrrhus deserts her, and she pours out her bitterness, and Pyrrhus then rejoices that he pains her little, since, after all, she has not loved him—

> ' Je ne t'ai point aimé, cruel ?   Qu'ai-je donc fait ?'

was wonderful; she put into the words an eternity of abandoned, hopeless love. Her voice and action were from the inspiration of a soul. Then she runs on with a rapid reminder of the sacrifices that her love had made, and presently comes another wonderful line :

> ' Je t'aimais inconstant; qu'aurais-je fait fidèle ?'

Imagine how such an idea would be expressed by a person able to manifest by voice and action the whole depths of the feeling it implies. Thereupon the audience goes wild with enthusiasm. Ah, *such* acting is equal to Beethoven.

Another thing Mr. Forster did for him was to tell him not to rewrite his MS. for the press, but to put down straightway what he meant to stand. Writing poetry with much revision and alteration had caused him to do the same for prose; but it was not long before he acquired the power of writing remarkably quick, clean 'copy,' and both before and after he came to London he was often grateful to Mr. Forster for having made him learn one of the important arts of journalism.

On the Saturday he called at the office of *Household Words*

and made the personal acquaintance of his correspondent,
Mr. Wills, who did most of the editorial work for Dickens,
and who told him that ' Skitzland ' had ' made a sort of
sensation.' He also saw Dr. Gavin, who furnished him
with sanitary papers to read during the long railway
journey with a view to an article for the *Examiner*, connected with application to Parliament for fresh powers in
a Contagious Diseases Prevention Act. On Wednesday,
the 17th, he returned to Liscard, and met his scholars the
following day.

He reopened his school in capital spirits, and was grati-
fied to find how pleased one of the parents was with the
improvement noticeable in his son. The lad had been
singularly dull and heavy, evidently crushed by injudicious
treatment, and Mr. Morley's school was a new world,
where his imagination and emotions were roused to
activity. Arrangements were nearly made for the lad to
continue at the school as a boarder, but this plan fell
through. The next letter, however, begun July 22,
announces the promise of a boarder to come the following
Michaelmas. This was Fred Estill, who did come, and
became a lifelong friend. Mr. Morley now sent to the
Examiner an article on ' Steaming to the New World,'
including to Australia. It contained some timely remarks
on ocean racing, but a debate unexpectedly sprung that
week in the House of Commons caused part of it to be
belated, and he is delighted to find how ably Forster has
added to and altered his article, so as to prevent its having
the appearance of coming the day after the fair. Alas !
he had suffered from the gentleman who did the poetry
for *Household Words*, whither he had sent one or two of
his poems, every word of which had been weighed, every
line polished to his utmost capacity. And this poetry had
been mangled ! He suffered in silence (except to his lady-
love). Mr. Wills had told him how they were bothered
by contributors, especially ladies, objecting to alterations ;

II

contributions were not signed, and they were well paid
for; but henceforth he would send no more poetry; no,
it should be prose to the prosy; and he adds some reflec-
tions on what he should do if he were editor, which are
amusing, seeing how soon he was to be asked to undertake
editorial work, and how unconscious he now is of any such
impending fate.   Chapman and Hall published his book,
'How to make Home Unhealthy,' on July 27, and he
hears that the articles have been extensively copied in
American newspapers.

He continues to write regularly for the *Examiner* a
leader every week, and often an additional article as well;
and as Liverpool merchants greatly respected the journal,
he found this a good testimonial for his school.   Forster
asked him to write about the Canterbury Settlement as a
piece of High Church bigotry which deserved ridicule.
This he did with a brilliant paper much praised and
quoted, following it up the next week with a similar
attack on Low Church bigotry and the Post-Office.   But
after he had done the work, he strongly felt that ridicule
was not the right weapon wherewith to attack bigotry,
and this was the last time that he ever put his talent to
such a purpose.   The case of a country curate, who was
said to have refused a dying woman's request to go and
pray with her, because she was a sinner, draws from him
two paragraphs, one of narrative, the other of comment,
'short, severe, Christian.'   Then he writes three articles
for the *Examiner* on investments for savings, laws of
partnership, and laws of land, dealing with reforms required to encourage honest enterprise, and with the importance of restricting the powers of settlement which
prevent land being easily saleable.   Each of these papers
he feels to be a genuine ' H. M.'   He knows that Forster
and he heartily agree, and he has simply to put forth his
strength in his natural manner.   The *Spectator* and the
Globe take his writing to be that of Fonblanque, and as

Fonblanque had raised the *Examiner* to its leading position, this was a satisfactory mistake. He also wrote on the same subjects a long paper for *Household Words* in accordance with a plan suggested to and approved by Mr. Wills in London, turning the blue-book into a fairy tale. But after spending many hours over the work, he had his paper, 'A Penny Saved,' returned, with a request that he would 'cut out the fairies' and give only the facts conveyed in his 'agreeable and much-admired style,' which meant shortening the paper by three guineas' worth of labour lost. He complied, as always, without a murmur audible in the office, but sends to Newport, and to Fred in London, many complaints of the way they mangle his papers. He at once plans other papers, for which they keep asking, but he feels that he shall write under constraint. 'Dickens has great genius, but not a trained and cultivated reason. I can never answer for his opinions: they are always dictated by good feeling; but feeling, without judgment, blunders often.' Mr. Wills, he thought, was too much afraid of offending subscribers.

Forster is quite another thing. In spite of difference in age, there is like-mindedness enough to make us friends. In all my own characteristics he excels me, except fancy only. He has a quick imagination, but mine's quicker, but in a great degree less under the control of judgment. If mine were in all things a mind like his own, of less stature, he could then think but little of my qualities; but, luckily, there is one thing in which I am able to excel, and so we pull together.

At a later date he would probably have admitted there was more reason for the prunings and alterations made in his *Household Words* papers than he now saw. From many quarters he gathered his material for new papers. The leading incident in his poem 'The Hermit's Toy' he worked into an article specially bearing on Ireland, entitled 'The Irish Use of the Globe in One Lesson.' Over this *Household Words* was enthusiastic. He is

II—2

determined, if possible, to earn £2 a week from *Household Words*, as his only chance of getting through the coming quarter without increasing debt, because in October heavy payments have to be made for interest on a loan and for life insurance. He and Miss Sayer had had much financial conference at midsummer. He gave her a list of all debts that he could remember, and now reports to her all particulars of income and expenditure, and what he can devote to lessening indebtedness. So the letters henceforth deal much with monetary consideration ; there are small misunderstandings to be explained, and, small as they are, they have some painful features, indicating how serious is the strain. More than once Mr. Holland advances money to meet some pressing creditor, being paid back when the quarter's school bills come in, and it is still hope deferred in regard to proposals from Forster about a salary. Several favourable reviews of his ' Home Unhealthy' appeared in the *Athenæum* and other leading papers; but he soon found that his chance of remuneration from the little book was as small as authors usually do find it on the half-profit system, in which, he says, half means one-fifth, or even one-tenth.

He devotes a good deal of time to reading about prisons and the social condition of Europe, and thinks on the subject till it interferes with his sleep. Fred obtains for him a multitude of facts relating to Parkhurst Reformatory, which was by no means successful in the treatment of its boys. Another topic touched on in his letters is the rough handling of Marshal Haynau by the men employed in a London brewery. He is glad of the unpremeditated outburst of indignation against a brutal tyrant, but does not like the continued gloating over the men's achievement and the daily ovation they receive in the press. This is the conclusion of a letter on Sunday, September 22 :

I laughed at the Sunday crowd upon the George's Pier in coming home, and loved the dear, gay, love-making, and warm-weather-enjoying crowd. No gentlemen and ladies of seven days a week, but birds gay only on a Sunday or a holiday. The gentlemen in patent - leather boots, check trousers, and *such* sky-blue ties. The ladies, in all the most vivid colours—no half-tints, I promise you, except some with prettier faces; but most faces were plain, and dresses which belonged to these were not plain, I assure you. A cobalt blue silk or satin dress, and bright orange shawl, red ribbons, and white lace bonnet, and a green gorgeous parasol, was one costume, and most were in that style; moreover, nearly all the parasols were up (mostly bright blue), though it was 5 p.m., quite cloudy, and no sun. But they all looked cheerful in the face, and the sweethearts looked innocently conscious, and the patent boots carried the blue parasol, when it was not up, and I loved them all heartily, but not as I love you. You are my sweetheart, and I'll carry your parasol, but won't wear patent boots.

The next week he tells that a 'rival' schoolmaster is about to flit. His pupils were always in a chronic state of sore knuckles from raps with a ruler, and at length he had hit a boy so severely on the back of the head that the father, his principal supporter, withdrew his sons, who were now running about all day on the shore. They were not sent to Mr. Morley because of his heterodox theology.

This brings us to the end of September, when he gave his school two days' holiday, and spent it himself reading, sorting papers, and arranging for his boarder, who arrived on October 8. Fred Estill was then thirteen, a healthy, happy lad, just the age and disposition to derive full benefit from living with Mr. Morley, who soon won his unbounded confidence. A difficulty arose in the school, owing to some of the children' being much slower than others, and Mr. Morley had no one to help in the teaching. So he met the difficulty by giving an extra hour from six to seven each evening to those who liked to come for it. From seven to nine he devoted to Fred Estill, teaching him, with other extras, Anglo-Saxon and Spanish. This meant giving twelve hours every day but Saturday and

Sunday to the school ; for meals, we are told, as if it was something virtuous, only took about twenty minutes, much of which was generally employed in reading or writing; and books of history, such as Gibbon and Milman, and of natural science, had to be read to supply material for the many hours of oral teaching. Once he sat up half the night enlarging a map of Central America to illustrate schemes of the Panama or Nicaragua Canals, which then attracted attention, and were being discussed in school. This inspired Fred Estill with a desire to draw maps; and one evening, while he was engaged on a map of England, Mr. Morley, who always thought play with his children useful employment, sat with him drawing demons, some two hundred of them, on the margin of the paper, with a stout old lady fighting her way through them, and labelled it ' Purgatory.' This was carried off home in triumph by the boy the following Saturday. Fred's lively whistling and singing about the house prevented there being any quiet time for writing till he was in bed, and then the journalistic labours began. The teaching was happy work. The mutual examination class* was answering admirably, and he says: ' I grow fonder of my duties every month.' Hard work and sea-air gave him a good appetite, and he reports that he is getting quite stout, and that an old fellow-student of King's said he would not have known him, so different is he now from the pale, thin youth remembered at college.

On October 6 he heard of the death of his grandmother Morley, and writes some beautiful words about the character of one whom he had always deeply reverenced and loved. Soon after this he had an opportunity of repaying some of the kindness he had received from the Hollands. One of their younger sons was taken seriously ill, and Mr. Morley went to see him twice a day, and became convinced that he was being wrongly treated.

* See ' Early Papers,' p. 309.

By his advice, Mr. Holland called in one of the leading Liverpool physicians, who supported the treatment hitherto adopted. The boy had a fever, he said, and must have lowering treatment. Mr. Morley believed the fever to be only a symptom of another disease which required quinine and stimulants. The local doctor came round to his opinion, and the treatment was changed just in time to save the boy's life, the improvement with the change being so marked as to convince the Liverpool physician of the incorrectness of his previous diagnosis. Mr. Morley adds, 'Nothing could have saved him without the devoted self-abandonment of his mother, who tends him sleeplessly,' and who afterwards herself had a severe illness from the overstrain. He thought that the regular medical system was far too mechanical. Every illness must have a definite name, and to every name there was attached a particular treatment with fixed rules. He knew that he had often understood and successfully treated cases through the power of a quick intuition which could not be reduced to rule and system. However this may be—and of course he is speaking of medical practice in 1850—he was undoubtedly right in this instance, and, apart from his professional skill, the comfort and encouragement afforded by his presence were very great all through this sore trial.

Among the papers that he wrote at this time for *Household Words* was one called ' Views of the Country,' which appeared on November 16. It is a clever, hopeful treatment of a number of political questions, full of brilliant fancy, but certainly suggesting that he has much to learn as a journalist. His illustrations include reference to a host of curious facts, gènerally unknown, about which he had recently been reading, and, being unknown to the general public, they are of doubtful value to illustrate topics which are themselves much more familiar. Here is one paragraph from it which will be read with interest at the present day:

It is a great pity that any quarrel about indoctrination into creeds should impede education for our poor. Everybody who has intercourse with children knows that they are incapable of understanding theologic subtleties. We may put into their mouths and make them roll about a form of words, as we may get them to suck pebbles; but they can no more extract sense out of the words than savour from the stones, nor are we able to compel them so to do. Nor have we any need to engage in the hopeless trial, with the record of the life and lessons of Christ lying ready to our hands, and His own prayer an eternal model to us in its grand simplicity.

Another of his papers possesses a good deal of biographical interest. While at Dunster he had written a story in which a certain Phil Spruce had expressed some of his own opinions, which he now regarded as false and unjust. But the machinery of the tale was good, and he uses it to argue against his former views. Dickens thought the additions he now made very beautiful, and sent the paper back to him that he might amplify them, which he does, 'showing no mercy to my former self, preaching truth, charity, self-reliance, and the sacredness of trouble out of a very earnest conviction.'

The story is 'The King of the Hearth,' and it will be found reprinted in the volume of fairy tales called 'Oberon's Horn.'* In regard to both the title and the setting of the story, he had no doubt that Dickens helped him to make real improvements, and as this was not always his feeling, it is pleasant to be able to note it here.

On November 25 he writes to Fred Sayer:

We are all too weak in being unable to act up to our ideal; but how much weaker we should be, if we had no ideal on before—a holy thing to follow, at a distance even, a spirit of God beckoning and pointing out the path! But deeds so horribly fall short of pure intentions. Oh dear, what an emphatic warning, and how veritably necessary ' *Watch* and pray'! Well, God is good; and with our hopes and our short-

---

* Published by Routledge.

comings, we have no need to tremble at the scrutiny of Him who knows the heart He judges.   Sayers, hows'ever, with all our blunders, quarrels, sins, man too is good, and bears the impress of his Maker.   I doubt whether you see that now so vividly as you will come to see it, for, positively, 'tis a thing which one has to discover.   There is an odd evidence of my discovery detectable this week ; you know how I thought of the world at twenty in ' Lilybell,' etc. : love drooping, deserted, selfishness the world's curse ; and at Madeley, I don't know whether you remember Mr. Spruce's philosophy, which stated my opinion of human nature five years ago.   I have outgrown that error, and recanted so completely as to recast Mr. Spruce for the purpose of holding up my old opinions to distinct condemnation, as false and unwholesome.   Faith in my fellow-creatures grows with knowledge of them.   Mr. Spruce modelled into a Christmas sketch will be in next Thursday's *Household Words*, and if you come across that 'ere work, just read him.   It will edify you to see how much of my old self-experience has been lopped away as morbid.

He has also been writing to Fred earnestly about the Bible, to make him feel that he need not regard himself as less religious because he is less superstitious, and cannot look upon the curses in the Psalms as inspired.   It is the *life of Christ* that is to be chiefly valued ; and in the rest of the Bible Fred may find much else of value, where it, too, shows the spirit of the Master.

England's two most pressing national wants at this time he considered to be land reform and universal education. In regard to both matters, much was to be learned from Germany.   He had said his say in *Household Words* about Stein and Hardenberg, and the ease with which an industrious, sober Prussian peasant could become the owner of a plot of land.   Next he wants to give an account of Prussian education, and this is how he finds time to do his work.   He hears on Sunday morning, December 1, that another paper is wanted, and he begins it that evening at 10 p.m., and writes till 2 a.m.   On Monday the two hours between school are devoted to it, and it is finished that evening in time to post in Liverpool, on his way to the Philosophical Society. Here a paper is read on the Egyptian Pyramids and square roots, which he thinks is full of absurdities; and so, having read a good deal about Egypt during the last twelve months, he makes his first speech at the society, and puts in a plea for common-sense. Then he returns home to read a lengthy correspondence, and write an article on it for the *Examiner*, which he finished by 3 a.m. Tuesday, after school, he went to the annual meeting of the Renshaw Street Book Society, where he was made auctioneer, and had to talk much about books, and where he formed several new acquaintances. He finally reached home by midnight, 'very tired.' The article in *Household Words* is called 'Mr. Bendigo Buster on our National Defences against Education.' It is an ironical attack on our national ignorance, 45 per cent. of the population being unable to read and write; while in Prussia education was practically universal; and the German system under which this was secured is fully and clearly described. They were much pleased with the article at the office, and it appeared in *Household Words* for December 28, along with another paper called 'The Death of a Goblin,' which at their request he had written on the subject of ghosts and drains.

For the *Examiner* he had written on 'Reformatories,' using the information Fred had obtained for him about Parkhurst, and much else that he had been reading with deep interest. He would have gone into this question even more fully than he did, but this winter the attention of the nation was absorbed for months in an anti-Catholic scare caused by the Pope's appointing Roman Catholic Bishops with territorial titles. Lord John Russell's letter to the Bishop of Durham on Papal aggression appeared on November 4, and rendered useless some light banter Mr. Morley had written for the *Examiner*, because Forster took the matter up with all the seriousness of an outraged

Protestant. Mr. Morley did not disagree with these views, but he felt at once, what everyone felt later, that far too much fuss was being made of the incident, and he preferred not to write about it himself, especially as he was resolved never to use ridicule in order to inflame passion against bigotry and superstition. He would not encourage bigotry on his own side to fight against bigotry on the other side. Forster would have welcomed his vigorous advocacy of the popular cry, and it must have needed strong conscientiousness to withhold it, for Christmas was approaching, when he would see Forster in London, and the question of the salary would, he hoped, be settled. Nothing more had been said about payment since midsummer, and it did seem a pity that it should be discussed just when his assistance seemed of less value than usual; but that was no reason for writing a line which would not carry the full approval of conscientious conviction.

Holidays began on December 18, none too soon, for a few days before he had written that he felt overworked: 'am obstinately black under the eyes and somewhat nervous, have outrageous dreams and unrefreshing sleep, with a constant sense of headache for the past fortnight'; and this though he had been very good in going to bed at eleven o'clock for a whole week. But he had real progress to report before coming to Newport. His school, with the help of his boarder, now brought him £216 a year, and *Household Words* he knew he might count on for at least another £60. There was a genuine surplus of income over expenditure, and every debt paid meant a step nearer marriage.

He came up to London on the 20th, and breakfasted with Forster, having a conversation which he describes as satisfactory, though it resulted in nothing more than a promise of a salary some time, Forster also saying that he did not think of using his services this year without returning payment for them. He spent Christmas at

Midhurst, on January 1 went to Chichester, where he
stopped with Mr. Jaques, and the next day went on to Newport. Here a happy time was passed till January 12, when
he left for London.   Travelling second-class from Southampton, he was impressed with the moral and intellectual
inferiority of his companions compared with those with
whom he went third-class the next day, when the train
leaving Euston at 7 a.m. brought him to Liverpool by
7.45 p.m. He calls the contrast a sad example of the
imbecility of the agricultural mind ; certainly the amount
of liquor consumed by Sussex farmers in the trains was
surprising.

He reopened school on January 14, and found his
children quite tired of their holidays.   He writes:

I am strong for work, and with the blessing of God will
work to the utmost of my ability, so that by midsummer we
may have made as great a stride as possible towards the attainment of our dearest wish.

This was to be his last half-year as a schoolmaster, but
he would have been much astonished had he been told so.
The proposal he received in June came to him as a complete surprise, and it was earned by an exercise of industry,
perseverance, and good temper which deserves due recognition.   There were serious disappointments during the
early months of this year.   Fred Estill returned with
' radiant face,' but no new scholars were offered till nearly
midsummer, and his present ten day pupils did little more
than pay his current expenditure.   The *Examiner* was
absorbed in the anti-Papal crusade, and Forster, though
glad of occasional articles, was still unable to offer any
remuneration for them.   His hopes of redemption lay in
Household Words, and here, with all his efforts, he had not
yet established satisfactory relations.   While at Newport,
he had begun an article called ' Mr. Napperday.'   As soon
as he returned to Liscard, he finished and sent it off, and

kept hoping for a remittance. But week after week nothing was inserted, and no cash came, and Mr. Holland had to be asked to advance money to meet a pressing claim. He sent off another article, on 'Central America,' before the end of January; and, having repented of his determination never to send them any more poetry, he let them have a poem, 'Wealthy and Wise,' which appeared on February 6, 'without the alteration of even a comma.' On the 16th he received back his paper, 'Mr. Napperday,' because the topics it treated had already been dealt with in *Household Words*. This was a severe disappointment, but he at once acknowledged the justice of the ground of its rejection, and admitted that what he had written amid various distractions at Newport was not as good as it should have been. He determined immediately to write a paper to represent the best he could do, and sent them 'A Plea for British Reptiles.' 'Central America' appeared on February 20, and the 'Plea' on March 6, when he received a remittance of £7 7s. for the two. How welcome this was may be gathered from the fact that he had been selling some of his books for a few shillings, and that ever since January 18 he had been wearing a pair of shoes so broken and shabby that he would not go to Liverpool in them by daylight, and always crossed the water for the news-room, or worship on Sunday, in the evening, till he bought a new pair after March 6. It is no wonder that he could not get rid of a bad cold during these seven weeks of broken shoes. But these two papers immediately re-established his position with *Household Words*. He was asked for further contributions, suggestions were made of subjects thought suitable, and material sent to him for study. A paper inserted in January had started the idea of a phantom ship visiting various parts of the globe, and had described 'Negroland.' In April this phantom ship visited the Polar regions, and the same month *Household Words* inserted two other papers on 'The Cape and the

Kaffirs,' and on 'Free Public Libraries.' In May four papers were published: 'The Last of the Sea-Kings,' ' Phantom Ship: Japan,' ' The World of Water,' and ' The Wind and the Rain '; in June two more: ' Madagascar,' and ' Phantom Ship: China.' All these papers teem with interesting information, conveyed with many a bright flash of wit, or light touch of humour, to aid the attention or stimulate the imagination. Fanciful machinery is, for the most part, excluded. It had not been appreciated at the office, and Mr. Morley's object was to find out what was wanted there, and to supply that. He cannot be wrong in supposing that the appreciation of his services was aided by his being easy to deal with, and accommodating. He never grumbled to them when his articles were altered, not even when his poetry was mangled. When the payment received was less than the usual rate, or, as twice happened, when nothing was paid for a short contribution, he asked for no explanation. He never pressed papers on them, and more than once lost money by not sending as much or as soon as he might have done. When he knew what was wanted, he was diligent and prompt in supplying it. His reward came in increased demands for his services, and, at length, in the proposal which brought him to London.

To the *Examiner* he was able to render a real service, and in the cause of public health. Early in February, Forster wrote asking if he had any private knowledge of the secret difficulties which obstructed the Board of Health in the matter of the Interments Bill. Editing *King's College Magazine* had made Henry Morley a public character while yet a student, and he now found the value of his reputation. He wrote to the City Officer of Health, Mr. Simon (afterwards Sir John Simon), whom he had known at college. There was not time to wait till he had received an answer before beginning an article, so he wrote the bulk of it at night, and had it ready to be modified and finished between school the next day if he received important news in the morning. This did take place. Mr. Simon's reply was most cordial and communicative, and enabled him to conclude what proved to be a very useful article for the *Examiner*, too plain-spoken, indeed, for Forster, who toned down some of its statements into hints, perhaps, not less effective. In order to write this paper rapidly, and while depressed by a cold, he took his third and last pill of opium, telling Miss Sayer :

Sure, I'm a good boy for taking it so very, very seldom, seeing what a certain way it is of getting the best fruit of my brains. I wrote a brilliant paper. Simon's letter next morning told me all the secrets I required, and S. offered to put his eyes and ears quite at my service in future.

So he worked in the information, and posted his paper, feeling that he had come out strong at a seasonable juncture.

Among other contributions to the *Examiner* this spring was one on lodging-houses and cellar-dwellings in Liverpool, which called forth protests in the Town Council. He found, however, that he was perfectly right in his facts, and, without directly contradicting any statement made in the Council, he reiterated his evidence in thoroughly convincing fashion, and materially aided a subsequent change in the law. The following letter refers to this matter, and is also a good illustration of his relation to the *Examiner*. Forster had expressed a wish to talk over the question of payment if Mr. Morley came to London at Easter.

Liscard,
Monday, March 24, 1851.

MY DEAR SIR,
    I return the proof. The surgeon to our borough prison, a friend with whom I have several times visited the prisoners, commented to me last week on the former paper

without knowing it was mine. He said it was true. He had been often grieved by the number of cellar victims in the gaol. I asked if there were many still, and he said that he had not noticed it of late, so I have no doubt the Health Committee have been doing as they say.

I give my 'Easter holidays' in *autumn*, so that I had no thought of coming to town. If you think it particularly desirable, I can of course run up on a Saturday, but perhaps that will not be necessary. I speak most unaffectedly in saying that I set a very trifling value on the aid my services can render to your constant energies. I feel that I could be dispensed with altogether by you very easily. I am glad to write, because I think it the most useful way in which my leisure can be spent, and should feel that quite independently of any thoughts into which money enters. If by the same work, or play, which is in itself a pleasure, I can collect a faggot or two to put under my pot, of course I'm glad of that; the rather as my pot has been a long time boiling, and I'm not the only person watching it. So any arrangement you may make with me will give me pleasure, and I shall be glad to receive tidings of it. Whatever you propose I shall be quite sure is the result of proper judgment. I have no false pride to hamper you with, mindful as I must be of my own deficiencies; I see so much that I can't do, that I am pleased if anyone is satisfied with what I can.

As for my part in our arrangement, you can depend pretty well on the regularity of my leisure enabling me to reply to your suggestions promptly, and within the compass of my strength and conscience—beyond either of which I am not afraid that you would wish to go; any kind of help that I can render to the *Examiner*, I am prepared to render cheerfully. You can propose or suggest nothing that will vex me so long as I have reason to feel assured of your goodwill. . . .

Ever, my dear sir,
Yours very sincerely,
HENRY MORLEY.

John Forster, Esq.

He tells Miss Sayer how he caught his last cold, adding a piece of news which should serve as a warning to people who have an old chapel to sell:

Talking of Catholics, I forgot to tell you, or to remember, what I believe really gave me cold—a true Briton who dropped anchor in our porch one night last week at one in the morning, extremely drunk, and kicked pertinaciously for two hours, till 3 a.m., at the street-door for admission. He had been attracted, moth-like, by the candle in my window. I was in bed, but reading. At his first hammering I got up, thinking somebody in excitement to be wanting me—a Holland suddenly ill, or so—but finding it was only a chap who 'threw himself on the protection of Britons in the house, and wanted to be let in and sheltered,' I spoke to him and went to bed again. Afterwards he was so extremely pertinacious that I got up to see whether the window-shutters had been fastened, thinking it might please him to smash a pane or two, and try to push in through the window. So I made good the fastenings, and went up again, but it was a damp night, and slipping about the house half-dressed I think gave me cold. What has he to do with Catholics? Why, he serenaded me with abuse and nonsense all the time, and among his expostulations were, ' I'm none of your b—— Catholics, I'm not ; I'm one of your true Churchmen, and I'll let you know it.'

I laughed to myself, and thought the Papal controversy has come home now to my door. This man might be an incarnation of it, senseless, drunken, noisy and pugnacious. Our good Englishmen are only drunk with zeal. This man, too, made a great boast of his British blood. And now, love, while I think of it, I'll tell you a bit of news at which you will be shocked. The old chapel in Paradise Street, deserted by Mr. Martineau and his congregation for their new church, has been converted by the person who has purchased it into a saloon for singing, dancing, and refreshments. The pews are in great part left ; the shelves for prayer-books being tilted up, now serve as supports for the porter-pot or gin-and-water, in which visitors indulge. It is one of those low places, 'admission free,' where you are expected to spend a certain number of pence in refreshments. Music and dancing are the entertainments, beer and tobacco the accompaniments from which the proprietor derives his return. I cannot tell you how much I was shocked when I came through Paradise Street a day or two after my return to Liverpool. They tell me that, from motives of economy, very little of the old chapel furniture has

12

been removed, only a platform is erected for the dancing; those
who look on still sit, with pots in the place of prayer-books, in
the old pews.

As soon as he returned to Liscard, in January, he began
thinking about writing a new book. First he thought it
should be called ' Party Cries.' He says:

> I mean to take a series of the most important topics of the
> day, and treat them in a succession of essays, after the style of
> ' Home Unhealthy,' that is to say, the tone will be throughout
> ironical, and enlivened with the greatest possible number of
> quaint illustrations. The first is to be ' Of the Church being
> in Danger'; others will be, ' Secular Education,' ' A Fair Day's
> Wages for a Fair Day's Work.'

A week later he has written the first essay, and thought
of a new title, ' The Cries of Babel.' But a few days after
this, on February 8, he writes: ' Laugh at me, my dear;
my " Cries of Babel " are still.'

The second essay was to have been on education; and
when he came to think the subject out, he felt that he had
so much to say about it, and that the one subject required
treatment from so many points of view, that it demanded
a book to itself. This book he proceeded to write, calling
it ' The Defence of Ignorance.' It was nearly finished by
Easter, when Forster kindly undertook to revise the MS.,
and suggested sundry alterations. These abolished the
introductory machinery, and threw the bulk of the essays
into the form of dialogues. For the interlocutors, Mr.
Morley revived the names of the members of the Owl Club,
Aziola, Ulula, and Screech, and in this form the book
was published by Chapman and Hall, and is reprinted in
' Early Papers.'* On the title-page is this quotation from
Barrow's ' Sermons Against Evil Speaking ':

> ' Many who will not stand a direct reproof, and cannot abide
> to be plainly admonished of their fault, will yet endure to be
> pleasantly rubb'd, and will patiently bear a jocund wipe.'

---

* Pp. 95-180.

This saying admirably expresses the spirit of the book, which is an earnest plea, conveyed in gentle satire, for improved education. After a lively introduction, the first dialogue deals with the ignorance of the middle classes, and is full of the experience of his own school at Liscard. This portion of the work greatly interested Forster. It also contains many keen reminiscences of his own school-boy days. The next dialogue is on the ' Ignorance of the Poor,' which is a castle with iron gates glowing white-hot in the furnace of religious zeal. It was not easy to touch those gates without burning your fingers. Here illustrations were, alas! only too plentiful, and some very striking ones are taken from the ' Domestic Mission Reports,' written by the Rev. Francis Bishop. Then follows a dialogue on ' Ignorance at the Universities,' for which the unreformed Oxford and Cambridge, with a glance at the perversion of free grammar school endowments, furnish abundant material. The last dialogue is called ' The Ladies' Drawing-room,' and is devoted to an exposure of the shallowness and frivolity of what was then deemed a proper education for girls. The school kept by the Misses Mimminipimmin strongly resembles one to which Miss Sayer went for a short time in 1844 as a teacher; and no doubt she may be recognised as the governess, who, ' a comely maiden, has a sweetheart somewhere labouring to earn her for his wife.' The condemnation of waltzing expresses a decided conviction, though, with characteristic breadth of view, he never enforced it on those who felt differently. He gives an account of the origin of this particular dance:

Aziola. You may well be reminded of a witches' Sabbath, for you, of course, know that we are indebted to the healthy imagination of the painters in the Middle Ages, who depicted such scenes, for the origin of waltzing. Their bold genius invented waltz-figures to heighten the devil's fun upon the Brocken, and a bolder genius transferred their graces to the drawing-room, and made that dance to be polite for ladies, which was drawn for fiends to make them look uncomely.

Buho. I enjoy a waltz.

Civetta. Certainly, and, above all things, it is for ball-practice that ladies should be trained; I do not say for balls alone, because their sphere of duty also should include shirt-buttons and pastry. There we stop, however.

He utters some generous appreciation of Miss Martineau's 'Deerbrook,' and her writings on political economy, and then follows a caustic reference to mesmerism and her pet cow, and her 'enormous donkey, who eats Bibles up instead of thistles.'* His cut at homœopathy is due to his having had to spend a Sunday evening with some friends who would draw him into the sort of argument that he hated. His banter about the Peace Association is fair sarcasm on the impracticable dreamings common in 1851, but destined to be followed by twenty years of great wars. The whole paper is full of shrewd common-sense, sparkling wit, and right feeling; but he could never write about women without expressing his reverence for true womanhood, and, with other illustrations of his thought, he gives this gem from his studies in natural history:

Civetta. A bit of pure air sticks about a woman, let her go where she may, and be she who she may; the girl most deeply sunk in misery and vice retains it, and can rise by it when opportunity shall come. A little creature lives far out at sea upon the gulf-weed—Litiopa is its name; often there comes a wave that sweeps it from its hold, and forces it into the deep. It carries down with it an air-bubble, and glues to this a thread, which, as the bubble rises to the surface, it extends. The little bit of air, before it breaks out of its film, floats on the water, and is soon attracted by the gulf-weed, towards which it runs and fastens alongside; up comes the Litiopa by her thread then, and regains the seat for which she was created. A bit of pure air sticks like this about all women—from the Queen on her throne, down to the world-abandoned creature on the pavement.

---

* The 'Atkinson Correspondence' had just been published.

These last words recall a passage in one of his letters which expresses the natural feeling of a pure-hearted young man. He confesses:

I am less free than I ought to be from sensual regards in looking at such women as are calculated to excite them—imagination spurs on youth, and I cannot subdue flesh and blood—but there has been no time of my life at which I would not have shrunk with horror from the notion of promiscuous embraces; the poor girls in the town I regard with deep sympathy and pity. I would do much to raise one of them, nothing to sink one lower.

What he felt about unprofitable argument is expressed in two or three of his letters about this time:

They will argue against 'Allopathy.' You know how I detest all arguments of the kind which convince nobody, and spoil good time.

Of theological discussions, he says:

The Christians who were to give a reason for their faith were to give it to those who had not Christianity. Our Lord never taught theology, and cannot desire that His disciples should waste their time in empty discussions about His essence, etc., among each other.

He had now made many acquaintances in Liverpool, and acquaintance in some cases was ripening into friendship, the only obstacle being the extent to which his engagements occupied him. At a meeting of the Philosophical Society a schoolmaster had made a showy speech, full of Greek and Latin quotations, about the doubtful derivation of some word. Mr. Morley had been lately reading Gibbon, and could have quoted a passage from the 'Decline and Fall' which would have settled the · question, but refrained from doing so, because everyone would have thought that the schoolmaster ought to have known that passage himself. At the Natural History Club he is sometimes amused at the way certain members talk of their experiments and discoveries, while ignoring

what has been done elsewhere. He never 'collected,'*
and made no experiments, but he read and kept well
abreast of the scientific knowledge of the day.

When a proposal was made that the club should spend
£8 or £10 in dredging the Mersey to complete its account
of the Liverpool fauna and flora, he warmly supported
the scheme, and promptly offered a guinea towards the
expense, thinking a public appeal for subscriptions for
such a purpose would be paltry. Engaged as he was,
beginning his evening at 10.30, and then often sitting up
reading and writing till two and three in the morning,
not unfrequently troubled with an obstinate cold and
cough, finding his eyes not as good as they were, so that
he cannot now mend a pen by candle-light, nevertheless,
as soon as there is a little relaxation in the pressure, his
thoughts revert to the question of seeing Mr. Bishop about
domestic mission work, to which he thinks he might devote
two hours every Saturday, when he says, ' I am afraid I
rest too much.' This was before Easter. As soon as
warmer weather set in, he began to suffer much from
headache, and, as *Household Words* was now eager for all
he could write, the idea had finally to be relinquished.
But he continued to study the blue-book on prisons, and
qualified himself to write on this subject with the authority
of sound knowledge as well as earnest feeling.

On March 12 he enjoyed a musical entertainment.

Mr. Hudson, as an old scandal-making maiden, notes among
other things how Miss —— sings duets with the doctor at the
window over the way, and illustrates by *such* a burlesque in
two tones of voice our 'Du, du!' The other thing that delighted
me most was a snatch of 'Lieber Augustlein,' which came into
a medley, and was sung by Madame Thillon very prettily. It
was a memory of you. You sang that for me last Christmas.

* He once found a curious worm in the sand by the sea,
and, having failed to bring it home safely in a cockle-shell, he
twice went in search of it with a bottle, but could not again
find it. This was the beginning and end of his experience as
a natural history collector.

Not many of Mrs. Morley's friends knew her as a songstress, but as a girl she had a beautiful voice, and for some years after marriage she often sang on Sunday evenings, while her husband listened with quiet enjoyment.

All this time Mr. Morley had been wearing the white neckcloth, which made him look so ' good ' as well as clerical ; but in the course of this spring he solemnly weighed the pros and cons, and decided to abandon it for a black tie. Liverpool had forced him to wear a hat ; he no longer looked so wretchedly pale when tired as he did at Madeley, nor was it equally important now to look as old as possible and very steady. At Madeley, where everybody knew him, no one could suppose he wished to be thought a parson, but misunderstandings inevitably arose in Liverpool. So, having made a gallant fight for independence to wear what he liked on his head, and to compensate for an old coat ' by obtruding clean linen,' he now gave up the· contest, and henceforth dressed like other people of his own position.

Fred Estill was naturally a noisy boy, and some alarm was caused one morning in March by his being quiet. ' Such a change to see him dull, poor fellow, I shall be glad when he returns to noisiness.' He was suffering from influenza, which proved the initial stage of measles. The parents of all the scholars had to be consulted, and it was found that most of the children had had measles already. It would not have been safe for Fred to be sent home across the water, so he stopped, and was nursed by Mr. Morley in addition to all other work, with a care and skill which had full weight with both the lad himself and with Mrs. Estill. The illness made more prominent the utter incapacity of Mrs. S., and the census taken this year revealed the fact that her age was sixty-eight. Some of the facts narrated to Miss Sayer sound incredible. . She came down shortly before nine in the morning, and retired to rest most of the afternoon. On being shown cobwebs in the schoolroom, she remarked, ' Yes, they would be cleared away at the half-yearly cleaning.' Instead of making puddings, she used once a week to bake a quantity of pastry puffs, and give them twice a day to Fred for dinner and supper, saying, ' The little fellow likes a poof,' till the boy began to loathe them and rebel.   Mr. Morley could never touch them himself, and so much of her extra-ordinary cooking disagreed with him, that it must ever remain a mystery how he now contrived to grow stout. His incapacity to make a servant do what he wanted was indeed constitutional, and reappeared in later life. Another neglect led to a serious trouble.   The unswept carpet at length became so dirty that all movement on it raised a cloud of dust, and he insisted on its being taken up, and the floor cleaned.   That done, the carpet was pronounced worn out, and disposed of, and he did with bare boards for the rest of the half-year.   Then he found the noise intolerable, particularly in the afternoon, when he gave most of his oral teaching, and liked to walk up and down with his ' head full of names and dates, taking care to use good language, as the boys will learn to speak as I speak.'   It had not occurred to him how much ear-comfort and brain-comfort was due to a carpet, but he endured the discomfort till the holidays.   In front of the house the slope down to the sands had long been untidy, and he spent £1 in having it returfed.   He was laughed at for this extravagance by the neighbours, who said the children would destroy the new tidiness in a week.   This gave him an opportunity of testing his method of treating children.   He told them that there would be no punish-ment for walking on the grass, but that he put it in their charge, and trusted them to exercise restraint on them-selves and show that the neighbours were wrong.

All these months the school teaching was pursuing its regular course, and Mr. Morley succeeded in proving that there was time for teaching history and science in addition to more elementary subjects. He had now reached modern history, and would have finished the whole tale by the end of the three years as originally proposed. He taught what may be termed a religious philosophy of history. He had, of course, to deal with the history of the Church, and says he had previously no idea what a painful tale it is.

For the sake of religion, I am anxious to give priestcraft the benefit of every doubt, but the whole tale is so clear that I'll warrant any of my boys against Puseyism. The thing is to make them see that it is because few but the bold, ambitious, and contentious men use their religion as a political machine, that religion shows a false aspect in history. I do try as I can to lay the foundation of a true religious feeling, to explain matters that puzzle children; I point out the hand of God in history, not obtrusively, but habitually, so that the children consider it a thing of course to ascertain the use of any great calamity. We go upon the fixed idea that mankind struggles forward and upward to a higher future, and that God disposes of events; I take pains to let them see through the great theological difficulty of reconciling man's free will with God's direction, a difficulty which springs only from an inadequate sense of God's transcendent wisdom. I teach nothing inconsistent with *any* Christian belief, except, indeed, the right of private judgment; and, of course, it is inconsistent with each creed to speak with honour of its neighbour—that I can't help. When we talk of image-worship, which plays a large part in our period of history, I take as much pains as if I were a Catholic to disabuse their minds of an impression that Catholicism is idolatrous. I teach them to honour other men's opinions and put them in a mind which may perhaps lead them hereafter to investigate their own, when they get old enough to have any—some ten years hence.

In his scientific teaching, too, he dwelt much on the religious aspect of the relation between cause and effect. He believed in teleology, and to the end of his life would never admit that it was overthrown by Darwinism.

Another matter which had hitherto retarded the growth of his school now offered to make amends. Right opposite

Liscard were moored the magazines in which were stored several hundred tons of gunpowder. An agitation had been on foot for many months to get these magazines removed, which could not be effected without an Act of Parliament, a lucrative monopoly being involved. This discussion had served to arouse considerable local alarm, and schools in the neighbourhood suffered severely. At last one lady, who had kept a boarding school of some size, decided on retiring, with the result that four new scholars, two boys and two girls, were promised by Mr. Nathaniel Caine to Mr. Morley after midsummer. This would raise the number of his pupils to fifteen and afford a considerable increase of profit. He began to consider the propriety of removing to a more convenient house, especially with a view to marriage sooner than had hitherto seemed feasible. But no thought of leaving Liscard had entered his head before June 3, 1851.

By this midsummer he had paid off about £80 of debt from his literary earnings, and still owed about £470.

CHAPTER X.

BROUGHT TO LONDON, 1851.

On June 3, 1851, Mr. Morley received a letter, in which Charles Dickens offered him five guineas a week if he would come to London, and work on the staff of *House-hold Words.* His mind must have been in a whirl that day, and during the evening when the Natural History Club met at his house. Here is the letter which he at once began to Miss Sayer:

MY DEAR WIFE,

The enclosed letter you will be good enough to write your impressions upon by return of post. We must decide upon this matter *together,* for it deeply concerns us both. I will tell you my present thoughts. I have a living before me here, and it must not be thrown up lightly. I dread the spirit of change. Now this is how I see each side of the question.

He reckons that, so far as income goes, he may make £400 a year if he comes to London, with improved prospects of further increase.

If the office at *Household Words* is a permanent one, I could be sure to keep it, and the journal itself is safe as a lasting property.

I should be safer in London than here for getting my boarders, and I might or might not take day pupils; they could easily be had where I have so large a connection. So I think I could make a school more easily in a London suburb than here. . . .

Wednesday morning. Love, we had a very good club meeting last night. I have done this : I have written to *Household Words* stating my position, and requiring more particulars; I have written to Forster, telling him Dickens's offer (he knows my position, and I've asked for his candid advice); also I've asked distinctly how much I might expect from the *Examiner* if I should move to London. Well, dear, I've also seen Mr. Estill, who thinks I ought to move, and would be willing to send Fred to London with me; and I've seen the Hollands. To quit such friends is very hard. Mrs. Holland says I must go, but I must be guided by you ; if you approve the change, she does not see how I can hesitate. She had suspected what would come. London is a great monster that sucks into itself everything worth having. Mr. Holland says I had better go if the *Examiner* adds any satisfactory engagement, that a brighter prospect has opened than I could expect to see at Liverpool, and that in my position I am bound to take advantage of it. I have talked it over with Nisbet and Byerley. Nisbet prophesied a year ago that I should be fetched to London; Byerley thought I ought to go, and this moment I am crying at the notion. I have found so much kindness here, and it seems ungrateful to leave the Hollands. I told them I thought so ; that my heart was here, and not in London; but they generously urged me towards better fortune to their own hurt. They would not like to send Charley so far from home until he is a little older; and Mr. Holland suggested what I think is the best policy—that I should lay aside the school idea for awhile. If I go to London single, with a good income that involves no outlay, I can lodge somewhere and live at small expense, so as to save nearly the whole of it. If F. adds £100, there will be £373, out of which I could save nearly £300— quite £300, when it is considered that I cannot live a year in such relations without dropping into other odd bits of literary work. In breaking up here, I could sell my furniture, and pay perhaps another £50 out of the proceeds, so that I should get much sooner out of debt by this means, and thereafter should have a more solid certainty to marry on ; and then we could revive the school, and I could get two or three house-pupils no doubt from Liverpool. I think, love, that is *the* plan. You need not fear the instability of literature as a source of gain. The great number of journals and publications in our own time has made it during the last twenty years a safe profession in which ability and industry have their reward. My ability is guaranteed, if not by my own sense of power, by the way in which I have been *sought*. I have not asked for anything, but have been asked, and am now unexpectedly offered a safe start under the strongest patronage.

Dickens and Forster are the two best men in London for introductions, and I know I can secure them as firm friends. I think you would not fear my being tempted to extravagance in London; you need not, dear. Music might tempt me, but when I can go to hear it gratis, of course it won't be an expensive luxury. I should be more likely to screw too much, living alone; but I should send you all items of expenditure, and consider the chief part of my income as not mine at all, merely entrusted me to pay away. Love, here is material for earnest thought. We must know more before we decide—what Dickens says—what Forster says. When I ask you to reply by return of post, it is not to hurry you to a decision; I want only an indication of your thoughts as soon as possible. The question before us is, indeed, of deep importance, and one in which I have no right or wish to act without my dear wife's counsel.

He wrote this letter to Mr. Forster:

Liscard,
Tuesday, June 3, 1851.

MY DEAR SIR,

Mr. Dickens offers me five guineas a week if I will come to London and assist in the getting up of *Household Words*. I am in great perplexity. My school at midsummer will have been raised to £300 a year with certainty of increase. If I came to London, I should teach, and possibly might bring two pupils with me. I am afraid of making a false step. May I trust your kindness—I know I may—to advise me in this matter? And will you help my calculations by giving me an idea of what the *Examiner* would contribute to my store if I should come to London? I ought to make up my mind soon, because it will be necessary, if I *do* leave Liscard, to arrange with parents of my pupils. Will you please give me your opinion as to my best course?

Yours always obliged, and very sincerely,
HENRY MORLEY.

J. Forster, Esq.

A kind and thoughtful reply came from Forster by return, pointing out that the decision must largely be determined by Mr. Morley's own choice between the occupations of teaching or writing, as well as between town and country.

If education be really your passion, the prospect you mention is not to be lightly exchanged for one not more certain in its nature, though it may possibly be more remunerative, and for a kind of life undoubtedly more full of hurry and excitement than that you are living now.

He then speaks of the possibility of carrying on educational work in London. As regards payment from the *Examiner*, he contemplated something varying from £50 to £100 a year for occasional help, a sum which he would do his best to increase by introductions to other papers, and he mentions a daily paper which he believed would be glad of occasional leaders. He concludes with an assurance, afterwards amply justified, 'that Mr. Dickens is the kindest and most honourable of men; and that in whatever you do for him, you will be able to reckon steadfastly on his earnest acknowledgment, and liberal desire to make it more and more worth your doing.' Mr. Morley's reply says:

Of course, you may easily imagine that a literary life is only too congenial to my temper, but I have regarded writing hitherto very much as an amusement, and the notion of relying on my pen would have seemed wild until now, when it appears in a worldly point of view to present itself as my best helper. One pupil I am told I can bring with me if I like, but as I am not yet out of debt, and if I come to London unencumbered and take lodgings, a year or so of work would set me free, it seems to me that it would be better to let the school lie dormant. . . .

Having proved my notions by experiment, I should not care again to take very young children, and might confine myself to those who have already mastered elements. I am disposed, therefore, to come to London, and at first trust wholly to my pen, earn myself out of debt with it, marry, and then revive my teaching in such modified form as shall then seem advisable. So London will be chosen, I suppose, my only doubt depending now upon ' the missis's' opinion. I have not expected from the *Examiner* more than you name, but I feel more at home in it than elsewhere, and therefore find your articles such pleasant work that I am half ashamed to be paid at all for playtime. I am indebted to the *Examiner*, I know, for my connection with *Household Words*, and shall ever be indebted to you for all manner of kindness.

Meanwhile, almost every post brings something more to Miss Sayer.

June 4, 1851.

Wednesday night. I cannot settle to do anything, dear love. I have prayed to God that He will enable me to think wisely. I foresee how it will be. London will suck me in; over a boundless field I shall be running a more ambitious race; my aims will be fixed higher, and the future overshadows my spirit. I feel deeply sad. We cannot always analyze our feelings, but I love this place for all the kindness I have here experienced. I love my boys, and the vision of a London career, of all that is to be achieved, and of the ambition that will urge me on and up, contrasts with to-day's repose. Starting so firmly propped, facile as I appear to be in winning friends, with a strong spirit of work and ambition, alas! I shall prosper indeed; but I must watch jealously the gates of my heart. I must look up with double love and double reverence to you. I shall soon earn money, but the way is smooth, and it leads far. But it is not only worldly prudence that will lead me to the more prosperous road. If worldly advantage comes unsought to invite me where every talent can be turned to its utmost use, I should be false to my trust if love of ease and fear of temptation kept me in a simpler life. My talents are a trust from God, and to God's service I must consecrate them. It will be so easy to pervert them, to use them most for personal aggrandizement. In London I shall become intensely active; there is no fear of my health of body, but my health of soul. I must cultivate scrupulously a habit of private prayer; I must more than ever pour my thoughts into your heart, and listen to your counsels. It seems destiny, the way in which all the events of my life follow each other. Is it not strange, too, that I, being born a writer, and yet publishing at loss my verses which obtain me nothing but some agreeable reviews, should, by a course of events quite uncontrolled by myself, be led in the most desirable way that can be conceived, and yet without my own connivance, into the profession of letters? All comes of the ' Tracts upon Health,' which caused Dr. Guy to ask Dr. Sutherland to ask me to write in the *Journal of Public Health*, which led to the beginning of 'Home Unhealthy.' But if the *Journal of Public Health* hadn't broken up, I shouldn't have offered ' Home Unhealthy ' to the *Examiner* (which I did without a notion of the consequences). ' Home Unhealthy ' in *Examiner* made Dickens ask me to write in *Household Words*, and Forster ask me to write in *Examiner*, for money. Writing in *Household Words* makes Dickens ask me to come to London and help edit it, and F. becomes a firm kind friend.

It seems clear that what brought Mr. Morley to London was the prospect of more speedily paying off his debts. Apart from this, he would not have been tempted away from the teaching which he loved so well, and the friends whom he had found so true. Mrs. Holland was most unselfish in urging him to go, for to her and Mr. Holland his weekly visits, when all sorts of questions were referred to him as their 'walking encyclopedia,' and his presence and counsel in time of illness, had added much to their appreciation of his worth as the teacher of their children. But all the parents of his scholars felt how great their loss would be, and yet that they could not ask him to stay. On one occasion a slight misunderstanding about the course of studies had caused a parent to write to Mr. Morley a letter which a hot-tempered man would have so answered as to cause the withdrawal of the pupils. But Madeley experience had not been in vain, and Mr. Morley's reply drew from the father an ample apology, and now no man was more concerned than he at the prospect of parting. Various consultations were held respecting the possibility of finding a suitable successor. Mr. Morley resolved to ask nothing for the goodwill of his school, for he felt this would be like selling the friendship of half a dozen families; and he at once set about making inquiries, thinking that Fred Sayer might possibly know the right man among students leaving University College, London. Mrs. S. was not forgotten, and it was a relief to find that she knew herself to be unfit for a post of working house-keeper; there was a retreat ready for her much more suited to her strength; in fact, only her affection for Mr. Morley had induced her to stay as long as she had done at Marine Terrace.

So the work of the school was wound up, bringing history as far as the year 1000 A.D., and having a grand final burst of 'Mutual Examination.' He says (June 9):

The children to-day know all about the move, and express affectionate indignation. 'The Dickens take me !'. is their notion of the subject.

The last set of prizes were chosen and given, and good-byes said to many friends on the last Sunday.

Burnt stores of letters yesterday, including all the Madeley-G. correspondence. I'd such a swarm of letters, and it's no use keeping them *now*, except the box full of your woman's heart, your faithfulness and tenderness and loving care. I have kept nothing now but a few illustrative scraps—a host of early compositions went into the blaze. As Madeley papers went into the fire, I couldn't help contrasting my condition then and now. . . . *Then !* Ah well ! *those* days are gone. Good days and useful days, and God be thanked for them ! Thank God for *these* days, too !

On Saturday, June 21, he came to London. Miss Sayer was also in London, so there are no letters to describe what happened; but we may hope that he realized what he anticipated as the highest earthly bliss, which was for them to go and hear Beethoven's *Fidelio* together. He had lodgings to find, and business details to arrange, and work to begin at once for *Household Words*. Then there was the Great Exhibition to visit in Hyde Park, and

13

Forster had a transferable season-ticket, admitting two, which was freely at their service. Nor did he omit the search for a suitable teacher for the children of his friends at Liscard. Having found, as he thought, the right man, he sent him down to Liverpool with various introductions early in August, but too late. A Mr. Gibson had heard of the opening, and had secured a promise of most of the pupils, and for a time carried on the school in the old house.

The series of letters begins again on July 28, and gives a vivid picture of his work for *Household Words*, and for the *Examiner;* also of various attempts to find further literary engagements, the most successful of which was his undertaking to write the life of Palissy the Potter, his first important book. It will be convenient to note what he did between now and the following Christmas under three heads.

1. As soon as Miss Sayer left London, Mr. Morley began to put into execution his design of doing for *Household Words* a good deal more than he was strictly required to do, so that it should be impossible to accuse him of neglecting the work for which he was paid a weekly salary, when he afterwards made other engagements. His personal relations with all members of the staff were soon of the pleasantest character. Mr. Wills said he 'was the best fellow they ever had to do with,' and before long it became a rare event for anything that he wrote to be altered by editorial hands. This consummation, however, was not reached at once. Among popular 'shows' at the Exhibition were some models illustrating Goethe's *Reineke Fuchs,* and he determined to write a good version of the story for English readers. Someone else had forestalled the idea, but he knows he can do something better than has yet appeared.

My own humour jumps with the original, and I have put in touches of my own to clinch a paragraph occasionally. I shall take pains to go on and finish well, for if well done it will be a worthy addition to the prospective 'works.' I don't translate, but give a rendering of all the story, and, if possible, the humour, minus the hexameters.

On August 5 he writes about his work, and tells how it had to be curtailed till it was spoiled; he never seems afterwards to have cared for the condensed version of the poem.

Another subject on which he wrote a long paper was called " The Labourers' Reading Room '; it is an account of an institution established by some working-men at Carlisle.

I have not attempted to be clever, but to put clearly before working-men a statement of what they could do—and impress emphatically the spirit in which they should do it—to help themselves in the way of self-culture.'

A paper called ' Light and Air ' he speaks of as one on the philosophy of a summer evening; it is a simple scientific account of physical optics. But thinking he was getting too much into a jog-trot style, he let loose his fancy in a paper which he called ' Life in the Capital of Kratzebeissedingen.' He thought this a jolly paper, which they would like at the office; but, alas, three days later we hear that Wills wanted it levelled to the meanest capacity, so he withdrew it, and afterwards sent it to *Fraser's Magazine*. But the editor replied :

I am very sorry to find that the paper you sent me is not considered suitable for *Fraser*, because I very much wish to rank you among our contributors. I am sure you could easily write articles which would suit us admirably. The point of this paper, it is thought, would not be generally understood, but it is, I am told, very well written, and the opening capital.

Other papers of his in *Household Words* were entitled ' The Work of the World,' ' The Birth and Parentage of Letters,' and one of which we shall hear again on ' Pottery and Porcelain.' In the index to Vol. III., which ends Sep-

tember 20, he found fifty-five references to his own contributions: 'pretty good considering that I was half this
volume at Liverpool.' For October he had written a
paper on ' Associations ' as an antidote to socialism, but

Dickens, bother him! wants the combination paper altered
from a cheerful dialogue to a grave essay. I thought the
subject better treated in the other way, and think so still, but
I must put my taste in my pocket; and this alteration cannot
be made without a complete recasting, so that gives me extra
work to do.

Another paper is on ' Gold,' dealing with the recent
discoveries in Australia and California. He was also given
a number of articles by other people to look over and rewrite. There was a gentleman at Vienna who had a quick
eye for facts worth noting, and sent much interesting
information to the office, which Mr. Morley turned into
an article called ' A Black Eagle in a Bad Way.' Another
contributor wrote from Naples, sending material of value
which required more complete recasting before it was
suitable for the journal. A paper of his own, written this
month, is called ' John Bull at Home in the Middle
Ages '; it is on English comfort during that most uncomfortable period. In Noevmber he has a useful article
on ' Building and Freehold Land Societies,' clearly explaining their constitution, and the difference between
those established on sound principles and those which
were not safe. The same number (dated November 8)
contains a contribution of his on ' The First Time (and
the Last Way) of Asking,' dealing with matrimonial
agencies, which had already begun their career in
England.

Household Words for November 15 contains an article of
his, entitled ' A Free (and Easy) School.' It was written
in a style which Forster much admired, and attracted a
good deal of comment. Dickens was determined to do
something more to expose the abuses connected with the

endowed grammar schools of those days, and he had found
the right man for the work. But while others praised,
Miss Sayer frankly said she did not like the paper, and
Mr. Morley explains why these exposures had to be made.
But he is glad she does not like the paper, because it will
give pain to the master. 'I must sometimes give pain to
somebody, but I don't want you to say that I do it
cleverly.' It cost him considerable trouble. He was
busy reviewing books for the *Examiner* till 3 a.m., and
was up early to finish them, which he did by one o'clock.
Then, after a hurried meal, he went by train to Barnet.

Walked over the whole place, then to the school; walked in
coolly, looked at everything, and catechized the master. I
said a gentleman in London, who had seen one of his pros-
pectuses, had asked me to run down and ask him a few
questions. That was the precise truth. He put his own
interpretation on it, and disclosed the secrets of the prison-
house. I saw everything I wanted, played my part without
saying a word inconsistent with the bluntest truth, and found
the place an admirable pattern of free grammar school abuses.
It was four o'clock when I had done. The train left at five,
so I walked on three miles to Colney Hatch. There I got
into the train, and took back with me to London materials for
a most picturesque and interesting paper. Then I journeyed
home, and arrived *so tired*. I had determined upon writing the
Barnet article the same evening, in great hope of getting
Friday to myself. I lay upon the sofa for an hour and drank
green tea, but as Mrs. Lilly don't know how to make green
tea, I might as well have tried warm water. She puts about
a fifth of the right quantity. Then I began to try and write,
and my jaded wits wouldn't go; but it was yet early, and, in
fresh mood, there was time to get the paper written before bed
—and a day was a great gain. Opium would have got me
over the difficulty, but I felt afraid of that. I sent out for as
much brandy as I thought might do, and had brandy and
water with my supper. After that, by midnight I had written
two or three MS. sheets—not very well—and went to bed
despairing. This Barnet trip it wouldn't do to spoil. I had
found rich material, most easy to work up. My tact at getting

and employing such material would inevitably be noted down in Dickens's sconce as a mark for or against me as a useful member of the staff.

To write a good paper I was determined. So I got up, and rewrote my last night's work. Dinner put me out, but after dinner I went on, and, in fact, except three quarters of an hour spent on the tailor, that unhappy paper has occupied my whole and close attention until half-past ten to-night. Now it is done. Including the visit on which it is founded, it has taken me a full day and a half. Now I have leisure to feel faint and ill. This business was fairly not more than a half-day's work, but never mind. I've done the paper well. It does not contain an atom of invention—except names, of course —everything I describe I saw ; every syllable of talk, every minute incident is literally true. Writing about a mouldered charity, it was not out of place to give way to my present dumpy mood, and let the dull October sky, and the rustle of dead leaves communicate their influences to the paper. Still, I think it makes a picturesque and pleasant article—a true picture from real life.

The master of the school turned out to be one of Dickens' old tailors.

Poor Mr. C. has been several times to Dickens, having been, utterly to my surprise, almost ' snuffed out by an article.' Trustees had been down upon him, and parents were writing to remove their sons. A note from Dickens, with this paragraph, have set him right again—as nobody could wish to do him injury. The poor fellow appealed simply for pity—said every word was true, and was, said Dickens, ' quite awe-struck at the cleverness of the young man.'

He thought I must have been in the medical profession, for I said he was lax of fibre ; so he was lax of fibre—had been pulled down by constant rheumatics. I said he was fluffy, so he knew he was fluffy that day—he had been taking snuff, and he was not clean at all. Dickens imitated him, not mockingly —but you know his talent for mimicry—and he expressed quite touchingly the poor fellow's appeal, to which, of course, he had responded generously. Well, he's all right now.

Another expedition on which he was sent by Dickens produced a paper called ' Need Railway Travellers be

smashed ?'   It describes a most ingenious invention made
by a Mr. Whitworth for preventing collisions.   Mr.
Whitworth was an unfortunate ' inventor' who had been
trying for five years to get his plans adopted; but railway
companies at this time were more intent on denying the
existence of collisions than on doing everything possible
to prevent them, and the daily press was not yet awake
to its full duty as representing the public interest.   For
instance, after a collision and loss of life on the South
Coast railway, the coroner's jury had expressly recommended railway companies to adopt Mr. Whitworth's
invention, and every London paper omitted this recommendation from its report of the proceedings.   In a letter
Mr. Morley says :

It is characteristic of Dickens to have read in a true spirit
his long letters, perceived the chance of good in them, folded
and numbered and ticketed them, and sent them on to be
attended to at once.   I very much appreciate that spirit in
Household Words.

Dickens reads every letter sent to him, and not a note to the
office is pooh-poohed ; every suggestion that may lead to good,
however overlaid with the ridiculous, is earnestly accepted and
attended to.

Mr. Morley's paper opens with a lively description, put
hypothetically, but all drawn from Mr. Whitworth's
actual experience, of the difficulties which an inventor
might have to encounter, and then gives a plain,
thoroughly intelligible statement of how the plan worked
at its trial on the line near Woolwich.   Mr. Whitworth
was most grateful, and hinted at something ' more than
thanks,' an offer which was of course declined.

Special efforts were made to plan and publish an extra
good Christmas number of *Household Words*, and the
matter was discussed at a couple of dinners to which
Dickens invited the staff.   This consisted, in addition to
himself, of W. H. Wills, R. H. Horne, Charles Knight,

and Henry Morley. All were anxious to do their best on this occasion, and Mr. Morley, besides having a ' bothering Christmas paper from Naples to dress up,' wrote one which assuredly may be identified with the first paper in the number, entitled 'What Christmas is as we grow Older.'

Dickens had lately bought Tavistock House, and Mr. Morley went there early in December for 'a dish of tea,' which he found meant a pleasant evening party. Here are some of his comments on it:

His study leads out of the drawing-room by a sliding-door, and on the study side of that door and on a corresponding panel he has what Carlyle would call 'shams'—bound backs of books which have no bodies or insides—mock shelves between glass, for the rows on which he has amused himself over the invention of a series of ludicrous titles, such as 'Godiva on the Horse,' 'Hansard's Guide to Refreshing Sleep,' 'Teazer's Commentaries' (for Cæsar's), and so on. 'Toots's Complete Letter Writer'—you read Dombey, didn't you? He has a luxurious study, but not an overwhelming stock of books, though a good many. Among the people there were Mr. and Mrs. Wills, Horne and his wife. . . . Poor nice old Hogarth. I understood Mrs. Dickens to call her sister Miss Hogarth ; if so, there is a family connection with the good old simple-minded man who, you know, compounds the news of household narrative out of the papers. Forster does its leading article. Miss Hogarth —*if* Hogarth be her name—is a lively young damsel of twenty or twenty-four, rather good-looking. Well, there was Mr. Leech —*Punch's* artist and mainstay—with his wife. Leech is fond of putting pretty women into his pictures, and so you may suppose he has got hold of a pretty woman for a wife. She was the prettiest person in the room. There was Costello with his wife. Dudley Costello is sub-editor of the *Examiner* —does all *but* the leaders and reviews, compiles the news, etc. I really don't know whether he is aware of my share in the *Examiner*. He would be if he looked over my shoulder now and saw my handwriting ; but I saw him reconnoitring me through his eye-glass. He is a good sort of fellow, I dare say —handsome, I think, tall, etc. There were Egg the artist, and sundry others—never mind. Oh, there was my old friend, your neighbour, Mr. White, whom I had met at Forster's, a capital fellow, and *his* wife. Well, and if I had had *my* wife, she wouldn't have been at all frightened by the men of print, and still less by their ladies. Literary people do not marry learned ladies. Dickens has made evidently a comfortable choice. Mrs. Dickens is stout, with a round, very round, rather pretty, very pleasant face, and ringlets on each side of it. One sees in five minutes that she loves her husband and her children, and has a warm heart for anybody who won't be satirical, but meet her on her own good-natured footing. We were capital friends at once, and had abundant talk together. She meant to know me, and once, after a little talk when she went to receive a new guest, she came back to find me when I had moved off to chatter somewhere else. Afterwards, when I was talking French politics on a sofa, she came and sat down by me, and thereupon we rattled away; and I liked her, and felt that she liked me, and that we could be good friends together, and that she would like you very much. You will be just according to her own heart, and will like each other in five minutes. I also made friends with her sister, and with Dickens I am in good odour, so that's all right. I seem likely to make friends as easily in London as at Liverpool.

Among other work for *Household Words* in December, he wrote two long articles on the history of the Hungarian nation, which was an interesting topic in connection with Kossuth's visit to England this autumn.

2. We must now turn to the work he was doing for the *Examiner*. On July 30 he dined with Forster. 'Met there Maclise the painter, whom I liked thoroughly; a quiet, pleasant, unassuming man of genius.' Another guest was a master at Eton; famous for Greek; 'a self-satisfied, loquacious epicure.' The following Friday morning he called on Forster, who set him down at once to write an article on the Patent Laws, with very little opportunity of studying the question. The next week he says:

So I am to breakfast with him on Thursday, and after breakfast, I suppose, he'll play the old trick of giving me pen and paper in his rooms. He has great confidence in my quickness of perception—gives a handful of materials, and expects me to get out the pith intuitively; and he has much faith in my readiness of pen. But I wish he wouldn't adopt that way of showing it, because, if I come home, I can deliberate a bit, walking; then take off my handkerchief, kick off my shoes, wash my hands, and write a more refreshing sort of article. However, anything. The value of a journalist consists in being independent of such circumstances, and ready to write at any time and anywhere. So be it.

The same letter remarks that Forster has got to the 'my dear Morley stage of our acquaintance.'

On August 14 he is going to show up a pamphlet written in the King of Naples' interest, 'which has to be exposed to the scorn that it merits; an atrocious thing!' He sits up till 4 a.m. to do this thoroughly. He explains to Miss Sayer that the source of his private information is Panizzi, of the British Museum, and adds some stinging facts about the venal worthlessness of the hack who had been engaged to write the pamphlet. The next week he wrote again at length on Naples, and says in a letter:

The article last week has stirred up Gladstone himself to provide us further private information; so, between Gladstone and Panizzi, there was a great store found which I had only to pour out properly. That has been done in another long article, and now this Neapolitan manifesto is settled, every atom of it smashed. The King's party attempt now to disown M., and say they have an answer yet to come. There is no doubt, however, that they did make him their mouthpiece, and the Naples Minister did distribute copies of his pamphlet.

Some three weeks later he writes:

The Government of Naples is answering Mr. Gladstone, and the *Times* correspondent sends some early intelligence of the Naples pamphlet. When I saw that I knew there would be work for me as soon as the manifesto gets to England. Now Forster wants me to go in at once, and knock down so much of it as the *Times* has printed.

He found a stanza from Tasso which made a splendid quotation for his article, and wrote one of his best papers. It will be remembered that the chiefs of the Liberal party in Naples had been arrested in December, 1849, and, after a mock trial six months later, had been sentenced to imprisonment for life in horrible dungeons.

A case of miscarriage of justice in England next called for his attention, and he wrote on it with such effect that his articles were copied by the *Times*, and referred to in one of its own leaders. He had feared he was getting sleepy, and was writing only 'what would do,' so he says, 'It gives me heart to see how immediately and visibly progress appears when I have given myself a shake.' He now had an opportunity of heaping some coals of fire on the head of the gentleman who 'did the poetry' for *Household Words*, and had mangled his own verses, for he was given a novel, 'The Dreamer and the Worker,' by Mr. Horne, to review for the *Examiner*.

He had not anticipated giving more than about five hours' work a week to the *Examiner;* but on September 11 Forster asked him to do a number of reviews, and at 5 p.m. gave him three more books. 'I was reading all last night, and writing the review this morning till the boy came.' He had had a talk about an article for the *Edinburgh Review,* to which Forster promised him an introduction.

I must stake my reputation, then, upon my articles. . . . I feel that I shall suit 'em, and get well into their connection if I mind my P's and Q's. I'm made for *Edinburgh* articles. They pay gloriously.

In his next letter he gives this sketch :

I was amused at glancing over my work as it lies by me on the table just now. There's Gavin's *Cholera Report* from British Guiana, which he wants me to turn to use. There's a letter from a captain dated Bombay with particulars about Furlough regulations, and request for an article, which I recommended should be written, and which I am deputed accordingly to write. That is the next thing on hand. There's a tract forwarded from Ireland to be written upon by Monday at latest for the *Examiner*, and I'll do it gladly, for it's a step in the right direction that I shall be proud to help. There is a collection of letters from California which I'm to read and report upon by Tuesday, and a mass from Naples in a most unreadable hand, ditto. There's a cosmopolite collection. I've promised also a paper on Porcelain, which, in consideration of other work, I don't mind postponing. And Dickens's desire for an anti-communist article must also be met by Tuesday. So you see it's not to be wondered at if I don't take a holiday to-morrow.

He was now really overworking himself. He had had no holiday this summer. He once took a book to Harrow, and had four hours' reading in the fields. Dickens and Forster were together at Broadstairs for some time, leaving him the more to do in London. At the end of September we hear of his coming home with a splitting headache, resting a little, and then going to a party at Mr. Wills', where he was introduced to his host's father-in-law, Robert Chambers, of Edinburgh. A day or two later he writes that he took a book to review next week worth reading, but long, and to be reviewed elaborately. This was 'Vestiges of Creation'; but, of course, he had no idea that the Robert Chambers whom he had just met was its author. He found the book contained four hundred pages of close printing, fearfully metaphysical and condensed reading, and 'it wants to be reviewed elaborately and philosophically; but it is all of a kind to make me better qualified for work. I shall never buckle to reviewing, I fancy, that is to like writing frequent newspaper reviews which imply much promiscuous waste reading. I don't like reading to waste.' In the end he wrote what he calls 'no very complimentary review of " Vestiges of Creation," but I tried to grapple with the writer's theory, and point out some of its absurdities.' In his book on 'English

Literature in the Reign of Victoria,'* he says of the
'Vestiges' that it 'set many talking and some thinking,
and was one of the first signs of a new rise in the tide of
scientific thought.' But he was never convinced that the
direction taken by this new current of scientific thought
was entirely right.

When the *Edinburgh Review* for October appeared, he
found it contained an article on Naples, which quoted
with praise, and frequently referred to his papers, and
spoke of his 'terse, vigorous style, which fully maintains
the *Examiner* in its ancient reputation.' He had decided
on taking Martin Tupper's 'Proverbial Philosophy' as his
subject on which to write an article for the *Edinburgh*,
and, amid all other work, found time to do it this autumn.
He grudged 7s. 6d. for the book, but wrote a paper which
he thought a satisfactory exposure of much hollow
pretension.

On October 11 he received £15 from Forster, the first
he ever had from the *Examiner*, whose finances were
heavily weighted with pensioners. He says :

I shall take F.'s money with satisfaction, for, so far as that
goes, I have earned it, though I owe, and ever shall owe, a
deep acknowledgment of the aids we receive, and shall receive,
from Forster's friendship. While I was reviewing 'Civilization' this morning, and he was writing something else, F.
stopped again to marvel at the way my pen scampered. (He
thought himself one of the fastest writers, but I ran far ahead
of him.) I told him very truly that if I used my judgment as
much as he did, my pen would go a great deal more deliberately.
He said he acquired his power of scribbling rapidly after much
labour, but mine seemed never to have cost me any effort.
Whereupon I explained how I used always to toil and polish
and recopy, till he took upon his head the responsibility of
bidding me be careless. I don't mean that I consider my style
worse than Forster's ; but in the far more important quality
of sound judgment, and in its concomitants, compared with F.

---

* Page 332.

I am exceedingly deficient. He's just the man to give advice worth taking, and advice from him I do invariably take.

Carlyle's 'Life of Stirling,' and some big books on Afghanistan were among the works he reviewed for the *Examiner*, which now took up as much of his time for £1 1s. a week as he gave to *Household Words* for £5 5s.; but .his faith never wavered in the value of his connection with the *Examiner*, and of the services rendered him by Forster. Still, it was *Household Words* that found the money, and once when he was accidentally paid pounds instead of guineas, he triumphantly tells Miss Sayer that he had asked for the shillings, saying, 'He meant to have the moons by which his suns should be accompanied.'

He went with Forster to witness the close of the Great Exhibition on October 11. He says:

The anthem wasn't imposing, but the nine cheers were, and the crowd. The entire building was crammed with people; galleries, nave, and transept were one crush—*under* the galleries nobody. I started with the adventurous resolve to see the crowd thoroughly, and travel with the press down one end of the nave. In a quarter of an hour I had gone about twenty yards, squeezed hither and thither; so I gave up the adventure, and slipped aside under the galleries and out at a side outlet. Outside the throng was as great, and for a mile down Piccadilly vehicles moved four abreast at funeral pace. Verily it was a climax. I suppose everybody who went, went so as to be there at five o'clock, and hear the final knell. All London seemed to be collected in and round the building, the evening being sunny and cloudless, with a remarkably clear atmosphere.

On October 20 he went to the Adelphi, where there was a 'Bloomer' farce.

An ill-written thing; I saw twelve feminines in the twelve different varieties of the Bloomer costume, and very well they looked in it. I wish it could be introduced. It shall have my good word in the *Examiner* on the sanitary score, but I suppose there is no chance for it.

On Friday night, October 31, he begins :

There, dear, the month and Tupper are finished. Tupper
makes, I think, a very pleasant article, and will do if the *Edinburgh* don't think it *infra dig.* to notice him at all. I'm pleased,
however, on reading the paper over, which implies goodness in
it. I think it will fetch us £20. Take it to F.'s to-morrow.
F. asked me late yesterday for an article on Kossuth. I feel
as worn out as he does on the theme, and it was half-past ten
before I had finished, read over complete and corrected slips
of pen in Tupper. It was a pump to write on K., and F. was
going to send a small boy for copy at eight this morning. I
didn't finish the article till after half-past two, and then wanted
to go to bed, was going ; but I knew F. would be pleased with
a review of ' Fra Angelico ' that had stood over from last week,
and I thought of the trouble he takes for me, and will take over
the *Edinburgh* affair now ; so I rubbed my eyes and wrote the
review and did up my parcel, and left it for the devil, and went
to bed —a little before four.

The next, or rather the same morning, he was up at
eight to go on the ' collision ' expedition already described.

This autumn Kossuth visited England. He was received with an enthusiasm which caused the *Examiner*
to undertake a very difficult task. On November 13,
Mr. Morley writes that Forster

wanted me to go and talk over a political and friendly warning
to Kossuth, whose doings are not altogether satisfactory.
Going, coming back, and writing a very ticklish article—complaint of Kossuth from *Examiner* will attract too much attention
to be worded carelessly—took up the best part of my day.

Forster liked the article, and added some touches of his
own ' admirably done.' The result was a shoal of letters
from subscribers indignant at the attack on Kossuth.

The *Examiner* tries to be impartial in time of fever, and then
down comes indignant correspondence.

Forster thought that Kossuth was trying to draw
England into war, and determined to issue a timely warning on the subject.

3. The books which Mr. Morley had published had so far brought him no pecuniary gain. The sale of 'Sunrise in Italy' had been very disappointing; and though there was a second and popular edition this autumn of 'How to Make Home Unhealthy,' this brought him nothing but a little more fame. It had been reprinted in New York by Harper Bros.—of course without payment, and with the name of Harriet Martineau as the author. But he had the true literary instinct, which told him that he must go on writing books as well as do the work for *Household Words*, which found his bread and butter. In August he was thinking about a book on the laws of England relating to land, but a better subject for his industry was soon found. On September 20 he writes:

I have agreed to try my hand at biography. Chapman and Hall would like me to supply two volumes of that sort to their 'Library.'

On the 30th he says:

The life I should like best to write is that of Palissy the Potter, for which there exist good materials, but I fear they are not easily attainable in England.'

In writing his article for *Household Words* on 'Pottery and Porcelain,' he had come across Palissy, and at once felt that he had found a man worthy to be made better known. He soon learned more about him, saying (October 8):

I looked through some materials in the Museum yesterday, and find the subject even better than I expected—'Palissy the Potter,' you know. He was just the sort of man I can admire thoroughly—intensely energetic and original; a reformer utterly fearless, full of true manly dignity. When the king said that unless he gave up his religious crotchets, he should be compelled to give him up, Palissy regretted that he should be under such compulsion, but said no kings or councils could compel a potter to bow down and worship his own clay. Then Palissy, moreover, was a humourist, and that I love him for.

He was quaint in his originality, had a sly, honest turn of satire in his composition. Living through ninety years of eventful history, his life and times would find me abundant interesting matter. Only of his domestic relations no details are known beyond the fact that he had a large family, and that his wife was sorely tried during his years of struggle. If therefore I write ' Palissy the Potter,' I must weave him into private relations of my own invention—relations of a kind that will bring out his character, and give point to the facts of his career. The book will thus be two-thirds fact and one-third fiction. The biography which details public facts is romantic enough; the private relations induced by his public vicissitudes must have been also of a very interesting kind, and I think I can sketch nicely what they might have been. The result will be a book having the interest of a novel, but a fair exponent of a man who represented progress in his own age, and whose life I can so tell as to make it animate others to be bold and free men, struggling forward even now.

He talked this scheme over with Forster, who approved it, and assured Mr. Morley that Chapman would give him £100 for the first edition of such a book. This was double what Mr. Morley had expected, and strengthened his resolve to devote more of his energies to books, knowing that, if he succeeded there, he would be sought after by editors of periodicals, instead of having to ask them to take his articles. There were various negotiations with Chapman, which Forster carried on, securing for him more favourable terms than Mr. Morley would have made for himself, though not quite so good as had been hoped at first. He had to sell the copyright for the £100, but he was to receive £50 additional when a second edition was required. On October 21 he writes :

I have been to the Museum to work at ' Palissy.' There is such a deal to study. If I were not quick at catching leading features, etc., I could not get the mere reading through under six months. But the book will be ready in February. I am going into contemporary documents, etc., so that I may have minutely true details to make my picture life-like. It takes completely France in the sixteenth century.

14

He read much before he began to write. On November 12 he says :

Have read also for ' Palissy ' the history of France almost up to the year 1500, and have turned up at the Museum all I wanted to know about glass, and out of German and French authorities a sufficiently minute acquaintance with the scenery of Perigord, etc. Am going to Museum now, and finish grubbing ; work up French domestic life in the sixteenth century, and some Venetian history ; then I shall come home ready to begin writing. *Examiner* to-night, *Household Words* to-morrow morning ; but I shall probably begin ' Palissy ' to-morrow evening—at any rate, after to-day I'm ready to begin, so you will soon hear weekly reports of progress with our biography.

November 14.

I begin ' Palissy ' in earnest *writing* on Monday, and shall, at any rate, have a great deal of time next week at my own disposal. I have unearthed at the Museum a great store of old contemporary memoirs, but it is such a wilderness of old French in big volumes. Never mind, with rich material there's more trouble, but a better book. I shall be able to write continuously from Monday, but must work very hard.

It was some days later before he actually began writing the book, a talk with Forster having modified his plans ; and when he did begin, he says that at first he wrote very slowly. During this talk, Forster committed himself to a warmer expression of appreciation than he had previously ventured to utter, ' saying he thought me well started, with a career before me that he should take great interest in watching. Everything I did was done so well that he expected me to make a very solid position.'

On November 22 he reports :

' Palissy ' prospers. Very great progress has been made, but not in writing. The whole work has been recast since I talked with Forster. Then on Thursday afternoon I got the old quarto edition of his works, which I had caused to be rummaged for in Paris, and that soon showed me that the modern editor had misled me by his French way of jumping at conclusions.

I narrowly escaped having to rewrite what is already done, and couldn't add a syllable till I had worked up the Agenois. The old quarto is an invaluable friend, and will lighten my labour greatly. The amount of information which ' Palissy' will necessarily contain is likely to edify the public, but it will cost me not a little study.

Forster is impressed, as I am, with Palissy's bit of auto-biography, as the best thing of its kind in literature. How anything so exquisitely good and curious should have remained so long locked away from general knowledge is really odd. The multitude of readers, who are stupid enough, would no doubt miss all the touches that delight literary taste. I shall have to work out the points, and tell the story in my own way, putting the translations into an appendix ; but critics of good taste—*Athenæum*, for instance—will fasten greedily on Palissy's charming little narrative, the perfection of naïveté.

We have now seen the principal work which he under-took and accomplished during his first six months in London. For *Household Words* he did considerably more than was in the bond, and did it well. For the *Examiner* he not only wrote political articles, but important reviews, which entailed much heavy reading. For the *Edinburgh Review* he wrote an article on Tupper, which, though not accepted there, secured him a favourable introduction. It was soon published elsewhere, and effectively pricked a large reputation-bubble. For *Fraser's Magazine* he also wrote a paper, which the editor reluctantly had to decline, but which evoked an immediate request for other con-tributions written in a more humdrum style. Most im-portant of all, he had been commissioned to write a book, had found a subject worthy of his labour, and had plunged into the preliminary studies with successful energy. Writing ' Palissy the Potter' may be regarded as the beginning of the main work of his life.

Thus he carried out what was in his mind in a letter which he wrote on July 31 :

I am confident and happy. May God ever bless us, dear love ! I have deliberated a good deal now, and watched, and

14—2

I feel *perfectly safe* here in London. Our way is clear, but I must work—really work—not play at working. If I do that we are out and out safe; there is no question about it, but a man who don't work drifts behind, there is no mistake about *that*. Very well, I'll work and go ahead.

This letter is signed ' Your Hippopotamus,' an indication of girth which is frequently repeated in subsequent letters.

This autumn he spent a couple of days in Liverpool, crossing 'the dear old Mersey,' arranging with his successor, Mr. Gibson, about his furniture, and with various other creditors and debtors, and returned to London with his old boarder, Fred Estill. Mr. and Mrs. Estill had written in despair of finding the kind of teaching they wanted for their boy, and thought of altogether ending his period of education. Mr. Morley was very frank about the disadvantages there would now be in living with him in London, and could not offer to do much more than superintend the lad's education, and give him some teaching in the evenings, but this offer was promptly accepted. Lodgings were taken at 4, Stratford Place, Camden Square, conveniently near to Mr. Wills. Fred's companionship proved no hindrance to other work, the studies in Spanish, Anglo-Saxon, and in higher mathematics went on under Mr. Morley's tuition, and many theatres and other places of amusement were visited with orders from Forster.

On September 30, ' We went to the Zoological, and saw my brother the hippopotamus.' He spent a long time before the various cages, and says: ' I don't know how long it is since I have been so much interested by anything in the way of an exhibition.'

One serious difficulty arose, and was thus met: Fred Sayer was in London, and usually spent his Sundays with his future brother-in-law. How were the two Freds to be distinguished? Mr. Morley decided it by calling Fred Estill 'Toby.' 'Toby' 'discovered the retaliation' of

calling his teacher ' Tub.' Perhaps this seemed not sufficiently respectful for use outside the immediate circle, but
his inventive faculties were exhausted, and he could think
of nothing better to call Mr. Morley than ' Toby.' So it
became ' Toby,' ' Toby,' between the two friends during
the next forty years.

Many other friends were soon made in London. One
was Mr. Charles Tagart, of 47, Lincoln's Inn Fields, the
lawyer of one of his creditors. He says :

> Of all the multitude of lawyers I have been so unfortunate
> as to come across, I never found the lawyer and gentleman to
> coincide as they have done in Mr. Tagart. He does his duty
> as a lawyer, but takes care to be a gentleman as well.

He was the brother of the Rev. Edward Tagart, minister
of Little Portland Street Chapel, and he soon asked Mr.
Morley to dine with him to meet this brother and a party
of gentlemen, chiefly lawyers, who seemed to find it difficult not to talk ' shop.' There were other dinner parties,
one at Mr. Parker's, editor of *Fraser*, where he met ' Professor Blackie of Aberdeen, rather an original '; also
George Meredith, whose poems he thought showed much
promise. Another acquaintance he made, at a party at
Mr. Wills' was James Hannay, then a contributor to
Punch. But he says :

> The more I see of London literary society, the more I feel
> disposed to shrink into myself and pick my friends carefully.
> I do not like the style of average literary talk. I shall go
> about and make friends and multiply acquaintances, but keep
> my inner thoughts shut up, and my labours hidden from all
> but the few whom I see to be earnest and true-hearted men,
> The general literary tone, so far as I have seen yet, is too
> flippant. Forster and Dickens and Jerrold are the only three
> men I am sure about at present. Dickens at present likes me
> at a distance, but we shall become stout friends hereafter, I
> feel sure, far as his genius transcends mine, for he is a true-
> hearted man.

Douglas Jerrold I have not yet met so as to be introduced

to him, but I can't fail of coming across him, and he is a man
after my mind. When I have published 'Palissy,' and done
a little more to show what's in me, I shall be more able to
choose my friends than I am now, with two tiny brochures for
my credentials. I don't care a scrap for the accident of fame,
don't care to have for friends Macaulay, Carlyle, etc., but I
want men with progress for their aim, who have no cant of
literature, and don't mind being accused of cant while they are
labouring for humanity. Among literary people, great or
small, wherever I find such I want to make friends of them.

Work in the new year continued on the same lines.
For *Household Words* the most important of his papers was
one which he wrote after going on January 13 to Blackwall, to see a shipload of female emigrants sail for Sydney,
Australia. A scheme had been started by the Right Hon.
Sydney Herbert, M.P., for assisting needlewomen, and
other female workers, of whom there was a superfluity in
England, to go out to the Colonies, where their labour
was in real demand. He came home from Blackwall wet
through, with a splitting headache, only fit to go to a
pantomime : so the next night he sat up till 5.30 a.m.
writing his account ; and then, after two hours' sleep,
went to breakfast and work with Forster. On the 27th
he reports :

The Sydney Herbert people are delighted with my paper;
they want to print it in a pamphlet by itself. They have
bought up lots of the number containing it to be sent with the
girls to Sydney. They expect the paper to do the fund an
immensity of good here and in Australia.

For the *Examiner* he wrote regularly every week,
generally contributing one political article as well as
reviews.

He tried various Unitarian places of worship in London,
for he says, 'to join in worship with fellow-Christians is
indeed a duty.' But he was hard to please, and after a
while writes, 'my only hope is Dr. Sadler,' who was then
assistant-minister at Hackney, but whom, so far, he had

always missed when he went there. Dr. Sadler soon
afterwards became minister of Rosslyn Hill Chapel,
Hampstead, and was for thirty years Mr. Morley's loved
and honoured pastor.

Speaking of some vague slander, he writes:

I would not think ill of the devil himself on an archangel's
testimony, if it was only Hum and Ha! I'll think well on the
slightest hint so far as the hint will go; but to every man I'll
give the help—and it is a great help, moral and social—of a
good opinion till I have proof that it is unmerited.'

Referring to certain old treasures which he had kept
through all his wanderings, he says:

I do indeed by nature turn to the bright side of everything,
but nobody knows, because I never choose to talk of it, how
clearly I have always seen the black.

On March 1, he dined with Mr. Samuel Gaskell to meet
Mr. Proctor (Barry Cornwall), a fellow Commissioner in
Lunacy.

I've only to report, dear, the dinner last night, which, as
regarded eating and drinking, was remarkably good. I wonder
whether I shall ever catch the literary love for fish and flesh
and fowl and cooking for their own sake. Sam Gaskell I have
told you of before, a thoroughly good, clever fellow. Barry
Cornwall I liked quite, and I have no doubt he liked me, for
he is evidently more disposed to think well than ill of his
neighbours. He's no longer young, you know—probably past
sixty—but not at all infirm, and very genuine. You feel the
poet in his fresh and simple-hearted conversation, there's a
sense of fresh air in his talk, and if he is not a great poet, you
know he's a true one. Unluckily, since he was seventeen,
dinner has always compelled him to sleep, so after an hour or
two he tumbled off into a nap. Mr. Gaskell says he can't
hinder himself from doing the same at his own table. He
roused up before I left. As he is good friends with four or
five of my connections, we shall be sure to have him in our
own acquaintance, and you will be glad, for he's a genuine man.

Some hours of his precious time in February had been
given to lodging-hunting; for, after full consideration, it

was settled that they could not live in the rooms at Stratford Place.   He found that people who did not like to put
a card in the window, but advertised in the *Times*, were
ready to let apartments at a much lower rate than regular
lodging-house keepers required for the same accommodation ; and he finally settled on rooms in the house of a
doctor at 73, Connaught Terrace, Edgware Road.   Into
these he and Fred Estill moved on March 13, and the
same evening he writes to Miss Sayer one of his elaborate
descriptions of the rooms, with all details of the furniture,
that she might picture her future home.   He had done
the same at Madeley, at Manchester, at Liscard, and at
Stratford Place : and now, after the nine years' waiting,
the hopes were to be fulfilled.   Careful as he now was in
all expenditure, he wanted to do everything which would
fitly mark the great day in their lives.   The wedding was
at length fixed for April 15, and he devoted immense pains
to considerations about the wedding-cards—the best that
London could supply—suitable gifts to the bridesmaids,
and other matters which he could see to in London.   In
regard to drawing up a list of names to whom the cards
should be sent he felt his constitutional incapacity.

The most tremendous question still before us is where the
cards are to go.   I look hopelessly into a fog of friends.   I am
sure to do some blundering over all that.

The honeymoon they determined should be at Winchester, *i.e.*, they resolved to spend a week in lodgings
there.   In the marriage-certificate he decided to describe
himself, not as 'surgeon,' but as 'journalist.'   A long and
grateful letter to the Hollands was included among the
duties he undertook in the last days before the wedding ;
some time also was given to Fred Sayer, who was over-
done with work for examinations.   With him in the room
he could only write 'Palissy' at half-speed ; but even in the
last week Fred found his usual welcome.

On February 21 he wrote one of his most beautiful

letters, dwelling on the happiness that would reach its consummation in their wedding. He knew that marriage would not extinguish cares and solicitudes, but it would bless them with the privilege of being able to take personal counsel together, and with the rest and comfort afforded by their close and constant sympathy. He utters again one of his favourite thoughts, how the differences between them were the main foundation of their love, how it would take a little time to get accustomed to one another's ways, when they would sometimes fret one another in the midst of their bliss; this would be ' oftener in the first year than the second, oftener in the second than in the third, for after the third our union will be perfected, and our peace entire if we make good use of our time, take good heed of our faults, and walk hand-in-hand earnestly before God.'

He knew that they each had a decided character, the one strong where the other was weak, and this should enable them to be of the greatest help to one another. He spoke of the extreme sensitiveness which made each ready to feel or fancy the slightest breath upon their mutual love, but which was the condition of their having the capacity to feel as deeply as they did.

Let us hold our love as a strong bond of duty towards God, and peace that passeth understanding shall be in our home and in our hearts. I shall try when you are mine never to fret you with a syllable, but in such trials we may not, till we get our ways of maid and bachelor fused into one way, always be successful. Being face to face and heart to heart, we shall not grieve at that; the full sympathy, the real devotion of our love, will fill our home with the right atmosphere, and our two hearts will beat together with a harmony like that of heaven.

This is the spirit in which his wedded life began on April 15, 1852. How truly his aspirations were fulfilled during forty years is known to none but God.

PART II.

THE WORK OF LIFE.

CHAPTER XI.

JOURNALISM AND AUTHORSHIP, 1852—1857.

THE wedding of Mr. Morley and Miss Sayer took place at the Unitarian Chapel, Newport, the ceremony being performed by the Rev. Edmund Kell, M.A., and the witnesses being Anne Price Backshell and Fred Sayer. The married pair spent their week's honeymoon at Winchester, after which they came to London, and in their lodgings in Edgware Road entered on the final phase of their struggle to pay off the debt. At the end of a diary for 1852 there is an entry in Mrs. Morley's handwriting which is indeed eloquent of the spirit in which she took up the task, especially when we consider the position of a young bride brought to London and introduced to many new friends.

EXPENDED.			£	s.	d.
Honeymoon trip	...	...	...	9	3	4
Housekeeping from April	...		...	112	6	0
Debt paid from April		...	...	200	14	8
Interest from ditto	...	...	...	41	12	11
				363	16	11
Balance in hand		...	...		19	2

The £112 6s. must have defrayed the whole of their expenditure for eight months and a half, including Fred

Estill's board till the end of June, for the total sum expended, added to what Mr. Morley received previous to the wedding, closely corresponds to his entire income for the year. It meant living with great frugality in far from comfortable lodgings, which were changed more than once before they finally took a house of their own in August, 1853. But the strenuous effort received its due reward; after 1852 all pressure of debt became a thing of the past; and in 1856, the final payment of the loan raised on the life-insurance policy closes this important episode in their lives.

In October, 1852, Chapman and Hall published ' Palissy the Potter.' The reception was as favourable as even its sanguine author had dared to hope. So great was its popularity that it was extensively plagiarized. Mr. Morley considered that when facts were made public they became the property of the public, and might lawfully be used by other authors, but he resented the caricature of his grand old Potter given in a book which aimed at nothing but popularity, and which had the impudence to appropriate not only his hard-won facts, but much of the imaginary detail he had elaborated to add interest to his picture of life and times. Subsequent editions were called for in 1855, 1869, and 1878, and in them he modified his plan so as to leave no possibility of confounding fact with fiction.

No sooner was this biography off his hands than he undertook a similar task for another man equally little known, and deserving to be better known, Jerome Cardan. He tells us:

I was first attracted to the study of Cardan, from which this work has arisen, by the individuality with which his writings are all marked, and the strange story of his life reflected in them.

Cardan was the popular philosopher and fashionable physician of the sixteenth century, with Pope and Emperor, princes and kings, among his patients; a man lost behind judicial astrology, credulous over dreams, believing he had the friendship of a demon, but withal one of the most profound and fertile geniuses that Italy ever produced. His chief title to remembrance is that he was a doctor who made valuable discoveries in medicine. For twenty centuries there had been only two men who had done anything for the art of healing, Hippocrates and Galen; and in the sixteenth century, with Europe ravaged by the plague, the amount of ignorance and folly prevalent is well-nigh incredible. Cardan's folly belonged to his time, and those of his books which contained most folly sold best during his lifetime. His works, written in Latin, were at the British Museum in ten densely-printed folio volumes. Scattered all through these formidable pages were the facts of his life, and the task of picking out the facts and arranging them was now undertaken by Mr. Morley. He indulges here in no fiction, does not transform an incident, and gives references for every statement. All this work was done in the intervals allowed by his regular engagements for *Household Words* and the *Examiner*, and there are entries in a diary, week after week, noting when he secured three or four hours, or sometimes whole days, for Cardan.

The success of 'Palissy' brought a ready opening to some of the magazines. During 1852 and 1853 he wrote several articles for *Fraser*, including two studies of Conrad Gesner and Vesalius, which are reprinted in 'Clement Marot and other Studies' (1871). The sketch of Bergerac also reprinted in the same volume was written for *Fraser* a little later. The *Westminster Review* was now being edited by John Chapman, who asked Mr. Morley in April, 1853, to write a quarterly notice of contemporary English literature, and this subject was afterwards extended to include American writers, but the engagement seems to have been of short duration.

Meanwhile the work for *Household Words* continued its steady course, and on its behalf there were visits paid to the Aztec Liliputians, 'the last fashionable humbug'; to an election for the Blind Asylum; to the Old Bailey Sessions; to the *Zoological* Society 'to meet Mitchel and study zoophytes '; to Apsley House; to Messrs. Mayal for new processes in photography; to Redhill with Jonathan Crowley for railway signals; to Bradbury and Evans to do the printing presses ; to Professor Wheatstone for a paper on the stereoscope.   For the *Examiner*, besides writing reviews and a good deal of dramatic criticism, he went to the private views of the New and Old Societies of Water-colours and to the Academy.   As an art critic, he always felt special interest in the soul of a picture, but he was also a good judge of its merits from the purely æsthetic point of view.   He disliked the obtrusive, glaring style fostered by large and crowded exhibitions which tempt artists to indulge in eccentricities in order to attract notice.   He was also severe on pre-Raphaelite ugliness and bad drawing.   He liked pictures good to live with.·   But, for the most part, his comments, year after year, on the Institute and Royal Academy deal with little but the subject of the picture, describing the aim of the artist, and saying how far this aim appeared to a spectator to be realized.   Such comments furnish a curious contrast to the kind of critiques which have since become fashion-able.   But, then, one wonders what a writer who confined himself to the subject of pictures would find to say about many modern exhibitions..

The spring of 1853 brought the birth of their first child, and when the hot summer came, Mrs. Morley and the baby were taken to Midhurst, and then to Carisbrooke, where Mr. Sayer had just built a house beautifully situated on the rising slope of the valley north of the castle.   This he named Palissy Villa ; for now every shadow of the old estrangement was passed away, and Mr. Morley became more and more the strong son-in-law on whom the family were accustomed to rely in all difficulties. He took little holiday himself this summer. Dickens was away from London finishing ' Bleak House '; W. H. Wills during August was at Boulogne; Mr. Morley got away for a day or two now and then; and whenever he had a few hours to spare in town, they were wanted for house-hunting. Many days were partly spent in this pursuit; most of the suburbs of north and west London were visited; the house finally selected was at 20, New Hampstead Road, now 40, Castle Road, Kentish Town, the decision for this house rather than another, cheaper and more conveniently situated, being made on the ground that it furnished much better accommodation for a servant. Into this house they moved, September 24, 1853.

On October 4, Fred Sayer came to live with them there. He had nearly completed a most successful career as a medical student of University College. After winning there numerous medals and prizes, he went to Edinburgh to continue his studies. Nursing a fellow-student, he caught typhoid fever. Mr. Morley hurried thither to see after him, and writes some interesting letters from Edinburgh. Students' bedrooms in those days were mere cupboards. Fred was well cared for, first in the infirmary, and then in the house of a friend, Charles Jenner, a brother of Sir William Jenner. But when the fever departed, symptoms of consumption appeared; and on a second visit to Edinburgh, Mr. Morley has to report little hope of recovery. Fred died May 22, 1855, and is buried in the Grange Cemetery, near Newington.

So ended the earthly career of one of whom Mr. Morley writes*: ' He had the divine gift of genius, and none but noble aims. Had he lived, he would have been now among the honoured chiefs of his profession.' And he

---

* ' Some Memories,' p. 22.

adds words which mean much : ' I think of him when I read " Lycidas." '

Meanwhile, Mr. Morley's main work steadily continued. As soon as ' Cardan ' was finished, he found a subject for a third biography in Cornelius Agrippa. From a long series of old Latin letters it was possible to gather the details which give colour and animation to history, and to tell for the first time the story of a life which had till then been only misrepresented by enemies. This work completed a trilogy of sixteenth-century biographies of scholars, not political heroes, of different nationalities and social positions. He says* :

Palissy was a Frenchman, with the vivacity, taste, and inventive power commonly held to be characteristic of his nation. Cardan was an Italian, with Italian passions ; but Agrippa was a contemplative German. According even to the vulgar notion, therefore, they were characteristic men. Palissy was by birth a peasant ; Cardan belonged to the middle class ; Agrippa was the son of noble parents, born to live a courtier's life. All became scholars. Palissy learned of God and nature, and however men despised his knowledge, his advance was marvellous upon the unknown paths of truth ; he was the first man of his age as a true scholar, though he had heaven and earth only for his books. No heed was paid to the scholarship of Bernard Palissy, but the civilized world rang with the fame of the great Italian physician, who had read and written on almost everything—Jerome Cardan. Hampered by a misleading scholarship, possessed by the superstitions of his time, bound down by the Church, Cardan, with a natural wit as acute as that of Palissy, became the glory of his day, but of no day succeeding it. The two men are direct opposites as to their methods and result of study. In a strange place of his own between them stands Agrippa, who began his life by mastering nearly the whole circle of the sciences and arts as far as books described it, and who ended by declaring the Uncertainty and Vanity of Arts and Sciences. The doctrine at which he arrived was that, in brief, fruitful must be the life

* Preface to ' Cornelius Agrippa,' p. vi.

of a Palissy, barren the life of a Cardan, since for the world's progress it is needful that men shake off slavery to all scholastic forms, and travel forward with a simple faith in God, inquiring the way freely.

Agrippa found the life of a courtier as full of harassing disappointment as we should expect to a scholar who lived during the Renaissance, and who, though he could fight bravely, did not like war. All his fortunes are told with the minuteness which shows him to us as a living man, and are most instructive for the history of his age. The book was published in 1856.

The papers he wrote for *Household Words* during 1854 included one on 'The Quiet Poor,'* which attracted some attention. Dickens wrote to him : ' You affected me deeply by the paper itself. I think it is absolutely impossible that it should have been better done,' and forwarded correspondence from the secretary to an ' Association for Improving the Dwellings of the Industrial Classes,' a benevolent society which endeavoured to show that its object might be attained as a commercial enterprise, and complained that its progress was greatly hampered by the land-laws and the expense of obtaining a charter to secure limited liability. The Act for conferring limited liability on joint-stock companies was passed the following year. Another subject which received much attention both in *Household Words* and the *Examiner* was the question of public health, especially in connection with the cholera. This was very bad in London during the summer of 1854, and Dickens writes that he is determined the public shall not be allowed to forget its lessons in the excitement caused by the outbreak of the war with Russia. During this autumn Mr. Morley received a series of long letters from Edwin Chadwick, of which he made good use. Chadwick himself got into considerable trouble about this time, through trying, so Forster said, to do more than the

* Reprinted in *Gossip*, p. 91.

Sanitary Act authorized him to do. But he was an enthusiastic and painstaking reformer, and poured in a wealth of facts about trapping sewers, illustrated with gruesome anecdotes about the Westminster Law-courts, also about gross mismanagement at certain provincial towns, and the harm done by water company monopolies. Finally he wrote to say how pleased he was with Mr. Morley's article 'Omission and Commission.'

The cold early in 1855, it will be remembered, was terribly severe, and lasted long. On March 19 Dickens writes, 'I am very much touched by your article " Frost-bitten Homes," ' and makes a proposal to go with Mr. Morley and visit a number of poor homes. Several such expeditions were executed, and I well remember a vivid description of them given by Mr. Morley some thirty years later, when 'slumming' was become popular. He told us of the tenderness and keen insight with which Dickens made his inquiries, and how, as he left each room after getting his facts, he also left two half-crowns. Dickens was always generous in paying for whatever he received.

On June 21 Dickens writes to Mr. Morley: 'I think your idea of an almanac an excellent one.' The scheme was settled at a dinner at the office, and in due course Mr. Morley received a cheque for £25 for its production. A note warmly welcoming it came from Douglas Jerrold. This *Household Words Almanac* was continued for some years, and was always well packed with useful information.

There certainly was some holiday out of town this summer, as Dickens writes that Henry Morley and a small daughter had been seen at Folkestone, and complains that they had not mounted the hill to visit him.

In November Mr. Morley was requested to undertake a new journalistic engagement. He received a letter from Mr. J. R. Robinson, now the Sir John Robinson so well

15

known in connection with his brilliant management of
the *Daily News*, asking him to write a weekly article for
the *Inquirer*, the principal organ of the Unitarians, ' on
general topics, education, sanitary reform, philanthropic
progress.' This was begun with the new year, and continued till the spring of 1858, when it was terminated by
Mr. Robinson in a letter expressing the most cordial
appreciation of the work that had been done.

With the end of 1855 John Forster ceased to be editor
of the *Examiner*. Fonblanque was still the principal
proprietor, and various temporary arrangements seem
to have been made for carrying on the paper; but in
the course of 1856 the whole of the literary department,
with all dramatic and art criticism, was placed in Mr.
Morley's hands at a salary of £5 a week. The political
editorship was assigned to Mr. M. W. Savage, and this
arrangement lasted, with a certain amount of friction, for
the two editors were jealous of encroachment on one
another's space, till the end of 1860. Mr. Morley had
been assured that the arrangement with Savage was to be
regarded as temporary, and that with himself as permanent, and from January, 1861, till November, 1867, he
was the sole responsible editor of the paper.

During part of 1856 two of his old Liscard pupils,
Charley and Arthur Holland, lived with Mr. and Mrs.
Morley. He had in 1853 given some lessons to Charles
Dickens' son, Walter, but the pressure of other work
had prevented his carrying out any further scheme for teaching. He had not been forgotten at King's College, for in
April, 1856, Mr. J. W. Cunningham, so long its secretary,
wrote saying that the medical professors wished to submit
his name to the Council for election as an Associate of the
College. This was a recognition of the position he was
achieving in London, and may have assisted in the important step onward taken the following year.

Dickens now gives a cordial assent to the republication

of any of his papers contributed to *Household Words.*
Accordingly, in May there appeared a volume called
'Gossip,' containing forty-six reprinted papers, and twenty-
two little poems, 'wisps out of that stack of verse which
nearly every man builds in his youth, after infinite turning
and tossing of the green material from which it is composed.' Much journalistic work is of course intended to
be of only temporary value, and this volume may be taken
as Mr. Morley's own selection of what he thought worth
offering in book form; certainly it contains much of his
brightest wit. A much smaller selection of these writings
was subsequently reprinted in 'Early Papers.'

CHAPTER XII.

BACK TO TEACHING: KING'S COLLEGE, 1857—1865.

MR. MORLEY had not given up his school at Liscard
without profound regret. Journalism found him a livelihood, and a great variety of opportunities for useful
labour; but even when working his hardest at it, he was
never content with it; he kept steadily to his purpose of
carrying on real study, and then writing books which
should deserve a place in literature. His last two
biographies, however, appealed to a limited class of
readers; and forty years ago, more than now, there was
the need to educate a reading public before it would try
to take interest in studies which lie outside the beaten
tracks. The process of education could only be carried
on by lecturing, and Henry Morley was the man to begin
it; here, as in so many other movements, acting as the
pioneer. In this matter, as in all else that concerned his
progress, the new opening came as a result of the skilful
and conscientious discharge of some earlier duty. He
never had now to seek for work; others always came and
asked him to undertake some new task for which they
were sure he was well fitted. Had he ever felt inclined
to doubt the existence of a Divine providence, his own
experience, with its conquered troubles and successive
stages of onward guidance, would have seemed to him an
absolute refutation of such doubt.

Dr. Gairdner, of Edinburgh, whom he had met in connection with Fred Sayer's illness, had a brother in London, whom he introduced to Mr. Morley. This was James Gairdner, of the Record Office, and author of ' The Houses of Lancaster and York,' ' History of the Reign of Richard III.,' and other works. He called early in 1855 at the house in New Hampstead Road, and became a frequent visitor there along with George Buchanan, J. Furnival, Mr. and Mrs. Chadwick, Fred Estill, and a few others. Later on he found in the household another source of attraction, which ultimately led to his marriage, in 1867, with Mrs. Morley's younger sister, Annie Sayer. Mr. Gairdner has kindly furnished me with some recollections of the days we are now describing :

Well do I remember, indeed, the first day that I called upon him in what was then a rather quiet thoroughfare in Kentish Town named New Hampstead Road. At that time he had not been many years married, and had only one child—a bright frisky little girl. He himself was slender in make—very unlike the portly man that he afterwards became—and was still fighting his way uphill, to some extent, though with good heart and hope, having long left behind him the difficulties and burdens of his earlier career. But in one thing he was essentially the same, as he was all along. He was intensely sociable, always glad to make a new friendship, hearty and hospitable in a real, genuine, homely way that made his frugal board ten times more interesting than a rich man's table. And what shall I say of his conversation? Well, he was not a Dr. Johnson, or an ' autocrat of the breakfast-table,' or by any means garrulous. He was a very good listener if a man had anything to say. But what he had to say himself was always pithy and to the point, often humorous, but always gentle, and never, that I remember, sarcastic beyond the very mildest kind of irony. Above all, it was characterized by the most perfect sincerity of mind and heart, by a sincerity, indeed, that I should almost call unique ; for, humorous as he was, and dearly as he loved a little bit of nonsense, he was absolutely incapable of deceiving anyone intentionally, even for an instant, in joke ; and not only so, but I am perfectly sure he was incapable even of taking pleasure in seeing another man misled, even though he were the veriest simpleton. Indeed, I have a sort of recollection of some instances when persons of his acquaintance had fallen into rather ridiculous errors, possibly from taking him a little too seriously, though he seldom could have given any occasion for that, and when he immediately put the matter past a doubt by adding to the story something so extremely ludicrous that credulity was no longer possible. His high allegiance to truth was shown quite as much in the free play of his imagination as in his most serious utterances.

I had already read ' Palissy,' and was interested both in the *Examiner* and in *Household Words*. The former had been a favourite with my father, and though it represented an old school of Whiggery, which was possibly even then on the decline (so many reforms had been carried since its first editor, Leigh Hunt, was put in prison for quizzing the Prince Regent as a superannuated beau!), yet it still was interesting, with pungent articles occasionally by Fonblanque or Forster. Morley, as sub-editor, took charge only of the literary part of the paper, writing most of the reviews and dramatic criticisms; and I must say that his style was rather a contrast to that of the political writers, for if there was a fault in his criticism, it was too good-natured. Alike in literature and in social life, he was always willing to see the best of everybody; and now and then I fear his charity was just a little too expansive. He had, however, a high appreciation of all real merit, and nothing fared very badly with him, except pretentious and superficial nonsense that gained more credit than was due to it. I believe a popular and now almost forgotten author of that day, whose ' Proverbial Philosophy ' was selling by thousands, and whom tea-table-parties were accustomed to speak of as 'a very suggestive writer,' received his first douche of cold water criticism in the columns of the *Examiner*.

Ultimately he became editor of the *Examiner*, and wrote political articles as well—at least, occasionally, as he could not but do in that position. But here, though he acquitted himself fairly enough, he was scarcely in the right place for a man of his strong literary bent, and he was too good a fellow, besides, to enter with zest into political warfare. His thoughts were mainly devoted to literature. I saw this so clearly that, at an early period of our acquaintance, I expressed a hope that he would one day undertake a regular history of English literature, and I was delighted to find that the design was actually in his mind at that very time. It must have been about the same time that I was brought into close relations at the Record Office with the late Rev. J. S. Brewer, Professor of English History and Literature at King's College, London. At that college a new movement had taken place for the establishment of evening classes for the benefit of persons employed during the day. Happening one day to speak about Morley to Professor Brewer, I found that he remembered him as a student at King's College, and immediately thought of him as the very man whom he should like to take charge of an evening class of English literature. I was happy to be the medium of conveying this proposal to Morley, who very soon arranged to undertake the duty.

Thus was the step taken which brought Mr. Morley back to teaching, and made the history of English literature the study of his life. One of the first pupils at King's College evening classes, Mr. H. R. Fox Bourne, has also been kind enough to write out some recollections for which readers of Henry Morley's biography will be grateful. The teaching at King's College was begun under a certain disadvantage, for Professor Brewer had been announced as the lecturer. Mr. Fox Bourne writes :

To the momentary annoyance of the dozen or so of young fellows assembled on the first evening, a younger man than we expected entered the class-room, and informed us that Brewer had abandoned his intention of conducting the class himself, and had deputed him (Mr. Morley) to take his place. Our disappointment did not outlast the evening. The lecturer at once charmed us by his kindly manners, his unaffected and genial way of communicating the knowledge with which his mind and memory were so well stored, and above all his peculiar skill in interesting his pupils in every subject on which he discoursed. To myself his lectures, always chatty and always profound, were throughout two winters a constant delight. Whether he was giving us a smattering of Anglo-Saxon grammar or of the Norman-French components of the English language, whether he was enabling us to see how the varying

moods and temperaments of different times and races showed
themselves in the tale of Beowulf and later myths and romances,
in the old miracle plays and chronicles, in ' Piers Plowman ' and
Chaucer, or whatever else, there was more instruction in his
teaching than in any other of which I have had experience.
He has sometimes been blamed for not keeping pace with the
scholarship of the last two or three decades, for making
philological slips, and being occasionally at fault in his verbal
criticisms.   Whatever ground there may be for these allega-
tions, they scarcely, if at all, lessen the value of his work as a
teacher.   His teaching was the outcome of such thorough
understanding of his subject as no pedant and no mere antiquary
can boast of.   He had the rare power of putting himself in
sympathy with the circumstances and conditions of life and
thought out of which sprang the utterances of the great men,
and the little men, of whom he was, mainly by reason of his
doing that, so apt an interpreter.   This word ' interpreter ' best
expresses his speciality as a teacher.   He was more than that,
however.   His success in arousing his pupils' interest, in im-
parting to them some of his own enthusiasm, was all the more
remarkable because there was no attempt at eloquence in his
talk.   His lectures were always chatty, adorned by nothing
but his spontaneous wit and abundant humour.

The present Sir Edward Clarke, Q.C., M.P., was
another of his students.   He held an appointment at the
War Office, and was using his evenings for study and
preparation for the Bar.   Other students were Eccleston
Gibbs, afterwards clerk to St. Pancras Vestry, and for a
short time M.P ; another was Edward Arber, who has
himself become a learned Professor of English Literature.

Mr. Morley himself wrote the following in a diary at
Easter, 1858 :

On Tuesday, March 16, my winter course of lectures ended
at King's College, and I received twenty-one guineas and some
odd shillings as my share of the fees.   The lectures, which
began in October, have been so planned as to embrace, with a
more particular study of Spenser and Dryden, a general view
of the development of our language and literature from the

earliest of its days to the year 1700. They have so far succeeded with the students that I am asked to form a summer class. . . . I have enjoyed very much the delivery of the literature lectures, and the class has stuck by me so steadily that I expect next winter to find its borders enlarged, because I hope instead of three to have a dozen men who follow up the subject through a second course. Furnivall, who lectures upon English at the Working Men's College, dropped in upon my last lecture but one, which happened to be a mere clearance of scraps, etc.—no lecture at all. He admired the earnest working manner of the men, but said ' my pace was killing.' I know, however, of old, by my own experience as a student, that quick lectures are followed much more easily than slow ones. We have felt our way along, and I have known that the class followed me, while it is very certain that I have been able to include in the course at least one-third more information than there would have been room to get into it had I preferred a dignified walk to a sharp trot over the ground.

The subjects taken by Mr. Morley at King's College were as follows. His first courses were : Tuesday evening, ' The Origin and Structure of the English Language, illustrated by our literature from the earliest times to the invention of printing.' Friday evening, ' The Principles of Composition, illustrated by the history of English literary composition, from the appearance of Sir Philip Sydney's " Defence of Poesie " to the establishment of the *Edinburgh Review.*' These two courses, with sundry modifications, were continued year after year, other classes being added, and an assistant lecturer, the Rev. O. Adolphus, being appointed to take junior classes in grammar. In the session 1860-61 there appear a course on ' English Dramatic Literature, from its origin to the present day,' as well as two classes for the study of Anglo-Saxon. A new course next session dealt with ' Writers and their Times : Influence of Political and Social History at Home and Abroad upon Literature in England, from its origin until the present day.' There was also a course on the ' History of English Satirical and Comic Litera-

ture.' In 1862-63 he has a course entitled ' A History of
Taste in Literature, illustrated chiefly by the series of
English writers whose fame has been great, but not
lasting.' There is also a course dealing with writers from
1668 to 1862. In 1863-64 he lectured on the history of
English epic and heroic poetry and the literature of the
century from 1763 to 1863. In 1864-65 he takes English
literature from the Conquest to the birth of Shakespeare,
and also gives some ' Practical Notes on the Study of
English Literature : an outline designed to be useful to
those who would teach themselves.' In 1865-66, his last
session at King's College, his subjects are : Tuesday,
6 to 7, Gower, Chaucer, and other Writers of their
Times ; 7 to 8, English Literature in the Reigns of Elizabeth and James I. ; 8 to 9, Anglo-Saxon Literature.
Fridays, 6 to 7, English Literature : 1688 to 1866 ; 7 to 8,
English Composition.

This list of subjects shows how thoroughly he covered
the ground during these nine years at King's College.
The large number of lectures a week which he was able to
give at a later period was rendered possible by the solid
work he was now doing for these classes, and by the
marvellous memory which enabled him to retain facts
which he had once mastered, and knew to be important.
He was always adding to his stores, going further into his
studies of forgotten authors and the byways of literature,
and developing his own interpretation of men's lives and
thoughts ; but the main outlines of his learning were
now drawn, and the judgments he now formed probably
underwent little subsequent modification.

It need hardly be said that Mr. Morley threw all his
energy into every good work at King's College that
claimed his assistance. He wrote an article entitled
'Minerva by Gaslight,' respecting which Mr. J. W.
Cunningham, the secretary, says : ' It was very bright
and clever, and served to bring our evening classes into

notice.' He adds (1896): ' I have a delightful memory of my dear old friend.'

In March, 1860, Mr. Morley received a letter from Professor E. H. Plumptre, thanking him for his note about King's College, and wishing he could infuse his spirit into Rev. and Right Rev. friends 'who at present hold aloof because King's College, London, is not King's College, Cambridge.' Next year he delivered the introductory lecture to the seventh winter session of the evening classes.

A concluding reference in it to the higher education of women was prophetic of the task he was himself to undertake. Forster wrote to him about it : ' Capital lecture, too, you gave, so frankly genial and sufficient, manfully expressing your opinions, as manfully conceding everyone else's, and neither setting up your own back nor any other body's.'

On January 1, 1858, Mr. Morley began keeping a diary, and continued it for fifteen days. Its pages are full of family news, stories about his children, medical anecdotes told him by his father, and accounts of the fortunes of various cousins. There are notes of work done for *Household Words*:

January 4.—Till 5 p.m. reading for and writing a burlesque biography of the thief David Haggart.

Then he went to dine with Forster, and heard how Dyce had cancelled at his own cost the second volume of his Shakespeare, and seen every sheet of it destroyed, because, as he went on,

his scale of workmanship enlarged, and that volume was left out of harmony with those that followed. . . . Forster described a recent call upon Leigh Hunt (who could make any room beautiful for ninepence), whom he found in a mean, miserable room, with two plates laid upon a dirty tablecloth, knives and forks such as a labourer would use, and comfort nowhere, sitting huddled over the little fire with a silk cape over his shoulders, face so pinched that it was almost gone, and poring with great lustrous eyes over his paper as he wrote. He looked like an old French abbé. But the soul of Leigh Hunt was at work in him, for he was busy over his dear friends Chaucer and Spenser. Cardinal Wiseman had in some pamphlet called them sensuous, and the lover of old poets was with the eagerness of boyhood at work on an answer to the Cardinal.

January 5.—Breakfast late. Continued writing for *Household Words* 'The Short Life of David Haggart.' Dined at half-past seven with Savage at Kensington Gate. Met Robert Bell, Theodore Martin, the two publishers, Chapman and Parker junior, and a man of whom all I know is that he keeps a perambulator. There is no other point of sympathy between us. Talk weak. Sense in Bell's notion that if all the books in the world were to be destroyed, and he might save one—Shakespeare apart—he would save 'Tom Jones.' Perambulator read 'Tom Jones' last year, and thought it too heavy for the present age. Chapman would not have 'Tom Jones' because the copyright is out, and if there's to be only one book in existence, he wishes to own the copyright. . . . After dinner Bell got up a round game of cards. We all played loo until past twelve. I have not played loo till to-day, or played at cards at all for money since I was a boy, and had to join round games at children's parties. Dislike cards; the liveliness is all over one topic, and that a stupid one. Walked home part of the way with young Parker, who wants me to write again in *Fraser*.

This dinner was an exceptional dissipation. He always declined invitations if he could do so without rudeness. He sometimes expressed himself severely with regard to the 'weakness' in the topics of conversation among the men he met when he did dine out, and he rather resented the way that important matters were sometimes settled over the dinner-table by members of a committee, who afterwards came to a meeting with their minds made up.

January 6.—Breakfast late. Finished writing for *Household Words* 'The Short Life of David Haggart' by five o'clock; had some tea; took it to Wills; went on to town, bought bread, fetched books, took money, looked in at the newsroom, then home. After supper read through Landor's 'Dry Sticks' with a view to a review, which must be written to-morrow. There is all the old man's value in it, and there are all his faults. The book will expose him naturally to much narrow censure, and I have promised Forster that he shall have the satisfaction of a careful notice in *Examiner*, and get generous usage from his old ally.

The next morning a caller prevented his getting to work till nearly one o'clock.

Then began writing the review of Landor's book, ate dinner and wrote. Printers' boy here by my order soon after two; cold day; fetched the devil in to the fire, and wrote with him at my elbow; sent him off with part of copy; went on with review; had tea in a hurry; took the rest of the Landor notice myself to the printers. Read news; bought bread in the Strand; called for new books at the *Examiner* office; found a new edition of Dyce's Webster. N.B.—Bought yesterday the first folio of Dryden's plays, two vols., for eleven shillings. After supper looked over books for *Examiner* notices, wasting a little time in lingering over Webster, and wrote a short notice or two. A turn at baby-holding, and in bed at ten minutes to three, but kept awake a lot by Master Robert.

January 8.—Breakfast late. After breakfast went to Little Pulteney Court, wrote short notices there for *Examiner*, and corrected proofs. Took the proof of Landor notice to show Forster, as he had asked to see it. . . . F. delighted with the notice; gave me a special shake of the hand in thanks for it. Went to Fleet Street for dinner at the Cock; began *Inquirer* work; wrote a short article on the death of Havelock during dinner; then adjourned to a newsroom, wrote the rest of the *Inquirer* matter; went to *Inquirer* printers, having coffee on the way; left copy there; came home, and read new books, and attended to domestic requirements till half-past two.

The next day, Saturday, being one of comparative leisure, he devotes part of it to house-hunting up the Highgate Road. He found a place, Grove Farm House, which was sufficiently roomy for the growing family, and in many respects suitable. Then he went to town.

Called at Chapman and Hall's in Piccadilly; settled with Chapman to begin at once the printing and woodcutting for

'Memoirs of Bartholomew Fair.' I have ascertained the character and extent of materials, settled the general plan, and written a chapter. There I stand fast, and pressure of other work will keep the book unwritten for ever if I do not raise the printer's devil to get him to prick me on.

On Sunday morning he took nursemaid's duty while the nurse went to church. Some part of Sunday he always gave to his children. Later on it was generally the evening, when he was the most delightful companion and playfellow that ever children had. He did not at this time attempt to teach his own children, but he did much to stimulate and train their imagination. Of one of them he says :

She is a fidgety little mortal still, but clever, shrewd, lively, and source of great pleasure and happiness to us, and manageable enough when wits are brought to bear against her wits, which are incessantly at work. After dinner went to Hopley's to look at his picture, 'An Alarm in India,' which is to be sent on Tuesday to the British Institution. Hopley home with me to tea; left shortly before twelve. Letters and accounts. Bed at a quarter to two. Hopley excruciated at supper-time because I ate a multitude of apples with bread and water. My stomach has been out of order the last day or two, and the whisky-and-water that I have been used to take instead of beer, because it assists instead of impeding power of work, did not get digested last night. Therefore whisky is forsworn, an apple poultice is applied to the stomach, and this application causes torment to the beholders, Hopley and the missus, who think ten apples a poisonous dose. Why shouldn't I make an apple pudding of myself?

The reader will, it is hoped, excuse these medical details, and be glad to know that the application answered. The patient was very busy the next day, and among other things decided against Grove Farm House. After supper,

Read to the missus as much as she could bear of the last half of the 'Duchess of Malfi.' Horrors upset her. She has never heard or read the last scenes of 'King Lear,' and for the same reason will never know how the 'Duchess of Malfi' ends.

Read her some of Ben Gaultier's ballads (very poor they are, though !) to cheer her up.

January 12.—Worked till evening at Dyce's Shakespeare. Read the life and dipped about the volumes, having in view not only the *Examiner* notice, but also the renewal of lectures next week at King's College.

Then he gives a short account of his appointment there the previous autumn, and continues :

This morning Savage sent me a couple of stalls, which Charles Kean, a friend of his, wished to be used for the study of his Hamlet, in which part he was to reappear to-night. Savage begged me to be kind. I went accordingly after tea, alone, and bore my grief. Charles Kean's Hamlet is his most anxiously-laboured performance, and he is to be respected for the great pains he has taken, but I believe that there is not the faintest sense of poetry in his nature. He has no keen instincts to guide him ; I believe that he has no knowledge of, and no imagination to conceive, the subtleties that are the soul of a good play. The 'Hamlet' at his theatre was therefore precisely like a three and a half hours' eloquent discourse from drum ecclesiastic. I fidgeted, gaped, dozed a little, and, when released, came home about eleven wretchedly nervous ; was distressed and irritable till after reading MS. for *Household Words.*

In the ' Journal of a London Play-goer ' several notices will be found of Charles Kean's performances, which Mr. Morley could honestly praise, but he says nothing whatever about this Hamlet. Extracts from one more day may be given :

January 13.—Called at *Household Words* office ; had a talk over items of *Household Words* business with Wills. . . . Glad to find him even more ready than I was to postpone an article upon John Parry's scheme of a model Royal Academy and National Gallery building. John Parry gave us both not long since an hour and a half's entertainment in description of his beautifully-executed plans, which he prefaces with a set of clever caricatures of things as they are. But the plans represent his idea in different stages of its growth, and as he described with equal care what he had planned and abandoned, and what he had planned and abided by, the impression of his scheme that stayed upon my mind was simple enough, and clear as to main principles, but hopelessly incoherent as to its details. Wills says he is making a fresh plan of what he now really does mean; will wait for that. His scheme is in the main very ingenious, and I fancy right and feasible, with many clever little originalities in the detail. Went to British Museum Reading-room, read sundry things. Called at *Examiner* office for books. Home. After dinner and tea sundry reading, writing, and domesticities. This evening Hepworth Dixon forwarded a note from Dilke to him with a cheque for me, which he requested him to send me, because, on looking over the accounts of the *Athenæum*, he found himself so much in my debt. That is payment for little papers sent from Madeley ten or eleven years ago, and signed ' H. M.,' for which no money ever was expected. That is therefore the first writing paid for to me in cash.

On January 14 he is busy writing for the *Examiner*, and in the evening goes to Sadler's Wells, where 'the comedy was " The Clandestine Marriage," perfectly well acted— Phelps the Lord Ogleby, and Mrs. H. Marston the Mrs. Heidelberg. I wish Sadler's Wells Theatre were in the Strand.' He often thoroughly enjoyed Phelps' acting, but, as in other cases, shrank from a personal acquaintance with an actor whose performances it was his duty to study and criticise. He thought relations of more or less intimate friendship between public performers and journalists responsible for much bad criticism.

The above extracts will show how interesting an autobiography, full of shrewd observation, we might have had if Henry Morley had gone on with ' Vita Mea,' or had kept a diary such as this for more than one fortnight out of fifty years. As it is, we must pick up our facts from many sources as best we can. Before, however, he finally left the pages of this substantial volume an utter blank, he filled some of them with a summary.

AFFAIRS OF THE NEXT TWO MONTHS.

At Lady Day we take possession of, but do not begin to tenant, our new house. After further search, a suitable house was found at the top of Haverstock Hill, No. 4, Upper Park Road. It was one of an unfinished row, and was itself not perfectly ready for a tenant. We have, therefore, had some of our time occupied in business over the details of fitting up . . . and the arrangements of terms of lease, introducing a clause that shall make it void in case of my death, and so forth, has been part also of the two months' occupation.

He then writes the paragraph about his King's College lectures already quoted,* and after that proceeds: '*Examiner* work during the two months has gone on as usual.' He speaks very frankly about the weaknesses of his colleague, whose

appointment is now a confessed mistake. When he goes—for Fonblanque and Forster both assure me that his present position is but temporary—it is understood that I shall be left to work alone in managing the paper, with help from a body of political contributors. Had a stronger man been in Savage's place, I could not have hoped to become editor of the *Examiner* in a dozen years. Nevertheless, I should have worked most happily with any better man. *Household Words* work during the last two months has taken a pleasant turn. I have had too often the sense upon my conscience that the work I give to *Household Words* is not worth the pay I receive for it. *Household Words* never complains, never duns, never looks glum. My relations are all of the pleasantest, but though I try to earn my salt, I feel too often that I am not doing it ; and when that is certainly the fact, Dickens cannot be blind to it. Home calls, pressures of other work, swallow up time. *Household Words* never puts pressure on, and so *Household Words* is apt to come off worst. A fortnight ago the success of the King's College lectures, and my own interest in them, suggested to me that I might add to my *Household Words* work a constant source of papers for some time to come by beginning a series of literary articles—not professedly a series, yet really coherent and consecutive—illustrating English literature by anecdotes and sketches of old writers and writings from the earliest times onward. Dickens liked the notion, and I began straightway with an article on ' Celtic Bards,' then did the usual *Household*

* P. 232.

Words work, and now have Beowulf in hand. With a study
to myself in the new house, which I have never had here, I
may hope to get more work done, and, without relaxing effort
in any other directions, not only earn, but more than earn, my
Household Words money, which is what I should do for some
time to come until I feel that I've fetched up arrears.

The want of a separate study furnished the reason why
he went to bed night after night between two and three
o'clock in the morning, and for the almost continuous
entry, 'Breakfast late.' At Upper Park Road healthier
hours were generally kept, and while the study was in the
basement, the nursery was at the top of the house. In
the earliest years, at New Hampstead Road, he might
sometimes have been seen in the streets carrying a baby
in long clothes, quite regardless of the smiles of passers-
by, while one of his accomplishments may be said to have
been writing with the baby in his lap. 'Her first appearance in literature' is noted in connection with an infant's
smudge upon one of his papers.

The diary next gives a full account of correspondence
in connection with the *Inquirer,* for which, in consequence
of fresh editorial arrangements, he soon ceased to write.
He concludes: 'The matter has been settled on all hands
in the kindliest spirit.' He proceeds:

Book work is upon the 'Memoirs of Bartholomew Fair,'
which I hope to publish before Christmas. The time given to
it hitherto this year has not been great. I have obtained and
used permission to look through the records at St. Bartholomew's Hospital; after going through more forms than seemed
necessary, I found everything most courteously placed at my
service. . . . I have looked up the stores in the City Library
sufficiently to keep the woodcutter at work in advance, so that
I shall not have to wait for him when leisure comes for getting
forward with the text. Also—though there is now but a
chapter and a half written—I have sent the first chapter to the
printers, and must look to their devil for some extra stimulus
to keep me going.

At the end of June he notes that some of his King's College work on the drama

has been turned to account in an article for the *Quarterly Review* now at press. Editor of *Quarterly* was engaged to notice Dyce's Shakespeare; hadn't time to write himself, and nobody to ask. He told Forster that, and Forster suggested me. Therefore I was applied to, and this work, like every other of the sort, comes to my door wholly unsolicited.

The 'Memoirs of Bartholomew Fair' was published early in 1859, and proved a thoroughly successful book. It has been several times reprinted, and has been largely used as a quarry by later writers, who have thus been saved much trouble in original research. The Rev. William Rogers, then of Charterhouse, wrote to him on March 8, asking if he would give his lecture on Bartholomew Fair to the poor people at the Golden Lane Schools, where there had been a course of good lectures. This was probably the first of many acts of charity of a similar kind. In June he is in communication with an interesting man—Johannes Ronge, founder of the Catholic branch of the 'Freireligiöse Gemeinden' in Germany. Ronge gives him information about schools for an article in *Household Words*.

This summer there was a holiday at Felixstowe, where the Morleys made a common household with the George Buchanans. Mr. Morley writes from there to his father:

Savage came back last Monday, and is at work again, but he is no better in health. My five weeks of editing was very serviceable to me, as you will see by the enclosed note from Fonblanque, which you will be glad to read, but please return it.

In December, in time for the Christmas holidays, he published his first collection of fairy tales, entitled 'Fables and Fairy Tales,' illustrated by C. H. Bennett. This, of course, immediately proved a popular book. It was followed the next Christmas by another collection, called

'Oberon's Horn,' under which title the stories have all been republished. Charles Bennett was asked also to illustrate this second book, which he was delighted to do, saying, February 6, 1860 : 'Your fairy tales are fuller of notions, conceits, and good honest daring absurdity than anything modern that I know. Do not doubt my working with my boots on.' Mr. Morley considered the essential feature of a good fairy tale to be abundance of incident and rapidity of movement, and in such narratives he found ample room for his rich sense of fun and lively imagination. He did not forget, however, to put a soul into each of his stories, to make them illustrate the possibility of overcoming evil by good, and be 'stories of redemption'; and it was indeed a treat in later years to hear him read aloud one of these combinations of loving pathos and humour. The 'Chicken Market' tells of his own early struggles.

Mr. Bennett became a valued friend, and when his premature death occurred in 1867, and other friends—especially those connected with *Punch*—raised a fund for the support of the widow and the orphaned children, Mr. Morley became the acting trustee of this fund. John Forster was delighted with the fairy tales, finding '"Melilot," "Silver Tassels," and "Sissoo" positively charming—quite perfect in their kind.'

Mr. Morley saw Forster too frequently for the letters that passed between them to contain much of note, but they often encourage his literary work. In September, 1858, Forster expresses his admiration for a notice of Longfellow, and in March, 1860, for an article by Henry Morley on Fielding; and he helped to make the arrangements with Fonblanque by which Mr. Morley became sole editor of the *Examiner* from January 1, 1861. Soon after this an incident occurred which might have seriously disturbed a friendship less firmly rooted. The *Examiner* took the side of a Mr. Turnbull against Lord Shaftesbury, and Forster, who had the highest admiration for Lord Shaftesbury as well as a warm friendship, was much hurt thereat. He speaks his mind very frankly in two letters. Mr. Morley's replies have not been kept, but they must have asserted his right of independent judgment; and the real interest in the episode lies in the fact that the two men, having spoken out their own minds, then let the subject absolutely drop, and a few days later Forster is writing in the friendliest terms about Professor Lushington's poem. In May he writes about the violin-playing of Ole Bull, and 'a conspiracy to run him down by a clique of Jews who have the monopoly of musical criticism.' In the autumn he cordially approves some suggested plans for the paper, and thinks 'there is extraordinary improvement in the new arrangements.'

Mr. Morley had many communications this year from Charles Cowden Clarke about his wife's edition of Shakespeare, he being anxious that she should have the credit for the work she had herself done. An appreciative review calls forth a grateful acknowledgment, and Mr. Clarke is delighted to find that the editor is the author of 'Palissy.' He had given a copy of this book to a young Italian artist, who wished to paint one of the striking pictures suggested in the work, but who had gone off instead to be one of Garibaldi's volunteers. Mr. Clarke, writing from Genoa, gives a sad account of how Italy is being spoiled by the introduction of French manners and morality. In later years he writes about the 'Characteristics' and other Shakespearian studies.

Many, indeed, were the appreciative letters which Mr. Morley received from authors whose books were reviewed in the *Examiner*, and many were the acquaintances made which might have ripened into close friendship had other engagements and his home ties permitted. He may be said to have discovered George Macdonald, and placed him in the front rank of novelists by a review of one of his early works. George Henry Lewes was an old friend, and writes asking who is John Morley, and also welcoming James Gairdner as a contributor to the *Fortnightly* on Henry Morley's introduction. Shirley Brooks, Editor of *Punch;* W. Harrison Ainsworth; Edmund Yates; Elizabeth Drummond, sister of Thomas Drummond, the inventor of the lime-light; Andrew Halliday; James Knowles; J. O. Halliwell; S. Phelps, and many others, write to him during these early years of editorship, sending thanks or invitations, asking questions or favours, and opening relations from which many friendships would have sprung had time permitted. Another correspondent sends £5 for the Fever Hospital after reading an article in the *Examiner*, which the secretary asks leave to reprint in the annual report. Lady Shelley wishes to thank by name the writer of a review.

One of his early experiences as editor was sufficiently absurd. It may be gathered from the following letter from Dudley Costello, his sub-editor:

Saturday, March 9, 1861.

My dear Morley,

I am sorry to have suppressed a very interesting police case this week, but I give you the details as far as I know them, trusting to you to supply the rest.

Scene: An archway in a narrow street, near the Haymarket. Time: 3 a.m. Dramatis Personæ: An editorial character, with a bag; Policeman Lynx on the look-out. To them, later, Policemen Grab and Shakeum.

Policeman Lynx (as if giving evidence): ' Being on my beat, promiscuous, at the corner of Little Windmill, I sees a man with a beg, which he bolts out of the harchway hopposite, and runs like winkin' up the street. Whereupon I lays legs to pavement as fast as I can come it, gives the office to Grab and Shakeum, which they jines in the pursoot, and afore he can turn the corner, the gent is nabbed. On searching of his beg, we find it choke-full of littery rubbish—the contents of a printing office close to the harchway—we has him back for identication, which he said he was a editor,' etc.

Please let me not burst in ignorance, but say how you got
out of the hands of the Philistines, for this is all I heard.

Ever yours,

D. C.

Mr. Morley undoubtedly was arrested by a policeman
as he was running away from his own office with a bag-
ful of papers. On Friday nights he always stopped there
till two or three in the morning, and probably wished to
warm his feet as well as get home as quickly as he could.
Finding himself chased by a policeman, he ran harder for
the fun of the thing ; but at last the bobby overtook him
with, ' Now, my man, what have you got in your bag ?'
A return to the office together was required to make
matters quite clear to the arm of the law.

Mr. Costello was a real friend. In May, 1865, he lost
his wife, and sends Mr. Morley a ring to wear for her sake.
On September 29 of the same year he died himself, and
Mr. Morley, who had done much of his work during the
illness, came home about eight in the morning, having
been with him all the night till the end came.

It will be remembered that the *Examiner* was one of the
few English journals which took the side of the North
during the American Civil War, but it willingly gave a
hearing to the other side, and among the letters kept by
Mr. Morley is a long one from a Liverpool merchant in
1862, referring to a review, and giving excellent reasons
why the Northern States will never be able to conquer the
Southern.

Mr. Fox Bourne has sent me some notes. Speaking of
the time when Forster edited the paper, he says

it was then in its old shape, a sixteen-page paper of the size of the
Weekly Dispatch, only three or four pages in the front containing
original matter, the rest being news-cuttings supplied by Dudley
Costello, the sub-editor. Fonblanque continued to write now
and then (chiefly, I think, the ' Justices' Justice' articles), and
I believe the principal leader-writers were McCullagh (afterwards McCullagh Torrens) on Parliamentary subjects, Eyre

Evans Crowe on foreign affairs, and Edwin Chadwick on social
questions.   When I first began to write for the paper—December, 1858—Morley was responsible for about three columns
(a page) of book reviews, and a column or two of theatrical
and art notices, etc.

As a reviewer of books, Mr. Morley's rule (and his instruction to me) was : (1) To be as generous to the writer as justice
allowed, only finding fault when and as far as fault-finding
became a duty; (2) to bring out the gist of the book in as
readable and as instructive and suggestive an article as possible.
I sometimes thought he erred in being too amiable.   If he
could not honestly praise, he generally preferred to say
nothing.

As a theatrical critic, he kept up the best traditions of the
Examiner, following more in Leigh Hunt's and Charles Lamb's
steps than in Hazlitt's — instance his volume of collected
papers.

In or before 1860, as well as after, I suggested to Mr.
Morley that he should use influence with Fonblanque to
revolutionize the *Examiner*, abolish its news columns, and fill
it with original work, to compete with the *Saturday Review*,
which had been started in November, 1855.   The *Saturday* put
all the older weeklies at a disadvantage by giving so much
more original and smart writing for the money.   The *Spectator*
tried to face this rivalry by imitating it in a graver style.
The *Examiner* continued in its old groove, and necessarily fell
behind in the competition.   Mr. Morley, I think, favoured my
suggestion; but Fonblanque would not hear of it.   He had
grown to be a good deal of a conservative in his old age—at
any rate, he declared himself quite satisfied with the paper in
its old form, and declined to make any change.*   I am not

---

* On October 5, 1861, when Mr. Morley was well in the
editorial chair, advantage was taken of the repeal of the paper
duty to introduce considerable improvements in the *Examiner*.
Henceforth the news was arranged in a more convenient and
condensed summary, and a record of events was given in a
form which has since been adopted by many journals.   Out of
thirty-eight columns, twenty-seven are in this number filled
with original matter, and something like this proportion became
the rule.   In particular, the literary department was greatly

aware, however, that it lost much ground under Mr. Morley's skilful and zealous editorship, notwithstanding the fact that at least two-thirds of its space was taken up with digests of news which very few of its subscribers cared to read. Its decadence began to be rapid soon after it passed into Torrens' hands.

The concluding incidents in Mr. Morley's editorship, though belonging in time to the next chapter, may find here an appropriate place.

All through 1866 and most of 1867 he was doing a great deal of work for the *Examiner*, and the strain of the late hours on Friday night, when he was sometimes not home till 4 a.m., was considerable. He had undertaken the duties which Dudley Costello performed till his last illness, and was compiling the news and putting the paper together with elaborate care. Fonblanque, now an old man, was anxious to sell the paper, and various nibbles came from possible purchasers, one of whom—the late W. D. Christie—was desirous that Henry Morley should take a share in the venture. Mr. Fox Bourne, too, was most anxious to be allowed to buy the paper, and was greatly disappointed to learn that Fonblanque had suddenly sold it to McCullagh Torrens. The first act of the new proprietor was brusquely to inform the editor that his salary would be considerably reduced. ' In that case,' replied Mr. Morley, ' my engagement with the paper will terminate with the end of next week.' And after November 9, 1867, his connection with it entirely ceased. He made no complaint ; he was the last man to talk about a grievance. Hardly anyone at the time was acquainted with the cause of his leaving, but he knew what was now his own due, and he preferred to throw up his post rather than be treated shabbily and discourteously.

---

and permanently enlarged, and the paper used was much improved. Forster was emphatic in his congratulations on the change. It was further than this that Fonblanque declined to go.

Mr. Torrens engaged a young hack at about forty shillings a week to do all the literary work, while he tried himself to manage the rest. He soon found that this did not answer; the paper rapidly lost ground, and by August, 1868, he wanted to sell it again. Reynell, the printer, was willing to take a share if Mr. Morley would return, and also put some money in it. But this the Professor was unwilling to do, though he felt no doubt that he could again make the *Examiner* a valuable property if it were his own. But he could always secure pay for his labour without any speculation, and he was doubtless feeling more and more strongly that literature rather than journalism claimed his time and strength. Ultimately the *Examiner*, with a sale reduced to a hundred copies a week, was bought in 1870 by Mr. Fox Bourne. It was then considerably transformed, and became the organ of the opinions best known in connection with the name of John Stuart Mill. In politics it was radical; in religion it was agnostic. In 1873 Mr. Bourne sold it to Mr. P. A. Taylor, who in turn parted with it to Lord Rosebery. The last number appeared on February 26, 1881.

These facts are worth stating, for they show how far Henry Morley was from being responsible for the decline and decease of the paper. It was, indeed, a matter of very deep regret to him that it took a line opposed to some of his strongest convictions. Those who know his style at this period will not find it difficult to pick out many articles written by him during his editorship, and very good reading some of these are. But the only ones which he himself rescued from oblivion are the theatrical notices reprinted in 1866 in 'The Journal of a London Play-goer, 1851-1866.' This volume, after having been for some time out of print, was republished in 1891 by Routledge, and is valued as the contemporary judgment of a keen and kindly critic of the stage. Mr. Morley was always an enthusiastic play-goer, and often took his young children with him to share the enjoyment. These dramatic treats were continued after he ceased to edit a journal, and it is characteristic of his unwillingness to receive favours that, though offered a place on the 'free list' by the principal theatres, he refused every such offer after he had left the *Examiner,* and invariably paid for his seats.

With the year 1865 Mr. Morley's regular connection with *All the Year Round,* the successor to *Household Words,* came to an end. It had lasted for fifteen years, and had rendered him invaluable service. Nor had he been of less value to the journal. There are letters from both Dickens and Wills which show how they appreciated his work. In 1868 Wills was taken seriously ill, and Henry Morley supplied his place for some months. Dickens welcomed him back with rejoicing, and paid most liberally for his contributions, valuing, too, the assistance of several new writers whom he was able to secure. Wills himself wrote: ' I am not in a hurry to get back; all the better for *A. Y. R.,* I think. The numbers appear to me to be better than ever they were in my time.' It seemed as though work of this kind were still to absorb a large part of his energy. Fortunately, however, this temptation was removed. Dickens' eldest son had not met with the success he had hoped for in other walks of life, so his father now resolved to try him as editor of his weekly journal, and the new arrangement began in November, 1868.

A few more items may be chronicled as belonging to the period ending in 1865. A sister-in-law of Mrs. Morley's died in childbirth, and the bereaved infant, Geoffrey Sayer, was taken home by Mrs. Morley to be reared as a foster-child till old enough to be restored to his own family. We have already referred to the many cases in which Mr. Morley's help was invoked for persons mentally afflicted. One such sufferer was an inmate for a time at

Upper Park Road soon after the house was taken, and the kindness and attention of both Mr. and Mrs. Morley were very great.

In 1861 Mr. Morley had a piece of literary luck. He discovered on a bookstall a tattered copy in black letter of Lyly's 'Euphues,' and the copy proved to be a unique specimen of the earliest edition. He wrote an article on 'Euphuism,' which appeared in the April number of the *Quarterly Review*. For this he received a cheque for £42.

But the great work on which he was engaged as soon as 'Bartholomew Fair' was published was the first volume of his 'English Writers,' which appeared early in 1864. In this form it was never intended to be anything but tentative. It grew out of his studies for his King's College classes, and set forth a mass of information respecting the earliest literature of our land. As it is superseded by the re-issue begun in 1887, after twenty-three more years of study, it is not necessary to say more about the earlier issue. The chief interest of it is in the fact that Mr. Morley henceforth set himself to make the 'History of English Writers' the main literary work of his life.

On February 13, 1864, there appeared in a contemporary journal a review of his book which he felt to be grossly unfair, and he adopted a line of defence which few authors are in a position to take. He reprinted the whole of the review in the *Examiner*, so that his readers might judge of its merits for themselves, and replied to its statements one by one, taking a quiet impersonal tone, but showing with incisive effect the incompetence and ill-nature of his critic, and then signing his name to the whole article. Forster wrote to him: 'I see that you take the thoroughly right tone. . . . You ought to be thankful for the opportunity your enemy has opened to you.' It certainly was hard that one who was all his life helping others should be treated so shabbily himself. But he was never again served in the same way.

This year, 1864, witnessed the beginning of an act of kindness on his part worth much from so busy a man. At Cutcombe, near Dunster, the clergyman was the Rev. — King. He had two daughters, one, Alice King, being perfectly blind, but gifted with power of writing which eventually made her a successful authoress. There were happy memories of the ten months spent at Dunster, though he had not then known the Kings, and Mr. Morley practically undertook to teach Miss Alice King how to write novels. A story called ' Irene' was sent to him, and Mr. H. Blackett, the publisher, writes about his careful revision and condensation. This kind of help extended over several years till it was no longer needed, and there were pleasant interchanges of visits when the Kings came to London, and Mr. Morley found time once or twice to revisit scenery which he always thought the most beautiful in England.

We conclude the present chapter with a contribution from Professor Morley's eldest daughter :

My father was clever with penknife, scissors, pencil and brush, and always ready to use them in our behalf.

When I was eight or nine, I wrote what I called ' a book' of stories, and these my father illustrated himself. I used to leave a space for the picture, and tell him what it was to be, and he would draw and colour it for me. There was one clever picture, I remember, of three pigs carrying in the afternoon tea, to the astonishment of the lady of the house.

One picture I never could get him to draw for me. The story was of a lady who had told the doctor to bring her a baby, and gone to bed to receive it, according to custom. The doctor, however, was fond of practical jokes, and he brought her a cat instead! The picture was to show the doctor presenting the cat to the surprised and indignant lady. I never could understand why my father always put off drawing this picture, for the subject struck me as a very happy one.

He used to make dolls out of sticks of firewood, which were

a source of great delight to us. Their faces were carved and coloured, and always full of expression, so that you could not mistake the leading characteristics of the little firewood people.

The first to appear on the scene was Matilda. She was of humble origin; indeed, at first her only garment was a single one of paper, but it was evident from the scornful cast of her features that underneath the paper garment there beat an aristocratic heart.

She won the affections of Sir Decimus Doleful, a person of mature age, with solemn and somewhat lugubrious features, and 'a marriage was arranged.' Before the ceremony, Sir Decimus journeyed down to Framlingham, where he was kindly provided with a real tailor-made suit, by the father of our nursery governess, and he returned in all the added dignity of a black trouser, white shirt-front, and swallow-tailed coat stitched with red.

The fitting of these little people with garments was fraught with difficulty, for, as they had no waists and only one leg, their clothes had an awkward habit of suddenly slipping off them at critical moments. A little extra excitement or hurry would cause this to happen, which was trying and undignified, to say the least of it.

The marriage ceremony of Sir Decimus and Lady Doleful was performed by Parson Duncan, a clerical person with rosy cheeks, smooth black hair, a black suit (home-made), and bands. The happy couple set up housekeeping in a four-roomed doll's house, and engaged at first one servant to wait upon them—Jemima by name. She was an excitable person who often came out of her clothes, and she had a habit of repeating at all times, in and out of season, a verse which my father wrote for her:

> 'Jemima Cholmondeley is my name,
>   Sweetness is my natur';
>   Mudville is my native place,
>   And I can't abear pertater.'

Jemima, single-handed, proving unequal to the requirements of Lady Doleful, a cook was added to the establishment. She was made out of the thickest bit of firewood to be found in the house, and was a truly portentous person. When she got angry and stumped about in the kitchen the noise was considerable.

In due time children came to bless the home of Sir Decimus and Lady Doleful. When one was expected, we used to 'handy-spandy' to see if it should be a boy or girl, and then ask my father to make a little Doleful of the required sex. The first three were girls—Priscilla, who had staring eyes of beads, and hair made with a black tassel, and whose character was most inquisitive; Angelina, who had Roman features and a haughty disposition inherited from her mother; and Gloriana, whose hair was made with a red tassel, and who had the fiery disposition often associated with that colour. Sir Decimus despaired of a son and heir; but at last one came—Reginald, a mild youth with a flat, washed-out face, and not much character. A governess was now needed to educate the little Dolefuls, and she duly appeared upon the scene. The fun was to invent all sorts of adventures for this family, and make them behave as, according to their respective characters, they would behave. It was a 'character novel' in the nursery.

Parson Duncan, who was a frequent visitor at the house, fell in love with the governess; but, alas! here arose a great difficulty, for he being himself the parson, there was no parson to marry them.

About this time my brothers and I went to school, and with the advent of long frocks and Eton jackets our interest in the fortunes of the Dolefuls ceased, and I fear Parson Duncan and the governess are still unmarried. They, and the other fire-wood people, have played their part in life, and now lie quietly by, treasured possessions of their various owners, for the sake of the dear hand, now still, which fashioned them.

CHAPTER XIII.

UNIVERSITY COLLEGE, 1865—1878.

FROM 1852 to 1865 the Professor of English Literature at University College, London, was David Masson.* He began giving his lectures as usual in October, 1865, but soon after this moved to Edinburgh, where he had been appointed to the University Chair of English Literature. For some time the prospect of the vacancy at University College had existed, and Dr. Sadler, of Hampstead, wrote a testimonial dated February 27, 1865, which begins : ' Hearing that Mr. Morley is a candidate for the Professorship of English Literature at University College——' This testimonial, however, appears never to have been used, and I am told by Professor Carey Foster that Mr. Morley's application for the post was only received quite at the last, just before the appointment was made. It is said that he did not send in a single testimonial, only his book on ' English Writers.' This of itself would not have secured him the post, for, however much learning it showed, it proved no capacity to teach. Dr. Hodgson, however, who at this time was well known to several members of

---

* In 1852 Mrs. Holland had called Mr. Morley's attention to the vacant professorship, and he had answered, ' I'd like to have it, but would not like to ask for it and not get it. So I think I'll wait till the next time, and then, if I think I'd like it, perhaps I could be pretty sure of getting it.'

the Council, wrote unasked a letter which enabled them to decide that Henry Morley was their best candidate. He heard of the decision on December 6, and the following day began lecturing at University College.

It must have cost him a severe struggle to give up his connection with King's, and transfer his work to Gower Street. It had been a disappointment to him that Fred Sayer was sent there instead of to King's, and he must have had the same feeling in stronger measure in regard to his own teaching. After hearing of the coming vacancy at University College, and after perhaps deciding to apply, he evidently hesitated long. But there were strong reasons for the course he took. In the first place, he was only teacher of the evening classes at King's College, and the professorship of English there did not become vacant till 1877. But, in the second place, he never could have become a Professor at King's College, for he could not comply with the condition that in making application for the post he must declare himself a member of the Church of England. He had always the deepest love and reverence for that Church; his Unitarian theology did not greatly differ from the opinions held by many Broad Churchmen; but there was this difference, viz., that, holding these views, he deemed his right position to be outside, not inside, the Church, and the only name by which he would ever describe his religion was the name Christian.

The change once made from the Strand to Gower Street, the transference of his allegiance was complete; and while it was always a special pleasure to him to promote good fellowship or academical co-operation between the two colleges, University College was henceforth always first in his thoughts. Here he laboured for twenty-four years with enthusiastic loyalty, and with lavish expenditure of his time, strength, and money. He had a reward, especially during the middle period of his career, in a popularity and power of which his friends were very proud. He had

17

a reward, for which he cared more himself, in a good influence exerted over thousands of young lives, and an opportunity of developing their minds and souls through the study of the noblest literature that the world has ever known.

Some years elapsed before his fullest and highest activities came into play. He began with only five lectures a week. My own terms in his lecture-room were confined to the session 1866-67; and then, as he told me afterwards, he was still trying to carry on Masson's work rather than giving full scope to his own methods of teaching. Certainly, the full charm of his lectures, which were never read, but always spoken extempore, was only attained with the enormous amount of practice he had when he was devoting himself almost exclusively to lecturing. He once reckoned up the total number of the regular lectures he had given at 14,000. Excluding audiences who did not attend a course of at least ten lectures, he also found that he was teaching in one year no less than 2,000 persons. There was a time when he was giving twenty-two lectures a week at University College alone. Towards the end of the period with which we have now to deal, he undoubtedly overtaxed his strength. But he never wilfully undertook more than he could perform. He could do more than most men. *Punch* was quite right in dubbing him Professor More-and-Morley, and he learned with much difficulty the necessity of doing less and less. For many years he had wonderfully good health. In the early part of 1865 he did knock himself up, and we hear of his fainting at night; and some time after this John Forster writes in concern about him. But he was then bringing out the second volume of 'English Writers,' and such a book could not be produced in the intervals allowed by other occupations. He recognised the fact, and letting the issue wait till he could find proper time for this great work, he confined his activity to what he could do without any more breaking down.

Among the students who attended his classes for a considerable period was Mr. B. Paul Neuman, who since then has been actively engaged in literary work, and is known as the author of those delightful stories, ' The Interpreter's House,' and of a book which gives the results of much devoted labour with boys' clubs—' Raymond's Folly.' Mr. Neuman has written the following graphic account of the days of his studentship :

It is not an easy task to reproduce in a few words impressions that range over a long period. The difficulty lies in seizing the salient and rejecting the insignificant. It is certainly not any lack of material that hampers me. For many years Professor Morley, to use the title that rises most naturally to my lips, was a constant, almost a pervading, influence. Four or five times a week, sometimes oftener, I met him at college, and besides this, I was privileged to join those Sunday evening gatherings that are delightful memories to so many of his old students.

It was in the autumn of 1868 that I went to University College. I was then just turned fifteen. From that time University College meant to me Henry Morley—that, and little more. When I recall those days, his figure rises first of all. He comes along the corridor from the professors' common-room to his class-room. As he walks, he hugs the wall. I never remember seeing him take the middle. He comes at a good swinging pace, for the bell has just rung. Under one arm, held akimbo, he carries a huge pile of books, tapering from a folio to a duodecimo. The weight of the pile is considerable, so that he leans heavily on one side. Now he enters the room. Most likely a scrimmage of some kind is going on, a struggle for a cherished seat, a baptism—by sprinkling—of ink, or a simple fusillade of pellets and note-books. Down go the books on the table with a bang. Then he stands for a moment watching the scene, and a smile lights up his face as he takes in the humours of the fray. But by the time he has sat down, taken out the roll, and begun to call the names, the noise is stilled and order reigns.

After the roll-call, the lecture begins. The lecturer springs to his feet, takes hold of the chair by the back, and, tilting it slightly forward on the front-legs, leans over, glancing at an

17—2

open book or a few brief notes on the table. From these he
reads out any necessary dates or facts, often leaving the chair
to write them on the blackboard, but generally returning to it
again before very long. Next comes the clothing and vivifying
of the skeleton outline. Without a note now he talks on,
thoroughly interested himself, and so taking our interest captive,
too. Even the chair is abandoned for minutes together, while
he walks up and down, his hands locked behind his back, his
eyes bright with enthusiasm, misty with quick sympathy, or,
oftener still, twinkling with merriment. Now he checks himself in full career to choose some special passage, which he
reads out in his own natural but often singularly impressive
manner. This is the tit-bit, generally kept to the end, and so
liable to be cut short by the importunate bell. Last of all
comes a brief levée at the table. Most of those who can, wait
behind for a word with the Professor. They thumb his books,
make inquiries, pertinent or otherwise, ask advice with reference
to their exams, bring their notes to have lacunæ filled up. And
he, with a nod and a smile and a cheery word for all, makes
everyone welcome, answers every question he can, and if he
doesn't know the answer, says so, without any beating about
the bush.

To this hasty sketch of the Professor in his class-room, I
will add a few notes by way of supplement.

He was a born teacher who obviously loved his work, and
this was one of the great secrets of his success. Another lay
in the sympathetic interest he took in any of his pupils who
showed the least readiness to reciprocate his friendly advances.
How kind and patient, how generous in praise, and yet how
frank and fearless in his criticisms, he could be, I have very
good reason to know. It was delightful to see the pleasure
and pride he took in the success of any of his pupils. He
might well have been the author of the words he often quoted
from Ben Jonson, 'My son Cartwright writes all like a
man.'

Perhaps his crowning merit as a teacher was his power of
communicating to others something of his own enthusiasm and
love for literature. And next to this I would place the breadth,
and generosity, and sanity of his literary judgments. Less
important, perhaps, but, as subsequent experience has shown
me, hardly less remarkable, was his way of maintaining order

in his classes. There was in him nothing of the martinet ; I
never remember seeing him lose his temper for a moment.
But neither can I call to mind a single instance in which a
class got out of hand, or broke loose from an easy but perfect
control.

He was so simple and natural that his lectures were a
revelation of the man. I well remember how, when he was
lecturing on Victorian literature, we noticed that he seemed to
avoid dealing with Dickens. When at last he had to speak of
him, we understood his reluctance. Before he had finished
the biographical details, his eyes were full of tears, and that
day he came very near indeed to an absolute breakdown. ·

Outside the class-room, he threw himself with the utmost
heartiness into all the interests that made for *esprit de corps* and
good-fellowship. Time, work, money, he gave freely to any
and every cause that could contribute towards the progress
and success of the college of his adoption.

But what strikes me as most characteristic of all is the fact
that, after twenty-five years of happy intercourse as pupil and
friend, I cannot recall one spiteful or ungenerous remark such
·as will sometimes escape the lips of even the genial and the
good. His nature was the kind of soil that starves ill weeds.

The value of such a picture as is here drawn lies partly
in its relation to the statistics of his classes ; figures, which
would otherwise be comparatively barren, become eloquent
indeed if we use them to multiply the kind of influence
which Mr. Neuman enables us to realize in his own case.

The prosperity of University College was at this time
advancing with remarkable strides. The number of students
in the Faculties of Arts and Laws in the session 1866-67
was 365. By 1873-74 it had risen to 571 ; in 1877-78 it
had dropped to 470, but the following year rose to 731 ;
and in 1884-85 it reached the highest point, 841. Turning
now to the number of Professor Morley's own students,
we find the following list : For the session beginning
October, 1865, the number is 52 ; 1866, 52 ; 1867, 57 ;
1868, 67 ; 1869, 68 ; 1870, 95 ; 1871, 97 ; 1872, 108 ;
1873, 104 ; 1874, 95 ; 1875, 68 ; 1876, 89 ; 1877, 79 ;

1878, 191 ; 1879, 203 ; 1880, 203 ; 1881, 194 ; 1882, 188 ; 1883, 148 ; 1884, 156 ; 1885, 159 ; 1886, 107 ; 1887, 128 ; 1888, 109.

The remarkable rise in the session beginning October, 1878, is mainly, but not wholly, due to the admission of women students. On the other hand, the opening of the University College at Cardiff in 1883 is indicative of a movement which has greatly affected the fortunes of the London colleges. With the excellent teaching afforded by so many new provincial colleges, there has been a marked falling off in the number of students who have come to London, especially from South Wales and the West of England.

On October 2, 1867, he delivered the introductory lecture of the Faculty of Arts, his subject being ' College Work.' The lecture was subsequently printed in the volume entitled ' Clement Marot.' Here is a characteristic extract from near the conclusion :

Plato says that 'a boy is the most ferocious of animals.' The ferocious animal which he resembles is, I think, the domestic kitten. When, at his first passage out of boyhood, the young student suddenly enjoys the freedom of that trust which a college puts in his own powers of self-restraint, he is likely to be sometimes so ferocious as to play when he should work. Yet even that occurs but seldom. Would it ever occur if it could be remembered always that this personal indulgence is only to be had at the expense of others whose work it disturbs? After a year's contact with the college work it does, so far as I know, become a point of honour with all students to deal fairly by their comrades and themselves in this respect.

Professor Morley's abandonment of journalistic work, in 1865 and 1867, meant a loss of income of about £700 a year. The professorship at University College was at this time unendowed, the remuneration coming entirely from a share of the fees paid by the students. He had taken a house for which he had a heavy rent to pay, and the education of his own children was beginning to cost money. But, as always happened to him now, so soon as he had time and strength for new work, it appeared and claimed his full energies.

The year 1868 saw the beginning of an important new development of University Extension and of the Higher Education of Women. To the *Oxford University Extension Gazette* for July, 1891, Professor Morley contributed the following letter:

THE PIONEERS OF UNIVERSITY EXTENSION.

DEAR SIR,

You ask for my recollections of the classes held in various provincial towns before the beginning of the University Extension movement. The idea of that form of University Extension which you are now on the way to realize came first, as you have shown, out of the Universities themselves. You will find it suggested in evidence before a Parliamentary Commission in or before 1851-52. The classes of which I now send one or two recollections opened the way for the work now being done by Oxford, Cambridge, and London. Their first founders were women; their one aim was the higher education of women.

In 1868 Ladies' Educational Associations were formed in several towns of Lancashire and Yorkshire for bringing teachers from the Scottish or English Universities to give courses of about ten lectures to women only. In the same year, but, I think, a few months later, such a Ladies' Educational Association was established in Edinburgh. Professor Masson gave a course upon some subject in English literature, and another of the Edinburgh University professors gave a science course. The lectures were to ladies' classes, which were formed and controlled by this association as an independent agency outside the University. The example of Edinburgh was, in another month or two, followed in London, when there was formed a Ladies' Educational Association that also began with two courses—one in science, one in literature—which were given by Professor Carey Foster and by me at the Beethoven Rooms in Harley Street. These courses opened in March, 1869. Among some of us there was an intention from the beginning so to direct the work of the London Ladies' Educational Association that it might prepare the way for as complete an opening of the Science and Arts Classes of University College to women as experience might show to be practicable. Our two courses in the Beethoven Rooms were followed in November by six courses in St. George's Hall, and they were not confined, as was then usual in such classes, to eight or ten lectures in a course. We ventured upon courses of thirty-six lectures, and they were well attended. The next step was taken in the winter session 1869-70, when, on condition that the classes met and separated at the half-hours, it was agreed to be convenient—for readier access to the apparatus necessary for experiments—that two of the science classes should meet in the college, the other classes all still meeting at St. George's Hall. In the next session, 1870-71, there were three such science classes, instead of two, held in the college, and in 1871-72 prejudice was so far removed that, with consent of the council of the college, we brought all the classes into our lecture-rooms, and increased the number of the women's courses from eight to twenty-one. They were classes of professors of the college, not of the college, and they were held under the superintendence of a ladies' committee, the Committee of the London Ladies' Educational Association, working in concert with us. To have gone farther in that year would have been to reap before the corn had ripened. We then moved step by step in the next successive sessions, opening first to women as well as men one or two small college classes upon subjects chiefly attended by elder students. In this way, tentatively but with firm advance, by gradual experiment extended over ten years, all the old prejudices were so far conquered that in 1878 the University of London opened its degrees to women, and University College, which had obtained in 1869 the necessary modification of its charter, was fully prepared to teach all who desired knowledge, and was open to women as to men, except, of course, in the Faculty of Medicine.

It was during these ten years, from 1869 to 1878, that Ladies' Educational Associations, formed in very many of the chief towns throughout England, were preparing the ground for that extension of University teaching which is now being controlled by University syndicates, and is now slowly bringing

within sight the realization of an ideal first suggested at least
forty years ago.

The classes of those ten years began in each town with the
formation of a Ladies' Educational Association, by which the
subject of study was selected, the class formed, and the lecturer
invited. The lecturer received either a fixed fee, usually of
5 guineas a lecture, which included travelling expenses,
except for long distances; or a minimum fee of 5 guineas,
with a division of any profits after payment of expenses. In
that way, I remember that I had £100 for ten lectures at
Liverpool, and I think £111 for ten lectures given on the
evenings of the same days at Birkenhead. The whole movement was very vigorous. The courses were of ten lectures;
the students were all women; the season for lectures was in
the two terms between October and Easter. I ceased altogether to take classes out of London when the battle for
higher education of women, so far as I had anything to do
with it, was won by their admission to the Arts and Science
classes at University College. But during the ten years when
that work was in hand, I was one of the band of workers in
the provinces, and in the greater part of the time gave three
days a week to that work. When I went far North, I found
Scotch professors coming South upon the same good errand.
We took the same thought then that you take now for the
fitting of our little rounds of work, so that more than one town
might be taken in one day, and invitations were received a year
or two years in advance, whilst there were some towns in
which courses on the same subjects of study were carried on
by the same teacher from year to year. In nearly all the
classes exercises were written and marked and certificates
given, with an order of merit in the honours list, based upon
the marking of the class work, and the number of students
who in those days wrote papers was considerable. There
were, indeed, some towns in which nobody who came to the
classes would do paper work; but there were others with large
classes in which, except some four or five, every student wrote,
and if she missed her paper for one week sent two for the next.
In one of the years between 1869 and 1878, I had the curiosity
to add up the number of students in my classes for that session,
in and out of London, omitting any who took fewer than ten
lectures, and found they were about two thousand.

In the latter part of this period of ten years the attention of local committees was more and more drawn to the suggestion of a permanent organization of their work by transformation of it into a system that would bring University teaching from Oxford or Cambridge home to the doors of the people in, the provinces. Cambridge was then chiefly in question, and I most heartily admired the energy with which Professor James Stuart was acting then as a pioneer in the new movement. The old Associations for the Higher Education of Women had provided starting-points for the establishment of classes bound together by affiliation to a single alma-mater, open equally to men and women, and placed under the care of a University syndicate that would be able to assure not only their permanence, but their development. My recollections, you see, are of the first stages of a process of evolution that is on its way to such substantial results as, I hope, your *University Extension Gazette* will have to record in the years to come.

Wishing success to you all in the attainment of your highest aims alike at Oxford and at Cambridge,

I am,

Faithfully yours,

HENRY MORLEY.

Carisbrooke,
  Isle of Wight,
    May 25, 1891.

In this letter we have Professor Morley's summary of the new work which he undertook during the ten years of which he speaks. It might be largely supplemented from letters which he wrote to his eldest daughter, who in September, 1869, was sent to school with Mrs. Phipson at Stuttgart. None of the children had previously gone to a boarding-school. It was the first break-up of the home circle, where all had everything in common, and the father resolved that the absent one should not lose her share in the family life. So while others wrote weekly budgets of home tidings, he rarely failed to send an account, sometimes running into several sheets, of his own doings, and for nearly a year we have his own words telling of the joyous energy with which he entered into his new fields of labour. In the first letter he wrote to her (August 5), he touches on a deeper subject :

After your departure, we travelled with you by help of the continental time-tables, saying, ‘ Now Vi is here, now Vi is there.’ You will be often in our minds every day, and often connected with our thoughts of God, as we must be with yours. I do not care about kneelings and set times and formal holdings forth to God for His information and edification as to what we think He ought to do. But every fresh glimpse of the beauty of the world should give us a thought of the lovingkindness of its Maker that sometimes sends our hearts up to Him with a conscious emotion of love and worship. Every little effort to do right that *is* an effort can be made with just one little thought glancing to God for blessing on it. God can be thanked in some one minute of a happy hour, even while we are in the midst of talk and laughter. That is what I read in the admonition to ‘ pray without ceasing,’ and so we may feel the nearness of God, and help ourselves to act from worthy motives, exalt every happiness, and lessen every trouble, while we may be so far from Pharisaism that the narrow pietists may think us naughty for never ‘ saying our prayers.’ You will have so much in your new life to help in strengthening a little habit of that sort, that it would grow of itself, I think. It only comes into my head to speak of it because I love all my little household very tenderly and miss anyone, and am happiest in remembering that the nearer we all keep to God, the nearer we are to each other.

He sends this account of his first provincial lecturing :

At Winchester I left Aunt Lizzie in the train and my overcoat in the cloak-room, and took my dear old umbrella and lost myself a bit up and down the town before I found out Mr. Awdrey’s quarters in the college. Winchester College, you know, was established in the days of Chaucer. It is the oldest of our public schools, and some part of the building is as old as the cathedral. It is the wife of Mr. Awdrey, the second master, who manages the ladies’ lectures, and the headmaster, Dr. Ridding, who asked me to repeat my lectures for his senior boys. Mr. Awdrey lives in delightful old panelled rooms belonging to the ancient part of the college ; has drawing-room, study, etc. ; is youngish and studious, and has a nice little wife.

I found with them Dr. Ridding, the headmaster, who had given up a busy hour in the school to meet me, and we four sat down to a lunch which, I suppose, was Mr. and Mrs. Awdrey's dinner with its name altered, for there was a hare and a boiled leg of mutton and a pie. Now, when we had lunched, and Dr. R. had gone to his duties, Mr. Awdrey took me round the college, and showed me the fine old chapel, rich with painted glass; and the old library, like another chapel, with some treasures of MSS. and old books; and the cloisters, in which old students now known for their works had carved their names in schoolboy days; and the old school-room, now not half big enough; and a delicious green for cricket, football, and fives-court, and so on. Then I washed my paws, and went with Mrs. A. to lecture. The ladies' lectures at Winchester were first started last February, and they made a bad start with a man who was a failure. Then they got a lecturer on Ancient History, and, not venturing again to form a class of ladies only, made the lecture open to both sexes, and got about a hundred to attend. Now they again try ladies exclusively, and it remains to be seen what class I shall get. On Friday the lecture was open, and the numbers of the class will not be settled for a week or two. They had taken the lecture-room of the Mechanics' Institution, which is the biggest in the town. It was not more than half full—fifty or sixty, perhaps—when I began, but more kept coming in, and I suppose there were about a hundred when I finished. I saw they liked the lecture, and Mrs. Johns, who was the original promoter of the movement and the original inviter of me, told me it was exactly what they wanted. As I was waiting at the door of my little retiring-room for the ladies to get downstairs (and they seemed to be a great many going down), I was greeted very cordially by three damsels, who proved to be the Miss Kingsleys. Their father was at Bristol, at the Social Science Association meeting, and they were staying meanwhile with a friend at Winchester, properly grieved, of course, that they shouldn't be able to hear all my lectures. I talked with them till all the ladies were out, and then went a little way with Mrs. Awdrey and Mrs. Johns, but wouldn't go back to the Awdreys', because I had to lecture again in three-quarters of an hour to the college boys, and what I had been doing was special introductory for ladies, so the next had to be different, and I wanted to make up my mind quietly as to what was to be put into it. So I turned into the Cathedral, where service was going on at the other end and organ-playing. Then I turned out into the town, and in due time appeared at the headmaster's quarters. They are modern, and on a very handsome scale. The lecture was to be given in his study—a large room with three great windows, down which hung delicious festoons of Virginia creeper, rich in autumn colour. It is a handsome room, well furnished, and chairs for fifty had been ranged all round the study table, and behind the study table were chairs for the headmaster and second master, with me between them. Then the boys trooped in, only those of the highest form—pretty much of the same age as my college students—a lot of nice young clever-looking fellows that it was pleasant to see ; and when they were all settled, I stood up and said my say, and enjoyed it.

The lecture began a little after five, and as it came to a close the light waned, and the soft evening gloom came through the creeper, and the students couldn't see to take notes, and I couldn't see my watch ; but when I had done, I found that I hadn't gone many minutes beyond an hour's talk, which I had very much enjoyed. Then I was shown to a grand bedroom to wash for dinner ; dined with half a dozen pastors and masters of the college with some dinner-party state ; got after dinner a little nervous about my quarter to eight train, but was told that a fly was ordered to call for me and take me to the station. The fly duly carried me off, but Winchester time being slower than London time, I went off with a little sense of hurry, and left my beloved old umbrella on a visit for a week at Dr. Ridding's.

On October 19 he announces that he has really found out the way from Winchester Station to the college, but so many hospitalities are offered that he has to learn a new route each time.

Winchester Fridays turn out very pleasant, and I haven't had a headache from them since the first. My duty seems to be to give two lectures, eat two dinners, and have a cup of tea between.

He is looking forward to the re-opening of the ladies' classes in St. George's Hall, London, which

will hold 800 or 1,000, so if we get only fifty or sixty, we shall look lively. In the evening the original Christy's Minstrels perform there, and if we fail by ourselves, we may get up a coalition with them.

On October 26 he writes much rollicking fun, telling of his good health and spirits. Work on all sides was prospering. Of Winchester he says :

Mrs. Johns was the getter-up of the Winchester ladies' class. Her husband is a man who has written books of natural history for the young, one or two of which I have, and he keeps a high-class school for boys between eight and fourteen whom he prepares for public schools. He gets well paid, and lives in a big house with grounds on the hill outside Winchester. On a tree at his entrance-gate is stuck up a notice : ' To Trespassers —Scolopendras and Serpenturias are set in these Grounds.' They are names of plants, but sound like dreadful instruments of torture. I liked the people there much ; but there is a school of ten girls attending the class who all send notes of lectures that require an enormous quantity of correction. I had begun the exercise work in the week, and gone on with it in the train ; but these damsels gave me so much to do that I had still three or four exercises uncorrected when I got to Winchester. Then there, woe, woe ! were Mr. Johns and Kingsley at the station, so I couldn't finish my correcting as I walked up to the house. But after dinner, alias lunch, I told Mrs. Johns my difficulty, and got leave to go on with them. Then I went with her to lecture in their carriage, correcting as I went. Was put down at Dr. Ridding's for a book I had left there, and as there was still one exercise uncorrected, I wouldn't go on with her, but walked to the lecture-room correcting it, and got done just as I reached the door and as the clock struck three. Then the rest was as usual. Only when I had come out of the ladies' class, and was in the little side-room, I heard a great noise of tumble-cum-stumble like a legion of polter-geists, and thought there was a troop of boys at work somewhere. Then the ladies came out, and Mrs. Johns said: ' Did you hear our little attempt at applause ?' The other lecture was as usual, with the little dinner-party after it and the fly to take me to the station. My college work is getting on wonderfully well: a new student enters every day I come, and as my classes have been going up every year since I came, I hope they'll go on doing so in years to come, in which case some day we shall be able to afford nuts on state days and holidays. Next week I've to go to Newcastle, and shall have news to tell you about that. At present I look forward with bewilderment to the two lectures to be given there, for I want to write them, and have only written about a third of the first. When or how the rest is to be written the Fates will decide for me. What is to be goes ever as it must. Then come the ladies in the next week after that, and if I do really get a larger class than last year, we may possibly, supposing increase to continue, live to afford on high days and holidays ginger wine with our nuts.

We should like to have heard more of what passed between him and Kingsley, but he only tells us that he did not flinch from his victuals, though he ate them before the Canon's mouth.

On November 9 he sends an account of his visit to Newcastle. The letter is dated ' Inky Villa,' by which name his house had begun to be known. He stayed with Mr. Watson and gave two lectures on Sir David Lindsay of the Mount, at the Literary and Philosophical Institution, with Sir William Armstrong in the chair. But though very favourably received, he was not himself satisfied with what he had done. One of his lectures, which had been partly written, was too much like a book, and the other was brought too abruptly to a close when he found people were leaving to catch last trains. He saw Durham on his way home, and much enjoyed the old castle with its stately hall, antique carved staircases, and tapestried galleries, the home of a University not ' three dozen years old, heavily ecclesiastical,' all very unlike University College. He brought away these stories with him :

There's a place by the Tyne in Newcastle called Paradise, and some twenty or thirty years ago the old bridge was swept away by a memorable rising of the river. A man was asked in a court of law: ' What is your name ?' ' Adam.' ' Where do you live ?' ' In Paradise.' ' How long have you lived there ?' ' Since the flood.' Another is this: A witness began his evidence before a judge at assizes with : ' As I was coming out of a chair-foot I met a hoddy-doddy.' Judge looks like a scared owl. ' Coming out of a chair-foot ! Is the man drunk ? How could he have come out of the foot of a chair ?' Counsel explains : ' My lord, a chair in Newcastle is the term for a narrow passage leading to the river, and a chair-foot is that end of the passage which abuts upon the river. A hoddy-doddy, my lord, is the popular term in Newcastle for a commotion which eventuates in blows.'

The following week he gives another lively account of his trip to Winchester. Other places were beginning to ask him to give courses of lectures, and he suggests the idea of going about in a caravan.

As for the ladies at St. George's Hall, I shall know to-morrow more about them than I do to-day. My class isn't bad, and I expect it to be better. I exhibit myself on a tub or other small article covered with a bit of carpet, upon which I balance myself with a table and a bottle of water. The object is to show that I can stand there without upsetting the table or spilling the water. Ladies sit and wonder that the table's not upset until the hour is up. Then they go away, but return in a day or two, anxious to see the trick repeated. To-day additional attraction was provided. The gymnastic professor robes and unrobes in a box to which hitherto he has ascended by three steps. To-day the steps were removed, and the professor performed the difficult and dangerous feat of the ascent of the box wholly without help of machinery. It's difficult to explain to you how he did it, but he did it, and afterwards jumped out of his box without falling on his head, and went through the table and water-bottle trick as well as ever. But when he came away he found he had lost the skin off his hands, only it wasn't his own skin, but only some other poor beastess's. This is the clearest account I am able to give you to-day of the present condition of the ladies' lectures. I've just been reading ma's letter with awe and admiration. What a fund of information ma has got ! That's a grand law in Germany for fetching the police to people who dance after supper. It *can't* be good to shake the stomach too much after eating, and if the police come and hold you still until your supper is digested your own father couldn't do more, and wouldn't do so much, most likely.   Ma says of course I've told you about the lectures.

In spite of counter-attractions at South Kensington, these ladies' lectures were promising well, especially his own, for which he had seventy-five students, and we are glad to hear that a platform of reasonable dimensions was soon provided.   At Winchester he heard the following :

The boys are obliged to write English verse whether they can or can't, and have now and then distinguished themselves greatly.   One boy began a poem thus :

> As when a lion, twixt two tender calves,
> With bloody talons rends them both in halves.

Another began a poem about Egypt, with a fine reference to Apis, etc. :

> The gentle Ibis and the sacred bull
> In peaceful pastures now may eat their full.

Another, in a poem on the Ganges, had this poetic gem :

> A long and scaly beast came trotting down the Nile ;
> It caused them much alarm, it was a crocodile.

In January, 1870, an important opening was afforded him, when he was asked to lecture at the Midland Institute, Birmingham.   If he had made any mistake at Newcastle, he was resolved it should not be repeated here. He took for his subject ' King Arthur in English Literature, from the Earliest Legends to the completed " Idylls of the King." '   His last lecture at University College was over at four o'clock ; he dressed, caught the five o'clock express from Euston, and was at the door of the Institute at Birmingham three minutes before the lecture was due. ' It is a large theatre, with the seats banked up steeply, and was as full as it could be, all the standing room being occupied.   I lectured for an hour and a half, and they seemed to like it.'   He came back by train at 1.20 a.m., reached his home by a quarter to five, had a little sleep,

18

and then went off to the reopening of his London ladies' class, which now numbered ninety students.

On January 26 he writes about Birmingham :

When I went down to the second lecture, I was hailed on the platform at Rugby by a gentleman who had been at No. 1, and was going down to No. 2, greatly impressed with the fact that I had lectured 'without a note.' I got there in good time, and found, instead of about three members of the committee, the little private room well stocked with committee men: and big-wigs of the institute, and the lecture-room ten minutes after I had begun was full to the doors, standing room and all. As I went on with an account of the treatment of King Arthur by successive writers on the way to Tennyson, with the committee of the institute just under me, a paper was put on the table before me inscribed, 'Take another lecture for Tennyson. We can give you an evening in March.' So I got to Tennyson at ten o'clock, and then said what was proper to ascertain whether I should take another lecture, or give, as could be done in ten minutes, the points that concerned Tennyson, and so finish at once. Everybody seemed to be game for another lecture, so I stopped there, and am going to give a special lecture on Tennyson's 'Idylls of the King,' at Birmingham, on March 7. After the lecture I got more emphatic expressions of satisfaction than I had expected, for I was more conscious of what I had 'been obliged to leave unsaid than of what I *had* said, and wasn't much pleased with myself. However, the people seemed to like the lecture, and Messrs. of the Committee spoke as if they really looked upon it as a great success.

The third lecture, on Tennyson's 'Idylls,' was given to so crowded an audience that there was not even standing room some time before he began. What he said is well reported in the *Birmingham Daily Gazette* for March 10, 1870.

In January, 1870, he also began a set of lectures in Yorkshire. On every Thursday he went straight from lecturing at University College to Bradford, where he generally stayed with Mr. and Mrs. Hertz, and lectured Friday morning at the Mechanics' Institute to a ladies' class of about 130, 'nearly twice as big as any they have had before,' and most energetic in raining exercises. At 1.15 he left for Leeds, where he had ten minutes for dinner, and reached York at 2.55. There the lecture-room belonged to the Philosophical Society. 'Last week I began there, solemnly introduced by the Dean and some local dignitaries,' to a class of about fifty. After the lecture he dined with Mr. Fitch, now Sir J. G. Fitch, whose acquaintance, thus begun, soon ripened into friendship. At night he left for Huddersfield, where he lectured Saturday morning at 11.30.

There have been two attempts before to get up a class at Huddersfield, both turning out dolefully, but I've got more than the little room engaged will hold, and next Saturday we are going to move to the Assembly Rooms.

Home was reached about 8 p.m. on Saturday, his principal trouble being that the railway carriages were so badly lighted that he could not see to read in them after dark.

Week by week he tells a similar tale of pleasant hospitalities, and growing classes and hearers eager that he should go on talking long beyond his appointed hour. He was singularly easy to listen to, having a very unusual power of retaining the attention of his hearers without strain on their part.

The success of all the lectures he was now giving led immediately to further invitations for the autumn. Birmingham, Leeds, and Bradford all applied for ladies' courses, and, later, Southport, Alderley and Coventry were added. He saw that he must pack his London lectures into three days, and keep from Thursday to Tuesday morning free for country lecturing and writing. By the end of March his ladies' courses were coming to an end, and he looked forward to buying a new bottle of ink and bundle of pens.

I gave the York ladies an hour and three-quarters instead of an hour, and they seemed to like it; went out of their quiet

18—2

way to applaud when I'd done—that was for exercise after sitting so long.

He managed with some difficulty to escape the hospitalities which were pressed upon him, and went for what he dearly loved, a quiet prowl by himself about the city, and bought some good stereoscopic slides.

On April 13 the Easter holidays began, and he finds time for a long letter. There were some people who believed that his lectures could not mean real work because they were so interesting, and who thought more of a course on astronomy which had been made so dull as to land the town where it was given in a considerable deficit. Indeed, the association which started these ladies' lectures in the Northern towns nearly ruined the whole cause by engaging young men who could not lecture, and whom people would not continue coming to hear. Professor Morley's tours at this time were of great value in proving the possibility of making lectures pay.

A special course of lectures was being given this spring (1870) at University College. Of one of these he says:

It was by Mr. Ralston, our best authority here on Russian matters, translator of Kriloff's fables, etc. He gave a good end I hadn't heard to a very old story. Fine sense of the force of circumstances. A Russian bragging of his native province said much of its honey; said its bees were as big as pigeons. Asked about the beehives, said they were much as elsewhere. The holes into them? Oh, much as usual. But if the holes are no bigger than usual, and the bees as big as pigeons, how do the bees come in and out? He stopped to consider of this, and soon made the end of the difficulty with, 'They must.' If there was nothing for it but they must go through the little holes, of course they did. That's great philosophy, as well as a good Russian sense of absolutism. There are not many things one can't do if one *must*. Another story was of a great house with some old coach harness hanging in its grandest room. The owner had once gambled away his land, and then gambled away his house, and then his serfs, and then his horses, and then his carriages, and then, having nothing, went

out to hang himself, when his eye was caught by the glitter on
the silver ornaments of some old harness that he had forgotten
to gamble away; so he went back and staked that and won,
staked his winnings and won—won back his carriages, won
back his horses, his slaves, his house, his land, and as much
land again.   So he paid honour to the old set of harness all the
days of his life after.

On May 5 he mentions his election as examiner in
English for the University of London, and says: 'I have
had a nice note from my colleague, Mr. Fitch, with whom
I shall be good friends.'   He held this post for the usual
five years, then was ineligible, but on the next vacancy, in
1878, was re-appointed for another five years.

On May 11 he tells how the ladies' classes for
Chemistry and Physics had been allowed to be held in
the college for the convenience of apparatus, the ladies
being let in and out at a time when all the male students
were supposed to be safely shut up in their lecture-rooms,
and how it was proposed to continue this plan the next
session, and to apply the same principle to some language
classes and to the Fine Art classes.   At St. George's
Hall, his class, which had reached a hundred, proved the
only one really profitable, and he generously gave up
£40 of his fees to meet other deficits.   His income was
as yet barely equal to his somewhat heavy expenses, and
sacrificing this money meant a necessity for writing something that would sell at once instead of giving spare
time to his books.   He was president this year of the
University College Athletic Club, and one of the judges
at the annual meeting on May 17, when Mrs. Morley gave
away the prizes.   Mentioning this, he adds some thoughts
on what his children owe to their mother :

Mamma came out very nicely as Queen of the May in a
moiré dress and a light bonnet, and looked well, and did her
presentation with all grace, so as to earn her 'Three cheers for
Mrs. Morley!' also I like to see her trotting about with
Cousin Flora.   As you all grow up, and mamma gets more

free, and the world goes well with us—which it promises to do
.—we'll see how much rest and holiday we can give her after
all her care of you.   We shouldn't be so happy as we are in
you all if she hadn't given herself up to mother's duty as she
has done.   But we are happy in all our children.   Somebody
said of your carte de visite that you still had a child's face, and
I hope you'll keep it and die with it long after we are gone.
The only preservative is a light heart that comes of simplicity
of life, quiet truth, and a childlike endeavour to be good that
is above the highest results of philosophy when they are of a
sort that doesn't lead to that.   What a stupid blunder men
and women make who go in for false dignity, shallow gravity,
and labour to look old and wise.   It is great happiness to see
the child spirit unspoilt in all our five, and I am grateful for
it above everything to mamma's simple sincerity of nature and
her long and close devotion to her duty.

Writing on June 8, he gives this proof of the pains he
was prepared to take for his students :

I had rather a long holiday, having no lecture from 4 p.m.
on Thursday to 3 p.m. the following Tuesday, Whit Monday
being a holiday always.   I could have done lots of things, but
I had promised one of my classes to answer with pen and ink
any difficulties left unexplained in Books I. and II. of the
' Faerie Queene.'   While others sent reasonable little questions,
one student, who is painstaking but not poetic, deluged me
with questions, many of them foolish ; and as one mustn't
refuse any help that's asked for, I had to give up just the whole
of my holiday to that young gentleman.   However, it didn't
matter in the long-run.   It's instructive to me to find what
unimaginable difficulties a prosaic mind can find in reading
Spenser's poetry, besides being blind to two-thirds of the
allegory, as most people are.   As I hope some day to edit
Spenser, the hindrance was a help, perhaps.

The next letter contains sad news :

Work looks well, but I have had a very great grief since I
wrote last, in the sudden death of Charles Dickens.   It brings
tears to my eyes to write it, and I can't talk of it.   He was a
good friend to me before you were born, and but for him my
life might have been less happy than it is.   He had a stroke of
apoplexy at six in the evening on Thursday, lay insensible till

about the same time next evening, when he died. There have been nineteen years of goodwill between us that time has deepened, and in all our intercourse never an unpleasant word, and many a cordial word or sign of trust and confidence. I understood him and he me, but until he was gone I hardly knew the strength of the regard that had grown up so quietly. How hard it must be for those who have no children to lose old friends of their past. Well, our chief happiness remains in you young mortals.

He has also this characteristic bit :

There's an unusual crop of roses, and you'll get pears in the gorilla's nest. That tree which was allowed to mount skyward after long nailing and training to no purpose, is this year loaded with fruit. A parable for educational folks. How many children are nailed and trained according to art to some dead wall of formal doctrine, and never yield a morsel of fruit, but turn out famously if Nature is not thwarted !

Stuttgart days were drawing to a close, and Mrs. Phipson took her pupils to Munich before arranging to bring them home. At Munich, during a great plague, persons were said to have been buried alive, and it was now the law that every corpse should be brought to the morgue and left there for three days, being so placed on wires that the slightest movement would ring a bell. The tourists saw this place as one of the sights, and an account of it calls forth this reply :

Your first impression of death was the true one, and it was good to take into the Cathedral and to feel it as you did. I have seen many dying and many dead, and terror is one of the last thoughts I should associate with death. Love generally shines out of the dying and surrounds the death-bed. From the dead face all petty expressions vanish, and there comes into it a still, natural beauty that suggests the innocence of child-hood, often upon the most rugged features. And what energy of the soul behind the veil drawn between us and it ! Death is beautiful, and to be welcomed in its time, but not by the indolent as a better bedtime. There is God to be loved by active service here and hereafter. In His time it is very good to be taken; but meanwhile we must put all our souls into the day's work here and do our utmost—not that we may get a better bargain for the life to come, but for the love of God, simply because it is most natural that we should do so, as *it is.* The longer I live, the more I believe in the natural goodness of the desires and impulses of men, obscured as they may be by conventionality and false shame, or distorted by bad education and the weakness that in too many allows bold and hard people to take the lead. Well, never mind.

The sudden declaration of war between France and Germany on July 15 changed a good many plans, but did not prevent the safe home-coming and hearty rejoicing over the family reunion which ended this correspondence.

Professor Morley was now fairly launched on his work of incessant lecturing for eight or nine months in every year. On Thursday, January 28, 1871, he started for Bradford, and did not return home till the following Monday at midnight, and this represented his regular round except when he did not get home till 5 a.m. on the Tuesday. At the Midland Institute he gave two lectures on February 27 and March 6 in the Masonic Hall on 'The Spirit of English War Literature, Past and Present.' He was, of course, no lover of war; but he often told his classes how a noble literature can only spring from the heart of a nation deeply stirred to noble deeds. He also gave in the same town, in the Lecture Theatre, a Monday morning course to ladies on 'The Spirit of English Literature from the Birth of Wordsworth to the Death of Byron.' This was followed by another course in the autumn, and for eight or nine years these Birmingham lectures were regularly continued, and many were the letters of appreciation of them that he received. Other places at which he gave courses of lectures in 1871 were Huddersfield, Southport (which afforded him a whiff of sea-air), Banbury, Leamington, Stourbridge, and Stratford. At New Brighton also he gave two lectures, with the feeling that his audience was somewhat stiff. He says, however:

Coming out, I heard an old lady say to her daughter, as they stood in the lobby waiting for their carriage, that it was very amusing. Ah, but I made them applaud some things that I put my soul into.

He could be very amusing. Of a Southport lecture he says:

Buckingham's *Rehearsal* (which is fun) being a part of it, I went in for fun therewith, and did what I have not done before in lectures, read parts of it with dramatic change of voice, and made them all laugh unreservedly.

These quotations are from letters to Mrs. Morley, written on the Sundays when he could not get home. Consequently, Mrs. Morley had to fill up the census paper, and writes, March 31:

I shall put myself at the head of the list. I suppose you will go down wherever you locate on the Sunday night. Don't you feel an alien?

One of these Sundays he spent at Stratford-on-Avon, and writes:

I have been sitting on the old bench whereon Shakespeare and Anne Hathaway made love, and send to my own love violets and a bit of barberry out of Anne Hathaway's garden.

Surely it must have been then that he resolved to interpret the soul of every one of Shakespeare's plays. John Morley, writing to him January 17, asks for another literary contribution, and suggests one of these plays as a subject. It may be well to state that the two men were in no way related, often as the contrary was asserted. In this letter John Morley says:

Why not agree to be brothers? We cannot resist destiny. I hear so often that we are brothers—sometimes cousins for a change—that a genuinely fraternal feeling is growing up in my bosom.

A letter which he received on January 28 shows the sort of social life that would have been open to him had he not deliberately turned from it. Mr. W. P. Pattison writes from Brooke Street, asking him to dinner to meet Farrar,

who goes to Marlborough next Friday. I am asking a *few* friends, those who I know he will care most to meet, and I class you among the number, as he always affectionately carries you in his memory. The others asked are Stansfield, Arthur Helps, Ruskin, and Lushington.

But evening parties did not suit Mrs. Morley. The occasions when she did go to one are recorded with a note of triumphal rejoicing, and for her sake, as well as for his work's sake, he declined nearly all such invitations.

One form of rest and change he did allow himself in 1871 and almost every succeeding year, and that was a good summer holiday. Funds were available. His classes in London had grown considerably, and the provincial lecturing, on the scale on which he could undertake it, was profitable. So this year the family party were at Barmouth.. In 1873 the place chosen was Westward Ho; in 1874 it was Sandown, Isle of Wight; in 1875, Dawlish; in 1876, the Lakes; in 1877, Llanfairfechan; and in 1878, Tenby. It is a relief, amid the record of so much work, to name these places, and summon up the associations connected with the happy days spent with a cavalcade of friends amid such scenes. His children's education involved hard study at school and college, and the social festivities which he shunned himself made large demands on their time and strength. Each summer he gave them a splendid holiday, and added tenfold to their happiness by setting aside for a time much of his own work, and entering fully into their enjoyment. His plan was himself to visit the chosen place early in the summer, and look for apartments in a house well up on a hill, and affording airy accommodation, often sharing the house with friends. When settled there, he was great on expeditions, wishing his party to see all that was worth seeing while in the neighbourhood. His knock at the bedroom doors, and summons, ' Expedition morning,' were a frequent incentive to early rising. He never enjoyed being in a rowing-boat, and had a nervous dread of anything like a precipice, but everywhere else was a delightful companion.

During 1872 the lecture round was not less important than the previous year. At the Midland Institute he gave two lectures on John Milton ; but he managed to shift his ladies' classes to the Friday, and so return home for the Sundays. Halifax, Liverpool (the Philharmonic Hall), and Manchester (the Athenæum) were new centres for lecturing.

We shall better realize what it was that he was doing during these years if we note how his lecturing influenced some of his students. Mr. Leonard Montefiore, whose early death will be remembered with sorrow, writes to him on June 25, 1872, a letter of warm appreciation :

I cannot tell you how grateful I am for your sympathy for the best I have tried to do, and the interest you have taken in me ; and I must thank you once more for all that I have learned from your lectures—something besides English literature, for your teaching is better than any sermons. The letter which you have written to me, and the notes of your lectures which I have, I shall keep and read and prize as long as I live.

Dr. H. Bond, now of Trinity Hall, Cambridge, was a lively young student of University College at this time, and he writes to me :

The memory of his lectures is by far the most pleasant association I have with the college. I was disgracefully idle in those days, and his lectures were the only ones I attended regularly and thoroughly enjoyed. He had in a remarkable measure the chief excellence of a good lecturer—the power of making his hearers as much interested in the subject as he was himself, and of driving them to the books he talked about by his enthusiasm for authors of the most widely differing aims and styles. His sympathy with everything which could show any claim to the name of literature was a great lesson to those whom youth and ignorance would naturally have driven into narrowness and partisanship.

He must have exercised a great influence for good by the simple kindliness and humanity of his criticism of life and literature. Looking back at it all now, I can see what a difference it might have made to hundreds of students—full as we were of the elements out of which prigs are made—if, instead of hearing Henry Morley, we had listened to a more academic lecturer with possibly a finer sense for finish of workmanship, but without his sympathy. I did not intend to write all this, for it is just what every one who ever heard him lecture would see at once; but I have always felt grateful to him, and have wished that I had known him personally.

Most valuable, too, is the following contribution from Miss Elsie Day, mistress of Grey Coat School, Westminster. We have seen the interest he took in women's higher education, and have still to learn much more of the efforts he made on its behalf. We may take what Miss Day says as representing the feeling of a very large circle of students.*

Grey Coat Hospital,
Westminster,
June 29, 1896.

DEAR MR. SOLLY,
        I understand that you are writing a memoir of my dear old friend and master, Professor Henry Morley. May I, as an old student, send you a few notes of the impression he made upon his pupils? I first joined what he called his ' Maidens' Class ' in October, 1872. The authorities at University College did not recognise us as students of theirs; we were somehow smuggled in under the wing of a Ladies' Educational Association. Some of the professors looked a little askance at us —we were to be dreaded as an unknown and irregular body—

---

* In 1875 a handsome three-handled ' loving-cup ' was presented to him, bearing this inscription : ' To Professor Henry Morley, from the ladies of his evening class, with hearty thanks for his kind help. University College, London, June, 1875.'

but Professor Morley neither doubted nor hesitated ; he gave us a hearty welcome, and helped us to the uttermost.

Looking back nearly a quarter of a century, I can recall with perfect clearness the delight his lectures gave me. His strong personality made the 'professor' be lost in the intensely living 'man.' His love of all that was strong and pure and good was always present with us. The very first impression he gave me was not that he was 'over' his class, but in it, working 'alongside' of it, and heartily enjoying it, as we did. Tired he must often have been when he came to lecture, but he never let us feel that we wearied him. He was always ready to help, willing to be questioned, glad to praise if we gave him the opportunity.

His old students would all support me in saying that his persistent determination to find something good to say of every one of whom he spoke was a very marked characteristic of his teaching. Even of so unsavoury a person as Mrs. Aphra Behn he contrived to say some words of deserved praise, bidding us remember her as one of the first to protest against slave traffic. Except in cases of downright meanness or cruelty, he seemed incapable of severity in judgment ; not that he called black white, but if, as almost always the case, white was mixed with the black, it was to the white that our attention was directed. The type of mind to which he dealt the hardest measure was that which found its rest in dogma, not realizing that truth has many varying aspects, and that 'God fulfils Himself in many ways.' Yet even here I can remember his fear lest anything he might say should cause pain to some 'Sisters' who at one time attended the lectures. Several phrases I can remember his often repeating to us ; one from Quarles he delighted in : 'If a man would see the light of the sun, let him first put out his own candle ;' and in Sir Thomas Browne's last sentence in the 'Religio Medici': 'Dispose of me according to the wisdom of Thy pleasure—Thy will be done, though in my own undoing.' Certain passages in Bacon's Essays always recall to me his voice and face, most of all, now, that in which Bacon declares 'the *Nunc Dimittis* the sweetest of the canticles.' An introductory lecture on Henry VIII. made a lasting impression on many of us. Speaking of the play as a series of falls of great men, of turns of Fortune's wheel, he suddenly paused, and said very quietly :

'And yet were they falls, when they roused in these men the Diviner hope? Is it not a series of illustrations of the words in the Psalm, "Man walketh in a vain shadow, and disquieteth himself in vain; he heapeth up riches, and cannot tell who shall gather them. And now, Lord, what is my hope? Truly my hope is even in Thee"?'

Very soon after I joined the classes the Professor invited me to make my way to Upper Park Road some Sunday afternoon. The hearty simple kindliness I met with there—from him and from his dear wife—is one of my most cherished recollections; their devotion to each other, and the restful sense of 'home,' gave such an atmosphere of peace to the house.

Another marked characteristic of our friend was his love of serving. Instances came at various times to my knowledge of his giving painstaking continuous help. I do not mean the help that is, a mere matter of writing a cheque, but of work done at the expense of personal and inconvenient service.

When he left college for his well-earned rest at Carisbrooke, his old students gathered round him to say 'good-bye.' Professor Arber spoke as the representative of the men who had worked under him, and it was my privilege (I believe by Mrs. Morley's wish) to speak for the women. I said then that during all the years that I had known him he had constantly reminded me of the famous saying of St. Francis de Sales, 'You will catch more flies with a spoonful of honey than with a gallon of vinegar.' He won people into goodness by being so good to them, and so entirely believing that with all their failings they somehow meant to be good. Divinity, of course, was outside the scope of his lectures, but whatever was his subject he never failed to impress us with an absolute sense of his living faith, and his overflowing love to God and man. As Bede says of St. Aidan, so may we say of him, 'He lived none other than he taught.'

In January, 1874, he began lecturing at Reading at Miss Buckland's School for Girls. This was his first engagement of the kind in the neighbourhood of London, and was an important beginning, for it was work which grew rapidly on his hands, and enabled him to fill up all available time profitably without the necessity for long railway journeys. Miss Buckland writes to me:

It is indeed a great pleasure to me to speak to you of Professor Henry Morley, and of his work in connection with our school. He began to lecture for us in January, 1874, and gave two courses of lectures in every year for more than twelve years. I had thus the opportunity of hearing him give about 250 lectures, in which were included every period of English literature, with special treatment of the principal writers and their chief works.

In dealing with the history of literature, he sought to show how the good seed sown in one period brought forth fruit in the next, and at all times he was as full of hope for the future of English literature as of love and reverence for its past. In the treatment of special works, Professor Morley was a faithful *interpreter*, rather than a critic; his great aim was to reveal to his hearers the inner thought which was the soul of the work, and so to open their eyes to the perception of the ideal, that seeing ' the highest,' they might ' love it,' and aspire towards it ; but at the same time he always kept in view that aspiration could only lead to the ideal through duty.

In his estimate of literary work Professor Morley constantly taught that the merely artistic treatment of an unworthy subject gave the work no claim to a place in the higher ranks of literature. His intense love of moral beauty, and his quick sympathy with humanity in every phase of feeling, enabled him to make the teaching of literature one of the most important and fruitful subjects of education. It may have seemed to some people almost a waste of his distinguished scholarship and talents to be introducing our great writers to school-girls, but Professor Morley's work can never be justly estimated by the immediate help it gave in understanding and appreciating English literature, great and valuable as this was ; the whole results of his teaching require a much larger summing up than this ; and I can speak from the close personal knowledge I had of its influence over my own pupils, who were residing with me, during the twelve years he was their teacher. It was, I believe, for many of them as the seed-time of their spring, and is now ' bringing forth fruit in happy lives of love and duty. His influence in the cultivation of the imagination was to create a taste for everything that was pure, simple, and sweet, without affectation or exaggeration; he awakened feeling that was truthful and healthy, free from every touch of

sentimentality or morbidness.   Whilst calling forth admiration
for the older ideal of womanhood in its devotion, tenderness,
and home affections, he recognised the claim on women for
wider sympathies, and their power for receiving a higher and
more intellectual culture.

Among his University College students was Charles E.
Moyse, now Professor of English at the University of
Montreal, Canada.   He also writes to me some valuable
recollections :

October 25, 1896.

Dear Sir,
        You ask me to write something about Henry Morley,
and I do so with pleasure.

In my college days Henry Morley took possession of me
entirely.   I came to him fairly well read in English poetry,
and with very definite ideas as to what I liked—a fair specimen
of a youth of eighteen who had been straying in modern literature
without guidance or illumination.   The classical languages were
my favourites, and I had resolved to devote most of my time
to them, but my intentions began to change as soon as I was
brought under his influence.   The result was that during the
five years of my stay at University College (1869-1874) I
attended, I think, every course which Henry Morley delivered.
To me he seemed an apostle then, and in many ways he seems
so still.

I see now that his mind was largely of the Teutonic order.
He was never rhetorical, and anything like academic pyro-
technics was to him both an impossibility and an abomination.
Eloquence, even in the popular sense of the term, he did not
possess.   He spoke slowly, and sometimes with deliberation
that bordered on hesitancy ; but this was in some measure due
no doubt to the requirements of the class-room.   With that
eloquence which is not so much heard as felt, he was greatly
gifted.   When, leaving biographical fact, he had to disclose the
real intent, or, as he was fond of calling it, the inner spirit of
a book, his words, earnestly uttered, seemed to lay bare the
very impulse of the writer.   Earnestness, which might be
defined as massive rather than impetuous, lay at the root of
his character, and made him so potent an influence on young
minds.   This essentially Teutonic quality of massive earnest-

ness stands out to me now as one of the most prominent things in Henry Morley. His strong sense of what I might call the moral purpose of good literature was Teutonic likewise. Here was seen his great strength, and, in certain cases, his weakness. Form was to him a secondary matter, and while he did not overlook finish, his eye preferred to dwell on something didactic. Literature in the truest sense, he would often say, is not written to amuse, but to elevate—' to find out the right and to do it, the wrong and to undo it,' has been the aim of our English writers from the first. We are accused of preaching on any and every thing. Our accusers are right; it is our characteristic, and we do it well. Life is not a jest or a long guffaw, any more than a dinner is whipped syllabub. Whipped syllabub is very nice in its own little place, but a man who professes to live on it, lives neither wisely nor well. Views like these naturally made Henry Morley regard himself as an interpreter of literature, and not as a critic in the ordinary meaning of the term. And when he had to deal with writers of temperament similar to his own, his power of interpretation was marvellous. First interpret, then criticise, he would often say. He passed over the average critic with just a word. ' The critic is the little man who climbs on to the big man's shoulders, and waves his cap to the people.' The sentiment expresses a feeling which was not really unkindly. I remember asking him once if he had read a certain review of Tennyson's ' In Memoriam.' ' No, I have not,' he replied; ' why should I ? If ' In Memoriam ' were unknown to me, I should read it for myself; but I think I know it as well as, and even better than, the reviewer. Life is too short to be wasted in scampering over magazine articles in the attempt to find novelties.' I asked him if there were not critics *and* critics. ' Certainly,' he replied, ' but those whose duty it is to look after the streets of literature should be properly trained, and should know weeds when they see them. The average reviewer knows everything, and hence his readers know little or nothing. Keep your reviews chiefly on the shelf: take your books, and use your brains.' Some of Morley's criticisms were little paragraphs of interpretation. He would trace the way through such works as ' Utopia' or ' Hamlet' or ' Maud' or ' Christmas Eve ' and ' Easter Day ' with unerring instinct, and you could not help feeling that he was mainly right. Of course, all the world knows how he divided up his

19

subject. The comparative view of literature as he presented
it, and it was never so clearly presented before, threw a flood
of light on the development of English thought. His students
often heard more about Italy and France than about England.
The English are a part of Europe in their literature, but they
have generally the national mark to show. So he said, time
and again.

His biographical matter I found, on the whole, apposite. It
was oftened lightened by little personal incidents which prevented it from becoming dreary. Scores of such come floating
before me now. I can never think of Selden without remembering that he used to scribble on bits of paper while the barber
was cutting his hair. As Henry Morley grew older, and his
biographical material accumulated, he seemed to attach more
importance to the biography of an author than is visible in his
earlier professional work. A man lives in his time; first of
all, then, let us examine the time, and then speak of the man.
When I am told that a genius is altogether independent of his
age, I ask for facts, and the facts mostly lean the other way.
Richard Rolle of Hampole is one person, and William Godwin
another. To know *them* you must know their times.

Fun he thoroughly enjoyed. One thing struck me in my
early student days—his appreciation of humour and his detection of it. For instance, he brought out Carlyle's humorous
flashes—imbedded often in the very heart of a grave paragraph
—as but few men could do.

Henry Morley is not by any means confined to his books. I
have detected pilferings from him, time and again, without the
slightest trace of acknowledgment; in fact, some of the commonplaces of our teaching look back to him as their discoverer. If
they were discovered before, I am not aware of it. The details
are often old enough, but they stood in isolation, and he first
brought them together and made them instinct with light and
meaning. You have doubtless heard from Arber, and Arber
has doubtless told you that Morley was of professors, the world
over, *facile princeps*. That is indeed saying much ; but when I
regard the man in every light, I find myself saying the same
thing. Henry Morley is not confined to his books, as I said
a moment ago. He lives on in the lives of hundreds of pupils
who venerate his name.

Of our more private and personal intercourse I ought not,

perhaps, to speak, as it is beside the purpose for which I write. But I cannot close this letter—put together, I fear, in a very disjointed way on the spur of the moment—without alluding to our meeting, when I was in doubt as to my ability to fill the post I now occupy. One evening in May I went to his house at Hampstead, feeling perplexed and impotent. I had been working in schools for some three years, and now there was a chance of my getting a chair in English in a distant colony. Should I go? Morley must decide, I thought, and so I turned Hampsteadwards through Regent's Park, which looked, I fancied, more beautiful than I had ever seen it. ' Come down into the den, Moyse, and tell me all about it.' I told him a hundred things. He walked up and down the room for a minute or two, and then turned to me and said : ' Moyse, you can do it ; go, and my blessing goes with you.'

With reference to what is here said about Henry Morley detecting Carlyle's humour, I well recollect his annoyance at Froude's incapacity to detect it. One instance was when Froude reproaches Carlyle with want of feeling for telling his wife that all would be well if she would keep her mouth shut. Professor Morley said that the Carlyles had had a joke between them about somebody's theory which represented evil influences as flying down the throat and being baffled by a shut mouth. Carlyle's remark was a humorous allusion to this joke intended to help his wife keep up her hope and spirits.

An important series of annual lectures began in 1874 at the London Institution. We have seen that he was not satisfied with his public lectures at Newcastle. This meant taking greater pains to do the thing as well as possible next time. The King Arthur lectures given shortly afterwards at Birmingham were a brilliant success, and led to a long series of engagements there. At the London Institution a first idea of beginning with Chaucer was rejected in favour of a more popular subject, and he gave five lectures from April 8 to May 13, on 'English Poets of the Nineteenth Century.' This course left his audience ' asking for more.' In 1875, May 13, 20, and 27

19—2

are the dates of three lectures on 'The Inner Thought
of Shakespeare's Plays.' After this, his lectures there
had to be confined to one or two evenings early in January
before college term began. They are—1876, January 3:
'The Study of English Literature'; 1877, January 4
and 11: 'The History of the English Novel'; 1878,
January 10 and 17: 'English Novelists of the Nineteenth
Century'; 1879, January 2 and 9: 'The English Stage
as it has been' and 'as it is'; 1880, January 1: 'The
Future of the English Stage'; 1881, January 6: 'Our
Living Dramatists'; 1882, January 5: 'The Essay in the
Nineteenth Century.' The librarian at the London Insti-
tution all these years was Mr. Edward W. B. Nicholson,
now of the Bodleian Library, Oxford. He writes to me:

Professor Morley was one of the best lecturers I ever heard,
always interesting in matter, always charming in manner. A
lecture by him at the London Institution was sure of a large
audience, and the pleasure with which they heard him may be
gauged by the fact that when he was unable to cram all he
wanted to say into the usual hour, they always let him see that
he might go on. At last he and we took it as a matter of
course, I think, that his lectures would considerably exceed the
time, and on one occasion he beat all previous records, to the
delight, I believe, of everyone present, by lecturing for two
hours and two minutes.

Another incident from 1874 must be recorded. It
occurred on September 4, 'Death of Boddles.' Boddles
was a cat, I may say *the* cat long and honourably connected with No. 8, Upper Park Road. Rarely did the
Professor write to any member of the domestic circle
without mentioning the state of his health and the tenor
of his ways. The letters to Whitby (1867) and those to
Stuttgart (1870) contain many particulars. And during
all these years neighbours could tell how the Professor's
step was heard crunching the gravel of the garden-path at
midnight, while his voice uttered in alluring tones the
persevering cry, 'Bod, Bod, Bod!' as he sought night

after night to induce this animal to sleep at home. Boddles was buried in the garden; a handsome tombstone marks the spot, and bears the inscription:

REQUIES
CAT.

While they were at Sandown this year they made the acquaintance of Mr. C. L. Dodgson (Lewis Carroll). The Professor's youngest daughter was a small child, fond of digging in the sand, and he one day received a very pretty picture of her, drawn by Mr. Dodgson, and sent 'with apologies for infringing the author's copyright.' The child and the artist after this became for a while close allies, and he soon sent her a present of 'Alice in Wonderland.' But it is well known that his interest in the fair sex did not survive their entrance into their teens, and this particular friendship proved no exception. Professor Morley much admired ' Alice,' and sent its author a copy of his own fairy tales containing, Mr. Dodgson writes, ' an inscription so complimentary that I am almost shy of leaving it about.'

On May 27 and June 3 and 10, 1876, he gave his first lectures at the Royal Institution, Albemarle Street. He chose the same subject as had been so much liked at Birmingham, and spoke on ' King Arthur's Place in English Literature.' This was succeeded year after year by the following courses, generally delivered on Saturday afternoons in May and June, and very numerously attended:

1877—February 24; March 3, 10, 17, 24: Effects of the French Revolution on English Literature.
1878—May 4, 11, 18, 25; June 8, 15: Richard Steele. (The lectures on June 8 and 15 were on Joseph Addison.)
1879—May 24, 31; June 7: On Swift.
1880—May 8, 15, 22, 29; June 5: The Dramatists before Shakespeare, from the Origin of the English Drama to the Year of Death of Marlowe, 1593.
1881—April 30; May 7, 14; June 7: Scotland's Part in English Literature. (June 7 was on Thomas Carlyle.)
1884—January 19, 26; February 2, 9, 16, 23: Life and Literature under Charles I.

Mr. Henry Young, the assistant-secretary, writes : ' It was my privilege to be present at the last three courses given here by Professor Morley, and I have a pleasant remembrance of the genial and interesting way in which they were delivered.' They were lectures for which he made careful preparation, though given in his usual easy style. Had he lived to complete ' English Writers,' all his accumulated store of information concerning our literature in these later centuries would have there found its place; and would have added immensely to the popularity of the volumes ; but he left no notes of use to anyone save himself, and his ' winged words ' are flown.

On July 1, 1877, James Knowles wrote to him about a scheme for a recent literature department in the *Nineteenth Century*, and was anxious that he should begin it in the August number. Professor Morley complied with this request, and sent an introductory article expressing the main thoughts which he had developed in his recent course of lectures at the Royal Institution on ' Effects of the French Revolution upon English Literature.' Here, therefore, we have the argument of this set of lectures, and the article should be read by those who would understand his contribution to the interpretation of our nineteenth-century literature. He shows how in earlier centuries our English struggle was for liberty; how, with the new sense of freedom that dawned with the close of the last century, a new endeavour had arisen in the noblest minds ; and how Wordsworth had expressed the master-thought of the present century in the passage which contains the lines :

> ' What one is,
> Why may not millions be ?'

Freedom is for a purpose, and that purpose is the development of individual character, and this not only in selected specimens, but throughout the human race. He touches lightly on Byron, says more about Shelley and Keats, and then has something on Carlyle, Tennyson,

Browning, Dickens, Thackeray, Jane Austen, and George Eliot, showing how each contributed to the fulfilment of this same high purpose. He developed this thought in an address on Wordsworth given to the Liberal Social Union on October 25.

The next two articles are in the *Nineteenth Century* for November, 1877, and for February, 1878.

The fourth and last of these articles appeared in September, 1878. This deals with dramatic literature, a subject which he had made to an exceptional degree his own, and there was special interest in it at the time because of Tennyson's recent production of 'Queen Mary' and 'Harold,' and the attempt which Henry Irving had made to produce 'Queen Mary,' or, rather, certain scenes from the play, at the Lyceum Theatre. Professor Morley greatly wished to see our best actors again performing plays written by our best living poets, and what he says in this article is interesting as criticism, and suggestive for any future endeavour in this direction. When 'The Cup' was produced at the Lyceum, he carefully studied its performance, and ascribed its comparative failure to the fact that the principal actor and actress, however good in their way, were not good in the way intended by the author. Irving should have been genial, even jovial, when allowed to do as he liked, and Ellen Terry should have uttered 'loud tones,' after the manner of Mrs. Siddons. But these two performers, with all their fine qualities, were physically incapable of representing the characters designed by Tennyson. Something like this was the criticism expressed by Professor Morley one day as we returned home from the theatre.

The four articles in the *Nineteenth Century* give us some of his maturest thoughts on recent writers, and they brought him into pleasant relations with Lewis Morris, who was glad to encounter so appreciative a critic and so able an interpreter. They also led, as we shall see later, to some pleasant personal intercourse with Tennyson; but they were written under heavy pressure of other work, and were at the start interfered with by an event which brought much sorrow into the closing months of 1877.

On September 19 his father wrote to him in good health and strength for a man on his eighty-fifth birthday, but a month later Joseph Morley writes from Midhurst to say that his father is very ill, and had resigned all appointments at the Apothecaries' Hall. Till then the old man, much valued at the Court meetings for his shrewd sense, as well as his geniality and courtesy, had regularly done his duties in the management of the institution. All his life he had taken deep interest in the society, and in 1871 had written to congratulate his son Henry on his election to the rank of Liveryman. The example set by the father was not without important influence on the son's last years of life. On Thursday and Friday, November 8 and 9, 1877, Professor Morley gave two lectures at the Philosophical Institute, Edinburgh, and Mrs. Morley accompanied him there. They saw some of the sights of the place, and visited Fred's grave. Dr. Hodgson asked a number of headmasters of schools and colleges to meet him at dinner on the Saturday; but worse tidings came from Midhurst, and instead of waiting for this congenial gathering, husband and wife started back together for London by a night train immediately after the second lecture, and as early as possible on the Saturday he was with his father. After this for many weeks he regularly went to Midhurst every Saturday, returning Sunday night looking very gray and haggard. His father's illness was gout, which had long been kept at bay by most careful rules of living. Now the attacks were agonizing; each seemed as though it must be his last, but his constitution was still vigorous at eighty-five, and he did not find rest until the very end of the year. The funeral was at Midhurst on January 3, 1878. His daughter Mary writes of the comfort which his son's visits were to him, and very faithfully they were paid. But the strain was great, for it is hard to see the sufferings of one we love, and be able to do but little to relieve them; and Henry Morley's heart was full of love and gratitude to the father who had done everything for him in early days, and who stood by him even when his own hopes were disappointed, and much labour and sacrifice seemed thrown away.

After the spring of 1878, we reach the period when he gave up his regular provincial lecturing. The University Extension Movement in the Northern towns was by this time firmly established, and many able lecturers had been trained for the work. So, except for special occasions, he confined his speaking to the neighbourhood of London. As far as travelling was concerned, this meant a great relief, as may be judged from the following memorandum. It is not dated, and may belong to any year between 1873 and 1877.

> Wednesday.—To Hitchin 1.10: On with Wordsworth, Byron, Montgomery, and Campbell. Leave 5.16; leave Peterborough 7.12, Darlington 11.33.
> Thursday.—Darlington 12: John Locke's Philosophy. Leave 1.40, Redcar 2.40; or leave 2.40, Redcar 4.40. Redcar 6.30: Later Elizabethan Dramatists—Dekker, Chapman, Marston, etc. Leave Redcar 8, Stockton 8.45: Shakespeare's Comedies, Merchant of Venice.
> Friday.—Leave Stockton 6.30. York: Dryden; Defoe's Early Writings. Leave York, London and N.W., 12.40, viâ Leeds; Liverpool 4.15. Lecture New Brighton 8: Ideal Commonwealths. Leave Lime Street 11 p.m., Birmingham 2.30.
> Saturday.—Leave Birmingham 7.30. Reading carriage slipped 9.30. Lecture 11: Jeremy Taylor. Leave Reading 12.45, Moorgate Street 2.20, Fenchurch Street 3.10, Leytonstone 3.45: Richardson, Fielding, and Smollett.

He once had a narrow escape of his life when the floor of the railway carriage came out while the train was travelling at a considerable speed, and he had to mount the seat and hold on by the hat-rail till they came to the next station. On another occasion he had for a companion an old gentleman who had been trying to make himself more comfortable with the aid of a somewhat deflated air-cushion. Professor Morley was going to blow it up for him; but his action was arrested by the exclamation, 'Stop, sir, stop! that cushion contains my deceased wife's breath!'

During these years (1865-1878) Professor Morley enjoyed splendid health. There was, however, one exception. He was very liable to take bad colds, which were generally accompanied with splitting headache; but he never allowed this to be a reason for breaking an engagement, though there were times when it was as painful to his audience to listen as it was for him to speak. He was able to make an effort of will which carried him through such seasons at no small cost.

For two or three sessions he had 'students' evenings' at his own house, which were greatly valued. After his week-day evenings became so fully engaged as to render the continuance of the original plan impossible, he and Mrs. Morley made their Sunday evenings for thirty years a very happy time to the large number of students and others who were invited thus to share their bright and simple home-life.

Three or four months each year were comparatively free from lecturing, and then the time was devoted to writing. In 1868 he edited for Routledge Addison's *Spectator*. It was, as he says, 'a long job,' and the small type tried his eyes. After this he had to use glasses, never needed before. But it became at once the standard edition, 'as, apart from its notes, the only one for the last 180 years that is not full of blunders in the text.' He had an article in the *Edinburgh Review* and several in the *Fortnightly*. He also wrote for a short while for the *Saturday Review*, but not approving its treatment of some of the books it noticed, he ceased sending contributions.

The first part of his own 'Tables of English Literature' appeared this year. These are a series of charts ruled horizontally to show years, while vertical lines represent the lives of authors, with the titles of their works inserted in the year of publication, different colours being used to give greater clearness. The 'Tables' were produced by lithography by Chapman and Hall, and sold well, but have been for many years out of print. The firm in whose hands Professor Morley wished to place the series doubted if it would sell by tens of thousands, and he did not care to give it to other publishers who asked for it. So the matter remains, much to the regret of students who are still inquiring for these 'Tables.'

Another work undertaken in 1868 led to unexpected consequences.

Sampson Low and Co. were then publishing, and Mr. Hain Friswell was editing, the 'Bayard Editions,' a well-printed series of pleasure-books, and Professor Morley was asked to undertake one entitled 'The King and the Commons: Cavalier and Puritan Songs.' He carried out this engagement with his usual thoroughness, and by so doing made a discovery which he thus announced in a letter to the *Times*, July 15, 1868:

University College, London,
July 14.

SIR,

As the discovery of an unpublished poem by Milton is matter of interest to all readers, and the authenticity of such a poem cannot be too strictly and generally tested, I shall be obliged if you will give publicity to the fact that such a poem has been a found. It exists in the handwriting of Milton himself, on a blank page in the volume of 'Poems both English and Latin,' which contains his 'Comus,' 'Lycidas,' 'L'Allegro,' and 'Il Penseroso.' It is signed with his initials, and dated October, 1647. It was discovered in this manner: I had undertaken to contribute a small pleasure-book of literature to a cheap popular series, and in forming such a volume from the writings of the poets who lived in the time of Charles I. and the Commonwealth, where I did not myself possess original editions of their works to quote from, I looked for them in the reading-room of the British Museum. Fortunately, it did not seem to me useless to read a proof containing passages from Milton with help of the original edition of his English and Latin poems published in 1645. There are two copies of that book in the Museum—one in the General Library, which would be the edition commonly consulted, and the other in the noble collection formed by George III., known as the King's Library, which was the copy I referred to. The volume contains first the English, then the Latin, poems of that first period of Milton's life, each separately paged. The Latin poems end on page 87, leaving the reverse of the leaf blank; and this blank I found covered with handwriting, which, to anyone familiar with the collection of facsimiles in the late Mr. Sotheby's ' Ramblings in Elucidation of the Autograph of Milton,' would, I think, convey at first glance the impression it conveyed to me, that this was the handwriting of John Milton.

It proved to be a transcript of a poem in fifty-four lines, which Milton, either for himself or for some friend, had added to this volume. It is entitled simply ' An Epitaph,' and signed by him ' J. M., 1 Ober, 1647.' He was then in his thirty-ninth year. As the page is about the size of a leaf of notepaper, the handwriting is small. Thirty-six lines were first written, which filled the left-hand side of the page, then a line was lightly drawn to the right of them, and, the book being turned sideways, the rest of the poem was packed into three little columns, and the other two lines at the top of the third column, followed by the initials and date. Upon the small blank space left in this corner of the page the Museum stamp is affixed, covering a part of Milton's signature.

The book is in the one place in the world where it is most accessible to the scrutiny of experts, and inquiry will no doubt be made into its history. Its press mark is 238 h. 35 in the King's Library. The poem, I think, speaks for itself. I need hardly add that the following copy of it has the MS. contractions expanded and the spelling modernized; but it should be stated that the word here printed ' chest,' as the rhyme shows it was meant to be pronounced, was written ' cist,' and that the last three syllables of the last line but two, though close to the edge of the binding, and almost effaced by the sticking to them of some paper from the cover, are consistent, in the few marks that are visible, with the reading here conjectured and placed within brackets.

I am, sir,

Your obedient servant,

HENRY MORLEY.

AN EPITAPH.

He whom Heaven did call away
Out of this hermitage of clay
Has left some reliques in this urn
As a pledge of his return.

Meanwhile, the Muses do deplore
The loss of this their paramour,
With whom he sported ere the day
Budded forth its tender ray.
And now Apollo leaves his lays,
And puts on cypress for his bays ;
The sacred sisters tune their quills
Only to the blubbering rills,
And while his doom they think upon
Make their own tears their Helicon,
Leaving the two-topt mount divine
To turn votaries to his shrine.

Think not, reader, me less blest,
Sleeping in this narrow chest,
Than if my ashes did lie hid
Under some stately pyramid.
If a rich tomb makes happy, then
That bee was happier far than men,
Who, busy in the thymy wood,
Was fettered by the golden flood
Which from the amber-weeping tree
Distilleth down so plenteously :
For so this little wanton elf
Most gloriously enshrined itself.
A tomb whose beauty might compare
With Cleopatra's sepulchre.

In this little bed my dust
Incurtained round I here intrust,
While my more pure and nobler part
Lies entomb'd in every heart.

Then pass on gently, ye that mourn,
Touch not this mine hollowed urn.
These ashes which do here remain,
A vital tincture still retain ;
A seminal form within the deeps
Of this little chaos sleeps ;
The thread of life untwisted is
Into its first consistencies ;
Infant nature cradled here
In its principles appear ;
This plant, thus calcined into dust,
In its ashes rest it must,
Until sweet Psyche shall inspire
A softening and prolific fire,
And in her fostering arms enfold
This heavy and this earthly mould.
Then as I am I'll be no more,
But bloom and blossom [as] b[efore]
When this cold numbness shall retreat
By a more than chymick heat.

J. M., 1 Ober, 1647.*

This letter started a discussion which ran through the
principal daily and weekly papers during the next few
weeks, and also overwhelmed Professor Morley with
private correspondence. Dean Stanley, Sir J. Eardley
Wilmot, and many others, besides writing to the *Times*,
send him questions and suggestions. Lord Winchilsea
contemptuously scouted the notion that the poem could be
Milton's, and called forth numerous rejoinders from critics
who in turn discovered his lordship's mistakes and weak
points. A more formidable opponent was Mr. W. B. Rye,
Assistant-Keeper of the Department of Printed Books,

* In the words 'thus calcined' and 'prolific,' I have given
the reading finally adopted.

British Museum, who wrote to the *Times*, July 17, to say that the signature was ' P. M.,' not ' J. M.,' and that the handwriting was not Milton's. He adds that in this opinion he was confirmed by Mr. Bond, the Keeper of the Department of MSS. Professor Masson, too, appeared on the scene, stating that he had known of the existence of this poem, and had copied it two years previously. In doing this he had rejected a suspicion that it might be Milton's; it was not likely, therefore, that he would now accept this authorship. Professor Morley has another letter in the *Times* of July 20, dealing chiefly with the question of handwriting and signature, the doubtful ' J.' being nearly obliterated by the Museum stamp.

After this the controversy continued. Professor Masson wrote again more emphatically adverse; Professor Brewer concurred with him; W. V. H. (Sir William Harcourt), A. de Morgan, and Gerald Massey took the same side. Sir J. Eardley Wilmot, Hepworth Dixon, Hain Friswell, etc., supported the authenticity. The comic papers revelled in the sport. On July 27 Professor Morley replies in a letter to the *Times*, which is an admirable specimen of learned and courteous argument.

He has another long and able letter in the *Times* of August 4. Finally a facsimile of the poem was published in ' The King and the Commons,' with an introduction in which Professor Morley summed up the discussion and gave his own judgment. Much of this introduction is the same as the letter to the *Times* of July 27, but the follow-ing paragraph is additional explanation :

The suggestion of revival from the dust, with which the poem closes, is directly taken from the old doctrine of Palin-genesis, by which, says Isaac Disraeli, in his chapter on 'Dreams at the Dawn of Philosophy,' ' Schott, Kircher, Gaffarel, Borelli, Digby, and the whole of that admirable school, discovered in the ashes of plants their primitive forms, which were again raised up by the force of heat.

. . . The process of Palingenesis, this picture of immortality, is described. These philosophers, having burnt a flower by calcination, disengaged the salts from its ashes, and deposited them in a glass phial; a chemical mixture acted on it. . . . This dust, thus excited by heat, shoots upward into its primitive forms.' As the heat passes away the form fades. Hence the allusion to the 'more than chymick heat' that shall produce the last great Palingenesis of man.

He did not, however, convert Professor Masson, whose lifelong study of Milton gave him some right to pronounce the final verdict.

In 1868 we also find Professor Morley giving private lessons to Hindoo students, and helping one of them out of a serious difficulty, connected with the limit of age, in which he was involved with the India Office.

This August is also memorable in another way. A favourite book at Upper Park Road had long been Mr. Ballantyne's 'Gorilla' book, in which 'three of his heroes, being now advanced from boyhood to whiskerhood, go off to Africa to see the gorilla, or to prove him a myth.' So the learned Professor and his two sons started off to try and find the gorilla in the New Forest. This they failed to do, but they found a name for themselves which stuck, and henceforth these three Morleys on a tramp were always known as the Three Gorillas—the name indicating their farewell to the usages of civilization—and some lively letters were written home recounting their adventures. They aimed at walking round the English coast, taking different sections in successive years, and accomplished several tours in the Southern counties, the Professor always carrying the bulk of the luggage in his Gladstone bag.

1870 was the year of the first election of the London School Board. Professor Morley went to support the candidature of Mrs. Garrett Anderson at a meeting which proved to be of a very rowdy character. Several distinguished gentlemen failed to get a hearing, and had to sit down; but when Professor Morley rose he was greeted with loud shouts of ' John Bull! John Bull! We'll hear him.' And hear him they did.

About the end of 1870 ' Clement Marot ' was published. It deals with another life from the sixteenth century, but is less of a biography and more of a study of literature than his previous books dealing with the same period. The second volume contains a lecture which he gave at Dublin in 1867 on ' The Influence of the Celt in English Literature.' He highly valued the influence of the quick Celtic imagination on the solid Saxon mind, and more than once attended meetings of the Celtic Society in London. Ireland in turn was grateful for the notice of her authors in ' English Writers.'

In 1873 he published his ' First Sketch of English Literature.' This has been the most widely read of all his books, its circulation being now between 30,000 and 40,000, and it may safely be described as the only original work which paid him financially for the labour put into it. In the preface he expresses his conviction that the political and social history of England should be studied along with any chosen period of its literature, while direct acquaintance should be made with one or two of the best books of that period. ' Whatever examples may be chosen should be complete pieces, however short, not extracts, for we must learn from the first to recognise the unity of a true work of genius.'

In 1875 he began issuing his ' Library of English Literature.' The Introduction expresses much of his maturest judgment respecting our literature, and in the five handsome, well illustrated volumes he was able to give abundant examples of the works, both prose and poetry, which he wanted students to read. The series proved popular, more than 20,000 copies having been sold.

In December, 1875, Mrs. Sayer died at Carisbrooke.

Her last years were spent in chronic ill-health, which prevented her even walking across a room; but there were remains of the old spirit to the last, only now this never failed to include the warmest appreciation of her son-in-law, whose early prophecy that he would become a favourite with her had been thoroughly fulfilled.

In 1876 he lost a dearly valued friend, for on February 1 John Forster died. Some years later the authorities at the South Kensington Museum asked Forster's literary executor to write a biographical sketch of him for the Handbook to the Dyce and Forster Collections. This was delayed for a year and a half, and then Professor Morley was asked if he would write it at once. He undertook the task as a tribute of gratitude and affection, and early in 1880, amid great pressure from other work, completed a very beautiful and most appreciative little memoir. He says in a letter:

Now, I hope that nobody who reads my little sketch of the story of his life in the Museum handbook will use his gift without a little love and respect for his memory.

CHAPTER XIV.

UNIVERSITY COLLEGE, 1878—1882.

THE year 1878 is a good point to begin a new chapter in the account of Professor Morley's life. He now gave up most of his provincial lecturing, and redoubled his activity in London. In the letter to the *Oxford University Extension Gazette* already quoted,* he describes the ten years during which University College gradually prepared the way to open all its classes, except those in the medical faculty, to women as to men. On March 4, 1878, the University of London received its supplemental charter enabling it to confer degrees on women. A committee at University College promptly considered the situation, and on May 25 presented a report, drafted by Professor Morley. This document could speak of the extent to which male students had become accustomed to the presence of women in the college, and to work with them as fellow-students in some of the classes. There was now also a considerable body of women accustomed to look to the college as a place for their education. It was, therefore, proposed that the London Ladies' Educational Association† should be considered to have done its work, and asked to transfer its whole interest in these classes to

* Pp. 263-266.
† The name of Mr. J. H. Mylne deserves to be remembered as its devoted honorary secretary.

the college; that the classes hitherto held for the association be held in future as college classes, strengthened and
supplemented where necessary, so that the full curriculum
necessary for a liberal education with such special training
as might be required in preparing for graduation should
be offered at once to women as to men.

It was further proposed that this should be done not by
suddenly converting all classes into mixed classes, but by
the method hitherto followed of gradual experiment in
that direction; and that each professor should suggest
and explain what appeared to him in his own subject to
be the best method of securing full instruction both to
women and to men.

The first ' mixed' class allowed had been one on Post-
Biblical Hebrew, a subject which was thought incapable
of encouraging frivolity. I happen to have been one of
the students attending it, and can testify how successful
was the choice.

The report was adopted, and the new scheme introduced, women now becoming, in the full sense of the
term, students of the college. Thus was the final step
taken in one of the earliest and most important movements for the higher education of women.

In every stage of this movement Professor Morley had
taken an active share. He had a conviction that men
and women ought to be taught together, and might learn
together in a college precisely as they go together to
lectures in every place but a college. His was the moving
impulse of the whole advance, and his practical cautious
temper was its guiding spirit. He never troubled about
uniformity; he preferred to ' hasten slowly,' gradually
acquiring experience; and when in December, 1879,
Owens College, Manchester, had thoughts of following in
the footsteps of University College, London, and wrote for
information, a large amount of useful experience was
available for the benefit of the northern town. It was a

great pleasure to him to find how well the women passed their first matriculation examination in June, 1879.

In 1878 Professor Morley was appointed to the chair of English at Queen's College, Harley Street. He began lecturing to the ladies there in the autumn, and held the post for eleven years. In the *College Magazine* for June, 1894, Miss Evaline Shipley contributes some recollections of the time when she attended his lectures.

A Few Reminiscences of Professor Morley.

Among the many benefits connected with a broader scheme of education than can be obtained at home or in a small private school is one that can hardly be too highly appreciated by the students of Queen's College. It is the privilege of listening to and coming into contact with the men and women who are an influence upon their generation. Foremost among such, during the years in which I studied here, stood the revered figure of our dear Professor of English Language and Literature, Dr. Henry Morley, whose recent death has saddened so many hearts. It is difficult to express in a few words what has remained in my mind as a most striking personality. But there are two aspects of his character which were very dear to all his pupils.

To all who attended his lectures the sound of his name conjures up one of the brightest, most cheery of pictures; the sound of his footstep as he hastened (always a little late) up the stairs and along the landing towards No. II., the hearty greeting with which he entered the room, and the comical glance towards the clock, followed by some half-humorous, half-penitent explanation of the causes of his quite regular delay—all this remains stamped on my memory. And then the fun over our 'papers'! How invariably he kept them week after week, making at each lecture some fresh excuse (which was sure to make us laugh) for not having corrected and returned them, until at the end of the term we had the long-expected delight of seeing the Professor enter the room, clasping great bundles of papers—veritable armfuls!—to be distributed with many a little joke. It was this cheery kindliness that went straight to our hearts.

And then there was that other aspect of his nature which

exerted an equally lasting and possibly more helpful influence upon those who heard him—I mean his earnestness. It was this that carried us unwearied through the less interesting parts of his lectures (where interest was never wholly lacking); it was this that revealed itself most clearly in his treatment of the more serious parts of literature, when he seemed to enter within holy ground, encouraging us tremblingly to follow. And this earnestness displayed itself most clearly in his appreciation and love of all that is good; his face kindled, his voice deepened, his manner became almost reverent, as he drew our attention to some noble thought, or led us to contemplate some noble life, deepening in us a love of all that is good, and inspiring us to take, as our guiding principle in *all* our reading, St. Paul's words, 'Whatsoever things are true . . . honourable . . . just . . . pure . . . lovely . . . of good report . . . think on these things.'

From October, 1877, to October, 1879, Professor Morley was Dean of the Faculty of Arts at University College, and a 'working Dean' in a new sense, discharging, not only the old duties of the office, but many new ones as well, as a representative of the Professors. The ruling authority at the college is the Council, which is annually appointed by the Governors. The Senate is a body consisting of all the Professors, with a member of the Council as its chairman, and Committees of the Senate considered and reported on the qualifications of all applicants for vacant professorships, besides dealing with many other subjects of academic interest. Professor Morley was always a hard-working member of such committees, and his ready pen was frequently employed to draft the reports, especially after the death of Professor Malden; and now, while he was Dean, much of his time was taken up in this way and in conferences with committees of the Council. It was a period of active development at the college, and Professor Morley writes joyously about it to his son Forster, who was then at Bonn, studying chemistry.

Thus he says:

There's a good deal of activity at University College, London. Last year I embodied in a report Kennedy's aspirations for an engineering school, and suggested step by step work for the realization of a very big scheme. It was too late for consideration then; but this year the report was trotted out by the Council, printed for distribution among themselves, and adopted altogether, though it involves a spending of £300 or £350 to start with, but on the strength of the start it is expected that money will be got out of the great engineers. Part of this scheme is the development of a technical school, and that has advanced to the point of making Graham a full Professor, for next session, of chemical technology or something of that sort. Lodge also is just beginning to be worked in, and has taken a house in London on the strength of better prospects. Also the Council has accepted all our library reforms, and the college has now £400 a year for maintenance of its libraries. Last Saturday I had to get to town as soon as I could to meet a Committee of Council upon the Greek and German chairs!

Planning the time-table for all the College Lectures in Arts, so that they should interfere as little as possible with one another, was the occupation of an evening when he had a bad headache, and was not fit to go out and do anything else.

On July 9, 1878, Lord Granville laid the foundation stone of the extension of the North Wing, and there was a luncheon in a tent erected in the grounds in front of the college. In the autumn of 1828 University College had been opened as the University of London, so that in 1878 the college celebrated its Jubilee, and resolved to commemorate the occasion by a further extension of its premises.

The real anniversary was, however, the opening of the session 1878-79, and for this Professor Morley was asked to deliver the introductory address. He gave, on October 3, a full history of the college, going back to the first inception of the design by the poet Thomas Campbell, and explaining at considerable length the aims that were in the minds of the founders, and the spirit in which they endeavoured to provide London with a grand unsectarian University of its own at a time when Oxford and Cambridge were the exclusive property of the Established Church, and even Catholic Emancipation had not yet been granted. Step by step the full story of the early stages of the movement was exhibited; and then the tale was continued of the subsequent fortunes of the college and the hospital down to the year 1878, when it had reached a hitherto unexampled height of prosperity that called for a further extension of accommodation for its teaching.

The council were grateful for this splendid address, and passed a resolution of thanks, with many expressions of ' genuine good feeling and gratitude,' as Mr. Ely added in a letter conveying their resolution. They decided that the address should be printed and given away. This procedure, though convenient at the time, made the address subsequently difficult to procure, and Professor Morley therefore reprinted the substance of it, with sundry additions and corrections, in the *University College Gazette* for 1886-7.

This autumn Professor Morley's two sons went to Munich, Forster for chemistry, Robert for painting, and his letters to them are full of fatherly interest in the careers they have chosen. He also tells them much about his work. The following is the time-table of his classes for the new session. With the exception of going to Birmingham, he is wholly occupied in or near London.

> Monday.—10 to 11, University College: History and Structure of Language (Women); 11 to 12, Literature, 1760-1815 (Women); 1 to 2, St. Mark's Square; 3 to 4, University College: Literature, 1547-1603 (Men); 4 to 5, History and Structure of Language (Men); 5 to 6, First English (Mixed); 6 to 7, Governesses Class.
>
> Tuesday.—12 to 1, University College: Early English (Mixed); 2 to 3, Literature, 1660-1714 (Men); 3 to 4, Literature, 1547-1603 (Men); 4 to 5, Single Works: Othello and Henry V. (Mixed); 6 to 7, Composition (Mixed).

Wednesday.—10 to 11, University College: History and Structure of Language (Women); 11 to 12, Literature, 1760-1815 (Women); 1 to 2, Composition (Men); 3 to 4, Literature since 1815 (Mixed); 4 to 5, History and Structure of Language (Men); 7 to 8, East End, Finchley, November 1 and December 4.

Thursday.—10 to 11, Queen's College: Literature of Eighteenth Century; 11.15 to 12.15, Language.

Lectures at Forest Hill (6), St. John's Wood (4), Sydenham (4), and Croydon (6), afternoons and evenings.

Friday.—Birmingham, 3 to 4, and 6 to 7.

Saturday.—Princess Helena College (2) 10.30 to 12.

Public Lecture, Sheffield, Thursday, November 14.

The revision of his Introductory University College Lecture was one of his occupations during January, 1879, and he then received an interesting letter from A. N. Goldsmid, Esq., who remembered the first suggestion made to his father by Thomas Campbell for the establishment of a University in London, and also remembered the site being nothing but fields.

Other college matters occupy much time and thought, such as writing reports from committees of the Senate on the Mathematical and Physics chairs, and on the Roman Law chair, which was then vacant, and for which there were sixteen candidates, of whose claims he gave in each case a careful epitome. Interviews with the Council or its committees, too, were now frequent, and as Dean he had some delicate negotiations to conduct in connection with the Greek professorship. On March 28 he has an address from the old students of his literature classes at Birmingham, expressing their appreciation and regret that the class could no longer be continued. On April 29 he gives an address on Text-books at the newly-formed Teachers' Union, which brought together the professors of the college and the masters of the school. The circular calling the first meeting was signed by himself along with Professor Williamson, as well as H. W. Eve and E. R. Horton, the head-master and the vice-master of the school. Dr. Oliver Lodge was perhaps the leading spirit on the committee, and there was hope at this time of retaining his services permanently at the college.

The sons came home this Easter—1879—and Robert promptly seized the opportunity of painting a picture of his father in the study. On April 14 Professor Morley writes to his wife:

He planted himself at the study window while I was at work, and has got me writing at my table, with a background of books. The swiftness of his work is wonderful. Already the picture is done, except work at accessories. He has cleared me off, and Forster and the girls declare the likeness very good. By Thursday he'll have finished the picture, which he does not mean to sell, though it may be exhibited as a ' professor at home,' slippers and all.

The picture attracted a good deal of attention and much commendation at the college soirée on June 19.

Forster Morley returned after Easter to Munich, and on May 14 his father writes to him:

I'll finish with a little scribble to you a desperately busy week that has come to an end at last. It was no joke to squeeze a Society of Arts examination into a full work time; pound away at the soirée, and have a soirée committee; pound away at the preface to the library catalogue and rules; have a library committee and a long talk with the committee of management to explain things; also throw in an extra lecture at Walthamstow; speak at an evening meeting in the Hampstead Vestry Hall, and be ready with my ' Library of English Literature' number, which was in ever so much arrear; yet turn up smiling at the Royal Institution to-day with a lecture that wanted preparation. However, it's all done, and I not only gave them a good lecture in Albemarle Street, but trotted thence in a hansom so briskly as to be at the Stamford Bridge grounds by half-past four to do my part as president this year of the athletic sports. They had fine weather, and the mother gave away the prizes, bringing away the most magnificent of bouquets. Coming home, in the rush to the train at the station, somebody relieved me of my watch. His taking is worse than my losing. Luckily the

mother's chain is left me unhurt.   The watch was a good
watch, but I have had some twenty years' service out of it,
which was worth a pound a year, and it was not a gift or
keepsake. *Hin ist hin.* Our college news is pretty lively.
Two of the three volumes of the catalogue—to O inclusive—
will be out on June 10. We got our prospectus for next
session out a fortnight ago in provisional shape, and students
have been making good use of it. The £400 a year to technical
studies, given us by the City Companies Committee, will be
divided between Graham and Kennedy most likely.   The
soirée promises to be all right.   I shall be very busy over it at
odd times.

The preface to the college library catalogue is by Professor Morley.

On June 8 he writes another letter to Munich full of
details of college work. . . . He had recommended Mr.
Arber as his successor at Birmingham, and given him
some time over subjects for lectures and books. Soon
after this he nominated him assistant examiner in
English at the London University.

On June 17 another letter follows, telling of long and
difficult negotiations with the Council.

If all goes well, it will have been a jolly finish to my official
life as Dean, for there will have been difficult points won, and
I shall have helped to leave the college stronger in many
ways for all the work I've given to it, to say nothing of the
building works at the new wing, the Jubilee subscriptions
being a notion of my starting. Cassal says he means to follow
the new customs and be a working Dean, giving up time and
thought to the advancement of the place, in which, as his vice,
I will quietly aid him.   What I look forward to next is that
in the session 1879-80 steam will be put on to pull up classes
of mathematics and physics, with more engine power.

On July 6 the annual prize-giving was over, and he notes :

We could report in arts and science an increase of 261
students, of which 211 were women, so that, leaving the women
out of account, we had on our male students an increase of
fifty.   The increase last year was only ten.

He seconded the vote of thanks to the chairman, who was Lord Kimberley, president of the college, and

contrived to say what we wanted said. Indeed, I have heard much since of the little speech, which seems to have given general satisfaction. Its aim was to show on the part of the professors appreciation of the work done for the college by the president and council, to give among our reasons for wishing to have the president for chairman, a desire to bring together once a year all parts of the college machinery, president, council, senate and students, and so go on to a few words on the work yet to be done for strengthening the sense of fellowship throughout the college. That is now one of the jobs I set myself to work at during the next sessions. We have got this session the ' Teachers' Union ' to bring together masters and professors. Next year we shall develop that, and peg away at the relation between professors and students. I shall think out my plans in the holidays.

We have new possibilities that arise out of the dismissal of K. He is to be replaced at the beginning of next session by the proprietor of the Holborn and Crosby Hall restaurants, two of the best known and best managed in London. He will put enterprise into the work, and make the students' refreshment-room a pleasant place. Professors, as well as students, will frequent it. We shall have also a way open to little inexpensive gatherings, without the fear that has deterred us hitherto of their being cheap and nasty.* Now that I have dropped the country courses, I shall revive my students' evenings at home, and I am not at all sure that I shall not propose the setting up of something of the nature of a students' committee empowered to send facts and suggestions to the Senate. The cloisters now enclosed can be made into a pleasant place for students to sit and talk together, and the square behind— that is Hayter Lewis's idea—with a little ivy to cover the brick walls, and some trees planted, can be made into a garden. Everybody seems ready to support active movements in this direction, and there is no reason why, as to its inner life,

---

* A dinner given by the professors of University College to those of King's College was ' capitally served ' the following December, and was the kind of gathering that Professor Morley rejoiced to promote.

University College should not in the course of five or ten years become thoroughly humanized, and at all points humanizing to the student. My chief work for the college next year will be in that direction and in the endeavour to establish a full system of teachers' classes, for schoolmasters as well as governesses, meeting in the evening.

For the session beginning October, 1879, he has a carefully compiled record of his University College students, noting the classes they attended, and the academic distinctions they gained. Here are the names of Mr. G. A. Aitken, Mr. W. H. Griffin, and Mr. A. M. J. Ogilvie, each followed by an impressive list of honours. The whole list includes 203 students, a number also reached the following session, and the highest ever attained.

Forster Morley was now at Berlin, and some more letters to him begin on October 29 :

My dear Forster,

    I haven't been able to sit at my table, more's the spite, until to-night, and now I have to get through a lot of work for the college, to rub up my knowledge for Q. C. and U. C. I've got to my sorrow five lectures to-morrow, and letters to write if I'm able to-night. Happy months to you in Berlin, and good fruit out of them! Home news is various. Mother took the chair at the Women's Debating Society, and is reported to have distinguished herself. From what I hear she must have succeeded admirably in keeping order and good humour. . . . College is vigorous, and my own work brisk. I felt my tongue curling up on Saturday night, and thought it was tired, so counted the lectures, and found I had given twenty-seven in the week, the greatest number yet. Two extra had added themselves to the usual twenty-five. The Saturday night lecture was to the Working Men and Women's College, on ' Newspapers,' and on Monday there was report of a part of it as ' Professor Morley on Society Journals.'
    At the Working Women's College on the preceding Saturday, when I praised Maurice as founder of such places, and said that his book on ' Learning and Working,' containing the lectures written by him to promote them, ought to be in all

their libraries, Macmillan, who was in the chair, made a
mem. in his mind, and I had soon after you left a pretty little
note from him, offering in the name of himself and his partner
to send me one hundred copies for Working Men's Clubs, if I
would distribute them.   Of course I will.   I have just set two
new ideas going in the college.   One is to solve the difficulty
of the students' common room.   What I propose is to pay
out any vested interest of the Reading-room Society in their
exclusive use of a room, give notice that the college will
resume the room next session, keep up the supply of papers,
etc.; and provide for all the students the same comfort that a
few are now providing for themselves.   The other is only a
pushing of the Council on to what, of course, has to be done, a
grand beating of gongs and cymbals for the building fund.   I
propose, as soon as they can be organized on a big enough
scale, two meetings for the building fund, one in the City, at
Guildhall or the Cannon Street Hotel; the other at Willis's
Rooms, with separate committees formed at each for raising
funds from east and west.   You'll see that £100,000 got, and
more than that done if I live.   I've a workable scheme growing for residence of students.   But the time for starting it is
not yet.   My talk, you see, is generally shop.   Home is, thank
God! so happy that I'm able to give thought to the shop, free
from care.   God bless us still with peace, and you with long
life and happiness.

The City meeting for raising funds was held at the
Mansion House, July 2, 1880.   The same evening he
writes :

I ought to be at work, but the release from anxieties about
the Mansion House meeting, which is over now, makes me
unable to settle down to ' Library of English Literature,' so I
will write to you now instead of to-morrow or Sunday.   Such
a session as this has been for work I've never had yet.   There
never was such a tight fit of lectures all the week through, and
the whole active work of executor had to be done in the midst
of it, besides the going to Carisbrooke when poor grandpa died,
and the going to Edinburgh for the LL.D., and working on
every committee at the Arts end of the college, and setting on
foot the stir we are making for the building fund.   I not only
set the machinery going, but had to *keep it going*.   There was a

good deal of inertia to turn into force active enough to set other forces going. There's no telling how many feeble suggestions I have tried to put the necessary pluck into. However, I have got the appeal made to-day in my own way. To the very last five minutes there was faint-heartedness. X. lamented we had asked for the Egyptian Hall, and wanted even then to move the people off to the Long Parlour. If the meeting had been a failure, I should have had all the fault laid on my shoulders, for again and again I had resisted any lowering of our flag, and stuck by the big room and the big claim for £105,000. We worked at the meeting every way, we professors; if we hadn't it *would* have failed. I wasn't without lurking doubts and dreads, of course; but nothing is to be done if one lets them come to the front, and the result will give us heart for going on. The meeting went all to our wish. Lord Kimberley spoke admirably: we had two Conservative aldermen to the fore; got just such a committee as I had planned, with full consent of the men wanted, and a table full of reporters scratching away. I have made up my mind to collect that £105,000 within the next fifteen years, and see the college buildings finished, if I live to threescore and ten. And that's not all I hope to see accomplished, but that will do for the present to talk about in the way of stone and brick and mortar.

At University College he began the new session, 1880-81, with 136 students. A good many of these come only for a single class, but the majority take three or four subjects, and some take as many as nine. The previous session some of his classes had been very small; this year, though he still offered subjects which could not be widely popular, he secured a remarkable record of attendances. For a class on the History and Structure of the Language, meeting twice a week, he has 34 names, and very regular attendants most of them are; for First English, Junior, he has 23 students; for Icelandic he has 6 names, and 5 fairly regular scholars; for Early English there are 31; for Composition 32; for Literature, Period from 1558 to 1603, there are 19; for the period 1603 to 1660 there are 40 entries, with scarcely a lecture missed by any of the class; for the period 1660 to 1689 he has 12 most regular students; for 'The Last Thirty Years' there are an equally diligent 32.   Then there are classes on Single Works, one taking 'King Lear,' for which the number is 38; another 'Hudibras,' with 18; and a third class for 'The Faerie Queene,' with 20.   In his evening governesses' class he has 28.   Mr. Arber helps him by taking an exercise class for which the entries number 22.   Exclusive of this last one, the total number of entries is 333.

More students join at the beginning of 1881, raising the total number for the session up to 203, the same number as the previous year.   Mesogothic appears to have been offered in vain, and the students of Icelandic, and those in the Early English, Senior, are very few, but all the other classes are large and very regular in attendance.   With the exception of the evening class for governesses, all are now open to men and women.

On February 16 a dinner at University College celerated the opening of the north wing.   Many most distinguished men were present.   Their names and the speeches will be found at p. 152 *et seq.* of the *University College Gazette* for 1886-7.   Professor Morley proposed the toast 'Art and Literature,' coupling with it the names of Sir Frederick Leighton and Robert Browning.

Leaving now University College, we may notice other matters which occupied Professor Morley between 1878 and 1882.   In 1878, when reappointed Examiner in English to the University of London for another five years, he was able to secure some reforms for which all subsequent students have had reason to thank him.   In setting questions his leading principle was always to find out what a student knew rather than what he did not know, to avoid all catch questions and small technicalities, and give each candidate the best opportunity of showing what he could do.   He was, of course, most careful to avoid coaching his own men to answer the questions he was going to set, and

was glad to secure the services of Mr. Arber to take a class
for matriculation and First B.A.   He knew that his own
students were at some disadvantage for lack of the direct
coaching which, while he was examiner, he could not give.
But he writes, April 28:

My men have only missed the exhibition twice in the last
nine years, and out of these two times there was one of them
marked as qualified for exhibition, so that in nine years I have
failed only once to provide a man up to exhibition mark.   If
Arber's coaching supplement my teaching, we ought never to
fail.

Later he writes :

The revised regulations are good for English. . . .   In
the First B.A. pass there is no longer to be a roving of questions over English history, to the end of the seventeenth
century, but a period of history set, as in honours, and generally
corresponding to the period of literature.   That is a distinct
gain.

Another letter says :

In settling the subjects for examination in 1881, I made all
the reforms I wanted in the way of directing English studies.
Knight Watson opened his eyes at some of the innovations
while politely assenting, and I thought it as well to supply the
University Senate with a little explanation of the meaning of
the change, which laid down one or two principles that I wished
to see adopted permanently.   As they have met to consider
these things, and I have had no note of objection to my proposals or to any part of them, I suppose all's well.   If so, I
hope for the blessing of all good teachers who prepare men in
English for the First B.A. of the present, or shall prepare them
for the Second B.A. of the future.   The students too, I think, will
bless me, for their work will be all the easier for being better
harmonized, made more compact and thorough.   What I want
is that both in Pass and Honours the period of history, with
about fifty years for its outside limit, shall correspond exactly
with the period of literature set for study, and that (except
what is given for language study and *one* play of Shakespeare,

in the B.A. pass) every book set shall be a book of the period studied, and shall be given as a complete work to be read as literature, with an assurance against diffused fidget over petty details, by limiting to one small stated part of it the questions on language, etc.   What can a teacher do whose students are required to read the eleventh book of 'Paradise Lost'?   He is like an artist who is told to explain a cartoon of Raffaelle's by reference only to the right leg of St. Paul.

New employment was continually being found for him. On January 7, 1880, he writes to his son Robert, then at Rome :

On New Year's Day I had to lecture at the London Institute on 'The Future of the Stage.'   Having forced leisure in the trains to and from Halifax, I occupied it in working out a definite scheme for a Dramatic Institute or Academy to put forward in the lecture, copied it out when I got home, got it printed on slips to give to the reporters so that they might have it right, and the result was that the papers all flamed out with it next morning.   Then I was surprised to find that my scheme actually satisfied the theatrical profession.   H. J. Byron wrote a cordial endorsement of it in the *Telegraph*, and I have had to take the consequences of being definite in my ideas. Have been to one little caucus, and next Tuesday there is to be a meeting of the chief actors and dramatic authors, which I have agreed to attend, and at once we go to business.   In a month, I believe, the thing will be well launched, and what I asked for is to be done.   There have been one or two flabby leading articles by writers who wanted to say something, and hadn't got their cue—didn't know how 'the profession' was going to take it.   But it seems clear now that the cue will be to all their friends, 'back it,' or 'back her,' *not* 'stop her.'

On January 18 he writes to Forster :

We had a meeting on Tuesday of the managers and actors. I was voted to the chair.   It was agreed that there should be a Dramatic Academy, and a committee was appointed of Hare, Kendal, Neville, Herman Vezin, Ryder, and H. J. Byron to work out a plan and submit it to a meeting of the whole profession. The *Theatre* (monthly magazine) is in new hands, and accepted well as representing higher interests of the profession. Its editor wanted me to write a few words for next number on my scheme ; I have done so to-night, and secured quietly, I think, fair understanding of my meaning. The only man against the plan, so far as I can find, is Burnand, who disports himself with me in *Punch* good-humouredly, and whose banter helps at any rate to keep the question alive.

Having set the ball rolling, and having seen the scheme cordially welcomed by dramatists such as H. J. Byron, and by actors such as Mr. John Hare, Professor Morley was sanguine of its success. Mr. Hare offered the use of the foyer of the St. James's Theatre for their meetings.

This National Dramatic Academy is not yet established, and any further history of attempts to start it hardly belongs to this biography. Professor Morley was promptly offered numerous suitable 'premises' from enterprising house-agents, and two years later he received from Mr. Hamilton Aidé a letter announcing that a School for Acting was about to be founded. The following draft of his reply shows what he thought of this :

> 8, Upper Park Road,
> Haverstock Hill,
> *January 7,* 1882.

DEAR SIR,

My heartiest goodwill goes with your scheme of a School for Acting, and I am quite willing to join, as you suggest, the general committee, and contribute, if it be thought worth while, an occasional lecture on dramatic literature. My willingness comes of the information you kindly give as to the extent of co-operation by actors and actresses themselves. I dwell with especial satisfaction on the facts that the 'management' will be by members of the profession forming a body of dramatic direction, and that the large and influential general committee represents only the public interest and support, and the natural fellowship of literature and art with the higher efforts of the stage. Every scheme, however generously meant, that touches in any way the self-respect and independence of a profession that when rightly followed may stand side by side with the noblest of intellectual pursuits, is a scheme to be avoided. As writers, you or I would not choose to be patronized, and I am quite sure that the success of your school will be in proportion to the confidence with which actors and actresses shall feel able to regard it as their own. I learn from your note that this feeling guides the plans of its promoters, and in that faith am most willing to do what I can in aid.

> Believe me, dear sir,
> Faithfully yours,
> HENRY MORLEY.

Hamilton Aidé, Esq.

We now return to the letter which he sent to Rome on January 7, 1880. In this he gives Robert advice about a picture which the young artist was thinking of painting to illustrate a subject taken from the 'Faerie Queene.' This was the kind of connection between painting and literature in which Professor Morley found much delight.

About the team of the devil's driving, these are my ideas: Get a good typically *Roman* model for Lucifera herself. Spenser has for underthought that she is the pride of the Church of Rome, though in the larger allegory she is the Pride and Lust of the Flesh to which we give ourselves as servants when we fall away from truth. You want a head and bust, luxurious, handsome, and as far as may be distinctly Roman in type, You could make a study fully worked out on a separate canvas from a well-chosen model, which should be a picture by itself, and afterwards work from it for your composite. The garlands on the chariot should include foliage and flowers of Italy, and the suggestion you give in the distance of her 'stately place' might be of a palace with hints of the architecture of St. Peter's. That must not be prominent, but if you can get any recognisable though subdued characteristic of St. Peter's or the Vatican available it would not be unfit. Idleness wants no comment. His 'portesse' is his breviary, a word derived

from 'porte hors,' the book carried out and about, which contained for ready use the different offices of prayer. You should
keep the monk in view in his hair by giving him not the tonsure, but an imperfectly bald crown, such as people may get
without tonsure. The shaven head typified by the constant
use of the razor the constant effort needed to repress the
sprouting vices of the flesh. So Idleness, whom Spenser
associates with the monk's life, should have his crown hairily
bald, if one may put it so, a little lawn of hair set in a bushier
surrounding, shaggy and neglected—that is, of course, so far
as the drawing of the figure leaves such a suggestion possible.
'Esloyne' means, of course, remove himself; 'essoyne' means
exemption. Gluttony beside him needs no comment, and
would compare well. In Lechery the 'whalley eyes' mean
what we now write as wall eyes, which means eyes faded in
colour. Calling Jealousy the green-eyed monster is allied to
this, so you should plant Lechery's head in a way to show
this old proverbial feature. Avarice, of course, must be lean
and cadaverous; and now, as you have them placed, you can
make Envy and Wrath slip across the traces, the wolf strain-
ing towards the camel, and the rider eagerly observant of the
heaps of gold counted by griple covetise, towards which he
also strains. The cross-movement of the wolf would make the
lion rear; and then you get Wrath, who may look any number
of daggers at the Counsellor thus getting across his way and
backing him to the devil. As for the devil, couldn't you find
a pre-Raffaelite picture in the Vatican with a fine mediæval
devil in it to give you the image as it actually existed in the
mediæval mind? The devil's ugliness will, of course, make a
grand foil to the beauty of Lucifera behind him on her chariot
of pride.

These letters to his sons abroad contain many beautiful
proofs of his fatherly love and confidence.

You must bear in mind always, in case of any bother or
difficulty, that you have a firm and safe base of operations while
your father and mother live to love and help you, that nothing
we believe it possible for you to do can vex us. You must
change your nature before you can become a care, or we desire
anything but to aid all your endeavour. So God bless you,
and that's all about that!

In another letter he says:

What most fathers would doubt about I am in no concern over at all, for I know well that I have two good young gorillas who are at one in all essential things with the old Go.

He had indeed reason to be proud of the perfect trust with which he could send his boys to study by themselves in these Continental capitals. His system of making trustworthy by giving trust succeeded absolutely in his own family, as, indeed, it did with almost all with whom he had much personal intercourse. It must not be supposed, however, that he was only good-natured at home. He had a sense of scorn quickly roused for everything weak or unworthy, and an emphatic way of giving it utterance. His 'Pooh!' was final, and if accompanied by a little stamp of the foot it was catastrophic.

He was a strong opponent to Jingoism, and no lover of Disraeli. He was asked about this time to write a life of Gladstone, and felt tempted by the opportunity of sketching such a career. Some of his political feelings were relieved in the following poem, no doubt written in 1878:

ROBIN GOODFELLOW,

TO A BROTHER WILL O' THE WISP.

Mar a nation, make a phrase,
>	Peace with honour!

Get some aldermen to raise
>	Peace with honour!

Labels over dirty ways,
>	Peace with honour!

In big letters on red baize:
>	Peace with honour!

Turkey, plundered, hardly says,
>	Peace with honour!

Greece knows whose fair word betrays,
>	Peace with honour!

Austria bleeds, and deeply pays,
>	Peace with honour!

India next we'll set ablaze,—
                              Peace with honour !
Russia, faint from bloody frays,
                              Peace with honour !
Stab in back and steal her bays,
                              Peace with honour !
Pile the cost of evil days,
                              Peace with honour !
While an ass is left who brays,
                              Peace with honour !
Set up empire, freedom daze,
                              Peace with honour !
Up your sleeve a card yet stays,
                              · Peace with honour !
Play it ; set the world ablaze,
                              Peace with honour !
Dress shame in phrases, never mind detection,
                              Burn blue and crisp,
Dance till your light's out at the next election,
                              Will o' the Wisp.

Early in 1880 Professor Morley lost his father-in-law, whose death led to important consequences. Some months later Professor Morley bought his house and garden at Carisbrooke, and began to make it his country residence, looking forward to retiring there with his wife when he could afford to give up lecturing. It was entirely the strength of old associations which drew them to the spot. On September 23, 1869, he had written that Mrs. Morley was 'a little out of health, for Carisbrooke air never agrees with her or me.' Both needed a more bracing climate than is afforded by the centre of the Isle of Wight, and it is quite possible that they might have had better health and longer life after 1889 elsewhere than at Carisbrooke. But the mistake, if it was one, was due to memories of ' auld lang syne.' It is a proof of the ' clinging conservatism' in Mrs. Morley's affections, and of her husband's desire to give her happiness.

Professor and Mrs. Morley took possession of their new

house at Carisbrooke in September, and spent a month there. He soon began improving the property. He bought on the opposite side of the road land enough for a good-sized garden, and made a splendid tennis lawn and bowling-green at the top. Here, on the end of the long down, which stretches westward for many miles, the air seemed always fresh, and the view of Carisbrooke, with its noble church tower and grand old castle, and the long sweep of distant downs, was particularly charming. At one end of the lawn he built a substantial summer-house, where he meant to come and write, and whither in later years he did sometimes bring his work. He never played tennis himself, but would join in a game of bowls, and was often ' in ' with ' burly bumbo,' the largest-sized balls. He planted a great many good fruit-trees in his new garden, making it, as he said, ' one of the fruitiest bits of England.'

On April 21, 1880, the University of Edinburgh conferred on him its honorary degree of LL.D. This was a graceful recognition of his academic standing, and it gave him the right to wear a graduate's gown on suitable occasion, such as college soirées and Presentation Day at the University of London, which has itself no power to confer honorary degrees. He and Mrs. Morley went to Edinburgh for the ceremony, and had a hearty welcome from old friends.

The following July the first wedding in the family took place, when Professor Morley gave me his eldest daughter, and welcomed me as his own son. He liked the old custom of a wedding-breakfast, with the regulation speeches, and very beautifully he now spoke, though he came perilously near breaking down through emotion. Another speaker whose words were worth remembering was my uncle, William Shaen ; and Dr. Sadler, who had joined our hands at Rosslyn Hill Chapel, once more gave us his blessing.

In April, 1881, Professor Morley paid us a visit in Liverpool, where my wife and I were living. This was the occasion when we made our pilgrimage to Liscard, and explored his old house, and identified many an ancient site.* I was then Minister to the Poor in connection with the Liverpool Domestic Mission, holding the post which was held in 1851 by the Rev. Francis Bishop, whom he had desired to help, and much interested he now was in all the work of that useful institution.

He had the opportunity this May of helping two good men to secure important appointments. One was O. J. Lodge to the chair of Physics at University College, Liverpool; the other was J. Viriamu Jones to his professorship at Firth College, Sheffield. It can be imagined how many applications for testimonials he was always receiving, especially from old students. Often he could give them with complete satisfaction, as to W. W. Skeat and C. H. Herford; but this duty was never done heedlessly, and the following incident is very characteristic.

A professorship at Queen's College was vacant, and his old friend Mr. Fox Bourne, applying for the post, asked if he might use a testimonial written with a view to another appointment. The following letters are dated July 13 and 15, 1881.

MY DEAR MR. BOURNE,

I do not think the post at Queen's College would add much to your income, but there is no foregone conclusion as to the candidate to be appointed. One difficulty in your way, or in the way of my using what personal influence I could in your behalf, is that Queen's College, like King's College, lays stress on the religious element in teaching. It is very liberal indeed in being free from the dogmatism that passes with some for religion; but I think it would want its teacher of history to be in accord with those who think ' there's a divinity that shapes our ends,' and to be, in that sense, a little of a divinity student. You

* See p. 125.

may remember how strongly I used to feel where for me, in such recognition of its religious element, the life of literature lay. That feeling has gained strength with years. I have no right whatever to think you wrong for holding other views, but knowing that you do so, and that they would put you out of accord with the work at Queen's College, how could I tell my colleagues that you are the man they want? With no such special difficulty in the way, my help and heartiest good-will is always to be relied on.

Ever yours,
Very sincerely,
H. M.

My dear Mr. Bourne,

Only a line to thank you for your note, which has done away with a misconception. Some years ago some talk of yours here that I now forget left us with the impression that you had put away faith in a God altogether. Some of the friends whom I heartily respect have done so, and it is no part of my religion to think that God Himself weighs error as men do. My regard for you has not been less, but as the chief use to my mind of a study of English literature is to sustain the spiritual side of life, and it has been, at any rate, my chief aim so to teach it as to bring it into use as a natural corrective to the materialist tendencies of the age, as an embodiment of the religious life of England in every shape, and narrowed to the measure of no shibboleth, while giving honour to each form of earnest thought, I fancied I had lost you as a fellow-combatant. I am very glad to find that I was wrong, and have quite put away the misconception. In any case, you were entitled to send in the note written for Birmingham, for I only wrote what was due. But I can say now that I shall be glad if you become a fellow-worker at Queen's College.

With kind regards,
Yours always sincerely,
Henry Morley.

Do not answer this ; enough is said.

It was the tone of the *Examiner* on religious matters after it had passed into the hands of Mr. Fox Bourne that gave Professor Morley the impression to which he refers.

Till Mr. Fox Bourne received these letters, he tells me that he never knew how strongly Professor Morley must have disapproved of this tone. The letters express convictions which I have often heard uttered verbally, but I know not where else they are stated so clearly and forcibly in writing, and am grateful for permission to publish them.

Many other events of more or less importance contributed to the work of the year. He helped Miss C. C. Hopley, sister of his old friend the artist, to publish her admirable book on ' Snakes.' Along with many distinguished men, he withdrew from the New Shakespeare Society on account of its treatment of Mr. Halliwell-Phillips.

In connection with his study of Wordsworth, a short trip which he made in September, 1879, is of interest. He writes on the 18th from the King's Arms, Dorchester, to Mrs. Morley :

To-morrow we hope to do Lyme Regis and the Wordsworth ground at Racedown, etc.

In 1795 Wordsworth and his sister Dorothy came to live at Racedown Lodge, on the slope of Pillesdon Pen, one of the ' Alps of Dorset.' Here he began the ' Excursion,' and the whole scenery of its first book is laid in this neighbourhood. The common across which the Wanderer toiled is near Crewkerne, and ' the employment common through these wilds ' is the spinning of rope and twine as it has been practised for some centuries at Bridport and in surrounding villages. After the first book, the scenery changes without notice to that of the Lake District, and there are, or, at any rate, were, comparatively few readers acquainted with the locality of the earlier portion of the poem. Professor Morley points it out in the ' Library of English Literature: Longer Works,' p. 373.

There was one thing which Professor Morley found he could not do while incessantly engaged in teaching, and

that was go on with 'English Writers.' But he managed
to supply the printer with the material for the 'Library of
English Literature,' often at no little sacrifice. He must
have felt this when he hurried away from a visit to Tennyson at Aldworth because the printer was clamorous. The
first time he was asked to meet the Poet Laureate at
dinner he declined, because he thought it looked like
suggesting to him what he should write in a *Nineteenth
Century* 'Review of Recent Literature'; but shortly after
this he made Tennyson's acquaintance, and much enjoyed
hearing him read his dramas, and discussing with him the
interpretation of the 'Idylls.'

On January 5, 1881, Baron Tauchnitz asked him to
undertake volume 2,000 of his series of English and
American authors, and to write for it a short history of
English literature during the reign of Queen Victoria.
This task was accomplished by the end of the year, to the
entire satisfaction of Baron Tauchnitz and his son, though
their letters often tell a tale of hope deferred. The foot-
notes were 'made in Germany,' and rather resemble a
sporadic catalogue of the Tauchnitz series. The text
itself shows Professor Morley's method of dealing briefly
with the English literature of our own age.

We have passed over almost unnoticed the single lectures
which Professor Morley was constantly giving out of
London, especially during the Christmas and Easter vacations, as well as the short courses and occasional lectures
which he gave in the evenings at various institutions in
London. He was indeed a much-sought-after man.
Flourishing societies paid him well—12 to 15 guineas for
a single night—but when he could find the time, he was
always willing to do work for poorer institutions on very
generous terms, and the number of lectures which he gave
for nothing, especially at domestic missions and colleges
for working men and women, was very considerable.

All this time, too, his correspondence must have been

great. He has letters asking him to do extension work, which he had given up, and to continue to act as its examiner; letters from grateful students; letters from foreigners, asking his help in finding literary work; letters and newspaper-cuttings from Australia, where his ' Library of English Literature ' was much appreciated. Traces of all this, and of much else, are to be found among his papers, and there was more which disappeared and left no trace. He is leading a life very full of happy and successful industry. His lecturing brings in a good income, and enables him to save something on which to retire and write books. His relations with all his colleagues are most cordial; and the home-life, with his children finding their place in the world, is a source of profound and grateful satisfaction.

CHAPTER XV.

UNIVERSITY HALL, 1882-1889.

In every active useful life there is a period of greatest energy and widest influence. After this inevitably comes a decline of strength, which must involve either a curtailment of activity or some shortcoming and disappointment in the duties undertaken. In 1882 Professor Morley was sixty years of age, he had had a hard life, and the brain was slowly beginning to utter a protest against excessive strain; there were indications of the malady diabetes, which ultimately proved fatal, though as yet none knew this, and it is doubtful if he suspected it himself; yet for another seven years he continued to lecture at University and Queen's Colleges, as well as to hold classes in London schools, and to give numerous extra lectures, many of them gratuitously. Of course, lecturing was easy to him; his thoughts and words flowed freely in their well-accustomed channels, and he did not now attempt to fill the week with as many lectures as he had been wont to deliver. But the additional engagements to be spoken of in this chapter are indeed astonishing. He was appointed Principal of University Hall; he started and became secretary to the University College Society; he also established and edited the *University College Gazette;* he made an important contribution to the movement to establish a Teaching University in London. He accepted a request from Messrs. Routledge, and edited for them 'Morley's Universal Library' in monthly volumes; he accepted proposals to edit Cassell's 'National Library' in weekly volumes. He supervised a new edition of his own 'Library of English Literature.' He began the reissue of his own great work, the *magnum opus* of his life, 'English Writers.'

He undertook the editorial work the more readily because he knew that he could carry it on after leaving London, and he looked to it to help furnish an income when he retired from lecturing. Nor was he mistaken here. The movement for cheap reprints did indeed after some years pass on into other hands, and then, as usual, he was content to let it go, and look out for something new, which, as we shall see, did not fail to come, up to the very end of his life. The most noteworthy feature in his editorship is his inclusion of books which lie outside the class read by everybody. No publishers before or since have ever dared to offer such works to the public in a cheap form as he gave them in his 'Libraries'; and though there were inevitable drawbacks, the movement while he guided it was, at any rate, so successful that it always led to fresh proposals from enterprising publishers, and its widespread popularity was so great that there seemed real danger that he would be remembered after his death only in connection with his services for the diffusion of cheap literature.* Undoubtedly there was a

---

* Witness the following lines:

John Bull is not sweet on the type of ' Professor,'
But good Henry Morley was happy possessor
Of John Bull's respect, John Bull, junior's, love.
He made good letters cheap ! 'Tis a title above
Many dry-as-dust dignities told in strung letters.
Ah ! many who felt Iron Fortune's stern fetters
In days ante-Morleyish, look on the rows
Of cheap classics, in musical verse, and sound prose,

miscalculation of strength in undertaking so much. He was still oversanguine, as he had been when twenty years old. Where success depended on the co-operation of others, he counted too much on their agreement and support. Where all depended on himself, he attempted more than he could possibly perform. We are coming, therefore, to years which will tell of disappointments as well as of happy triumphs in good works.

The year 1882 opens with all this in the future. He begins the term with three lectures on Mondays, five on Tuesdays, six on Wednesdays, seven on Thursdays, and six on Fridays, while on Saturdays he goes to Stamford Hill, and runs down to Reading for Miss Buckland's school, and also to give there a series of lectures on ' The Course of Thought in Europe before the French Revolution.'

Then there are the ' extras ': Four at Highgate in February; March 1, on ' In Memoriam,' at the Birkbeck; March 13, Spicer Street Domestic Mission, on ' As You Like It.'; March 17, Blackheath, ' Queen Anne's Times ; ' March 20, Sheffield, ' The Tempest '; March 27, Haven Green Chapel, ' The Literature of To-day, with a Glance at To-morrow.' Respecting the visit to Sheffield, he had received on February 9, from the secretary to the Literary and Philosophical Society there, a request that he would lecture on one of Shakespeare's plays which

---

Which bear the well-known editorial ' H. M.,'
And sigh, ' If *my* youth-time had only known *them*,
These. threepenny treasures, and sixpenny glories,
These histories, treatises, poems, and stories,
Which cost in my time a small fortune, what thanks
And what joys would have swelled o'er their neat rangéd
    ranks !'
Ah ! studious boys must feel gratitude, surely,
To have lived in the times of the good Henry Morley.
Punch.

Mr. Brandram would afterwards come and recite; and the letter continues : ' I may observe that your fee last year was considered too small, and would suggest £15 as an honorarium, if that would be agreeable to yourself.' No doubt it was agreeable to find such appreciation of what he had to say about Shakespeare. He knew he had a message to deliver to the world about the inner meaning of Shakespeare's plays ; he had gone through every one of them in turn with his classes at University College, and while leaving to other commentators much useful criticism on the words used by the dramatist, he would condense into an evening's lecture what no one else had said, and what he wanted to say, about the soul of the drama.

In the autumn of 1882 my wife and I moved to Southampton, where we were on one of the direct routes between London and Carisbrooke, besides being much nearer both places than when at Liverpool. Visits consequently became more frequent, and on many an occasion he gave a lecture in the Kell Memorial Schoolroom, built by his old friend, the Rev. Edmund Kell, in memory of his wife ; and once we had a notable address in the Church of the Saviour (where Mr. Kell had ministered after leaving Newport) on 'The Story of Religion in English Literature.' Indeed, I feel something like remorse in remembering how often during a five years' residence there we availed ourselves of his ever-ready help in connection with our congregational work ; but it is a proof that we none of us realized how he was being over-taxed. He enjoyed the meetings as we did, and we certainly had a right to feel that if not engaged in one place he would be busy in some other. His lecture on ' In Memoriam,' which he once gave us there, made a deep impression, his voice and manner, as well as his earnest words, bringing out most beautifully the spirit of hope and trust, which rises higher with each return of the season in the

22

circling years described in the poem. He told me afterwards that when this had been announced as his subject
somewhere else, he found right in the middle of the front
row of his audience three ladies in deep mourning, with
pocket-handkerchiefs all ready, come purposely to enjoy
the luxury of a good cry. For one so emotional as the
lecturer himself, this was a severe ordeal. So was another
occasion, in the neighbourhood of Windsor, when he had
to discuss the cutting off the head of King Charles I. in
the presence of Royalty.

But at Southampton, as in most places, no subject was
so popular as a play of Shakespeare. He lectured so
often on ' As You Like It ' that at last he rebelled, and
was willing to take any play but that.

Turning now to his work in connection with women's
education, we find on January 5, 1882, Miss A. L.
Browne writing to him about a Hall of Residence for
Women Students at University College; and from that
time till October 1, when this Hall was opened at 1, Byng
Place, he took an active interest in all the arrangements
for the establishment of this valuable institution. On
March 25 he writes :

DEAR MISS BROWNE,

If I were not under an old engagement to lecture at
Haven Green on Monday evening, I should be glad to attend
your meeting on behalf of the proposed Hall of Residence for
Women Students in London. You will have to start, I
suppose, at once your list of donations and subscriptions. I
cannot do much in that way, but will most gladly subscribe
£5 5s. a year for the three years during which you try the
Hall as an experiment. In another way I may also have some
little opportunity of being useful. It is practically certain,
although not formally settled, that an arrangement will be
made for the conduct of University Hall that involves my
doing what I can as principal of the Hall to associate it closely
with the college as a place of residence for students, and so
carry out my own wish to establish residence as an essential

element in our college system that has hitherto been too little recognised. Such an arrangement might open the way, in several respects, by friendly co-operation, towards success in the endeavour to establish at the same time a Hall for Women.

He took an active part in the subsequent development and incorporation of College Hall, as it was called. For several years he was chairman of its Council, and guided many of their decisions to wise issues. Its vice-principal was Miss Morison, who was soon appointed lady superintendent at the college, and who has sent me the following contribution :

Very soon after my appointment as Lady Superintendent at University College in 1883, I had the opportunity of seeing in what esteem and affection Professor Morley was held by all with whom he came in contact.

This feeling was noticeable not only in his students generally, but specially in those who attended the teachers' classes which were at that time being given by him at University College, and which were attended by students of varied ages and of different nationalities. Many of them expressed to me the almost reverent affection which they felt for Professor Morley, and their sense of the lifting up to higher things with which his teaching inspired them. It was also a feature worth noting that many teachers from American schools and colleges, when taking a year's leave, were eager to join Professor Morley's classes for the session from October to June.

His sympathy and willingness to give advice and help wherever he was able were appreciated to an extent that must have made great inroads on his time. On more than one occasion when he was being waited for to take the chair at some College Society meeting, those of us who were waiting would be told by one who had been an eye-witness: ' He started in good time from University Hall, but so many people have stopped him on the way that he is late in arriving.' This is typical of his constant willingness to lend a willing ear to any who needed his help, without any regard to his personal convenience.

Others will have told of his invaluable services in connection with the foundation of the College Hall of Residence for Women Students.   As chairman of its Council he was unfailing in his interest in all its affairs, constant in his attendance at the Council meetings, and had the special gift of gathering in the varying opinions of differing members and finally uniting them into a harmonious whole.

We can now deal with his appointment as Principal of University Hall, Gordon Square, a large red-brick edifice built by the Unitarians to commemorate the passing of the Dissenters' Chapels Act in 1844.   It was founded in 1847, as a Hall of Residence for students attending classes at University College; and in 1853 it also became the home of Manchester New College, where students were trained in liberal theology.   It had varying fortunes under different principals ; many of the old residents there would speak in high terms of the benefit they received from sharing its common life, and the session I spent there, 1871-72, was a happy and valuable addition to my college experience.   But from various causes there had been a considerable decline in its prosperity; and at length its trustees, unable any longer to carry it on, handed it over to a joint Board, composed partly of themselves and partly of the trustees of Manchester New College, to hold it in trust for this college so long as the Hall should be occupied and carried on by the college.   It was then placed under the authority of the Committee of Manchester New College, which determined to put forth every effort to make the place succeed in accordance with its original design, and all through the early months of 1882 its secretaries were in communication with Professor Morley with the view to his becoming Principal of the Hall.   His difficulty was that, for family reasons, he could not give up his house in Upper Park Road.   At one time he thought that this might be managed ; but he became convinced that it was impossible, and then he could only become Principal of the Hall by sacrificing his home life.

This was a heavy sacrifice to make, for home, as we have seen, meant much to him.

Nothing but his intense interest in this opportunity for developing this side of college life, and the conviction that here was a call of duty which he could not refuse, would ever have taken him to Gordon Square. He made himself a poorer man by accepting so onerous a post. But for years he had desired to develop this element in a collegiate education. Men might come to lectures, and sit side by side, hardly exchanging a word, and then separate and see no more of each other. He knew the value of residence at Oxford and Cambridge ; and these Universities were now open to Nonconformists as well as to Churchmen, and were drawing many young men thither of the class who had previously come to Gower Street. He knew that the value of University training largely consists in its human intercourse, and it became the passion of his last years at University College to establish there the fullest opportunities for enjoying a vigorous and healthy social life.

So the post was accepted. His son Forster was appointed Dean, and came also to live at the Hall, so that one of them might always sleep on the spot ; and the wrench was made. There is a pathetic entry in Mrs. Morley's diary, dated October 14, when a van had come to carry off furniture: 'I mourned long into the night, and could not be comforted.'

The Rev. H. Enfield Dowson, of Gee Cross, Hyde, was honorary secretary to the Committee of Manchester New College, and no man can speak with such fulness of knowledge as he concerning the work which Professor Morley did at the Hall. He has kindly sent me a valuable statement showing how the Hall flourished under Professor Morley's management. Sets of rooms had to be divided, and an extension of accommodation built at the back to take in the students now anxious to enter.

Mr. Dowson concludes:

One memory was left to those who were privileged to be in constant communication with him during the seven years he held the office of principal, and who had the joy of meeting him month by month at the house committee of the Hall, and it was a memory of a beautiful character, full of hope, never discouraged, knowing no bitterness, as gentle as earnest and brave, and it was the memory of one whom to know was to love, as the very embodiment of all that was kindly, all that was generous, with whom to agree was delightful, and from whom to differ was no less delightful, for with him difference meant no break for a moment in the most cordial relations; it was the memory of a noble Christian man that lived in the hearts of his colleagues in the management of University Hall, and that made them better for life for this association with him.

By the side of this statement, representing the views of secretary and committee, we place the recollections of an old student, now the Rev. L. P. Jacks, M.A., of Birmingham:

HENRY MORLEY AT UNIVERSITY HALL.

University Hall was vaguely known to the public as a place where young men resided while attending the classes of University College. Henry Morley made it his object to give the Hall a far higher function. It was his aim to raise it from the condition of a mere place of residence for those who were being educated elsewhere by making it the home of a vivid common life, which itself should be a liberal education. This description is not the mere retrospective inference of one who, twelve years after the event, collects his memories and reflects on their meaning. As Principal of University Hall, it was the very essence of Professor Morley's plan to impart his aim to the students who filled the building, and to enlist their deliberate efforts in carrying it out. He told us frankly that his intention was to make the Hall a place of true social education for all concerned. Again and again both in public and in private he appealed to us to realize that we had an individual responsibility, and no pains were spared by him to keep the aim of the Hall life clearly and constantly present to all our minds, and to impress it upon us that he not only expected us to be partners with him in its accomplishment, but that he relied upon our partnership in his hopes of success. Each man was to understand that he had a part to play in making the atmosphere intellectually vivid and morally healthy, and that by playing this part he could help to make the Hall a place of education for all the rest. For those who would understand the University Hall chapter of Professor Morley's life it is essential that this aspect should be clearly seen.

His aims went far beyond the level of giving a democratic semblance to the organization of the Hall life. It was the vital heart of his scheme to make the men conscious fellow-labourers with himself in the doing of a noble moral work. The idea was as splendidly conceived as it was heroically carried out, and in those days there were few men in the Hall whose hearts were untouched by the greatness of mind which prompted the attempt and the patient courage with which its author sought to carry it out. The realization of such an ideal deserved the hearty co-operation of all good men, and I venture to say that none of the old Hall men who understood what Professor Morley was aiming at—and the majority did understand—can think of the interruption of the work and the transference of the Hall to other purposes without a pang of very genuine grief.

As Professor Morley's ideal for the Hall was other than that which usually prevails in a residential establishment of the kind, it necessarily follows that his methods of dealing with the students were also different. Those methods have been, both then and later, the subjects of considerable criticism; but the critics have not perhaps sufficiently reflected that, granting the rightness of the end in view, traditional methods of dealing with young men would have been quite ineffective. For my own part, while seeing, as everybody must see, the dangers associated with them, and while remembering some instances in which they may be said to have failed, I am still convinced, after all that has been alleged on the other side, that Professor Morley's methods were not only sound in themselves, but the only methods of which the employment was possible in such a case. To begin with, it must be obvious that the end could be attained only by putting in force a much larger measure of trust than is usually reposed in youths who have just come up to college. A system of iron restraint, attended with bull-dog watchfulness and involving sharp notice of every little irregularity, with the usual apparatus of fines and rustications, would have been absolutely fatal to the spirit which he wished to infuse into the Hall life. We were all put upon our honour, and the motive to which appeal was made was not the fear of unpleasant consequences, but the sense of what the good of the whole body living in the Hall required. If this had been accompanied by the severe administration of a cut-and-dried code of rules, not a man in the Hall would have believed in the genuineness of the idea which was constantly being set before us by Professor Morley. As it was, the genuineness of the system was always above suspicion, and though the trust reposed in us was often abused, yet it was more often honourably respected, and even when abused there was always a sense of shame which will never desert the memory of the abuse.

Professor Morley never made but one type of appeal, and that was to good sense and right feeling. As I write the words a score of memories rise before me. I recall one or two occasions when the situation bristled with difficulties, and I see the figure of the brave old man standing like a steady rock in our midst, and I hear again the quiet, cheerful, generous words in which he would reaffirm his trust in the wayward youths around him, gradually rising to a tone of enthusiasm as he proceeded to tell us once more of his aspirations concerning the Hall and his unaltered determination to carry on the work in the spirit in which he had begun. The point of chief significance is not that there were some failures, but that there was such a large measure of success.

His methods could only succeed in the hands of one who possessed confidence in human nature, and a power of discriminating between what is essential and irrelevant in character. But these are gifts without which no man were fitted to occupy Professor Morley's position, let his methods be what they might. A timid and suspicious man succeeding Henry Morley would have failed of a certainty in his attempts to continue the Hall work; but such a man would have failed equally if he had followed anyone else. After all, the qualities on which he based his action—manliness, large-heartedness, and trust that the good must win—are not so very rare in the

world. There are plenty of men to be found who are capable
of displaying them; but it is rare to find them made the basis
of policy in dealing with young men. That Professor Morley
dared to do this is a crown of glory to his memory. What he
did was something new, difficult, something which exposed the
doer to constant criticism by the fearful and the timid. But
the way having once been opened, it is easy for us to follow it
up. The path which Professor Morley cut through the forest
may have been a short one, but it is the deliberate conviction
of one, at least, of his old students that he cut it in the right
direction.

In the Hall, as I remember it—between 1882 and 1886—
there was a strange and varied mingling of human types,
perhaps as varied as could be found in any place of similar
compass. In addition to the students of Manchester New
College, whose numbers were comparatively steady, there was
a considerable body of candidates for the Indian Civil Service,
the intellectual pick of the best schools of the kingdom, a somewhat greater number of medical students, and a miscellaneous
body of men training for various professions connected with
art, science, law, engineering, and education. To enumerate
the various types of character represented would be impossible;
enough that they comprised, as might be expected, the good
and the bad, and many shades of each variety. The list of
nationalities represented by one or more students would also be
a long one. I remember French, German, Spanish, American,
Hindoo, Parsee, Burmese, Cingalese, Japanese, Negroes.
This mingling of many types was one of the circumstances on
which Professor Morley relied most as a means of creating a
vivid social life. And there was in the Hall a continual clash
of mind and attrition of man with man, both on the intellectual
and moral side, which made the mental atmosphere highly
stimulating. Life in the Hall was never dull. In addition to
the general interplay of mind with mind, each department was
organized on its own democratic basis. The library and the
reading-room had their separate committees; there was an
excellent debating society, and, chief of all, an important body,
known as the House Committee, whose resolutions were moved,
seconded, and carried concerning matters great and small,
down to the cooking of puddings and the making of beds. At
the meetings of each of these, the Principal was uniformly

present, not as a dictator, but with a mind open to conviction,
and as the equal friend of all.   The amount of small detail
work which he performed in these ways was enormous, and
would itself have filled the time of most men.   Into everything
in which he took part he threw himself with the utmost heartiness, and made his personality a centre and source of life.
Rarely was he absent from the head of the table at any meal.
After carving for a score or two of men, during the whole
of which operation he was ready to converse on any topic,
grave or gay, saying many a wise word, provoking and joining
in many a hearty laugh, he would hastily take his own portion,
and, dinner over, away he went at express speed, to tackle one
of the endless tasks that were always awaiting him.   But in
spite of the many other labours he had to perform, we all felt
and knew then, as we know even more fully now, that at this
time the Hall was the subject nearest to his heart.   Already
fully occupied, according to any reasonable standard, it was
wonderful that he should have the courage to undertake a new
responsibility of such magnitude and of a nature so exacting in
detail work.   One aspect of the case was only too evident,
namely, that his last thought was to spare himself.   I cannot
avoid the conclusion that his work at the Hall was in essence
a great self-sacrifice ; and I wish to bear testimony that never
was work of that kind done with cheerfulness more unruffled
or with devotion more entire.   Only recently have I learnt
that during the whole of this time, when he was full of plans
and aspirations, and working at their fulfilment with extraordinary vigour and hopefulness, the disease which ultimately
proved fatal was slowly sapping his strength.   He was too
wise a man not to have known the actual state of the case ; he
was too brave to let it give him a moment's pause in the ever
forward march of life.

But few men have been privileged to sacrifice themselves for
a nobler object.   For he was not only confident of success, but
he firmly hoped that his own success would lead others to
follow his example.   University Hall was to become an object
lesson to all who had to solve the problem of associating young
men together in a healthy common life.

The question, ' Did Morley succeed ?' is one which I do not
hesitate to answer in the affirmative.   No doubt there were
errors in his management, but they were errors of detail and

not of principle. , They were capable of remedy ; many of them were remedied by him during my own term of residence in the Hall ; the rest would have set themselves straight in course of time. Looking back now, I see how enormously difficult some of the material was with which he had to deal. Anyone who should suppose it possible to carry out Professor Morley's principle without occasional failures can have no knowledge either of the material or the conditions that were before him. It was impossible that all the men should understand his aim ; it is even less likely that in so mixed a body none should be un-willing to co-operate with him in giving those ideas effect. But a sufficient number to ensure ultimate success did under-stand and did co-operate. To believe that ideal was intrinsi-cally unrealizable would imply profound disrtust of human nature ; but even if that distrust were indulged, it might be confuted by the memories of Hall men under Professor Morley's régime. The majority of the men did respect the trust imposed upon them, and they retain memories of a vivid and quickening social life which it is hard to believe could have been created by any other method. Professor Morley did succeed in making the associated life of the Hall a priceless educational benefit to all save a few. The enterprise was interrupted, but it is perhaps not too much to believe that the example will neither be lost nor forgotten. Whether or no the undertaking be ever renewed in other places, it is certain that many Hall men are now living in whose minds the heroic, loving, generous spirit of Henry Morley has left an ineffaceable impression, which may be trusted to reproduce itself in one way or another, and that per-haps is the noblest element in his success.

On taking office, the new Principal promptly burnt an elaborate code of regulations. In its place he issued the following :

GENERAL CONDITIONS OF RESIDENCE.

1. University Hall is open to students of Manchester New College and of University College, London, and its arrangements are adapted to the needs of modern student life.
2. Trust is put in the readiness of all who reside in the Hall to join the Principal in' daily endeavour to make resi-dence in the Hall pleasant and useful to themselves

and to one another.   There is no attempt at management by fines or trivial restrictions or by other discipline than that of a well-ordered home.

3. Any resident in the Hall who is out of accord with its
arrangements may give or receive a month's notice to
quit.

4. Prayers are read by the Principal at 8 a.m.   Attendance
at prayers is voluntary, but it is hoped that it will be
usual with all residents in the Hall who are not withheld by conscientious objection.

5. The Principal and students breakfast together in the
dining-hall at ten minutes past eight.   At nine o'clock
the breakfast-table is cleared.   For a special breakfast
after nine o'clock, a student who is in his usual health
pays additional one shilling.

6. There is a common room for the use of students in the
Hall.

7. Lunch can be had by each student in the common room
at any time convenient to himself, from half-past
twelve till half-past two.

8. Fixed hours are assigned at which students who live in
the Hall can apply to professors of the college for
advice and aid.   On the days and at the hours of
which notice is posted attendance for an hour and a
half in each week during the session has been promised
by the professor of each of the subjects in which aid
is most commonly required—namely, Greek, Latin,
pure mathematics, applied mathematics, and physics.
At known times, therefore, each of those five professors, as well as the professor of English, may be
found every week in the Principal's room, ready to
welcome and give help to any student who may come
to him for counsel or for explanation of a difficulty.

9. Notice is posted every Monday morning of the hours
during the week at which the Principal can be seen in
his room, without appointment, upon any business of
the Hall.

10. The Principal and students dine together at half-past five.
Any student who has chambers in the Hall may
occasionally bring a relative or a student friend to be
his guest at dinner.   A student who wishes to bring a

guest must obtain leave from the Principal not later than at breakfast-time on the same day, and deliver to the steward before noon a dinner-ticket, of which the price is two shillings. About once in each month there is a special guest-day. There is under no circumstances an additional charge for their dinner, or for any part of it, to students resident in Hall.

11. Tea is supplied in the evening to students in their rooms, or in the students' common room to such of them as may prefer to take their tea together there. Various opportunities will also be found of bringing students and Principal of University Hall into friendly personal relations with one another, and with students and professors of University College.

12. On Sundays the breakfast hour is half-past eight ; the dinner hour is half-past one, and there is supper instead of lunch.

13. The Hall is closed every evening at eleven o'clock, by which hour all students who have been out during the evening should have returned to their rooms, and any friends of theirs who have been visiting them should have left. Extension of this time can be obtained on any special occasion, by showing reason for it that shall seem sufficient to the Principal.

14. The most considerate quiet is to be maintained throughout the Hall at all times.

15. The occupant of rooms is answerable for the cost of any damage done within them to the furniture or building beyond reasonable wear and tear.

16. A student resident in the Hall, whose health fails in any way, though it be slightly, should make the fact known to the Principal without delay. Full attention will at once be given and continued, and, where medical aid is necessary, it must be called in.*

17. All responsibility for management within the Hall rests on the Principal, who does not doubt that the students will lighten it by free exchange of confidence. What-

* Cases of illness, if not severe, were always treated by Professor Morley himself, whose 'surgery' was once more revived.

ever complaint they have to make, though it be only
of a servant's inattention or the cooking of a dinner,
should be made to him.

18. All students living in Hall are asked also to remember
that their comfort as a household depends greatly
upon those who wait on them. Inefficient servants
will not be retained, but even these, while they are
in attendance at the Hall, should be treated with
courtesy, while those who do their best earn, besides
their wages, kindness and respect.

HENRY MORLEY

June, 1882.   (*Principal*).

'Prayers are read by the Principal at 8 a.m.' If there
was one form of self-indulgence which Professor Morley
did enjoy—one survival of the natural indolence which
was his old Adam—it was a late breakfast, with some
lingering over the newspaper before beginning the work of
the day. This utterly ceased during the seven sessions at
the Hall. There he always rose early, and was punctually
in his place ; and on the occasions when he came home to
sleep, a cab was always ordered to bring him to the Hall
by 8 a.m. He believed these morning prayers might be a
religious reality to his students. He carefully selected a
passage from Scripture, and then wrote a collect expressing the aspirations which he felt himself, and in which he
believed that others might as truly join.

Many examples might be given from Professor Morley's
letters to illustrate the spirit in which the work of the
Hall was carried on, but two must suffice. The first was
written on November 4, 1882, about a month after he had
taken charge.

DEAR DR. MARTINEAU,

You will be pleased to hear that two students, who are
about the youngest in the Hall, came to me of their own
motion after the meeting of the Manchester New College
Debating Society, and apologized for having turned down the
gas during the meeting. They said they did not know that you
or any professors or visitors were there, and that they thought

they were only playing off a small joke upon fellow-students. The prompt and frank confession and apology was, of course, to be at once accepted, but I took the opportunity of saying a few friendly words to the students generally after dinner next day, with that incident for text, and good-will has come, I hope, out of that little bit of schoolboy mischief. I did not think it likely that any student here would show disrespect to a meeting over which you were presiding, and am very glad to have been confirmed in that opinion.

Believe me, dear Dr. Martineau,
Always faithfully yours,
HENRY MORLEY.

More serious troubles than this had afterwards to be met, and the words of Mr. Jacks show how they were met. He was determined to put down evil, and equally resolved to 'overcome evil with good.' Here is a post-script to a letter to Mr. Dowson, September 14, 1886, delightfully characteristic of his estimate of the comparative value of different kinds of discipline :

I have been instructed in the mysteries of the Manchester New College students' common room and the wreckages there. The result is respect for the traditions of that institution. It is certainly good that men who have tiffs should be forcibly rubbed together by way of smoothing their angles, which I understand to be one of the brilliant ideas that make the common room a wholesome place for compelling students to understand themselves and one another. As gymnastics form a large part of this moral discipline, I shall make no more attempt to keep the room tidy, but have everything made clear for them, with only a table and forms till one o'clock, after which, on the days of Manchester New College lectures, the room can be put together in decent order for the use of our day residents who need a place of study. When Manchester New College hours come again they will be prepared for by taking out the better furniture, tying the curtains out of reach, and bracing up for a storm. This sounds absurd, but it will not be difficult to do, and I seriously think that it would be wiser not to put impediment in the way of clearly profitable fun. I only wish they had more elbow-room.

Mr. Talfourd Ely speaks of the Indian School as a matter in which Professor Morley took a special interest. At this time thirty or forty 'selected candidates' for the Indian Civil Service were required to spend two years of further study in England before being finally examined, and if successful sent out to India. At first it was intended that these two years should be passed either at Oxford or Cambridge; but University College, London, obtained so much recognition from the authorities as to be placed also on the list, the candidates being required to live in the house of one of the professors. Teachers of Indian vernacular tongues were provided at the college; the London Law Courts, where the candidates had to study legal procedure, were close at hand, and in the final examinations it was frequently found that those who lived in London passed extremely well. In 1885 Professor Morley was dubbed 'Censor' by the Council of University College, and the entire management of the Indian School placed under his control; but for three years previous to this he had given much time to making the arrangements necessary for its success. The men then had to pass the examinations at an earlier age than is now required, and probably needed more control than is now the case; but they were then, as now, picked men, of high intellectual attainments, and Professor Morley rejoiced to have them for his college and his Hall.

What else has to be said about University Hall may be left to the conclusion of the chapter, after we have noted his other work during these last seven years of his London life. Lecturing, of course, continued. At the London Institution he had usually given one or two annual lectures during the Christmas holidays; but in 1883, by some untoward arrangement, he agreed to lecture on January 18, after term had begun, and on a Thursday, when he had already seven lectures to give. His subject at the Institution was 'English War Poetry,' and he would no doubt have given an interesting address on it, but his voice was overstrained, and failed before the end. He did not lecture there again till December 12 and 19, 1887, after which he was invited every year till his death, but always had to decline. There were many more 'extra' lectures, including another at Sheffield on March 19, 1883, during the Easter vacation.

At University College various causes of friction cropped up during his last six years; and during the last three, 1887-89, Professor Morley comparatively rarely attended the meetings of the Senate. Many changes had taken place since the decade when the college was making most splendid progress, and holding so distinguished a position in the examinations of the University. He was willing to let younger men have their opportunity, and not to stand in the way, even though he could not approve their proposals or further all their wishes. What is most noteworthy is that never for a moment did he lose faith in the college, or slacken in his affection. He knew that there must be ups and downs in the life of every institution, and that rates of progress must inevitably vary. He was far too sanguine to doubt that there was a good time coming; he had too deep a faith to dream of abandoning any of the principles of his own life and labour.

He did not, however, thus resolve to stand aside until he had made a most energetic attempt to realize his great ideal of truer fellowship at University College, and to this he devoted the three years 1884-85-86. Early in January, 1884, he issued his draft scheme for a University College Society.

Mr. T. Gregory Foster, who had a close personal knowledge of the events he describes, has kindly sent me the following communication:

The University College Society was instituted at the beginning of the session 1884-85 by the late Professor Henry Morley, and was active during the remainder of his tenure of the chair of

23

English, until the end of the session 1888-89. The aim of the society was to promote fellowship throughout the college.

Previous to its establishment there had been a number of independent societies and clubs in the college, each of them appealing to small groups of students, but there was no general society to represent the whole body of students. In process of time these small societies and clubs, together with the administrative subdivisions of the college into faculties and departments, destroyed the sense of *esprit de corps* that ought to belong to one great institution.

Professor Morley therefore planned the College Society on the widest possible basis; it was to utilize the existing clubs and societies and ' to take such measures as it may think best to sustain and increase their individual well-being.'

The advantages of such a society were at once seen, and its membership speedily rose to over a thousand.

Not least of the many good works of the college society must be reckoned the establishment of the college *Gazette*, which ran with great success from 1886 to 1889. During its first year it was edited by Professor Morley under the *nom de plume* of John Gower.

The twelve numbers of that year are full of interest; they show the generous sympathetic spirit that inspired all that Henry Morley did, and are full of those touches of delightful humour with which he often cleared up misunderstandings and prevented bickerings.

The articles on the question of the development in London of a teaching University are of very special interest. The session 1886-87 was one of crisis in that important question. All through Henry Morley held to the broad, far-sighted policy, in preference to the immediately expedient, that there should be one University in London and not two, and that University College should be made the chief teaching institution in a University worthy of the capital of our great empire. Referring to the magnificent resources of London for such a University, he wrote:

' On such foundations, working with the heartiest co-operation of the teachers, it will be possible for the Senate of the University so to build, so to enlarge its powers in aid of higher education, that before two generations shall have passed London will have a University, at once local and imperial, for breadth and fulness of efficiency without a rival in the capital of Europe.'

Mr. Foster gives further details with regard to the society and its present successor, the 'Union,' and concludes:

On all hands the present social and athletic life of the college is mainly the result of Henry Morley's work, and I am glad to say that in reaping the fruit of his labours the present generation of students and of staff do not forget him.

T. GREGORY FOSTER.

(Student 1884-88, Fellow of the College, Lecturer and Quain Student in English.)

In starting the *Gazette*, Professor Morley assumed all pecuniary responsibility, as well as the editorship, and was ultimately left quite £100 out of pocket by his enterprise. But the early numbers are full of interest to all who care for the college, as well as to those who wish to understand the spirit which he tried to infuse into its activities.

The year 1883 was his last as examiner to the University of London, and in 1884 he is thanked for his past services as examiner to the Society of Arts, in which capacity he can no longer act. But compared with the new duties he was continually undertaking, these retirements seem like Falstaff's half-pennyworth of bread by the side of his intolerable deal of sack! Certainly few men have ever lived to whom such a load of work as he went on accumulating would not have proved intolerable. In 1883 a re-issue of his 'Library of English Literature' began, and continued coming out in monthly parts for the next four years. This involved careful revision, if not much fresh writing.

In May, 1883, appeared the first volume of an important new series. Messrs. Routledge and Son, who had already distinguished themselves by publishing good literature at popular prices, determined to do something better than had ever yet been done, and to publish a series of volumes, well chosen, with 400 well-printed pages, well bound, and with valuable original introductions, at one shilling. Nothing like this had ever been attempted, and if still cheaper issues have subsequently succeeded, they owe success in some degree to the new interest in our literature aroused by this enterprising venture. Professor Morley was appointed editor. Sheridan's plays was the first volume, and after this, month by month, appeared a new volume of 'Morley's Universal Library,' each containing four pages of original introduction. Here Professor Morley gives tersely, and with many a bright sparkle of his old humour, the facts about the author and his time needful for the understanding of the author's works. We have, indeed, lightly written reminiscences of his lectures. He did a certain amount of expurgation. He resolved to publish something of Rabelais, knowing and wishing others to know his importance in the history of literature; but Rabelais could not be admitted to speak for himself in decent society till he had wiped his feet on the mat at the door. So with regard to Boccaccio's 'Decameron.' These tales had played a most important part in literature, and greatly influenced our Elizabethan age; but this was a case in which the half is better—in fact, much better—than the whole. Professor Morley, however, never altered in his conviction as to the importance of publishing, wherever possible, complete works; and after the 'Universal Library' had run to sixty-three volumes, he was glad that it was succeeded in December, 1888, by the 'Carisbrooke Library,' where he could find space for some longer writings than he had hitherto been able to produce. In this series his introductions are much fuller, and he gives many valuable notes.

The success of the scheme started by Routledge naturally led the way to similar undertakings, with many of which we have no concern. But an article in the *Daily*

News in the summer of 1885, calling attention to the fact
that we had nothing in England corresponding to a
famous threepenny series in Germany, promptly produced
a request from Cassell and Company that Professor
Morley would undertake to edit such a series.   He
accepted their proposals, and Cassell's 'National Library'
was the result.   Here the issue was in weekly volumes,
and continued for about five years.   At a cost not exceed-
ing the gas or water rate, a constant supply of good
literature could be 'laid on' to any house in town or
country, and a circulation varying from 50,000 to 100,000
copies for each volume attests the popular appreciation of
the enterprise.   Letters, which Professor Morley greatly
prized, came from the far West in America, and from
other lands on the borders of civilization, expressing
gratitude for these cheap and handy volumes, which
seemed almost as ubiquitous as Palmer's biscuits.   Here
again short introductions, now for the most part very
brief, give the reader the information he most needs to
understand his author ; and if all these introductions could
be fused into one compact whole, they would form a fine
treatise on our literature.

One set belonging to this series bears a character of its
own.   Shakespeare's plays are all given, each in a single
volume, with a carefully revised complete text.   Here
there was abundant room for a full introduction, telling
everything known about the dates of composition, of
printing, or of performance, and then dealing at considerable length with the inner meaning of the play.   In impressive and beautiful language he here wrote out the
thoughts that had made his lectures on Shakespeare of
such deep and lasting interest.   He gave no notes of the
ordinary kind.   Many others had done this task so well
that he left it to them, and rather recklessly threw away
his chance of producing an edition of Shakespeare containing all that an ordinary reader needs.   Most readers,

and certainly all students, require much more explanation
of a verbal or archæological character, and comparatively
few people like reading two books at once. Apart from
this drawback, it may safely be said that Professor Morley
is at his highest and best in his interpretation of our
greatest English writer, and no one knows the mind of
Henry Morley who does not know his exposition of
Shakespeare's religion. This he sums up in the three
precepts : Love God, love your neighbour, do your work ;
and one or other of these he found taught in every play.
In most of the little volumes he had space to print some
earlier work used by Shakespeare as a foundation for his
play, and occasionally this source of the drama is given in
a companion volume. The essential aim of Shakespeare's
own work is elicited by showing how he modified what he
borrowed from some predecessor. What he left unaltered,
what he changed, and why he did so—here are all-important contributions to our knowledge of Shakespeare's real
religion.

Professor Morley defined a play as

the story of one human action shown throughout by imagined
words and deeds of the persons concerned in it, artfully developing a problem in human life, and ingeniously solving it after
having excited strong natural interest and curiosity as to the
manner of solution. It must not be too long to be presented
at a single sitting.*

. This definition is open to the objection that in a tragedy
the problem is seldom solved, and the dramatist exhibits
only the evils arising from the failure to find a solution.
I do not know how Professor Morley would have answered
this objection in regard to many tragedies, whether he
would have made his definition cover a negative solution
—*i.e.*, a clear indication that the course pursued was
wrong, and that its opposite would be right—or whether

---

* 'Library of English Literature'—Plays, p. 1.

·he would have denied that certain modern compositions, like most of Ibsen's prose dramas, are true plays. But there is considerable interest in this concluding paragraph of his introduction to ' Hamlet,' the first he published of Shakespeare's plays :

> How many Hamlets are there in the world with intellectual power for large usefulness, who wait day by day and year by year in hope to do more perfectly what they live to do: die, therefore, and leave their lives unused, while men of lower power, prompt for action, are content and ready to do what they can, well knowing that at the best they can only rough-hew, but in humble trust that leaves to God the issues of the little service that they bring. It is a last touch to the significance of this whole play that at its close the man whose fault is the reverse of Hamlet's—the man of ready action, though it be with little thought, the stir of whose energies was felt in the opening scene—re-enters from his victory over the Polack, and the curtain falls on Fortinbras, King.

We cannot fail to read here something of an *Apologia* for Professor Morley's own literary career. As a young man, his ambition had been to write and polish his own poetry till it was worthy to give him a lasting place in literature. He had sacrificed this aim, and undertaken many an active engagement in which he knew he could only rough-hew; and he had made this change with deliberate intent, as the best service he could render with his powers, trusting to God to shape the issues of his life. Shakespeare said to him, ' Do your work,' and all his days this is what he tried to do.

On August 4, 1884, a conference on education was held at the International Health Exhibition, South Kensington, and Professor Morley was asked to read a paper in the University section. In the spring of this year the subject of a Teaching University for London had been discussed in private conference, and he took this subject for his theme. He took the same subject for his last two lectures at the London Institution on December 12 and 19, 1887.

Here, again, he was one of the pioneers to rough-hew a scheme of very great educational value. He was, of course, too sanguine in expecting its speedy triumph. He thought three years would suffice to reconcile opposing interests, and bring the matter into a shape which would be generally acceptable, and he would have been much surprised if he could have foreseen that February, 1898, would see nothing but a bill introduced in Parliament. He did not altogether admire the way in which the scheme was discussed and promoted, and after a few years he was content with having made his contribution. His experience as a teacher and examiner of his own classes, and also as a University examiner of candidates who included his own scholars as well as others, had impressed upon him the superiority of class examinations over such University examinations as tests of knowledge and good work. He was well aware of the danger of favouring his own students, and once wrote severely of a college teacher who had been a London examiner, and had shamelessly prepared his own students for the questions which he meant to set. But, on the other hand, Professor Morley found it difficult to give his own advanced students their fair chance at the University, and sometimes explained to them the principle on which he had to set his questions. These questions had to be such as could be answered out of text-books accessible to those who prepared themselves by private study. But in progressive studies text-books are inevitably in arrear of the teaching of living scholars, consequently the examinations could never be ' up to date.' The very features in his own teaching which made it specially valuable, and brought students to fill his class-room, were those which must count least when the candidates were assembled in Burlington Gardens. This disadvantage applied in greater or less degree to all teachers who were in advance of text-books, and whose teaching was valuable for some individual quality not to be found elsewhere. A good teacher examining his own class knows what his students have been taught, and what they ought to know themselves; and in colleges of sufficient academic standing the interests of education would best be served by allowing class work to count towards the attainment of a University degree. It may be most dis- heartening to a thoroughly able teacher to know that his students will have to compete with candidates who have been simply crammed to answer stock questions. The professors at University College, while selecting subjects in accordance with those announced for the London University, would repudiate the idea that their classes were merely preparatory for such examinations; and, in spite of all the University triumphs won by college students, there was a strong feeling that men and women who had had a college life, and enjoyed the living intercourse between the teacher and the taught, should not be fettered by the requirements of candidates who only read text- books, or were crammed in correspondence classes, and should not be labelled at the conclusion of their studies with precisely the same distinctions. How to provide proper safeguards when teachers were allowed to examine their own classes for University degrees, how to prevent the whole movement from degenerating into a paltry com- petition for fees—these were some of the problems to be solved in the establishment of a Teaching University for London. He wished to leave the present University free, as now, to examine all comers; he did not wish to see the establishment in London of a second University under any new name. He wanted new machinery added to the old, all under the same Chancellor and supreme govern- ment, but with new authorities competent to give dis- tinctive degrees to students who had had a thorough college training. After all these years, opinion has un- doubtedly been moving in the direction of his wishes, and he would gladly have seen Parliament pass the Bill of

1898. Possibly the cause might have advanced faster in its early years if it had gone more on his lines. He certainly possessed great power of comprehending the bearing of many adverse interests, and of inducing their advocates to accept the best available compromise.

In January, 1887, Professor Morley at last succeeded in carrying out his long-deferred plan to reissue 'English Writers.' The preface touches on several points noted in this biography, the issue of the first volume in 1864, 'part of the fulfilment of a young desire,' intended mainly as a popular history, but winning credit for sound scholarship, and opening to him a career 'in which the study of literature, until then the chief pleasure, became also the chief duty of his life.' This of itself rendered some change of plan inevitable, and at the same time the labours 'of many good scholars in England and Germany were beginning to make large annual additions to the knowledge of our early literature. In research over the whole field there were new energies at work. Their issues were worth waiting for.' . . . 'After waiting and working on through yet another twenty years, the labourer has learnt that he knows less and less. Little is much to us when young; time passes, and proportions change. But however small the harvest, it must be garnered ; scanty produce of the work of a whole life, it may yield grain to someone for a little of life's daily bread.'

His project was now to issue a series of half-yearly volumes of moderate price and convenient size. 'But as no labourer plans in his afternoon for a long day's work before nightfall, the proportions of the book should be on a scale that will not extend it beyond twenty volumes.' He lived to write ten volumes, and left material from which it was possible to publish the eleventh, comprising 'Shakespeare and his Time under James I.'

Thus the chief literary work of his life was again resumed. He had not secured for it the leisure that was indispensable, though he had packed most of his lectures into the Tuesday, Wednesday, and Thursday of each week, leaving the other days and most of vacation-time comparatively free for writing.   But he found it impossible to be punctual with half-yearly volumes till he had left London, and the sale, though it reached several thousands, was interfered with by the irregularity.

Another question is, whether it was possible, even for him, to do a scholar's work amid the rush of practical requirements which absorbed his time.   He called his book only 'An Attempt towards a History of English Literature.'   He never imagined that he had said the final word on his subject, but he studied for it more than some of his critics imagined, and had a reason to give for not accepting many of the new views which he was accused of ignoring.   There is something rather perverse in the criticism which drove him from his first design of composing a popular history of English writers by an over-estimate of its aim, and then refused to recognise the enormous amount of painstaking labour thrown into the book.   Of course he made mistakes.   The man who waits till he is sure of making no mistakes is a Hamlet. Inevitably, too, he had a tendency to abide by the judgments of his earlier years.   This is a tendency that exists in every steady judgment.   None of us can go beyond the length of our tether.   The length of his, at any rate, allowed him to present the world with a great wealth of information, carefully sifted and intelligibly arranged, where the inaccuracies are very few, and for the most part easily corrected.   To those who have enjoyed the easy reading of much of his earlier writing, the chief disappointment in this latest book is the demand it makes on the reader's close attention.   The sentences are heavily laden with the numerous facts which they convey, and several of such sentences have often to be borne in mind before their full meaning can be understood.   Only rarely

do the ingenious wit and bright fancy of earlier days come
now to sustain the interest and kindle the imagination.
No doubt this is partly due to a growing sense of physical
lassitude.   To the end of his days he could write as well
as ever, but not as readily.   It was now afternoon with
him, and later in the day than he knew.   The book would
have been different if he had not given so much of his
strength to lecturing ; but lecturing found him an income,
and was much more compatible with study than journalism.

At the end of the second volume of ' English Writers,'
Professor Morley wrote some ' Last Leaves,' and he
frequently continued this practice in subsequent volumes
as a means of making corrections and additions.   Here,
January, 1888, six months after it was due, he also wrote
some words which have a general bearing on literary controversy :

In this volume, and in its predecessor, I have differed greatly
in opinion from some fellow-workers for whose labours I seek
always to show the respect I feel.   I have tried, and shall
always try, to record truly and fully opinions entitled to be
heard, when I have not been able to accept them, and to keep
all oppositions of opinions within friendly bounds.   Wherever
I have failed, or may fail, to keep those right bounds, blame
should fall on me only.   I do not know why a student of life
or language in the obscure times of which only we have thus
far spoken should be so positive as he often is that all the
light is in himself, unless it be that with darkness around him
it is himself alone that he can feel or see. . . .   What is a
scholar ?   It should be a man or woman who scorns delight
and lives laborious days, to acquire by life-long labour knowledge of some matter of study for its own sake and its uses to
the world ; who is drawn by love of it into a sense of comrade-
ship that welcomes all who lead or follow in the chosen path,
who learns more and more clearly every year how little is the
most we can achieve ; whose hand, therefore, is swift to support
a stumbling neighbour, never put out to force a trip into a fall ;
whose word is clear of bitterness, who has digested knowledge
into wisdom, and who helps on the day to which Hooker
looked forward, when three words uttered with charity and

meekness shall receive a far more blessed reward than three thousand volumes written with disdainful sharpness.

If this is a true definition of a scholar, that title will not be denied to Henry Morley.

Vol. II. completes the story down to the Norman Conquest; Vol. III. was ready by June, 1888, and covers the ground up to Chaucer. Vol. IV., the first of two dealing with the fourteenth century, was ready by December, 1888. After this nothing appeared till May, 1890. In these early volumes he, of course, reprinted much from the first edition of his book, but he was mindful of the large additions made to our knowledge on the subject through the labours of other scholars, and much had to be re-written, after reading and digesting a formidable amount of their published pages.

This applied most of all to the controversies concerning the writings of Chaucer, and accounts for the long delay in the appearance of Vol. V. He kept his readers waiting fifteen months, during which occurred the removal to Carisbrooke, rather than publish what he had not thoroughly revised.

On April 25, 1883, his second daughter was married to Henry Ellis, grandson of the William Ellis well known as an educational reformer, and as the founder of one of the most successful of Marine Insurance Companies. The Professor duly performed his part at the chapel and the breakfast, but the same date is on a long important letter to Mr. Dowson, begun before and finished after the ceremony, and going elaborately into the question of building the additional rooms behind University Hall. On May 16 he was elected on the committee of the London library, and henceforth became a regular attendant at its meetings. He had joined the library in 1877, and had made much use of it, coming in person to consult and carry away its books. On December 8 he took the chair at the College for Working Women at a meeting attended by Lord and Lady Wolseley and Colonel and Mrs. Maurice. On January 11, 1884, he appeared as Old Father Christmas at the Rhyl Street Domestic Mission, and delighted many young hearts as a veritable embodiment of goodwill and good cheer.

He did not altogether abandon even provincial lecturing, for on April 27, 1885, he began a course of Monday evening lectures on Shakespeare at Brighton after teaching in the morning at Sydenham, and in the afternoon at University College.

In 1885 he wrote an introduction to ' The Tales of the Sixty Mandarins,' by P. V. Ramaswami Raju, one of his Indian lecturers at University College, who had followed his own example in writing fairy-tales. He enjoyed reading these Indo-Chinese stories, revised the proofs, and gladly gave them his commendation. And, oh! this incident recalls the bundles of MS. which other students brought and asked him to read and help them to publish. They left the precious papers with him at their own peril. Some were returned after years of waiting; some, whose ownership was difficult to trace, were found at Carisbrooke after his death. He was not an editor, and this additional burden proved sometimes the proverbial ' last straw.' During 1883-84-85 there are now and again notes in Mrs. Morley's diary, ' Father came home poorly,' and so on; once it is ' very poorly indeed,' but it was most difficult to induce him to take any care of himself. He allowed himself some holiday every summer at Carisbrooke, and excursions with friends to Freshwater, Sandown, and other parts of the island, were very enjoyable to all who went. In 1886 we hear of his writing in the summer-house on the tennis-lawn, and one long letter written to his wife on Sunday evening, July 18, is full of local gossip, and contains this picture towards its close.

This little epistle has occupied the time of service in the little chapel down below. They had sung their opening hymn when we settled to ink, and are now at the closing hymn. We watched the people going in, and it was very pleasant to see their friendly greetings and domestic ways together ; they go in, babies and all. Now we shall see them coming out, after I have given you my dear love, also in a domestic way. Pen and ink work for the printer has been going forward very well, and yet I feel as if I were resting in idleness.

This year he edited 'Florio's Montaigne,' and also 'Boswell's Johnson,' in five volumes.

On October 12 Sir Saul Samuel writes to him respecting the appointment of a professor to the Chair of Modern Literature at the University of Sydney, Australia. There are also entries calling to mind a large amount of correspondence and other work which he did as executor to his late brother-in-law, James Sayer, of Hastings. These were the years after he and the Old Neuwieders had discovered one another,* and when he regularly went to their annual gatherings, often with Mrs. Morley, and rejoiced to contribute something to the Moravian Missions.

On March 31, 1887, he lectured at Cork on 'The Celtic Element in English Literature.' A few days before this the foundations were put in for a new wing which he built to his house at Carisbrooke. The main feature of this addition was a fine library where he could stow ten or twelve thousand volumes, and where he could write in a bay window looking out across a pretty lawn with evergreen shrubs and fir-trees, to the noble ruins of Carisbrooke Castle. He dearly loved this view, and had his table right in front of the window. Behind, the room was somewhat dark, as all space was required for bookshelves, and two other small windows were filled with stained glass containing beautiful portraits of Dante and of Chaucer.

In Newport, Isle of Wight, Her Majesty's Jubilee reign

* P. 28.

was commemorated by the present to the town of a Free Library by the late Charles Seely, Esq., J.P., and Professor Morley was asked to select most of the books for it. Writing to Mrs. Morley on July 16, he speaks of a bad headache which stopped his reading, so he had been buying books for the Newport Free Library. The letter incidentally mentions that he is chairman of the executive of the Free Library movement in St. Pancras. We are more surprised to hear that he is declining invitations to lecture at Bradford and Alderley Edge in the coming winter. But he holds out hopes that, if they like, he will come to them the following season. He had for some time made up his mind that he would cease all regular lecturing in the summer of 1889; but his first intention was to send in his resignation at University College twelve months earlier, and to devote his last year in London to a series of farewell courses. This would undoubtedly have been profitable, but very fatiguing. Various reasons, among them the Quain bequest endowing the English chair at University College—though this proved of very small pecuniary interest to himself—induced him to abandon this idea, and to defer his resignation at the college till the time when he left London.

In the spring of 1888 my wife and I moved to Bridport, and were visited there by Professor and Mrs. Morley the following August. We all had some days of good holiday, and one incident is worth recording. We returned home one evening through the fields of a certain farmer, and met him and his men carrying hay. Eight years later this same farmer asked me who it was that he had once seen walking with me, and reminded me of an encounter between our respective dogs which recalled this occasion. He had been so struck with the appearance of a fine old English gentleman that he had always wanted to know his name. On being shown a photograph of the Professor, he immediately recognised the figure that had so impressed

his memory. On another occasion Professor Morley was
travelling in a third-class carriage (as he always did travel)
from here to Maiden Newton, and in the compartment
were a number of farmers, one of whom was very noisy
and whose lively humour was not always quite refined.
Professor Morley said nothing till they all changed at the
junction, when, turning to this man, he remarked: ' You
have very good abilities, but they need cultivation.' That
man knew him not, but had not forgotten the incident
some years later when he told me the story.

January 22, 1889, brought a request that he would write
for the new edition of ' Chambers' Encyclopedia' an article
on ' The History and Genius of English Literature.' The
next day he lectured for the Royal Manchester Institution
in the Memorial Hall, Albert Square, on ' Men, Women,
and Books.' On March 5, at the Athenæum, Camden Road,
he distributed the prizes for Hamilton House School, and
gave an address on Education, and on June 1 he did the
same at the Highbury Athenæum.   On June 26 he went
to Bangor to present the certificates and give the annual
address at the close of the session of the University College
of North Wales.   In August he lectured at the Oxford
summer meeting of University Extension students.   A
domestic event also occurred during his last session in
London.   This spring his third and youngest daughter
was married to the Rev. Edgar Innes Fripp, B.A., son
of George Fripp, the artist.

His last lecture at University College was attended by
several of his former students, men and women.

One who knew him well says:

He summed up in a few weighty sentences the thoughts of
a life spent in truly patriotic service. Glancing back at the
generations of writers who have succeeded one another with
scarcely a break for five centuries, he declared that he could
only condemn two as having wilfully perverted their talents to
the harm of their fellow-men. Those two were Sterne and
Byron. The judgment was characteristic in every sense.

24

He closed with a few simple words, telling his hearers
something of his own personal ambition :

As a young man (he said) I had a literary ambition; I
thought that I could make a name among the minor poets of
the day. I may be stupid in my estimate of my own powers,
but I think so still. Soon, however, I asked myself whether
it would not be of more service to my country-people to try
and bring others to love the great poets of England than to be
myself one of the small ones. I deliberately and entirely cast
aside my small ambition. I resolved—spite of the fact that I
did not then see my way before me—to become a teacher of
literature.

On July 1, after the annual distribution of college prizes,
a meeting was held in the Mathematical Theatre, presided
over by Mr. Justice Charles, to present Professor Morley
with the following address :

TO

HENRY MORLEY, LL.D.,

PROFESSOR OF ENGLISH LANGUAGE AND LITERATURE
AT UNIVERSITY COLLEGE, LONDON,

AND

PRINCIPAL OF UNIVERSITY HALL.

The undersigned past and present students of University
College and residents at University and College Halls take the
occasion of Professor Henry Morley's retirement for expressing
their feelings of esteem and regard for his character and their
admiration for the noble work which he has accomplished.

Professor Morley has laboured unweariedly for University
College for nearly a quarter of a century, and the high position
now occupied by the chair of English, and the college generally,
is largely due to his genius and industry. In everything that
he has undertaken, whether in teaching or in disseminating by
his writings a knowledge of, and love for, the best that has been
produced by the world's thinkers, he has been rewarded with
abundant success. The whole English people is indebted to

him as a great teacher of his time, but only those who have been under his personal instruction can adequately appreciate his peculiar charm in teaching, and the sympathy that his large-heartedness and catholicity of mind have enabled him to feel for all that is good in human literature and human character. Perhaps no teacher of our time has exercised a greater influence upon others, and there are many who are proud to acknowledge him as the best inspiration of their lives. In spite of his busy life, he has been ever ready to help and sympathize with others, and his kindly hospitality has continually been extended to those who were most in need of friends.

During Professor Morley's principalship of University Hall, he has shown the same sympathetic spirit. With the loyal assistance of Dr. Forster Morley, he achieved such immediate success that the building speedily had to be enlarged, and his unfailing energy for the well-being of all has won for him universal popularity.

The success of the movement for the higher education of women, and the opening to them of the doors of University College, and subsequently of other institutions, is largely due to his advocacy. Those women who have known him at the college, or have benefited by his interest in College Hall, gratefully testify to his constant kindness and support.

The unfailing interest which Professor Morley has taken in the prosperity of University College is known to all, and students of the college who have not been members of his classes wish to express their sense of indebtedness. Many of the benefits now enjoyed by the students are owing to his initiative, and every proposal for more widely extending the work of the college, and promoting friendly intercourse among the students, has had his active support.

All who have the good of University College at heart must regret that Professor Morley feels that the time has come for him to retire, but they know that he has given the prime of his life to his work at the college, and that no one is more deserving of rest. They know, too, that his labours will not stop, but that he will devote the leisure which he will now enjoy to the completion of his great book on English Writers, in which will be summed up the essence of his life's work.

They can only wish him God speed, and hope that he will be blessed with many years of happiness.

The chairman read these words, and said that he wished they were more emphatic. Assuredly they express a conviction of the value of his services that was very widely spread and deeply felt. Mr. Arber, then Professor of English at Mason College, Birmingham, spoke for the male students, and Miss Day represented the women. It was a trying ceremony for Professor Morley himself. He began with unsteady voice, ' My dear friends and fellow-students,' and told them that, in going to Carisbrooke, he was carrying with him there the friendships of a lifetime. He spoke of his associations at the college with the many eminent men who had guided its destinies during the past twenty-four years, and as his parting charge urged upon his hearers the duty of being loyal to the college, which, he said, had a great future in developing individual citizenship, and consequently national character. Hearty cheers for Professor and Mrs. Morley closed the proceedings, and his career at the college came to an end.

It was the more difficult for him to speak on this occasion, for during the last month he had experienced the greatest disappointment of his life.

University Hall had been sold by Manchester New College to Dr. Williams' Library. The trustees of Manchester New College had long contemplated moving their college to Oxford. Founded at Manchester, moved to York and back to Manchester, it had been brought to London and located in Gordon Square in order to take advantage of a close association with University College, Gower Street. When University tests were abolished at Oxford and Cambridge, many of its supporters began sending their sons thither instead of to London, and wished that their ministers should also graduate at one of these older Universities. For several years the Unitarian body heard much about proposals to make a final move to Oxford, and build there a home for their college. It was at last decided that this should be done, and the move was made in 1889. The joint board of trustees mentioned on p. 340 had therefore to make fresh arrangements with regard to the Hall. Professor Morley had always assumed that, when this probable removal should take place, University College should have the option of purchasing University Hall, and of continuing to carry it on as a place of residence for college students. He had corresponded on this matter with Mr. Dowson, and had talked it over among friends when, owing to shortness of funds, there seemed a better chance of the Hall being bought *for* the college than *by* the college. However, when the Hall was for sale, the college made an offer to buy it, and for some time this was the only offer received. But among the Unitarians concerned there were many who were most unwilling to let the Hall thus go. Here is a copy of an inscription in its dining-hall :

THIS HALL WAS ERECTED IN COMMEMORATION OF THE PASSING OF THE DISSENTERS CHAPELS ACT IN 1844 7 & 8 VICTORIA CHAP : 45 THAT STATUTE BEING THE FIRST RECOGNITION BY THE LEGISLATURE OF THE PRINCIPLE OF UNLIMITED RELIGIOUS LIBERTY. UNTIL THAT STATUTE THE LAW ASSUMED ALL WORSHIP TO IMPLY THE PROPAGATION OF SOME SPECIAL DOGMAS TO BE DETERMINED BY ITSELF IF NOT DECLARED BY THE FOUNDERS.

THE OBJECTS OF THE FOUNDERS OF THIS HALL WERE

TO PROVIDE FOR STUDENTS OF UNIVERSITY COLLEGE LONDON THE ACCOMMODATION AND SOCIAL ADVANTAGES OF COLLEGE RESIDENCE

To provide a place where instruction without reference to creed should be permitted in theology and other subjects not taught or not wholly taught in University College and disavowing all denominational distinctions and religious tests to maintain the sanctity of private judgment in matters of religion.

This particular mode, then, of commemorating the Act had been adopted with the express idea of supplementing the education at University College on the one side on which the Gower Street system was necessarily defective, viz., its religious side. No theology, not even religious philosophy, might be taught there. Manchester New College was subsequently located in the Hall in order that its students, both lay and divinity, might have their secular training at University College, while public classes for the free study of theology and every branch of philosophy were held at the Hall, and residence was provided there under liberal religious influences. All the conditions were now changed, and men as honourable and as clear-headed as Professor Morley felt themselves under no moral obligation to sell the Hall to be hereafter worked on the lines which mark the essential basis of University College. Dr. Williams' Library is supported by an old Nonconformist trust, the principal object of which is the education of students, of various Dissenting denominations, as Christian ministers. A building had been erected for it in Grafton Street, but now its trustees offered a higher price for the Hall than the offer made by University College, and a majority of the joint board with whom the decision lay thought that the trustees of this library, with its various educational and religious functions, were the fittest body to be allowed to purchase the Hall. Negotiations for this sale were therefore promptly concluded without giving University College any chance of raising its bid.   Professor Morley could not see the matter in the same light as the joint board.   He pointed to the first object stated in the inscription.   To him it seemed that providing a residence for University College students was the one essential purpose to which the builders of the Hall had originally given their money, and he looked on any other disposal of the building as a moral breach of trust.   He regarded the transaction as an instance of 'how the judgment of the best men can be warped by party zeal.'   After this he would never go on a public platform in furtherance of any Unitarian object. He could worship with Unitarians, he said, and he could be friends with them; but he would never again act with them in any denominational society.   This resolution he kept to the last.

This great disappointment did occasionally make him a little bitter; it was the only thing that ever did so since he was a young man.   Miss Morison supplies a true touch when she says that they could not talk to him about the success of College Hall and the good work it was doing for the women students; he felt so deeply the contrast with the failure of his own efforts for the men.   Perhaps he was beginning himself to recognise how great were the sacrifices he had been making for the Hall.   His health this last session was in a very precarious condition, and another year or two of his London life would certainly have killed him.   He rallied much at Carisbrooke, but he died with life-long purposes unachieved.

CHAPTER XVI.

THE college session was no sooner over than the move to
Carisbrooke began. Mrs. Morley calls July 15, 1889, 'a
terrible day of delivery, every place in utter confusion.'
All the Professor's furniture from the Hall, and much from
Upper Park Road, including 12,000 books, came down in
eight vanloads, and crossed the water to the Isle of Wight.
In due course, however, the house was put straight, and
many happy hours were spent by the master arranging
his library. Then began some pleasant social intercourse
with the neighbours; this was to be part of the retirement from lecturing and London. There were the Pin-
nocks, the Chatfeild Clarkes, the Eveleghs, the Hughes,
and other old friends belonging to the Unitarian congregation at Newport, and there was its minister, the
Rev. John Dendy, B.A., and his wife. Mr. Dendy was
a man of true culture and earnest religious feeling. He
had been educated for the ministry, and had occupied a
pulpit for some years, when the state of his health made a
change of occupation necessary. He then went into business in Manchester, and when I first knew him in 1875
was a prosperous merchant with a large family living
in a commodious house near Eccles, a valued member of
the Monton congregation, and greatly appreciated by our
ministers in Lancashire and Cheshire as a layman who

kept in close touch with religious interests. Mrs. Dendy was sister to the Rev. Charles Beard of Liverpool. Further changes brought Mr. Dendy back into the ministry, and in 1889 he was settled at Newport, I.W., where he and Professor Morley became warmly attached friends and fellow-workers. Mr. and Mrs. Dendy gave much time to the Jubilee Free Library already mentioned. A still more important common field of labour was an Association for the Maintenance of Higher Education in Newport, Isle of Wight. Professor Morley helped to found this society, and became chairman of its committee, while Mr. Dendy acted as its honorary secretary. For several winters its courses of Oxford University Extension lectures proved most successful, and various branches of work were continued by a students' union during the summer months. For some years, in fact, the Isle of Wight was a model extension centre.

No less cordial and helpful were Professor Morley's relations with three successive Vicars of Carisbrooke, and with members of the congregation there. In 1889 the Vicar was the Rev. E. Boucher James, M.A., who had held the living since 1858. He wrote, February 11 :

Allow me to write and thank you for the honour you have done to dear old Carisbrooke in attaching its name to your new library. Not only does it show your regard for the place, which will be, I hope, for many years your home; it also adds distinction to the time-honoured Wehtgaresburk.

Mr. James and Professor Morley had much in common. Mrs. James writes:

Professor Morley's friendship was one of the brightest parts of our happy Carisbrooke life.

With many other neighbours relations were most neighbourly. Mrs. Morley's health and strength did not permit much party-giving, but it was nevertheless a very hospitable house and garden.

Another occupation found for the Professor took him

back to the Madeley days of Tracts on Health. A parochial committee for Carisbrooke was formed in February, 1890, four years before the Parish Councils Act, and dealt with the main drainage of the village and the water-supply of Gunville. He was appointed chairman of this committee, where his personal influence was as valuable as it had been in dealing with larger interests in London; and only a fortnight before his death, a meeting was held at his house in order that he might preside, and do what no other chairman could do. He was made a J.P. for Newport in April, 1892, and with the aid of a 'Justice's Manual' qualified himself for these new duties.

In going to live at Carisbrooke he did not mean to desert London, where alone he could find the books and papers needful for his literary work. So he kept on his teaching at Laleham to pay for his journeys up and down every fortnight or oftener, and the British Museum again knew him as an industrious student. His duties, too, at the Apothecaries' Hall began to claim closer attendance. When he became Junior Warden in August, 1892, this involved going to town every week.

Such were some of the main features of his life at Carisbrooke. On the mornings when he stopped at home he could enjoy his breakfast comfortably, and read his correspondence at leisure. Then he would pass through a pretty greenhouse, full of bright flowers which Mrs. Morley took under her personal charge, into the large handsome library where he had accumulated his literary treasures of forty years. It was not all books and papers. In the centre of the mantelpiece was a beautiful terracotta figure of Hermes. This represented the spirit of literature. Around were grouped the oddest collection of quaint notions. A portly pig stood for the British public, a nodding Chinaman did duty for the learned lecturer, an ecstatic frog expressed a delighted audience, a stork with a long bill ready to stick into something told of the critics,

and half a dozen other little figures had some other meaning on which humorous discourse could be held. They
are not much without such living word of explanation,
but they serve to remind us of the bright fun often enjoyed
during the first three years of his retirement.   The
attractions of his study, however, by no means made him
a regular student there.   He revelled in his freedom from
fixed engagements, and the possibility of writing only
when he felt inclined. He would often spend the whole
forenoon over unimportant odds and ends in house or
garden, with hard labour at the pump-handle, or, maybe,
take a walk into Newport on some small errand ; and
then, after an early dinner, he would perhaps give some
hours to real work.   Tea at five and supper at nine were
regular institutions ; late in the evening he seldom worked.

   On the whole, this life was very good for him, diversified
as it was by frequent journeys to town, and full of the
varied interests which make a country life so busy.   But
it was not a good life for getting forward rapidly and
steadily with his writing. Now that there was comparatively little which he was obliged to do, he often
seemed to be postponing the more important to the less
important in a way that would be incomprehensible if we
did not know the secret of his insidious disease.   This
had been partially checked, and was for a while held at
bay, but all the time it was increasing his difficulties in
doing his real work as he knew it should be done.

   This, however, appeared chiefly in the last years.   For
some time he continued to do as much as would make a
very fine week's work for most men, and if ever man had
earned a right to an occasional rest, it was Henry Morley
at the age of sixty-seven.

   He was not allowed to retire without receiving many
tokens of appreciation for past services.   On July 6 the
council of University College appointed him Emeritus
Professor of English Language and Literature.

On December 6, 1889, he and Mrs. Morley went to Bedford College, where he was presented by the Shakespeare Reading Society with a very handsome tall lamp, which afterwards always stood on his library floor. He was for many years a vice-president of this society.

On January 4, 1890, he drafts the following letter of thanks :

DEAR MISS CROUDACE,

Will you kindly convey my warm thanks and best New Year wishes to the old pupils at Queen's College who added to my Christmas happiness by their beautiful and useful parting gift ? I had often admired that kind of dish and thought I should like one, and knew that I should never be so luxurious as to buy one for myself. It is a little sad as one grows old to become surrounded by mementoes of love and goodwill associated with work that is done no more, often with kindred and friends that are no more, though never with affection that is ended. I hope, however, that the loving young minds whose companionship made work at Queen's College a pleasure, and whose durable sign of goodwill should find its way down to my grandchildren, are all born to enjoy many years of happiness, and that opportunities will come to me sometimes of seeing one and another of them. For those of us who don't again meet face to face there will always be the feeling, on my part, that I have young friends scattered here and there who think of me kindly, on their part, that they have an old friend at Carisbrooke upon whom they can look in with certainty of a welcome whenever they may come that way and care to fish him up out of the bottom of his ink-pot.

On February 5 he sends a letter in reply to the communication he had received in reference to the more comprehensive scheme which had been started at University College. For this Mr. G. A. Aitken and Mr. T. Gregory Foster were joint honorary secretaries. Many old students were traced, and 322 subscribers contributed £279; but the movement was ' confined to those who had known Professor Morley in connection with his work at the college, and no attempt was therefore made to obtain assistance from the general public.' Mr. Aitken's final report appeared in February, 1891. It says :

After careful consideration, it was decided that a handsome bronze medal, bearing Professor Morley's portrait, should be established, and should be given annually with the Senior English Literature prize at the college, without special examination. This will in the most effectual way secure the connection of Professor (now Emeritus Professor) Morley's name with the chair which he occupied so long, and on which he bestowed so much honour ; and the council of the college were good enough to readily respond to the proposal. The work of preparing dies for the medal was placed in the hands of Messrs. N. Macphail and Co., Glasgow, with satisfactory results.

After providing a fund for the purchase of the yearly medal, and paying incidental expenses, a balance of £200 remained, and this sum has been handed over to Professor Morley as a personal gift. Subscribers will be glad to see, from the characteristic letter which follows this report, how entirely Professor Morley's wishes have been met.

Carisbrooke, Isle of Wight,
February 5, 1890.

My dear Aitken,

The album, which to me and mine is very precious, came safely on Monday morning as I was leaving for town ; and on this, the first evening after my return, I have read it through to the last man, with my eyes watering. I cannot say how many kindly, loving memories are stirred as I pass on from name to name subscribed to the warm-hearted godspeed that magnifies with so much generous affection the fruits of happy labour in the past, as if what had been aimed at had indeed been done. But the book shows how readily in all relations of friendship built on earnest fellowship of work the will is taken for the deed. And it is well that we so cheer one another as we toil upon our way. As I read each name in this list, I know that I can find in it the name of a friend to whose kindness I do with all my heart join an answering kindness, in many cases I might say an answering affection. I wish I could thank each individually by this one act of poor acknowledgment of a book that will, I hope, long after I am dust, have value for my children's children and their aftercomers.

The decision of the Testimonial Committee I accept as another expression of strong personal goodwill. Fog permitting, I will get for you, as you suggest, a profile photograph when I go to town next week. Nothing could please me more, or be in my own eyes a more covetable honour, than perpetual remembrance in connection with the English classes at University College by a medal given to the best man of each year, without special examination—for examinations are too many already.

Of the large personal gift that remains, let me say that I am happy in it because of the large personal regard that it implies. After consideration, I think that it will be best to accept it, and to invest it separately, using the interest of it during my life for the annual purchase of some permanent addition to my little possessions, which I shall regard as, for the rest of my life, an annual gift from my old friends of University College, University Hall, and College Hall, so that mementoes of old days of pleasant fellowship with them will from year to year—as far as years may go in an old man's life—be multiplying in my home. The fund itself will at my death replace what I have had to spend on the removal of my books and chattels to Carisbrooke, and putting the books up again in the library, which is my last workshop. The testimonial will thus have come into my life as a good fairy, the subscribers as a troop of fairies who have, by the magic of their kindness, moved house for me, and placed me here surrounded by my books, free of all tolls upon my basket and my store that would leave so much the less in the basket of my wife when I am gone. Meanwhile, so long as I live I shall indulge my fancy with a succession of keepsakes as visible signs of what I am little likely to forget. But there is pleasure in periodical reminders of a strong goodwill, though we may feel that it cannot be made stronger; else, why do we keep home birthdays?

With kindest regards to yourself and all of you,

I am, my dear Aitken,

Yours always sincerely,

HENRY MORLEY.

The investment of this £200 and the purchase of an annual present with the dividends was a happy idea, and was duly carried out. But the Professor generally bought something which others could enjoy as well as, or even more than, himself. For instance, one year his present was a set of iron rods and nets to surround the tennis lawn. In 1890 a large party of Sunday-school teachers and friends, chiefly from Northern towns, came in relays to spend a summer holiday at Newport, and his tennis-lawn was at their service and much used. On August 9 they send a letter to convey 'their very sincere and hearty thanks for the great kindness you have shown them.'

This spring he read a paper full of characteristic convictions at the Christian Conference, whose meetings he was always glad to attend, and where, once at least, he presided, and had the satisfaction of calling first on a Roman Catholic priest and then on Dr. Martineau to open a discussion. The wideness of this conference was just after his own mind. He afterwards wrote out his paper, entitling it 'Co-operation among Christians,' more fully for the *Christian World* for July 3, 1890.

On November 26 he gave the address at a first meeting of an Old Students' Association formed at University College. He sketches the history of the college, showing how it began by offering a University education to all men irrespective of creed, how it had next led the way in gradually opening all its classes to women, and how the work to be done now was to go forward with the organization of the new Teaching University on the broad lines he always advocated.

On December 20 he wrote to me, sending his last volume of 'English Writers' as a Christmas present with some earnest good wishes. He adds:

There's no news that the mother hasn't provided in epistles, unless it be about the ink messes of this old manufacturer of libraries. Next year it looks as if I should have six libraries running together, old and new. The 'Library of English Literature' is in course of monthly re-issue. There is to be a re-issue of 104 of the volumes of 'Cassell's National Library,' with a few new books interspersed. Re-issue is begun of the 'Universal Library' on fine paper in half-crown volumes. The 'Carisbrooke Library' goes on, and two new 'Libraries' are to be started, one of poets in a dainty little series, the other in big volumes of historians. This, with two volumes a year of 'English Writers,' and a good deal of odd work in London and Isle of Wight, keeps me from sucking my thumbs. God bless you both.

Affectionate
GORILLA.

The 'Carisbrooke Library' did not continue beyond eighteen volumes, and it was succeeded by nine volumes of these 'Companion Poets' published in 1891 and 1892; they are indeed dainty volumes for the pocket. Before this he had resumed his own important series.

In May, 1890, after the long delay already noticed, he brought out Vol. V. of 'English Writers,' which is wholly occupied with Wycliffe and Chaucer. With the latter he dealt at considerable length. A long review in the *Athenæum* is chiefly occupied with proving that the 'Court of Love' is not genuine, and that the theory of Chaucer's development, founded on the assumption that it is, must therefore be unsound. The controversy is more for experts than the general public, and cannot be discussed here. But no doubt the line taken by Professor Morley did disappoint many Early English scholars, who thought that he had not been sufficiently ready to modify the positions taken in the first issue of his work. The greetings given to the succeeding volumes were cordial enough in many quarters, particularly among the leading papers of the great provincial towns; but we miss something of the appreciation we should have gladly seen in the chief literary organs of London. Perhaps they were waiting till the work was finished. Professor Morley never worried over reviews, but he occasionally sent a guinea to a newspaper cutting agency to see what the world was saying about his book; so that he cannot be said to have deliberately ignored all criticism. With greater regularity of publication the sale of 'English Writers' considerably improved, even though the times now dealt with were comparatively little known. Vol. VI. appeared in October, 1890, and covered the ground from Chaucer to Caxton. Vol. VII. is the only one dated 1891. It deals with the period from Caxton to Coverdale, and connects the Renaissance with the Reformation.

In February, 1891, he paid a visit to Belfast, where Mr. and Mrs. Edgar Fripp were just settling under happy auspices. In responding for 'Our Guests' at a public luncheon, he was not too sanguine in predicting a prosperous future for his son-in-law. The beautiful new church, All Souls, built for his congregation in Elmwood Avenue, stands there to prove this, and Mr. Fripp's own success as a lecturer on English literature in Belfast and the neighbourhood is as marked as his ability as a preacher.

On March 3 Mrs. Morley enters in her dairy: 'Father came home at 6.45, and unfolded budget till we went to bed.' So the old habit was revived. Hour after hour he would pour out to his wife a most interesting tale of what both deeply cared about, especially if it concerned their children. If others of the family were by, they heard it all, but the full story was never told unless Mrs. Morley was there. On March 4 he wrote me a letter agreeing to come to Bridport at Easter for a special occasion. I had had a Confirmation class of over sixty young people, most of whom were going to take their first Communion on the Thursday evening before Good Friday. Unitarian Bishops do not exist in England, nor did we desire any but a very simple ceremony, and I thought if Henry Morley would come and speak to my class they would never forget his words. He says:

It will be a new thing to give lay talk in aid of a religious preparation for life, but one might do worse, and it is long

25

since I have seen you both, so I will duly turn up for the day you name.

On March 26 he came, and gave us one of his own beautiful and impressive lay sermons. At a congregational meeting on Good Friday, he gave us his address on Tennyson's ' Idylls.'

Shortly before he paid us this visit, he had taken the services at the Newport Chapel on March 8, when Mr. Dendy had been suddenly called north by the serious illness of a son. We found two sheets of note-paper on which he had carefully planned the morning and evening services—hymns, lessons, prayers, and sermons—leaving nothing to the spur of the moment. Extempore prayers, indeed, he greatly disliked. On this occasion he used some of Dr. Sadler's published prayers, and also preached one of his sermons on ' Memory and Faith ' in the morning; taking one of F. W. Robertson's, on ' The Pre-eminence of Charity,' for the evening. We may well ask whether services like this, using the noble devotional literature that is available, would not be preferable to the spiritual food sometimes provided in emergencies. In Nonconformist places of worship a wish is often felt that cultivated laymen would prepare and conduct a service with the aid of the stores that are so widely accessible. On May 3 Professor Morley again helped Mr. Dendy by reading the lessons in the morning, and taking the whole evening service.

This spring and summer there was a good deal of family visiting at Carisbrooke. Robert Morley painted there industriously, and one of his best known pictures, ' Henpecked,' showing the maternal fowl chasing a fox-terrier, reproduced with much vigour a scene he had witnessed in a neighbouring farmyard. In May Mrs. Morley took part in an expedition to Sandown and Ventnor. In August the French fleet visited Cowes. On the 20th we went round the ships in one of the excursion steamers, and the next day a party of us went to Ryde to witness the review. We like to remember now that days like these did carry out the plan of what was meant to be done at Carisbrooke, with its enlarged accommodation for guests. Too soon, indeed, everything was changed, but no cloud of coming sorrow darkened the summer of 1891.

On July 11 Mrs. Morley writes: 'Father read "Memories."' This refers to the ' Some Memories ' of which ample use was made earlier in this book. Professor Arber deserves thanks for having persistently urged ' the Master,' as he loves to call him, to undertake the task of writing these most characteristic pages. They were not written easily, smoothly as they read, and the MS., which happens to be preserved, shows a most unusual amount of correction. They were intended to lead to the fulfilment of a lifelong purpose. On November 19 Professor Morley writes to Mrs. Fripp : ' I shall send in a day or two the first volume of " Books and Papers, by H. M., 1850-1870." We have read his letter from Liscard,* telling his hope to some day collect and publish an edition of his ' Works.' This aim was before him in his early literary efforts ; after he had left Madeley, and had nothing but his brains to rely on for making his new start, he resolutely determined to write not only what would sell, but something that should deserve to live. Since that time he had, indeed, achieved success in paths then undreamed of, but this very success had broken the continuity of his literary life, and he now endeavoured to secure that unity which is afforded by a collected edition of an author's works. To his disciples it is a profound disappointment that this purpose so far remains incomplete. Three other uniform volumes were published—' The Journal of a London Play-goer,' ' The Fairy Tales,' and ' Bartholomew Fair '—but they were not vigorously advertised, and the publishers—Routledge and

* P. 152.

Son—stopped the series of works on the ground that the demand for them had practically ceased. So students who wish for 'Palissy,' 'Jerome Cardan,' 'Cornelius Agrippa,' or 'Clement Marot, and other Studies,' must take their chance of picking up these volumes through second-hand dealers. They seldom or never appear in catalogues of books for sale.

The result might have been different if reviews had been more appreciative. But newspapers found it difficult to appreciate Professor Morley in all his various forms of activity. He was before the public in too many ways. The enormous sale of the 'National Library' and similar productions caused him to be classified as an editor of popular reprints; and the lack of unity in his labours, which he hoped to supply in this very series, proved too great to be thus removed.

I never heard a word of complaint from the Professor's lips respecting any review, or about the stoppage of the series. Probably he never abandoned his purpose, but was only waiting. Time had often brought him what he desired, and in all his plans he still counted on many years yet to come of life and labour. Any vexation he may have felt on this score, moreover, would be swallowed up in the great sorrow which was soon to quench the light and joy of his home.

During the autumn of 1891 he helped to organize the Extension lecturing in the Isle of Wight. He also wrote a biographical sketch of his late much-loved and honoured pastor at Hampstead, Dr. Sadler. On December 23 he and Mrs. Morley came to spend Christmas with us at Bridport, and on the 30th he gave a lecture on 'Comus' in our schoolroom. This subject was chosen in connection with our temperance work, in which he was thoroughly interested. He was never a teetotaler, but he believed that different sections of reformers might co-operate in promoting temperance, and was glad that the rules of the

Essex Hall Temperance Association enabled him to join as an honorary member. ' Temperance Notes ' in the *Inquirer* he always looked for, and read with much appreciation.

This Christmas Mrs. Morley seemed in fair health and good spirits, though not strong. On January 13, 1892, they started for Belfast, where the Professor lectured on the 19th and 21st for an ' Organ Fund,' and on the 25th and 26th for the Extension Society. On February 10 and 11 he gave two lectures at Lancaster for the Storey Institute, and on March 3 he gave another lecture at Belfast before bringing Mrs. Morley home again. Soon after this signs of her serious illness became evident, and Mrs. Morley was confined to her bed. There was some obscurity in the symptoms, and his own hopeful temperament caused him to see continual improvement, and to write to us encouraging letters to the last. He gave up his town engagements, and nursed her with devotion and practised skill. Dr. Groves, too, attended her daily. On April 5 he thought her sufficiently better for him to go to London, leaving her in a daughter's charge. But soon after he left the house there was a change for the worse, and in the evening, shortly before eight o'clock, she died.

The blow at the time was most severe, and the loss was one which grew greater rather than less as the days went on. He bore up bravely at the funeral, which Mr. Dendy conducted; he gathered white violets himself to throw into her grave, though none of us then knew the special reason why he chose this flower. Only for a few minutes on returning to the house after the funeral did his feelings overpower his self-control. He accepted with the resignation of a true Christian what had taken place, and set himself resolutely to make the best of the life that remained. We were to come and see him, he told us, and be cheerful; there was to be no repining or cherishing of sorrow. He would not shut himself up away from kindly neighbours, but hoped to see more of them in friendly

hospitalities. One difficulty was most happily sur-
mounted. All his five children had their own homes
and engagements, which rendered anything more than
occasional visits to Carisbrooke impossible; but a niece,
Miss Ella Sayer, daughter of the late James Sayer of
Hastings, came to live with him, and was to him as a
daughter in all devoted service and affection. The singing lessons which developed her fine voice were a new
interest to him, and he found much happiness in her
bright young companionship. Whenever it was possible,
too, some of us spent holidays or took work to do at
Carisbrooke.

We have spoken of his friendship with the Rev. E. B.
James. On April 9 he wrote this letter:

MY DEAR VICAR,
Warmest thanks to you and Mrs. James for all your
sympathy with me in my affliction, for your flowers from the
Vicarage garden woven into the symbol of our faith and hope
and best reminder of our duty in the time of sorrow, for your
beautiful letter, for your presence by the grave. I have lost
the life companion bound to me by fifty years of love from
sight and hearing till my time shall come to pass beyond the
veil that hides her from me now. My selfish grief for myself
is greater than it ought to be, but I know my darling is at
peace with God, and shall feel her living presence still about
me to the end; the footsteps of her life are still to be in mine
if God help me to strive to be worthy of that holy companionship. To you I may say that I have knelt by the deserted
house of flesh, and sought to make my great trial a consecration of the few years of my life here without her, that I may be
faithful as she was faithful till God bring us again together
where all tears are wiped away. I know that God's best
blessings come to us through the ministry of sorrow. My
darling was true and faithful. In all her life I think her word
was clear sincerity; she did not allow herself even to use the
social insincerities of speech that are admitted by convention,
and she clung to old friends and old loves while ready to make
new. To me she was all faith and truth, and she has filled
my life with memories that ought to help me in endeavour to

remain her life-companion in the everlasting life to come. I
do not repine. God filled our lives together here with blessings till we held our happiness in fear and trembling as too
great for earth. Our children have all been spared to us.
There was never a break in our immediate home circle till this
year, when my youngest daughter lost a month-old infant.
God is all love, and I do say from my soul, without a shadow
of reserve, His will be done. This loss will draw me nearer
to surviving friends and neighbours, and I pray that it may be
a consecration for the years that may remain to me on earth,
that I may work more strenuously and more faithfully and
always cheerfully, knowing how God brings light out of our
darkness, and that He is love.

With kindest thanks and regards to Mrs. James,

I am,

My dear Vicar,

Yours gratefully and affectionately,

HENRY MORLEY.

Rev. E. B. James.

The following August he lost this good old friend, and
wrote to Mrs. James:

August 29, 1892.

DEAR MRS. JAMES,

Out of the depths of fellow-feeling I must speak a word
of sympathy and try to say how I have felt with you and for
you during the last days of your great anxiety that closed in
what is now an overwhelming sorrow. I loved and honoured
your good, kind, wise husband when he was yet with us, as
we still do, now that he is with the spirits of the just made
perfect, lost to sight only for a while. Sorrow is not for those
we call the dead, whom God has taken. We sorrow for ourselves, from whom they have been taken. It must remain a
sorrow for this life, but is one that sanctifies the days remaining upon earth, and cheers them with a firmer tie to heaven.
The dear one lost for a few years from sight and hearing is
more alive than the survivor, for whom God has comforts that
He will surely pour into your heart, so ready by long devotion
to receive them. The affection of many friends, quickened by
sympathy with your great grief, will bring its little solace in this
world, while peace grows with the daily sense that the best

earthly love is bound for ever to the love of God, has grown to
be a part of heaven. God bless and comfort you! In that
prayer I am joined by all who are of this household.

My children all have grateful recollections of the Vicar's
kindness when their mother died, and my son Robert came to
Carisbrooke on purpose to represent his brothers and sisters
among the many loving mourners at the grave of one who
sought, not in vain, to be as a dear friend to every parishioner.

Believe me always,

Dear Mrs. James,

Yours very sincerely,

HENRY MORLEY.

Mrs. James, Vicarage, Carisbrooke.

He took much interest in a proposal to commemorate
the late Vicar's long incumbency, acted as the inter-
mediary between Mrs. James and the public meeting,
and was appointed secretary and treasurer to a committee
appointed to arrange for the placing of a brass tablet and
the erection of an eagle lectern in the church. ' It would
never have been done,' says Mrs. James, 'had he not
undertaken it.'

It was not long before he resumed his customary and
useful activities. In August he distributed the prizes at
the Nodehill Board School, and the *Schoolmaster* quotes
some words of his which have all the old ring. He
said :

Let them make the citizen, and the citizen would make the
State; but if they made the State, and never made the citizen,
then the citizen would make havoc of the State. In the year
before Waterloo Wordsworth wrote a poem in which he said
they must have every child in England taught, and he asked,
practically, for Board schools if they would have a wise and
free England. After many years these schools had been
obtained, and he believed they were doing the work which
God had appointed them to do—to be the teachers and civilizers
of the world. Those who felt that the difference between
political parties was simply the difference between tweedledum
and tweedledee must recognise that it was of the greatest
importance that in the days to come there should be citizens

using the privilege of the vote with a knowledge of what they were about, with faculties trained as those of the children in their schools were being trained, and who, instead of reviling those who did not agree with them, should be excellent friends, while using 'their own judgment in giving their individual votes. And so it was with temperance and other social problems : through those children,more than through anything else—more than through the Universities and higher teaching —was the future of the world to be made. Let those who had done well during the past year go on doing well ; and those who had been idle, don't let them be idle next year. Let them all remember that the day would come when England would have need of them, and that the best thought of the country was on them and on what they would become.

This same month, August, 1892, he succeeded by seniority to the post of Junior Warden at the Apothecaries' Hall, and entered upon his new labours there with zest. Thus began a three years' term of office to which he had long looked forward.

In 1892 he duly brought out his two volumes of ' English Writers.' Vol. VIII. appeared in February, and covers the ground ' From Surrey to Spenser.' It deals with the reign of Henry VIII. and the period of Italian influence ; it describes the origin of the English drama, and successive stages of the Reformation ; it gives some account of a large number of little-known authors, and special notice of such books as Ascham's ' Schoolmaster' and Lyly's ' Euphues,' and carries on the story through the earlier years of the reign of Elizabeth. It was favourably received, but his critics do not fail to point out certain disadvantages arising from its chronological method of treatment, which necessitated his leaving a subject and recurring to it again at a later date. This plan, they said, gives us materials for a history, not the history itself. To some extent Professor Morley would have admitted the charge, and pointed to his title-page, on which is inscribed, ' An Attempt towards a History of English Literature.'

But the chronological order was essential to his method of treating literature, and cannot be widely departed from by those who would study under his guidance. To understand the book you must know the man, and to understand the man you must know his time; that was his principle, and it involved the enormous mass of detail which he conscientiously accumulates for his readers.

In his 'Last Leaves' he explains the design he had formed for the rest of the work. Vols. IX. and X. were to deal with Spenser, and bring us to the death of Shakespeare; Vol. XI. to treat of writers between Shakespeare and Milton; Vol. XII. to be on 'Milton and his Times:' Vol. XIII. would bring us to the accession of Queen Anne, and Vol. XIV. to the death of George I. Vol. XV. would record the literature of the reign of George II.; Vol. XVI. would take the period thence to the French Revolution. Vols. XVII. and XVIII. should bring us to the death of Wordsworth; and the last two in the series, to see the light in 1897, were to deal with the latter half of the nineteenth century.

Vol. IX. duly appeared in the autumn of 1892. It contains no 'Last Words'; he did not again resume this friendly chat with his readers, but it opens with this dedicatory sonnet:

> The trembling movement of a joy too pure
>   To dwell with dust has ceased; gone is a joy
>   Whose memory no sorrow can destroy—
> The more than forty years of love as sure
> As God's high promises. Truth must endure.
>   Love crowns the bended head when no alloy
>   Of low desire rings base, no cares annoy,
> And the soul sits in sight of God secure.
> O wife with God, loved next to God, true wife!
>   To thee these careful words I dedicate,
> Which through long time pursue the path of life
> Where England treads the way which thou hast trod,
>   Of simple duty, glad to work and wait,
> And bring her children to the love of God.

He sends this volume to his son Robert, on November
25. At the end of his letter he writes:

Meanwhile I am doing what I can in the way of roses and
posies and finishing fruit-planting to make next summer cheerful, as I hope it will be; and I *can* be cheerful and resigned
to God's will, though time deepens instead of deadening the
sense of loss. The mother lives continually in my thoughts;
I think she is never for five minutes absent from them unless
when I am working at book or lecturing, and it is a curious fact
that I have never once known her as dead in my dreams.

This ninth volume, 'Spenser and his Time,' brings us
to many well-known works of the Elizabethan age besides
the 'Faerie Queene'; it is, in fact, the first volume that
deals mainly with writings which educated people feel
they ought to know something about. He had at last
begun to reach the periods on which he had been incessantly lecturing to audiences of most varied kinds for
thirty years. In these later periods he could have
assumed more knowledge of general history, and need not
have burdened his pages with all the detail of incident
that he deemed requisite in the earlier centuries. His
style would have more resembled that in which he spoke
to his students, and left a clearer impression of wide
survey and comprehensive generalization.

In 1893 only one volume appeared, the tenth; and this,
though larger than usual, did not cover all the ground
reckoned in the estimate. Now that he was in the
'spacious times' of Elizabeth, compression was not easy.
So he took the opportunity of drawing a definite line
between the reigns of Elizabeth and James I. by leaving
to a new volume everything after 1603. He used to say
that accounts of so-called 'Elizabethan' literature sometimes ran on into the days of Charles I., to the confusion of all clear understanding. So Vol. X. treats of
'Shakespeare and his Time under Elizabeth.' The
arrangement of the book affords a good example of his
method.

In dealing with the individual plays, Professor Morley
made large use of the Introductions which he had already
written for 'Cassell's National Library.' His analyses sometimes seem to run to disproportionate length ; but it must
be remembered that in these analyses he gives his interpretation of the play, and the grounds on which this interpretation rests. This is, in fact, his main contribution
to our appreciation of the great dramatist. Some of the
critics think there is too much moralizing in the interpretation, but he would have said it was needful to enforce his
exposition of Shakespeare's religion. The *Saturday Review*
of February 3, 1893, regards the Professor's views of
Falstaff as ' oddly unsympathetic, if not decidedly *borné* ';
and, by a curious coincidence, the critic in the *New York
Herald* of February 11 is ' struck,' not only with the same
ideas, but with identical words extending over several
sentences. But it was the earnestness in Shakespeare,
hitherto insufficiently noticed, that Professor Morley set
himself to bring out. He thus concludes the chapter
which deals with the ' Merry Wives of Windsor ':

Tradition about Shakespeare's deer-stealing at Charlcote—
which was not in his time a deer park—is as little supported
by fact as the idleness of the other inventions which have been
associated with his name. The Second Part of ' King Henry IV.'
has shown very clearly that into the first invention of Justice
Shallow Shakespeare put a deep religious earnestness. It was
a conception that had nothing in common with the petty spite
and ridicule which make part of the life that gives its narrow
bounds to the inventions of the gossip-mongers. He who
banishes out of his conception of Shakespeare all the unproved
small-talk, accepting nothing but the few proved facts, will not
find one fact out of accord with the spirit of the plays. No
writer can live up to the highest level of his own ideal. But
the man who has set before us, for all time, the purest and the
noblest readings of the problems of life must have had, in his
own life, more than Falstaff could well understand. Some
have found it easier to see Shakespeare as Falstaff would
imagine him than to see Falstaff as Shakespeare knew him.

This volume, then, of 'English Writers' is the last that
Henry Morley lived to publish. But all through 1893 he
was at work on the next volume. In March, 1894, he
writes that he hopes it will be out in April or May. Its
title is 'Shakespeare and his Time under James I.' The
first twelve chapters were left practically complete. For
chapter xiii. some preparation had been made dealing
with Beaumont and Fletcher. This has been ably supplemented by Mr. W. Hall Griffin, to whom the entire editing
of the volume was committed, and who has further enriched
it with two valuable additions—viz., chapter xiv., concluding the notice of the literature of Shakespeare's time
under James I., and describing his Sonnets; and a most
elaborate and carefully prepared Bibliography, which had
been promised, but which had been postponed till there
were now four volumes thus to supplement.

The entire work on 'English Writers' was thus rendered
complete to the year 1616, with a glance forward at the
later lives of some of the men then living, and with this
all was done that could be done. The main literary work
of Henry Morley's life must ever remain a fragment.

During 1893 Professor Morley was engaged on another
literary task which, unfortunately, was destined never to
see the light. By this time the movement for cheap re-
publications had largely changed its character, and had
passed into other hands. But, as usual, something else
came to take its place in its demand on his time and
strength. Messrs. Blackie and Co. asked him to undertake
for them a series of volumes of 'Tales and Songs of our
Forefathers.' The plan first suggested savoured too much
of the miscellaneous collection to approve itself to Professor Morley; but his counter-proposals were cordially
accepted, and in March, 1893, he and Mr. R. Blackie had
an interview at Carisbrooke, and came to an agreement
which seemed highly satisfactory to both sides, and likely
to result in a work of permanent literary value. There

were to be six volumes published between February 15, 1894, and March 15, 1896. The first was to give Tales of the Celts, Scandinavians, and Teutons, with Mediæval Tales and Church Legends; the second, the Rise of the Arthurian Romance, the Novel of the Fourteenth Century, and Tales of the Renaissance; the third, Tales of the Novelists and Dramatists from the Accession of Elizabeth to the year 1700; the fourth, Novels and Tales of the Eighteenth Century; while the fifth and sixth would give Novels and Tales of the Nineteenth Century, including American Stories, so far as copyright would allow. Songs and ballads were to be interspersed between the prose tales without strict reference to date. For doing this Professor Morley was to be paid £700, which he considered the best pay he was ever offered for this kind of work. He thought that he could do it when he was not in the mood for going on with 'English Writers,' and he was glad to look forward to having the money. He said about this time, ' I have enough to live on, but not to be liberal; and I like to be liberal.' One Sunday evening at Madeley, January 5, 1845, he had written to Miss Sayer: ' A strange being I should be without you, quite different from what I am, but I can't well fancy what. Reckless, for certain.' Now that he had to live without his wife, he found it difficult to take care either of his health or his money. His liberal donations were made out of capital, not out of income. He had always been able to earn; he expected this to continue.

But he had miscalculated his strength. In spite of all the efforts of will with which he still compelled himself to work, he could not get forward with these 'Tales and Songs.' Parts of the first two volumes were prepared, and some expense incurred for type-writing; but he left nothing ready for publication, and, of course, never received any of the payment.

During 1893 he was ready, as usual, to assist every good cause in his power. He gave several lectures and addresses in Ryde, Newport (on Tennyson and the vacant laureate-ship), and elsewhere.

There were meetings this spring of the Carisbrooke parochial committee, to consider precautions against fire. Another subject of considerable interest was taken up at this time by the new Vicar, the Rev. C. Eddy, M.A. On May 11 a vestry meeting was held in the church to consider the question of restoring the chancel. A committee was appointed, with Professor Morley as its secretary, and a public meeting called for the 25th, at which he gave a tolerably full history of the fine old church. He went back to the Norman Conquest and the connection with the Abbey of Lire, in Normandy; told of the founding of the priory church about 1150, and of the parish church alongside of it, of the building of the noble tower by the Carthusian monks of Sheen in the time of Edward IV., and of the destruction of the double chancel by Sir Francis Walsingham in the reign of Queen Elizabeth, by which he freed himself from the responsibility of having to keep it in repair. Professor Morley then gave an outline of the proposed restoration. The Rev. Clement Smith, M.A., Vicar of Newport, warmly supported the proposal, which was unanimously carried.

Among his visitors this summer was Mrs. Morley of Midhurst, widow of his brother Joseph, herself an invalid. For her he bought a wheeled basket-chair, and would himself take her in it about the Carisbrooke lanes, till he found the effort too much for his strength.

In August an event occurred which was to him a source of much happiness. This was the marriage of his eldest son, Henry Forster Morley, on August 3, to Ida, second daughter of Stephen Seaward Tayler. After this wedding only one member of the family remained unmarried, and Robert Morley's engagement in the spring of the next year to Miss Mary Hodgkinson, of Manchester, filled up the father's cup of joy.

This summer his old Neuwied schoolfellow, Mr. Ransome, gave him a very happy day by spending it at Carisbrooke and talking over old times. Another visitor, who spent several days with him, was Sir George Buchanan, now himself much broken in health, and it was touching to see the happy companionship of the two old men, friends of so many years.

In August, 1893, Professor Morley became Senior Warden at the Apothecaries' Hall, and began the second of the three years' term of management. During the summer, the weekly visits to London, though they took up time, were probably good for his health and spirits. But it was different when the winter came. Then the early start, the numerous changes, the bus, the train, the steamboat, and again the train, made the journey very trying in bad weather; but his regularity was unfailing. There were those who said that he lived too far from London to attend to his duties at the Hall properly. He was determined to show that this was not the case, and his power of determination when thoroughly aroused was very great. So week after week, and month after month, the work went on with ever-increasing strain, and with the postponement of whatever else could be put off. But every definite engagement was fulfilled.

On November 23 he gave his lecture on 'As You Like It' for Holy Trinity Church Union; and this, I think, must have been the last occasion when he delivered a lecture. When Christmas came, my wife and I spent some time at Carisbrooke. He was then grown painfully thin, and was not inclined for walks or excursions, but wanted us to go off without him. He was beginning also to admit an increased difficulty in getting through with work, and especially to lament the number of unanswered letters. Letters, indeed, continued to come to him from various parts of the world whither his books had penetrated, especially the little introductions to the popular libraries,

and many a 'cry out of the depths' came from some
unknown reader, who had found a source of strength or
comfort in his words, and wanted to draw more help from
the same source.   He was a preacher as well as a teacher,
and among the disappointed and the sorrow-stricken, as
well as the hopeful and the striving, there were those who
found his preaching good for their souls.

A treat I remember this Christmas was hearing him
read one of the old Scandinavian tales which he was
translating for Blackie's volume.   It was full of fresh
quaint interest.   There was no falling-off in the quality
of his work, though the effort required to do it was much
greater.   A note of invitation he sent at this time to Mr.
and Mrs. Dendy contains a sentence which recalls a recent
change.   The words are : ' The pastor has not tasted my
tobacco !'   Mr. Dendy was a confirmed smoker.   Professor
Morley not only never smoked himself, but used greatly
to dislike the smell, and Mrs. Morley had the feeling
customary among ladies of her generation.   Sons and
sons-in-law, too, might at one time have all been described
as anti-tobacconists.   But during this last year or so a
change came creeping in.   The Professor's sociability
overcame his old dislike, and the library was allowed to
know the scent of the once-banished weed.

There is not much to add respecting the early months
of 1894.   He had bad weather for some of his journeys,
and caught cold, and with this came the beginning of the
end.   He was thoroughly emaciated, and became so weak
that walking a few yards greatly fatigued him.   Yet it
seemed as though nothing would induce him to give up
his attendance at the Apothecaries' Hall, and it was hard
on his own children to see him struggling on so manifestly
overtasked.   At last they got his old friend, Sir George
Buchanan, to see him, and order him to take a rest ; and
the Master of the Apothecaries' Hall wrote most kindly,
urging him not to come again to town till he was really

26

better, and not to trust himself in this matter, but to be
guided by his medical adviser.

So he came home from his last journey, hardly able to
walk from the fly into his house, and the end was now
drawing near. Whether he knew it himself or not none
can tell. No word passed his lips which indicated a knowledge that he was soon to die; to the children gathered
round him he spoke only of the worth to him of their love.
But, then, he had ever been one ' so to live as never to be
afraid to die,' and since the loss of his wife, thoughts of
the other world had been a constant accompaniment of all
his activity here.

Undoubtedly he would have lived longer if he had taken
greater precautions during these last months, but it would
have been the life of an invalid, cut off from the fulfilment
of much that he longed to accomplish, and we cannot but
rejoice that he was spared this lingering trial.

Soon after Easter his friend and fellow-worker, Mr.
Dendy, died, somewhat suddenly, though he had previously had serious warnings of failing health. To Mrs.
Dendy, who was to return to the north, Professor Morley
wrote the following letter. It is a rendering of honour
where honour is due. It affords also insight into Henry
Morley's very heart and soul. By this time the weakness
had so increased that it was the labour of a day to write
these words :

Carisbrooke,
Isle of Wight,
April 7, 1894.

DEAR Mrs. DENDY,

I cannot speak the depth of sympathy with which I feel
for you in your sudden and overwhelming loss, and join with it
a yet vague sense of my own loss in one of the best and trustiest
of friends. This is my first attempt to write a note for many
days. My children, in loving concern for my break-down in
health, kept from me the day of the service in Newport.
Maggie went unknown to me as my representative. But my
love made part wherever any friends paid reverence to your

dear husband's memory. I loved and honoured him. No man was more trustworthy, kind, and faithful in every act of life. Full-hearted husband, father, friend, and citizen, true pastor, bringing fellowship with God into the daily ways of life, and following with patient care every line of duty, great or small, that brought with Christian kindliness some help to the common good of the community. So far as I can help in ravelling up any threads of unfinished business left in his many cares for the good of Newport, I hope in a few days to be well enough to be at your call.

For your own loss, dear Mrs. Dendy, I have a kindred feeling. I went up to the cemetery on the fifth, which was the anniversary of my darling's second birthday—the first to earth, the second into heaven. It is not great pain to wait for reunion with a life companion who has found the fulness of God's peace, and waits restfully to share it with us evermore. We live to try humbly to be good and worthy of the full fruition in His appointed time. Meanwhile you will live cherished among your children in your old haunts, widowhood coming to you in its softest form, with quiet blessings. There is no blessing that I do not wish you. You will go among old loves, but you will carry with you from your friends of the Newport congregation many a strong lasting affection. For me, I hardly think of you and your husband as parted. You are not, and will be my dear old friends for ever, joined together in my love.

Always yours affectionately,
HENRY MORLEY.

The next day he wrote a chatty letter to absent members of the family, rejoicing in the spring feeling that was in the air, and in the coming to Carisbrooke of his children. It seemed a good thing 'to have a breakdown and be so beset with love.' He says of himself

he is quietly recovering, but has learnt a little fact. Certain good-byes to lines of London work which he had planned to take next he has resolved to say at once, and so take in another reef of sail to come easily into port with ' English Writers.' I have been thinking it all out carefully while playing invalid, and got it quite clear to my mind. With everything else cleared away from round about it (and there was a good deal), I can finish my life at the Hall by taking the Master's year smoothly; there is interesting and delicate work to be done which I want to carry through. Then I have absolutely nothing except country duty to my neighbours, and till then very little between me and sunshine, with free leisure for the pen. This is a little report of the meditations of H. M. in which there are a multitude of little details that will be carried out during this week. The only other letter I have written is to Mrs. Dendy.

The final stage of his illness lasted from Easter to Whitsuntide. During these weeks he had the kindest attention from Dr. Groves. He bore his sufferings without a murmur. He would not keep his bed, but was helped to come downstairs almost to the very end, saying, ' It's easy going downhill surrounded by family angels.' He discussed parochial business with the new Vicar of Carisbrooke, the Rev. A. W. Milroy, M.A., and educational matters with the Vicar of Newport. As already mentioned, within a fortnight of his death, a meeting of the parochial board was held at his house in order that he might preside. He talked of restricting his future activities in accordance with diminished strength, but no word acknowledged how nearly all was gone. He rejoiced to have his children round him; almost his last words, as consciousness began to fail, were, ' I am beset with love.' Everything that affection could do for him was done, and he was grateful as a loving heart can be.

The end came on May 14—Whit Monday. The funeral took place the following Thursday. The grave is in Carisbrooke Cemetery, where he and his wife lie side by side in the spot he chose, each under a cross of the violets that meant to him so much. Carisbrooke and Newport came that day to do him honour. The Vicars of the two churches, Nonconformist ministers, the Mayor and Corporation, the Parochial Board, deputations representing the University Extension Centre and the Literary Institute, Captain Markland from the Castle, and other officials, with many, many other friends and fellow-worshippers were there.

Professor Arber had travelled from Birmingham ; Paul Neuman was another old student who stood beside the grave; James Gairdner, Geoffrey Sayer, and Henry Ling represented near relatives, and something more. Edmund Kell Blyth was there, a friend of many years. Wreaths and floral tributes were numerous, each really meaning the love and appreciation which formed its message. On one card were the words, ' An emblem of lasting affection for their lost friend from many former residents of University Hall. They will ever remember with gratitude his inspiring influence. Though a beautiful life has ended, its work will ever remain."

It fell to my lot to conduct this service. I did not know him then so well as I know him now, after four years' study of his life and the privilege of reading the letters which tell his inmost thoughts. Yet I knew him well enough to speak some words which shall conclude a task which has been to me very richly blessed. There is nothing in them to alter. There is much that I might now add out of the fuller knowledge. I have, however, tried to share this knowledge with all who read this ' Life,' and if the words have done their work, their readers already know the best that I could tell them.

ADDRESS AT CARISBROOKE CEMETERY, MAY 17, 1894.

We meet here to-day under the shadow of a great loss. It is the loss of one who will be missed wherever English writers are read. But we leave to other times the wider aspects of his work. He undertook the noblest work a man can undertake : he was a teacher of truth, of righteousness, and of love. Of one thing only would I remind you now. He felt the duty laid upon him to interpret to the English people the religion which runs through all our glorious literature ; and this great aim and purpose—to

bring out the religious element in the writings of other
men, and make it clear that all may understand—will be
found to characterize all he wrote himself, and to give a
unity to the teaching of his whole life. As one of the pure
in heart, he could see God, and he consecrated his powers
to helping others share the blessing. He delighted to
show that the lessons taught by England's greatest writer
are these: 'Love God; love your neighbour; do your
work'; and here he found a guiding principle which
governed the exercise of all the talents entrusted to himself. He loved God, he loved his neighbour, he did his
work. He knew the source whence this higher light has
dawned upon the world. He cared little what he was
called by others; but he cared much for the only religious
name by which he would call himself, the name Christian.
He was a disciple of Christ, a learner sitting at His feet,
and looking up with reverence to the face of the Son of
man who has been the light of the world. And he was a
disciple who took up his cross daily, and strove to follow
in the Master's footsteps; and having so learned Christ
himself, it was given him to help others to find the same
path that leadeth unto life. There are many here now
who know what has been the worth of his presence to this
neighbourhood since he made Carisbrooke his home. You
testify by your presence to the character of his influence
here. During a long course of previous years that influence was the same wherever he might be; and it has left
its mark on many generations of students. Our hearts are
indeed full of varied feelings, but there is one thought
which must and should predominate, it is the thought of
gratitude to God for the great gift He has given us in the
inspiration of such a life.

God calls our loved ones, but we lose not wholly
What He has given;
They live on earth in thought and deed, as truly
As in His heaven.
                                              WHITTIER.

INDEX

BILLING AND SONS, PRINTERS, GUILDFORD.

October, 1898.

Mr. Edward Arnold's
New Books and Announcements.

TELEGRAPHIC ADDRESS:
SCHOLARLY, LONDON.·

37 Bedford Street,

London,

NEW AND FORTHCOMING WORKS.

The Principles of Landed Estate Management.

By HENRY HERBERT SMITH, Fellow of the Institution of Surveyors, and Agent to the Marquess of Lansdowne, K.G. ; the Earl of Crewe ; Major-General the Lord Methuen, etc.

With Plans and Illustrations. One vol., demy 8vo., 16s.

It is hoped that this volume will prove invaluable to landed proprietors, land agents, and all interested in agriculture. Mr. A. C. Forbes, Wood Manager to the Marquess of Lansdowne, contributes an important chapter on Forestry, and Mr. W. Bowstead, Barrister-at-Law, upon Legal Matters affecting the management of a landed property. A portion of the book is devoted to Estate Architecture, the Construction of Farm Buildings, Cottages, etc., and is illustrated by several plates. Economic Science and Farm Practice, the methods of Agriculture, Surveying and Road-making, etc., are fully dealt with by Mr. H. Herbert Smith.

Amateur Clubs and Actors.

Edited by W. G. ELLIOT.

With Illustrations by C. M. NEWTON, and from photography. One vol., large 8vo., 15s.

This volume presents a lively record, by various contributors, of the history of the most prominent Amateur Acting Clubs, with reminiscences of the plays performed, and anecdotes of the players. Mr. Elliot, who has undertaken to edit the volume, deals with the Cambridge A. D. C. ; while Mr. J. W. Clark treats of the Greek Play at Cambridge. Mr. B. C. Stephenson records the doings of the Windsor Strollers ; Captain George Nugent the history of the Guards Burlesque. Mr. Yardley contributes some notes on the famous Amateur Pantomime and on the Canterbury 'Old Stagers'; Mr. Frank Tarver on Theatricals at Eton. Mr. Claud Nugent deals with the O. U. D. S.; Mr. P. Comyns Carr with the Oxford Greek Play ; Colonel Newnham Davis with Amateur Acting in India and the Colonies. The narrative of the doings of each club has been entrusted to one well qualified to undertake it, and the volume forms a valuable record as well as a most readable addition to the library.

Phases of my Life.

By the Very Rev. J. PIGOU, Dean of Bristol.

With Photogravure Portrait. One vol., demy 8vo., 16s.

The recollections of the Dean of Bristol are of scenes of clerical life, but of clerical life passed in many cities—in Paris, in London, at Doncaster, and at Bristol, and told with a wealth of anecdote and humour which will delight, not only the clergy, but their lay brethren. Dean Pigou's reminiscences touch human nature on many sides. His wide sympathies, his keen discernment, his humours and kindly satire, will appeal to readers of every class, while his serious criticisms will secure the attention which is due to his long experience and his calm and ripe judgment.

The Life of Henry Morley.

By the Rev. H. S. SOLLY.

With Photogravure Portrait. One vol., large 8vo., 12s. 6d.

The late Professor Henry Morley is best remembered for the great services he rendered to secondary and higher education, and for his successful endeavours to spread among the people an acquaintance with the English classic writers. The record of his life is certain to be welcome to the many students in every part of the United Kingdom who have valued his teaching and lectures at King's College, and when he filled the University Chair of English Literature at Edinburgh, or later at University College. But his diaries and letters will appeal to a still wider audience, with their record of his early struggles, his journalistic career as a contributor to *Household Words*, *Fraser's*, the *Examiner*, etc., and his friendship with Forster, Douglas Jerrold, and Charles Dickens.

Recollections of a Highland Subaltern

During the Campaigns of the 93rd Highlanders in India, under Colin Campbell, Lord Clyde, in 1857, 1858, 1859.

By Lieutenant-Colonel W. G. ALEXANDER.

With three Photogravure Portraits, seven full-page Illustrations, and several Plans. One vol., demy 8vo., 16s.

Colonel Alexander was actively engaged with his regiment in the relief of Lucknow, and in the subsequent Oudh campaign. He records his experiences from a diary which he kept throughout that time, and thus his account of the Mutiny, and of his experiences during it, has the charm of the feelings and opinions of an actor in the events noted while they were occurring.

3

Pages from A Diary of Travel in Asiatic Turkey.

By LORD WARKWORTH, M.P.

> With numerous Photogravure and other Illustrations from Photographs by the Author. One vol., fcap. 4to., 21s. net.

Lord Warkworth, accompanied by two other Members of Parliament, made in 1897-98 a journey of some months through Asia Minor, Armenia, and Kurdistan. The previous year he had visited Persia and parts of Asia Minor. In this volume he gives some record of his journey, and of his impressions upon some of the political aspects of the questions which still continue to be a disturbing influence in the near East, with an account of districts which are of supreme historical interest.

Tropics and Snows. A Record of Sport and Adventure in Many Lands.

By Captain R. G. BURTON, Indian Staff Corps, late of the 1st West India Regiment.

> With Illustrations from Sketches and Photographs. One vol., demy 8vo., 16s.

Captain Burton gives a spirited account in this volume of big-game shooting and of travel in Jamaica, the Punjab, Kashmir and Berar, on the Volga, at Hingoli, etc. Some chapters are devoted to Tiger Shooting, Bison Shooting, Panther Shooting, and the volume is full of records of successful expeditions after big game of all descriptions, which will render the work welcome to English sportsmen

Q's Tales from Shakespeare.

By A. T. QUILLER COUCH ('Q.'), Author of 'Dead Man's Rock,' etc.

> One vol., crown 8vo., 6s.

Tales from Shakespeare is a title inevitably associated with the name of Charles Lamb. But these tales, narrated by the charming pen of Mr. Quiller Couch, do not compete with, but are intended to supplement, Lamb's delightful book. Shakespeare's historical characters and plays were not included in the 'Tales' of Charles Lamb. It is with these that Mr. Quiller Couch will deal, with some of the plays omitted from Lamb's collection.

Newcastle-on-Tyne: its Municipal Origin and Growth.

By the Honourable DAPHNE RENDEL.

> With Illustrations, 1 vol., 8vo., 3s. 6d.

Miss Rendel in this volume carefully traces the history and development of Newcastle, and gives a most interesting survey of the fortunes of this border city in the past, and of its modern municipal growth.

Reminiscences of the Course, the Camp, and the Chase.

By a Gentleman Rider, Colonel R. F. MEYSEY-THOMPSON.

One vol., large crown 8vo., 10s. 6d.

Colonel Meysey-Thompson in this volume gives a lively description of his experiences of English racing and Irish sport, of bull-fights and racing in Spain, with reminiscences of school-life at Eton and of his military career.

Hunting Reminiscences of Frank Gillard, with the Belvoir Hounds, 1860 to 1896.

Recorded and Illustrated by CUTHBERT BRADLEY.

One vol., large 8vo., 15s.

The Reminiscences of Frank Gillard, the illustrious huntsman of the Belvoir Hounds, means a complete record of the Hunt during the thirty-six years he was connected with it. Such a record, teeming with accounts of spirited runs, and anecdotes of well-known hunting-men of the past and of to-day, with valuable hints on the breeding of hounds, and their management in the kennel and in the field, is a volume which will be a prized addition to sporting literature. Those who have hunted with the Belvoir, and hunting-men everywhere, will be glad to secure this work about the most famous of packs, and the book will appeal to a wider audience, to all who are interested in good sport. Mr. Cuthbert Bradley, who records these reminiscences of Frank Gillard, has also illustrated the volume with a quantity of portraits and pen-and-ink sketches in the field.

Days and Nights of Salmon Fishing.

By WILLIAM SCROPE. Edited by the Right Hon. SIR HERBERT MAXWELL, Bart., M.P.

With coloured lithographic and numerous Photogravure reproductions of the original plates. Large 8vo., 15s. Large Paper Edition, limited to 200 copies, Two Guineas net.

This is the final volume, Volume VII., of the popular Sportsman's Library. Scrope's 'Art of Deerstalking' has already appeared in this Library, and the present volume is a reprint of the companion work, which is even more scarce and more richly illustrated. Full justice is done to the original plates, which are all of them reproduced in this edition.

For a list of the other volumes in the Sportsman's Library, see page 16 of this catalogue.

The Frank Lockwood Sketch-Book.

Being a selection of Sketches by the late Sir FRANK LOCKWOOD, Q.C., M.P.

> Oblong royal 4to., 10s. 6d. Also an Edition de Luxe of 50 copies, printed on Japanese vellum, £2 2s. net.

This delightful volume, which contains a selection from the caricatures and humorous sketches of the late Sir Frank Lockwood, has been made possible by the kindness of Lady Lockwood, who put at the disposal of the publishers a number of the note-books of Sir Frank Lockwood, through the pages of which were scattered a host of his playful drawings. The various possessors of the caricatures and drawings which were brought together at the exhibition organized in London during the early part of 1898, also, at the request of the Barristers' Benevolent Society, gave consent to the reproduction of a selection from these sketches in the present volume. Some of the sketches reproduced have already attracted general notice for their masterly execution and playful fancy, but a large number have never before been made known to the public.

Tails with a Twist.

An Animal Picture Book by E. T. REED, Author of ' Pre-Historic Peeps,' etc. With Verses by 'A BELGIAN HARE.'

> Oblong demy 4to., 6s.

Mr. E. T. Reed's drawings in *Punch* are so well known and appreciated as to assure this picture-book of his a popular welcome. Many of the verses by 'A Belgian Hare,' which Mr. Reed illustrates in this book, though never before printed, have already gained some celebrity from being repeated by one person to another, and all are full of humour and vivacity.

The Modern Traveller.

By H. B. and B. T. B., Authors of ' More Beasts (For Worse Children).'

> One vol., 4to., 3s. 6d.

This is a new book of pictures and verse by the authors of the 'Book of Beasts,' who in that book ' discovered a new continent in the world of nonsense.' In this new book of nonsense they strike off on a new track, which is likely to be as fruitful of amusement as their former attempts.

BY THE SAME AUTHORS.

More Beasts (For Worse Children).

New Edition. One vol., 4to., 3s. 6d.

Verses.

By MAUD HOLLAND (MAUD WALPOLE).

> Crown 8vo., 3s. 6d.

Some of these Poems have already appeared in the *Spectator*, the *Speaker*, *Literature*, and the *National Review*, but the majority have not before been published.

The False Chevalier; or, The Lifeguard of Marie Antoinette.

By W. D. LIGHTHALL.

One vol., crown 8vo., 6s.

This historical romance by a new writer is founded on a packet of worm-eaten letters found in an old house on the banks of the St. Lawrence. The intrigues, the intensity of feelings, they rudely outline, have formed the basis upon which, the author has constructed this novel.

The Forest of Bourg-Marie.

By FRANCES HARRISON.

One vol., crown 8vo., 6s.

A romance of French Canada by Mrs. Frances Harrison, a Canadian author who has gained a reputation in Canada under the pseudonym of 'Seranus.'

The Delusion of Diana.

By MARGARET BURNESIDE.

One vol., crown 8vo., 6s.
A new novel by a new author of promise.

Various Quills.

A Collection of Poems, Stories, and Essays contributed by the members of a Literary Club.

One vol., crown 8vo., 5s.

This volume contains a bundle of literary pieces from various quills. The authors are anonymous. A few of the contributions have been published before in magazines or newspapers, but the great majority of them are now published for the first time, and among the pieces will be found poems and stories which will be recognised to be of exceptional merit.

Lectures on Theoretic and Physical Chemistry.

By G. R. VAN 'T. HOFF. Translated by Professor R. A. LEHFELDT.

With diagrams, 1 vol., demy 8vo.

Professor J. H. Van 'T. Hoff, of the Berlin University, is acknowledged to be the greatest authority upon Physical Chemistry; and this translation of his new work will be of value to advanced students and to all who are interested in a subject the importance of which is yearly becoming more fully recognised.

An Experimental Course of Chemistry for Agricultural Students.

By T. S. DYMOND, F.I.C., Lecturer on Chemistry and Agricultural Chemistry in the County Technical Laboratories, Chelmsford.

Crown 8vo., cloth. [In the press.

Elementary Physical Chemistry.

By CH. VAN DEVENTER. With an Introduction by G. R. VAN 'T HOFF. Translated by Professor R. A. LEHFELDT.

Crown 8vo. [*In the press.*]

NEW AND CHEAPER EDITION. REVISED THROUGHOUT.

Animal Life and Intelligence.

By Professor C. LLOYD MORGAN, F.G.S., Principal of University College, Bristol.

With 40 Illustrations, crown 8vo., 7s. 6d.

The continued demand for this important work has induced the publishers to issue it at a price which will place it within the reach of a larger public, and Professor Lloyd Morgan has taken the opportunity to revise the book, a large part of which he has entirely rewritten. [*In preparation.*]

BY THE SAME AUTHOR.

Habit and Instinct : A Study in Heredity.

Demy 8vo., 16s.

The Springs of Conduct.

Cheaper Edition. Large crown 8vo., 3s. 6d.

Psychology for Teachers.

With a Preface by SIR JOSHUA FITCH, M.A., LL.D., late one of H.M. Chief Inspectors of Training Colleges.

Second Edition. One vol., crown 8vo., cloth, 3s. 6d. net.

An Illustrated School Geography.

By ANDREW J. HERBERTSON, M.A., F.R.G.S., Lecturer in Geography at the Heriot Watt College, Edinburgh, and formerly in the Owen's College, Manchester.

With several hundred Illustrations, Relief Maps and Diagrams, large 4to., 5s.

This volume is the first attempt in this country to make the illustrations to a geography book as systematic and important as the text itself. The idea is based upon Frye's ' Complete Geography,' which has attained phenomenal success in the United States, and the material in that work has been put at the disposal of the publishers, and has been used by Mr. Herbertson in writing the English work, while a large number of carefully selected maps and illustrations have been added.

8

NEW AND CHEAPER EDITION.

A Book about the Garden and the Gardener.

By the Very Rev. S. REYNOLDS HOLE, Dean of Rochester.

One vol. crown 8vo, 3s. 6d.

A cheaper edition of this delightful work of Dean Hole is certain of a welcome and will form a companion volume to the popular edition of 'A Book about Roses.'

'A dainty book. . . . A profusion of jokes and good stories, with a vein of serious thought running through the whole.'—*Guardian.*
'A delightful volume, full, not merely of information, but of humour and entertainment.'—*World.*
'Dean Hole has contrived to make his book both amusing and of real practical utility.'—*Morning Post.*
'The papers are all written with that charming mixture of practical skill in gardening, learning in the literary art, clerical knowledge of the nature of men, and strong love of flowers, that is already familiar to this author's readers.'—*Scotsman.*

BY THE SAME AUTHOR.

The Memories of Dean Hole.

With the original Illustrations from sketches by LEECH and THACKERAY. Thirteenth thousand, crown 8vo., 6s.

More Memories: Being Thoughts about England Spoken in America.

With Frontispiece. Demy 8vo., 16s.

A Little Tour in America.

With numerous Illustrations. Demy 8vo., 16s.

A Little Tour in Ireland.

By 'OXONIAN.'

With nearly forty Illustrations by JOHN LEECH. Large crown 8vo., 6s.

A Book about Roses.

Fifteenth edition. Illustrated by H. G. MOON and G. ELGOOD. Presentation Edition with coloured plates, 6s. ; Popular Edition, 3s. 6d.

Addresses to Working Men from Pulpit and Platform.

One vol., crown 8vo., 6s.

Faith which Worketh by Love.

A Sermon Preached after the Funeral of the Princess Mary, Duchess f Teck. Bound in vellum, 1s. net.

🕮ecently published and Standard Works.

SCHOOL HISTORY.

Harrow School.

Edited by E. W. HOWSON and G. TOWNSEND WARNER. With a Pre-
face by EARL SPENCER, K.G., D.C.L., Chairman of the Governors of
Harrow School. And Contributions by Old Harrovians and Harrow
Masters.

Illustrated with a large number of original full-page and other Pen-and-
ink Drawings by Mr. HERBERT MARSHALL. With several Photogravure Portraits and reproductions of objects of interest. One
vol., crown 4to., One Guinea net. A Large-Paper Edition, limited
to 150 copies, Three Guineas net.

The volume contains articles by the following contributors :

E. E. BOWEN ; H. MONTAGU BUTLER, D.D., Master of Trinity College,
Cambridge, and late Headmaster of Harrow School; EDWARD M. BUTLER;
C. COLBECK ; Professor W. J. COURTHOPE, C.B. ; the EARL OF CREWE ; Rev.
J. A. CRUIKSHANK; Sir HENRY S. CUNNINGHAM, K.C.S.I. ; Sir CHARLES
DALRYMPLE, Bart., M.P. ; Rev. B. H. DRURY; SPENCER W. GORE;
E. GRAHAM ; W. O. HEWLETT ; A. F. HORT ; E. W. HOWSON; the Right
Rev. BISHOP JENNER; B. P. LASCELLES ; Hon. E. CHANDOS LEIGH, Q.C.;
Right Hon. W. H. LONG, M.P.; Rev. HASTINGS RASHDALL; C. S. ROUNDELL,
Governor of Harrow School ; the EARL SPENCER, K.G., D.C.L., Chairman of
the Governors; P. M. THORNTON, M.P. ; G. TOWNSEND WARNER; and the
Rev. J. E. C. WELLDON, Headmaster of Harrow School.

'Nothing could be more comprehensive or more satisfactory. The various topics suggested
by the fabric and history of the school are here admirably exhausted. Altogether, this is a
volume worthy of Harrow, and of which Harrow may well be proud.'—*Globe.*

'Not only Harrovians, past and present, but all who are interested in the history and inner
life of our great public schools, will welcome with gratitude this sumptuous and beautifully
illustrated volume.'—*World.*

'This volume is a model of its kind. Handsomely printed, profusely and charmingly
illustrated by the clever pencil of Mr. H. M. Marshall, and carefully edited by Harrovians in
love with their subject, it covers every side of Harrow history, traditions, and school life.'—
Daily Telegraph.

WINCHESTER COLLEGE. Illustrated by HERBERT MARSHALL.
With Contributions in Prose and Verse by OLD WYKEHAMISTS. Demy 4to., cloth,
25s. net. A few copies of the first edition, limited to 1,000 copies, are still to be
had.

GREAT PUBLIC SCHOOLS. ETON — HARROW — WINCHESTER —
RUGBY — WESTMINSTER — MARLBOROUGH — CHELTENHAM — HAILEYBURY —
CLIFTON—CHARTERHOUSE. With nearly 100 Illustrations by the best artists.
Popular Edition. One vol., large imperial 16mo., handsomely bound, 3s. 6d.

ART-BOOKS.

Old English Glasses.

An Account of Glass Drinking-Vessels in England from Early Times to the end of the Eighteenth Century. With Introductory Notices of Continental Glasses during the same period, Original Documents, etc. Dedicated by special permission to Her Majesty the Queen.

By ALBERT HARTSHORNE, Fellow of the Society of Antiquaries.

Illustrated by nearly 70 full-page Tinted or Coloured Plates in the best style of Lithography, and several hundred outline Illustrations in the text. Super royal 4to., Three Guineas net.

'It would be difficult to overestimate the value of this book to the collector. It would be but scanty praise to say that this book is a noble quarto. It is that and much more. With its beautiful type, ample margins and luxurious paper, its hundreds of illustrations, many of them whole-page lithographs of exceptional merit, it is an exceedingly fine example of typography, while its half-vellum binding is in admirable keeping with the care and taste which has been lavished upon the interior.'—*Standard.*

'An important contribution to the library of the serious antiquary and collector.'—*Times.*

'Mr. Hartshorne has been fortunate in finding a subject about which literally nothing was known, even by would-be connoisseurs, and he has risen to the height of his opportunity in a wonderful way. A fortnight ago the collector of old English Glasses was working in darkness . . . to-day such a collector has but to become the possessor of this sumptuous quarto and the whole sequence of glass-making, not only in England but on the Continent, from primitive times to the end of the last century, is before him. It is a monograph which must remain the one authority on English glasses.'—*Daily Chronicle.*

'No more sumptuous monograph on any artistic subject has been published this year than Mr. Hartshorne's volume.'—*Westminster Gazette.*

Clouston. THE CHIPPENDALE PERIOD IN ENGLISH FURNITURE. By K. WARREN CLOUSTON. With 200 Illustrations by the Author. Demy 4to., handsomely bound, One Guinea net.

Freshfield. THE EXPLORATION OF THE CAUCASUS. By DOUGLAS W. FRESHFIELD, lately President of the Alpine Club and Honorary Secretary of the Royal Geographical Society. With Contributions by H. W. HOLDER, J. G. COCKIN, H. WOOLLEY, M. DE DECHY, and Prof. BONNEY, D.Sc., F.R.S. Illustrated by 3 Panoramas, 74 full-page Photogravures, about 140 Illustrations in the text, chiefly from Photographs by VITTORIO SELLA, and 4 Original Maps, including the first authentic map of the Caucasus specially prepared from unpublished sources by Mr. FRESHFIELD. Two vols., large 4to., 600 pages, Three Guineas net.

Sparkes. WILD FLOWERS IN ART AND NATURE. By J. C. L. SPARKES, Principal of the National Art Training School, South Kensington, and F. W. BURBIDGE, Curator of the University Botanical Gardens, Dublin. With 21 full-page Coloured Plates by H. G. MOON. Royal 4to., handsomely bound gilt edges, 21s.

BIOGRAPHY AND HISTORY.

Talks with Mr. Gladstone.

By the Hon. L. A. TOLLEMACHE, Author of 'Benjamin Jowett,' 'Safe Studies,' etc.

With a Portrait of Mr. Gladstone. Large crown 8vo., cloth, 6s.

'An extremely agreeable volume, in the production of which Mr. Tollemache's rare talents for the difficult art which he practises claim a creditably large and important share.'—*Literature.*

'Reams have been written about Mr Gladstone within the last few weeks, but no sketch of him can approach in vividness and veracity such records as Mr. Tollemache preserves to us of his casual conversations upon everything under the sun '—*Daily Chronicle.*

'In these pages everybody, whatever his political opinions, will find much to interest him, for the " talks " cover an enormous amount of ground, from the human conception of time and place to the merits and demerits of " Dizzy " '—*Globe.*

'Mr. Tollemache is one of the wisest as well as most charming writers left to us. His " Talks with Mr Gladstone " is probably the best revelation of the inner mind of the great man that has yet been published '—*Liverpool Post.*

BY THE SAME AUTHOR.

BENJAMIN JOWETT, MASTER OF BALLIOL. A Personal Memoir. Third Edition, with portrait. Crown 8vo., cloth, 3s. 6d.

Many Memories of Many People.

By Mrs. M. C. SIMPSON (*née* NASSAU-SENIOR).

Fourth Edition. One vol., demy 8vo., 16s.

'A perfectly delightful book of gossip about men and women of historical importance. —*Truth.*

'Mrs. Simpson has something interesting to say about nearly every woman of note in the middle portion of the century. The whole book is good reading.'—*Athenæum.*

'This is a delightful book. A long succession of familiar names flit across Mrs. Simpson's pages, and she has something interesting or amusing to tell us about all of them.'—*Guardian.*

'There is not a dull page in it from first to last, and the present generation will have no excuse for ignorance of all that was best and most brilliant in the society of the middle of this century as long as a copy of " Many Memories " remains accessible.'—*Manchester Guardian.*

Letters of Mary Sibylla Holland.

Selected and Edited by her Son, BERNARD HOLLAND.

Second Edition. One vol., crown 8vo., 7s. 6d. net.

'A very charming collection of letters. Mrs Holland's letters not only make her readers love herself, they also make her correspondents living friends whose characters and lives we may well desire to know more of.'—*Guardian.*

'We feel sure that Mrs. Holland's letters will attract many readers by the force of that power of sympathy with which the writer was endowed It is as a reflection of human nature, with its almost startling depths of devotion and love, that we must judge them.'—*Spectator.*

'This book is one of a rare type in English literature. For its counterpart we must turn to French memoirs, to the touching story of " Reçit d'une Sœur," the Life of Madame Swetchine, or the Journals of Eugénie de Guérin.'—*Literature.*

A Memoir of Anne J. Clough, Principal of Newnham College, Cambridge.

By her Niece, BLANCHE A. CLOUGH.

One vol., 8vo., 12s. 6d.

'Her niece's work as editor has been done with admirable skill. Those who knew and loved Miss Clough will feel that not a word too much has been said, and that nothing has been left out which could help to make a rare and lovable personality more fully realized by those who would fain have known her better.'—*Guardian.*

'The memoir is thoroughly worthy of its subject, and must earn the gratitude of every reader. A complicated story has been clearly and simply told; a complicated character has been drawn with rare tact and sympathy.'—*Speaker.*

'Miss B. Clough has unfolded with singular discretion, clearness, and sympathy the early history of an important institution, and the personality of a great pioneer.'—*Spectator.*

Oman. A HISTORY OF ENGLAND. By CHARLES OMAN, Fellow of All Souls' College, and Lecturer in History at New College, Oxford; Author of ' Warwick the Kingmaker,' 'A History of Greece,' etc. Crown 8vo., cloth, 5s. Also in two parts, 3s. each. Part I., to A.D. 1603; Part II., from 1603 to present time. Also the PUPIL TEACHERS' EDITION in three parts. Division I., to 1307. 2s. Division II., 1307-1688. 2s. Division III., 1688-1885. 2s. 6d.

Pilkington. IN AN ETON PLAYING FIELD. The Adventures of some old Public School Boys in East London. By E. M. S. PILKINGTON. Fcap. 8vo., handsomely bound, 2s. 6d.

Ransome. THE BATTLES OF FREDERICK THE GREAT. Extracted from Carlyle's ' History of Frederick the Great,' and edited by CYRIL RANSOME, M.A., Professor of History at the Yorkshire College, Leeds. With numerous Illustrations by ADOLPH MENZEL. Square 8vo., 3s. 6d.

Reynolds. STUDIES ON MANY SUBJECTS. By the Rev. S. H. REYNOLDS. One vol., demy 8vo., 10s. 6d.

Rochefort. THE ADVENTURES OF MY LIFE. By HENRI ROCHE-FORT. Second Edition. Two vols., large crown 8vo., 25s.

Roebuck. THE AUTOBIOGRAPHY AND LETTERS of the Right Hon. JOHN ARTHUR ROEBUCK, Q.C., M.P. Edited by ROBERT EADON LEADER. With two Portraits. Demy 8vo., 16s.

Santley. STUDENT AND SINGER. The Reminiscences of CHARLES SANTLEY. New Edition. Crown 8vo., cloth, 6s.

Sherard. ALPHONSE DAUDET : a Biography and Critical Study. By R. H. SHERARD, Editor of ' The Memoirs of Baron Meneval,' etc. With Illustrations. Demy 8vo., 15s.

Recollections of Aubrey de Vere.

With Portrait. Third Edition. One vol., demy 8vo., 16s.

'The most genial, charming, and amusing volume of reminiscences of the year.'—*Truth.*

'It presents the portrait of a noble figure, a man of letters in a sense peculiar to a day now disappearing, a man of responsible leisure, of serious thought, of grave duties, of high mind.'—*Athenæum.*

'The recollections are likely to be widely read, for they will interest our readers.'—*Spectator.*

'There are brisk studies of character, quaint old stories, bits of exquisite descriptions, excellent jests, anecdotes of famous men.'—*Pall Mall Gazette.*

'These "Recollections" will appeal to many sympathies, personal, political, social, literary, and religious. As a Catholic the author enjoyed the intimate friendship of Cardinal Newman and Cardinal Manning, and these pages throw additional and interesting sidelights on the character and genius of each of these distinguished men. Few "Recollections" of late years, if any, furnish more pleasant reading than these.'—*Morning Post.*

Benson and **Tatham.** MEN OF MIGHT. Studies of Great Characters. By A. C. BENSON, M.A., and H. F. W. TATHAM, M.A., Assistant Masters at Eton College. Second Edition. Crown 8vo., cloth, 3s. 6d.

Boyle. THE RECOLLECTIONS OF THE DEAN OF SALISBURY. By the Very Rev. G. D. BOYLE, Dean of Salisbury. With Photogravure Portrait. One vol., demy 8vo., cloth, 16s.

Cawston and **Keane.** THE EARLY CHARTERED COMPANIES. A.D. 1296-1858. By GEORGE CAWSTON, barrister-at-law, and A. H. KEANE, F.R.G.S. With Frontispiece. Large crown 8vo., 10s. 6d.

Fowler. ECHOES OF OLD COUNTRY LIFE. By J. K. FOWLER, of Aylesbury. Second Edition. With numerous Illustrations. 8vo., 10s. 6d. Also a Large-paper Edition, of 200 copies only, 21s. net.

Hare. MARIA EDGEWORTH: her Life and Letters. Edited by AUGUSTUS J. C. HARE, Author of 'The Story of Two Noble Lives,' etc. With Portraits. Two vols., crown 8vo., 16s. net.

Lane. CHURCH AND REALM IN STUART TIMES. A Course of Ten Illustrated Lectures arranged to accompany a Series of 600 Lantern Illustrations. By the Rev. C. ARTHUR LANE, Author of 'Illustrated Notes on English Church History.' One vol., crown 8vo., 3s. 6d. net.

Lecky. THE POLITICAL VALUE OF HISTORY. By W. E. H. LECKY, D.C.L., LL.D. An Address delivered at the Midland Institute, reprinted with additions. Crown 8vo., cloth, 2s. 6d.

Le Fanu. SEVENTY YEARS OF IRISH LIFE. By the late W. R. LE FANU. New and Popular Edition. Crown 8vo., 6s.

Macdonald. THE MEMOIRS OF THE LATE SIR JOHN A. MACDONALD, G.C.B., First Prime Minister of Canada. Edited by JOSEPH POPE, his Private Secretary. With Portraits. Two vols., demy 8vo., 32s.

Twining. RECOLLECTIONS OF LIFE AND WORK. Being the Autobiography of LOUISA TWINING. One vol., 8vo., cloth, 15s.

TRAVEL AND ADVENTURE.

With the British Mission to Menelik, 1897.

By Count GLEICHEN, Captain Grenadier Guards, Intelligence Officer to the Mission.

With numerous Illustrations by the Author and a Map. Demy 8vo., 16s.

'Count Gleichen has produced a book which deserves to be read by everyone who cares for good tales of travel, for the record of a considerable English achievement, and for a first-hand account of an almost unknown and very interesting country.'—*Times.*

'A thoroughly entertaining book. Count Gleichen's book will be read by all who are interested in the greater affairs of the British Empire and the world.'—*Daily Chronicle.*

'To predict that the flash-light photograph of Abyssinia produced by Count Gleichen's instructive text and lively sketches will be as popular as it deserves is not faint praise.'—*Pall Mall Gazette.*

Bacon. BENIN, THE CITY OF BLOOD. An Account of the Benin Expedition. By R. H. BACON, Commander R.N. Demy 8vo., 7s. 6d.

Balfour. TWELVE HUNDRED MILES IN A WAGGON. A Narrative of a Journey in Cape Colony, the Transvaal, and the Chartered Company's Territories. By ALICE BLANCHE BALFOUR. With nearly forty original Illustrations from Sketches by the Author, and a Map. Demy 8vo., cloth, 16s.

Beynon. WITH KELLY TO CHITRAL. By Lieutenant W. G. L. BEYNON, D.S.O., 3rd Ghoorkha Rifles, Staff Officer to Colonel Kelly with the Relief Force. With Maps, Plans, and Illustrations. Second Edition. Demy 8vo., 7s. 6d.

Bottome. A SUNSHINE TRIP : GLIMPSES OF THE ORIENT. Extracts from Letters written by MARGARET BOTTOME. With Portrait, elegantly bound, 4s. 6d.

Bull. THE CRUISE OF THE 'ANTARCTIC' TO THE SOUTH POLAR REGIONS. By H. J. BULL, a member of the Expedition. With Frontispiece by W. L. WYLLIE, A.R.A., and numerous full-page Illustrations by W. G. BURN-MURDOCH. Demy 8vo., 15s.

Chapman. WILD NORWAY. By ABEL CHAPMAN, Author of 'Wild Spain.' With Illustrations by CHARLES WHYMPER. Demy 8vo., 16s.

Colvile. THE LAND OF THE NILE SPRINGS. By Colonel Sir HENRY COLVILE, K.C.M.G., C.B., recently British Commissioner in Uganda. With Photogravure Frontispiece, 16 full-page Illustrations and two Maps. Demy 8vo., 16s.

Gordon. PERSIA REVISITED. With Remarks on H.I.M. Mozuffer-ed-Din Shah, and the Present Situation in Persia (1896). By General Sir T. E. GORDON, K.C.I.E., C.B., C.S.I. Formerly Military Attaché and Oriental Secretary to the British Legation at Teheran, Author of 'The Roof of the World,' etc. Demy 8vo., with full-page Illustrations, 10s. 6d.

Knight-Bruce. MEMORIES OF MASHONALAND. By the late Right Rev. Bishop KNIGHT-BRUCE, formerly Bishop of Mashonaland. 8vo., 10s. 6d.

Macdonald. SOLDIERING AND SURVEYING IN BRITISH EAST AFRICA. By Major J. R. MACDONALD, R.E. Fully Illustrated. Demy 8vo., 16s.

McNab. ON VELDT AND FARM, IN CAPE COLONY, BECHUANA-LAND, NATAL, AND THE TRANSVAAL. By FRANCES McNAB. With Map. Second Edition. Crown 8vo., 300 pages, 3s. 6d.

Fire and Sword in the Sudan.

By SLATIN PASHA. Translated and Edited by Colonel WINGATE, C.B., Chief of the Intelligence Department Egyptian Army.

A new, revised, and cheaper Edition of this famous work. Illustrated. Price 6s.

In this edition the book has been thoroughly revised by the authors, omitting certain matters of temporary interest, and making it as far as possible a standard work of permanent value for young and old. The striking illustrations by Mr. TALBOT KELLY have been retained.

Also the complete work. Demy 8vo., One Guinea.

Pike. THROUGH THE SUB-ARCTIC FOREST. A Record of a Canoe Journey for 4,000 miles, from Fort Wrangel to the Pelly Lakes, and down the Yukon to the Behring Sea. By WARBURTON PIKE, Author of 'The Barren Grounds of Canada.' With Illustrations by CHARLES WHYMPER, from Photographs taken by the Author, and a Map. Demy 8vo., 16s.

Pollok. FIFTY YEARS' REMINISCENCES OF INDIA. By Lieut.-Colonel POLLOK, Author of 'Sport in Burmah.' Illustrated by A. C. CORBOULD. Demy 8vo., 16s.

Portal. THE BRITISH MISSION TO UGANDA. By the late Sir GERALD PORTAL, K.C.M.G. Edited by RENNEL RODD, C.M.G. With an Introduction by the Right Honourable Lord CROMER, G.C.M.G. Illustrated from Photos taken during the Expedition by Colonel Rhodes. Demy 8vo., 21s.

Portal. MY MISSION TO ABYSSINIA. By the late Sir Gerald H. PORTAL, C.B. With Map and Illustrations. Demy 8vo., 15s.

Smith. THROUGH UNKNOWN AFRICAN COUNTRIES. By A. DONALDSON SMITH, M.D., F.R.G.S. With Illustrations by A. D. McCORMICK and CHARLES WHYMPER. Super royal 8vo., One Guinea net.

Stone. IN AND BEYOND THE HIMALAYAS: A RECORD OF SPORT AND TRAVEL. By S. J. STONE, late Deputy Inspector-General of the Punjab Police. With 16 full-page Illustrations by CHARLES WHYMPER. Demy 8vo., 16s.

AMERICAN SPORT AND TRAVEL.

These books, selected from the Catalogue of MESSRS. RAND MCNALLY & Co., the well-known publishers of Chicago, have been placed in MR. EDWARD ARNOLD'S hands under the impression that many British Travellers and Sportsmen may find them useful before starting on expeditions in the United States.

Aldrich. ARCTIC ALASKA AND SIBERIA. By HERBERT L. ALDRICH. Crown 8vo., cloth, 4s. 6d.

AMERICAN GAME FISHES. By various Writers. Cloth, 10s. 6d.

Higgins. NEW GUIDE TO THE PACIFIC COAST. By C. A. HIGGINS. Crown 8vo., cloth, 4s. 6d.

Leffingwell. THE ART OF WING-SHOOTING. By W. B. LEFFINGWELL. Crown 8vo., cloth, 4s. 6d.

Shields. CAMPING AND CAMP OUTFITS. By G. O. SHIELDS ('Coquina'). Crown 8vo., cloth, 5s.

Shields. THE AMERICAN BOOK OF THE DOG. By various Writers. Edited by G. O. Shields ('Coquina'). Cloth, 15s.

Thomas. SWEDEN AND THE SWEDES. By WILLIAM WIDGERY THOMAS, jun., United States Minister to Sweden and Norway. Cloth, 16s.

The Chase, the Turf, and the Road.

By NIMROD. Edited by the Right Hon. Sir HERBERT MAXWELL, Bart., M.P.

With a Photogravure Portrait of the Author by D. MACLISE, R.A., and with Coloured Photogravure and other Plates from the original Illustrations by ALKEN, and several reproductions of old Portraits.

Large 8vo., handsomely bound, 15s. Also a Large-Paper Edition, limited to 200 copies, Two Guineas net.

THE SPORTSMAN'S LIBRARY.

Edited by the Right Hon. Sir HERBERT MAXWELL, Bart., M.P.

A Re-issue, in handsome volumes, of certain rare and entertaining books on Sport, carefully selected by the Editor, and Illustrated by the best Sporting Artists of the day, and with Reproductions of old Plates.

Library Edition, 15s. a Volume. Large-Paper Edition, limited to 200 copies, Two Guineas a volume.

VOLUME I.

Smith. THE LIFE OF A FOX, AND THE DIARY OF A HUNTS-MAN. By THOMAS SMITH, Master of the Hambledon and Pytchley Hounds. With Illustrations by the Author, and Coloured Plates by G. H. JALLAND.

Sir RALPH PAYNE-GALWEY, Bart., writes: 'It is excellent and beautifully produced.'
'Is sure to appeal to everyone who has had, or is about to have, a chance of a run with the hounds, and those to whom an unkindly fate denies this boon will enjoy it for the joyous music of the hounds which it brings to relieve the winter of our discontent amid London fogs.'—*Pall Mall Gazette.*
'It will be a classic of fox-hunting till the end of time.'—*Yorkshire Post.*
'No hunting men should be without this book in their libraries.'—*World.*

VOLUME II.

Thornton. A SPORTING TOUR THROUGH THE NORTHERN PARTS OF ENGLAND AND GREAT PART OF THE HIGHLANDS OF SCOTLAND. By Colonel T. THORNTON, of Thornville Royal, in Yorkshire. With the Original Illustrations by GARRARD, and other Illustrations and Coloured Plates by G. E. LODGE.

'Sportsmen of all descriptions will gladly welcome the sumptuous new edition issued by Mr. Edward Arnold of Colonel T. Thornton's "Sporting Tour," which has long been a scarce book.'—*Daily News.*
'It is excellent reading for all interested in sport.'—*Black and White.*
'A handsome volume, effectively illustrated with coloured plates by G. E. Lodge, and with portraits and selections from the original illustrations, themselves characteristic of the art and sport of the time.'—*Times.*

VOLUME III.

Cosmopolite. THE SPORTSMAN IN IRELAND. By a COSMOPOLITE. With Coloured Plates and Black and White Drawings by P. CHENEVIX TRENCH and reproductions of the original Illustrations drawn by R. ALLEN, and engraved by W. WESTALL, A.R.A.

'This is a most readable and entertaining book.'—*Pall Mall Gazette.*
'As to the "get up" of the book we can only repeat what we said on the appearance of the first of the set, that the series consists of the most tasteful and charming volumes at present being issued by the English Press, and collectors of handsome books should find them not only an ornament to their shelves, but also a sound investment."

VOLUME IV.

Berkeley. REMINISCENCES OF A HUNTSMAN. By the Hon. GRANTLEY F. BERKELEY. With a Coloured Frontispiece and the original Illustrations by JOHN LEECH, and several Coloured Plates and other Illustrations by G. H. JALLAND.

'The latest addition to the sumptuous "Sportsman's Library" is here reproduced with all possible aid from the printer and binder, with illustrations from the pencils of Leech and G. H. Jalland.'—*Globe.*

'The Hon. Grantley F. Berkeley had one great quality of the *raconteur.* His self-revelations and displays of vanity are delightful.'—*Times.*

VOLUME V.

Scrope. THE ART OF DEERSTALKING. By WILLIAM SCROPE. With Frontispiece by EDWIN LANDSEER, and nine Photogravure Plates of the original Illustrations.

'With the fine illustrations by the Landseers and Scrope himself, this forms a most worthy number of a splendid series.'—*Pall Mall Gazette.*

'Among the works published in connection with field sports in Scotland, none probably have been more sought after than those of William Scrope, and although published more than fifty years ago, they are still as fresh as ever, full of pleasant anecdote, and valuable for the many practical hints which they convey to inexperienced sportsmen.'—*Field.*

VOLUME VI.

Nimrod. THE CHASE, THE TURF, AND THE ROAD. By NIMROD. (*See above.*)

'Sir Herbert Maxwell has performed a real service for all who care for sport in republishing Nimrod's admirable papers. The book is admirably printed and produced both in the matter of illustrations and of binding.'—*St. James's Gazette.*

'A thoroughly well got-up book.'—*World.*

VOLUME VII.

Scrope. DAYS AND NIGHTS OF SALMON FISHING. By WILLIAM SCROPE. (*See page 4.*)

A Mingled Yarn. The Autobiography of Edward Spencer Mott (NATHANIEL GUBBINS). Author of 'Cakes and Ale,' etc. One vol., large crown 8vo., 12s. 6d.

'It is most interesting reading, and gives you glimpses of many strange byways of life and of all sorts and conditions of men.'—*Truth.*

'Uncommonly good reading.'—*St. James's Gazette.*

'Lively anecdotes crop up, like poppies in the corn, wherever one looks into this most entertaining book.—*Referee.*

'A very readable autobiography.'—*Literary World.*

Custance. RIDING RECOLLECTIONS AND TURF STORIES. By HENRY CUSTANCE, three times winner of the Derby. One vol., crown 8vo., cloth, 2s. 6d.

Hall. FISH TAILS AND SOME TRUE ONES. By BRADNOCK HALL, Author of 'Rough Mischance.' With an original Etching by the Author, and welve full-page Illustrations by T. H. MCLACHLAN. Crown 8vo., 6s.

Maxwell. MEMORIES OF THE MONTHS: Leaves from a Field Naturalist's Note-Book. By the Right Hon. Sir HERBERT MAXWELL, Bart., M.P. Crown 8vo., with five Photogravure Illustrations, 6s.

GENERAL LITERATURE.

Style.

By WALTER RALEIGH, Professor of English Literature at University College, Liverpool, Author of 'Robert Louis Stevenson,' etc.

Third Edition. One vol., crown 8vo., 5s.

'Professor Raleigh has produced a finished masterpiece, where the men before him, masters as they were, gave us brilliant sketches or clever studies. His ingenuity of thought, restraint of expression, austerity of judgment, his prudent counsel and wise suggestion are worthy of all praise. A model treatise on a most difficult and important theme.'—*Pall Mall Gazette.*

'In our judgment Mr. Raleigh's volume on "Style" is an amazingly good and pre-eminently interesting and suggestive book. His whole treatment of his subject is vigorous, manly, and most sensible.'—*Speaker.*

'As brimful of discerning criticism and fruitful suggestion as it is throughout lively and inspiriting.'—*St. James's Gazette.*

'Mr. Raleigh's volume is the fruit of much reading and more thinking. It is informed by the true literary spirit; it is full of wisdom, inclining now and then to paradox; and it is gay with quaintnesses and unexpected epigrams.'—*Times.*

'A fascinating little volume.'—*Spectator.*

BY THE SAME AUTHOR.

ROBERT LOUIS STEVENSON. Second Edition. Crown 8vo., cloth, 2s. 6d.

Bell. KLEINES HAUSTHEATER. Fifteen Little Plays in German for Children. By Mrs. HUGH BELL. Crown 8vo., cloth, 2s.

Butler. SELECT ESSAYS OF SAINTE BEUVE. Chiefly bearing on English Literature. Translated by A. J. BUTLER, Translator of 'The Memoirs of Baron Marbot.' One vol., 8vo., cloth, 5s. net.

Collingwood. THORSTEIN OF THE MERE: a Saga of the Northmen in Lakeland. By W. G. COLLINGWOOD, Author of 'Life of John Ruskin,' etc. With Illustrations. Price 10s. 6d.

Cook. THE DEFENSE OF POESY, otherwise known as AN APOLOGY FOR POETRY. By Sir PHILIP SIDNEY. Edited by A. S. COOK, Professor of English Literature in Yale University. Crown 8vo., cloth, 4s. 6d.

Cook. A DEFENCE OF POETRY. By PERCY BYSSHE SHELLEY. Edited, with Notes and Introduction, by Professor A. S. COOK. Crown 8vo., cloth, 2s. 6d.

Davidson. A HANDBOOK TO DANTE. By GIOVANNI A. SCARTAZZINI. Translated from the Italian, with Notes and Additions, by THOMAS DAVIDSON, M.A. Crown 8vo., cloth, 6s.

Ellacombe. THE PLANT-LORE AND GARDEN-CRAFT OF SHAKESPEARE. By HENRY N. ELLACOMBE, M.A., Vicar of Bitton. Illustrated by Major E. B. RICKETTS. Large crown 8vo., 10s. 6d.

Fleming. THE ART OF READING AND SPEAKING. By the Rev. Canon FLEMING, Vicar of St. Michael's, Chester Square. Third Edition. Cloth, 3s. 6d.

Garnett. SELECTIONS IN ENGLISH PROSE FROM ELIZABETH TO VICTORIA. Chosen and arranged by JAMES M. GARNETT, M.A., LL.D. 700 pages, large crown 8vo., cloth, 7s. 6d.

Goschen. THE CULTIVATION AND USE OF IMAGINATION. By the Right Hon. GEORGE JOACHIM GOSCHEN. Crown 8vo., cloth, 2s. 6d.

Harrison. STUDIES IN EARLY VICTORIAN LITERATURE. By FREDERIC HARRISON, M.A., Author of 'The Choice of Books,' etc. New and Cheaper Edition. Large crown 8vo., cloth, 3s. 6d.

Rome : the Middle of the World.

By ALICE GARDNER, Lecturer in History at Newnham College; Author of 'Friends of the Olden Time,' etc.

With Illustrations and Map. Crown 8vo., 3s. 6d.

' Miss Gardner's book on the Emperor Julian reconciled many readers to a singularly interesting personality of which they had previously heard little beyond the opprobrium of " apostasy.' In her present volume she addresses a younger audience, but in treating of a much wider subject she displays the same grasp and scholarship. We fancy Miss Gardner knows what youthful patience and attention are, and her method of appealing to the imagination by a series of strongly-lined pictures will probably do more to make Roman history a living thing to children than serried dates and a philosophical argument of causes and effects.'—*Saturday Review.*

BY THE SAME AUTHOR.

FRIENDS OF THE OLDEN TIME. Second Edition. Illustrated. Square 8vo., 2s. 6d.

Herschell. THE BEGGARS OF PARIS. Translated from the French of M. Louis Paulian by Lady Herschell. Crown 8vo., 1s.

Kuhns. THE TREATMENT OF NATURE IN DANTE'S 'DIVINA COMMEDIA.' By L. Oscar Kuhns, Professor in Wesleyan University, Middleton, U.S.A. Crown 8vo., cloth, 5s.

Lang. LAMB'S ADVENTURES OF ULYSSES. With an Introduction by Andrew Lang. Square 8vo., cloth, 1s. 6d. Also the Prize Edition, gilt edges, 2s.

Schelling. BEN JONSON'S TIMBER. Edited by Professor F. E. Schelling. Crown 8vo., cloth, 4s.

Sichel. THE STORY OF TWO SALONS. Madame de Beaumont and the Suards. By Edith Sichel, Author of 'Worthington Junior.' With Illustrations. Large crown 8vo., cloth, 10s. 6d.

WORKS BY THE VERY REV. S. REYNOLDS HOLE,
Dean of Rochester.

MEMORIES OF DEAN HOLE. Crown 8vo. 6s.

MORE MEMORIES. Demy 8vo. 16s.

A LITTLE TOUR IN AMERICA. Demy 8vo. 16s.

A LITTLE TOUR IN IRELAND. Large crown 8vo. 6s.

A BOOK ABOUT ROSES. Crown 8vo. 3s. 6d. and 6s.

A BOOK ABOUT THE GARDEN. Crown 8vo. 3s. 6d.

ADDRESSES TO WORKING MEN. Crown 8vo. 5s.

FAITH WHICH WORKETH BY LOVE. Crown 8vo. 1s.

WORKS BY SIR ALFRED MILNER, K.C.B.,
Governor of Cape Colony and High Commissioner to South Africa.

ENGLAND IN EGYPT. Popular Edition. With Map, and full details of the British position and responsibilities. 7s. 6d.

ARNOLD TOYNBEE. A Reminiscence. Crown 8vo., paper, 1s.

BY CONSTANCE MAUD.

WAGNER'S HEROES. Parsifal—Tannhauser—Lohengrin—Hans Sachs Illustrated by H. Granville Fell. Third Edition. Crown 8vo., 5s.

WAGNER'S HEROINES. Brunhilda—Senta—Isolda. Illustrated by T. W. Maud. Crown 8vo., 5s.

POETRY.

Ballads of the Fleet.

By RENNEL RODD, C.B., C.M.G.

One vol., crown 8vo., cloth, 6s.

'Mr. Rodd's ballads as a whole reach a high level of achievement. They have much of Macaulay's "go," and something better than Macaulay's rhetoric.'—*Pall Mall Gazette.*
'The verse is full of colour and animation and fine feeling ; simple withal, and vigorous without noise or brag.'—*Daily Chronicle.*
'Many-sided in its charm, no less than in its appeal.'—*Standard.*

BY THE SAME AUTHOR.

FEDA, AND OTHER POEMS, CHIEFLY LYRICAL. With etched Frontispiece. Crown 8vo., cloth, 6s.

THE UNKNOWN MADONNA, AND OTHER POEMS. With Frontispiece by RICHMOND. Crown 8vo., cloth, 5s.

THE VIOLET CROWN, AND SONGS OF ENGLAND. With Photogravure Frontispiece. Crown 8vo., cloth, 5s.

THE CUSTOMS AND LORE OF MODERN GREECE. With seven full-page Illustrations. 8vo., cloth, 8s. 6d.

Bell. DIANA'S LOOKING-GLASS, AND OTHER POEMS. By the Rev. Canon BELL, D.D., Rector of Cheltenham, and Hon. Canon of Carlisle. Crown 8vo., cloth, 5s. net.

BY THE SAME AUTHOR.

POEMS OLD AND NEW. Cloth, 7s. 6d.

THE NAME ABOVE EVERY NAME, AND OTHER SERMONS. Cloth, 5s.

THE GOSPEL AND POWER OF GOD. Crown 8vo., cloth, 3s. 6d.

Collins. A TREASURY OF MINOR BRITISH POETRY. Selected and arranged, with Notes, by J. CHURTON COLLINS, M.A. Handsomely bound, crown 8vo., 7s. 6d.

Gummere. OLD ENGLISH BALLADS. Selected and Edited by FRANCIS B. GUMMERE, Professor of English in Haverford College, U.S.A. Crown 8vo., cloth, 5s. 6d.

BY HENRY N. HUDSON, LL.D.

THE LIFE, ART, AND CHARACTERS OF SHAKESPEARE. Two vols., large crown 8vo., cloth, 21s.

THE HARVARD EDITION OF SHAKESPEARE'S COMPLETE WORKS. In twenty vols., large crown 8vo., cloth, £6. Also in ten vols., £5.

Hunt. LEIGH HUNT'S 'WHAT IS POETRY?' An Answer to the Question, 'What is Poetry?' including Remarks on Versification. By LEIGH HUNT. Edited, with notes, by Professor A. S. COOK. Crown 8vo., cloth, 2s. 6d.

Schelling. A BOOK OF ELIZABETHAN LYRICS. Selected and Edited by F. E. SCHELLING, Professor of English Literature in the University of Pennsylvania. Crown 8vo., cloth, 5s. 6d.

Thayer. THE BEST ELIZABETHAN PLAYS. Edited, with an Introduction, by WILLIAM R. THAYER. 612 pages, large crown 8vo., cloth, 7s. 6d.

COUNTRY HOUSE.

Poultry-Keeping as an Industry for Farmers and Cottagers.

By EDWARD BROWN, F.L.S. Fully Illustrated by LUDLOW.

New and completely revised Edition. One vol., demy 4to., cloth, 6s.

'. . . We are glad to welcome the appearance of an excellent volume by Mr. Edward Brown. The author has acquired so solid a reputation in connection with this subject that any praise of his work is superfluous.'—*Morning Post.*

'Mr. Brown is one of our best-known and most capable experts, and he has here presented the fruits of his wide knowledge and experience in, perhaps, the most useful form they could have taken. . . . His book is, indeed, a thoroughly practical and trustworthy guide to poultry in health and disease ; and whether a dozen hens be kept or a hundred, it will be their owner's own fault if, with Mr. Brown's excellent manual at hand, they fail to derive profit from their stock.'—*St. James's Gazette.*

BY THE SAME AUTHOR.

PLEASURABLE POULTRY-KEEPING. Fully Illustrated. One vol., crown 8vo., cloth, 2s. 6d.

INDUSTRIAL POULTRY-KEEPING. Illustrated. Paper boards, 1s. A small handbook chiefly intended for cottagers and allotment-holders.

POULTRY FATTENING. Fully Illustrated. New Edition. Crown 8vo., 1s. 6d.

BY COLONEL KENNEY-HERBERT ('WYVERN').

COMMON-SENSE COOKERY: based on Modern English and Continental Principles, Worked out in Detail. Large crown 8vo., over 500 pp., 7s. 6d.

FIFTY BREAKFASTS : containing a great variety of New and Simple Recipes for Breakfast Dishes. Small 8vo., cloth, 2s. 6d.

FIFTY DINNERS. Small 8vo., cloth, 2s. 6d.

.FIFTY LUNCHES. Small 8vo., cloth, 2s. 6d.

Cunningham. THE DRAUGHTS POCKET MANUAL. By J. G. CUN-NINGHAM. An introduction to the Game in all its branches. Small 8vo., with numerous diagrams, 2s. 6d.

Ellacombe. IN A GLOUCESTERSHIRE GARDEN. By the Rev. H. N. ELLACOMBE, Vicar of Bitton, and Honorary Canon of Bristol. Author of 'Plant Lore and Garden Craft of Shakespeare.' With new Illustrations by Major E. B. RICKETTS. Second Edition. Crown 8vo., cloth, 6s.

Gossip. THE CHESS POCKET MANUAL. By G. H. D. GOSSIP. A Pocket Guide, with numerous Specimen Games and Illustrations. Small 8vo., 2s. 6d.

Holt. FANCY DRESSES DESCRIBED. By ARDERN HOLT. An Alphabetical Dictionary of Fancy Costumes. With full accounts of the Dresses. About 60 Illustrations by LILLIAN YOUNG. Many of them coloured. One vol., demy 8vo., 7s. 6d. net.

Shorland. CYCLING FOR HEALTH AND PLEASURE. By L. H. PORTER, Author of 'Wheels and Wheeling,' etc. Revised and edited by F. W. SHORLAND, Amateur Champion 1892-93-94. With numerous Illustrations, small 8vo., 2s. 6d.

White. PLEASURABLE BEE-KEEPING. By C. N. WHITE, Lecturer to the County Councils of Huntingdon, Cambridgeshire, etc. Fully illustrated. One vol., crown 8vo., cloth, 2s. 6d.

SCIENCE AND PHILOSOPHY.

The Chances of Death, and other Studies in Evolution.

By KARL PEARSON, F.R.S. Author of 'The Ethic of Free Thought,' etc.

In two vols., demy 8vo., with Illustrations, 25s. net.

CONTENTS OF VOL. I.—The Chances of Death—The Scientific Aspect of Monte Carlo Roulette—Reproductive Selection—Socialism and Natural Selection—Politics and Science—Reaction—Woman and Labour—Variation in Man aud Woman.

CONTENTS OF VOL. II.—Woman as Witch—Ashiepattle ; or, Hans seeks his Luck—Kindred Group Marriage—The German Passion Play—Index.

'We have pleasure in welcoming a new work of extreme scientific value and of deep popular interest.'—*Saturday Review.*
'All of these Essays are well worth reading.'—*Times.*
'These brilliant volumes contain the most satisfactory work that Professor Pearson has yet done.'—*Speaker.*

Burgess. POLITICAL SCIENCE AND COMPARATIVE CONSTITUTIONAL LAW. By JOHN W. BURGESS, Ph.D., LL.D., Dean of the University Faculty of Political Science in Columbia College, U.S.A. In two vols., demy 8vo., cloth, 25s.

Fawcett. THE RIDDLE OF THE UNIVERSE. Being an Attempt to determine the first principles of Metaphysics considered as an Inquiry into the Conditions and Import of Consciousness. By EDWARD DOUGLAS FAWCETT. One vol., demy 8vo., 14s.

Hopkins. THE RELIGIONS OF INDIA. By E. W. HOPKINS, Ph.D. (Leipzig), Professor of Sanskrit and Comparative Philology in Bryn Mawr College. One vol., demy 8vo., 8s. 6d. net.

Ladd. LOTZE'S PHILOSOPHICAL OUTLINES. Dictated Portions of the Latest Lectures (at Göttingen and Berlin) of Hermann Lotze. Translated and edited by GEORGE T. LADD, Professor of Philosophy in Yale College. About 180 pages in each volume. Crown 8vo., cloth, 4s. each. Vol. I. Metaphysics. Vol. II. Philosophy of Religion. Vol. III. Practical Philosophy. Vol. IV. Psychology. Vol. V. Æsthetics. Vol. VI. Logic.

THE JOURNAL OF MORPHOLOGY. Edited by C. O. WHITMAN, Professor of Biology in Clark University, U.S.A. Three numbers in a volume of 100 to 150 large 4to. pages, with numerous plates. Single numbers, 17s. 6d. ; subscription to the volume of three numbers, 45s. Vols. I. to XIV. can now be obtained.

Paget. WASTED RECORDS OF DISEASE. By CHARLES E. PAGET, Lecturer on Public Health in Owens College, Medical Officer of Health for Salford, etc. Crown 8vo., 2s. 6d.

Perry. CALCULUS FOR ENGINEERS. By Professor JOHN PERRY, F.R.S. Crown 8vo., 7s. 6d.

Shaw. A TEXT-BOOK OF NURSING FOR HOME AND HOSPITAL USE. By C. WEEKS SHAW. Revised and largely re-written by W. RADFORD, House Surgeon at the Poplar Hospital, under the supervision of Sir DYCE DUCKWORTH, M.D., F.R.C.P. Fully Illustrated, crown 8vo., 3s. 6d.

Young. A GENERAL ASTRONOMY. By CHARLES A. YOUNG, Professor of Astronomy in the College of New Jersey, Associate of the Royal Astronomical Society, Author of *The Sun*, etc. In one vol., 550 pages, with 250 Illustrations, and supplemented with the necessary tables. Royal 8vo., half morocco, 12s. 6d.

Suggestions for a Scheme of Old Age Pensions.

A reprint of a scheme submitted to the Old Age Pensions Committee with an Introductory chapter on the Report of that Committee.

By the Honourable LIONEL HOLLAND, M.P.

Crown 8vo., 1s. 6d.

'Mr. Lionel Holland's dissection of the Old Age Pensions Committee Report is an exceedingly able and incisive piece of writing.'—*Westminster Gazette.*

'Will be read with interest by all sorts of politicians '—*Saturday Review.*

'An admirable introduction to the subject '—*Guardian.*

'A trenchant criticism.'—*Manchester Guardian.*

'Practical and well-considered suggestions.'—*Scotsman.*

Arnold-Forster. ARMY LETTERS, 1897-98. By H. O. ARNOLD-FORSTER, M.P. Crown 8vo., 3s 6d.

PRACTICAL SCIENCE MANUALS.

GENERAL EDITOR : PROFESSOR RAPHAEL MELDOLA, F.R.S.

Steam Boilers.

By GEORGE HALLIDAY, late Demonstrator at the Finsbury Technical College.

With numerous Diagrams and Illustrations.

Crown 8vo , 400 pages, 5s.

'A very good treatise . . peculiarly adapted for the use of those who have not time or opportunity to go deeply into the literature of the subject We do not know of any book on boilers more likely to be of use to the student than this.'—*Engineer.*

'A useful introduction to standard works on the subject.'—*Electrician.*

'The best elementary book on boilers we have seen. . . . The more we examine the book the better we are pleased with it.'—*Electrical Engineer*

Electrical Traction.

By ERNEST WILSON, WH. Sc., M I.E E., Lecturer and Demonstrator in the Siemens Laboratory, King's College, London.

With numerous Diagrams and Illustrations.

Crown 8vo., 5s.

'A valuable and interesting exposition of the principles of the subject, and of the more prominent and instructive instances of their application to practical purposes. Rich as it is in descriptions both of machinery and of experiments, the book cannot but prove welcome and serviceable to students of a subject the educational literature of which is as yet far from extensive.'—*Scotsman.*

Dymond. AGRICULTURAL CHEMISTRY. By T. S. DYMOND, of the County Technical Laboratory, Chelmsford.

Boulger. WOOD. By Professor BOULGER, late Professor of Botany in the Royal Agricultural College, Cirencester. [*In preparation.*

FICTION.

The Mermaid of Inish-Uig.

By R. W. K. EDWARDS.

Crown 8vo., 3s. 6d.

'A book of singular freshness and originality.'—*Spectator.*

'"The Mermaid of Inish-Uig" has been written with a very rare and curious art. From first to last it has been clear that Mr. Edwards' aim has been to suggest the wonderful, the incredible, and he has been completely successful. The idea is excellent; still more excellent is the way in which it has been worked out. Those who have essayed the *genre* of the wonderful know that the chief difficulty lies in devising a background of sober fact, in the harmonizing of wild and improbable incidents with everyday life. To tell a tale of frank impossibility is comparatively easy. But it does not convince, and is seen at once to be a mere fantasy outside of life as we know it. Here, then, is the difficulty which Mr. Edwards has overcome with such curious success; his novel is a fantasy, and yet it is convincing; it is a part of real existence.'—*Literature.*

'It is written with skill and genuine feeling for the pathetic and picturesque elements of peasant life on the coastline of Donegal.'—*Athenæum.*

A Reputation for a Song.

By MAUD OXENDEN, Author of 'Interludes.'

Crown 8vo., 6s.

'There is plenty of variety in Miss Oxenden's new story, and the threads of a very interesting plot are cleverly held together.'—*World.*

'It is a capital piece of latter-day fiction, and is calculated to add to the reputation which Miss Oxenden made in "Interludes."'—*Scotsman.*

'The cleverness of the story, the neatness of the style, and the liveliness of the dialogue show that the author is one to be watched.'—*Pall Mall Gazette.*

The King with Two Faces.

By M. E. COLERIDGE.

Seventh Edition. One vol., crown 8vo., 6s.

'We despair of giving to those who have not read this beautiful romance an adequate impression of the delicacy and variety of its portraiture, the freshness, subtlety, and distinction of its dialogue, and the poignant interest excited in the fortunes of the leading *dramatis personæ.* In the whole range of contemporary fiction we know of no more picturesque Royal figure than that of Gustavus as he is limned by Miss Coleridge. Above all, the book has to a quite exceptional degree the quality of glamour. Fresh from its perusal, and still under the spell of its magic, we are fain to re-echo Schumann's historic greeting addressed to Chopin in a review of his earliest published pianoforte works, "Hats off, gentlemen! A genius."'—*Spectator.*

'One of the very rare novels which yield so much pleasure that it almost stifles criticism. Miss Coleridge's quality is that of perfectly original brilliancy in romantic narration. Her style is at once placid and spirited, full of colour without heaviness and luxury, correct, rapid, adequate, with no tedious research of "the word," or preciosity. Her imagination is wonderfully vivid; for scenes and moments, colour, form, atmosphere, are all felt and conveyed in her pictures, which are not too numerous, and are never tedious.'—*Times.*

'One of the cleverest historical novels of late years.'—*Literature.*

'This is one of the most remarkable stories that we have read for many a day. . . . Gustavus is throughout a magnificent figure. . . . It is a bold thing to say, but we hardly remember in fiction the figure of a king more finely drawn. . . We desire to welcome this fascinating book.'—*Westminster Gazette.*

'**Adalet.**' HADJIRA : A Turkish Love Story. By 'ADALET.' One vol., crown 8vo., cloth, 6s.

Adderley. STEPHEN REMARX. The Story of a Venture in Ethics. By the Hon. and Rev. JAMES ADDERLEY, formerly Head of the Oxford House and Christ Church Mission, Bethnal Green. Twenty-second Thousand. Small 8vo., elegantly bound, 3s. 6d. Also, in paper cover, 1s.

Adderley. PAUL MERCER. A Tale of Repentance among Millions. By the Hon. and Rev. JAMES ADDERLEY. Third Edition. One vol., crown 8vo., cloth, 3s. 6d.

Blatchford. TOMMY ATKINS. A Tale of the Ranks. By ROBERT BLATCHFORD, Author of 'A Son of the Forge,' 'Merrie England,' etc. New Edition. Crown 8vo., cloth 3s. 6d.

Charleton. NETHERDYKE. By R. J. CHARLETON. One vol., crown 8vo., 6s.

Cherbuliez. THE TUTOR'S SECRET. (Le Secret du Précepteur.) Translated from the French of VICTOR CHERBULIEZ. One vol., crown 8vo., cloth, 6s.

Cholmondeley. A DEVOTEE : An Episode in the Life of a Butterfly. By MARY CHOLMONDELEY, Author of 'Diana Tempest,' 'The Danvers Jewels,' etc. Crown 8vo., 3s. 6d

Clifford. LOVE-LETTERS OF A WORLDLY WOMAN. By Mrs. W. K. CLIFFORD, Author of 'Aunt Anne,' 'Mrs. Keith's Crime,' etc. One vol., crown 8vo., cloth, 2s. 6d.

Collingwood. THE BONDWOMAN. A Story of the Northmen in Lakeland. By W. G. COLLINGWOOD, Author of 'Thorstein of the Mere,' 'The Life and Work of John Ruskin, etc. Cloth, 16mo., 3s. 6d.

Crane. GEORGE'S MOTHER. By STEPHEN CRANE, Author of 'The Red Badge of Courage.' Cloth, 2s.

Dunmore. ORMISDAL. A Novel. By the EARL OF DUNMORE, F.R.G S., Author of 'The Pamirs.' One vol., crown 8vo., cloth, 6s.

Ford. ON THE THRESHOLD. By ISABELLA O. FORD, Author of 'Miss Blake of Monkshalton.' One vol., crown 8vo., 3s. 6d.

Gaunt. DAVE'S SWEETHEART. By MARY GAUNT. One vol., 8vo., cloth, 3s. 6d.

Hall. FISH TAILS AND SOME TRUE ONES. Crown 8vo., 6s.

Hutchinson. THAT FIDDLER FELLOW. A Tale of St. Andrews. By HORACE G. HUTCHINSON, Author of 'My Wife's Politics,' 'Golf,' 'Creatures of Circumstance,' etc. Crown 8vo., cloth, 2s. 6d.

Knutsford. THE MYSTERY OF THE RUE SOLY. Translated by Lady KNUTSFORD from the French of H. DE BALZAC. Crown 8vo., cloth, 3s. 6d.

Lighthall. THE FALSE CHEVALIER. (*See page 6.*)

McNulty. MISTHER O'RYAN. An Incident in the History of a Nation. By EDWARD McNULTY. Small 8vo., elegantly bound, 3s. 6d.

McNulty. SON OF A PEASANT. By EDWARD McNULTY. One vol., crown 8vo., 6s.

Montrésor. WORTH WHILE. By F. F. MONTRÉSOR, Author of 'Into the Highways and Hedges.' Crown 8vo., cloth, 2s. 6d.

Oxenden. INTERLUDES. By MAUD OXENDEN. Crown 8vo., 6s.

Pinsent. JOB HILDRED. By ELLEN F. PINSENT, Author of 'Jenny's Case.' One vol., crown 8vo., 6s.

Prescott. A MASK AND A MARTYR. By E. LIVINGSTON PRESCOTT, Author of 'Scarlet and Steel.' Cloth, 6s.

Spinner. A RELUCTANT EVANGELIST, and other Stories. By ALICE SPINNER, Author of 'Lucilla,' 'A Study in Colour,' etc. Crown 8vo., 6s.

Williams. THE BAYONET THAT CAME HOME. By N. WYNNE WILLIAMS. Crown 8vo., 3s. 6d.

BOOKS FOR THE YOUNG.

FIVE SHILLINGS EACH.

SNOW-SHOES AND SLEDGES. By KIRK MUNROE. Fully illustrated. Crown 8vo., cloth, 5s.

RICK DALE. By KIRK MUNROE. Fully illustrated. Crown 8vo., cloth, 5s.

ERIC THE ARCHER. By MAURICE H. HERVEY. With numerous full-page Illustrations. Handsomely bound, crown 8vo., 5s.

THE FUR SEAL'S TOOTH. By KIRK MUNROE. Fully illustrated. Crown 8vo., cloth, 5s.

HOW DICK AND MOLLY WENT ROUND THE WORLD. By M. H. CORNWALL LEGH. With numerous Illustrations. Foolscap 4to., cloth, 5s.

HOW DICK AND MOLLY SAW ENGLAND. By M. H. CORNWALL LEGH. With numerous Illustrations. Foolscap 4to., 5s.

DR. GILBERT'S DAUGHTERS. By MARGARET HARRIET MATHEWS. Illustrated by CHRIS. HAMMOND. Crown 8vo., cloth, 5s.

THE REEF OF GOLD. By MAURICE H. HERVEY. With numerous full-page Illustrations, handsomely bound. Gilt edges, 5s.

BAREROCK; or, The Island of Pearls. By HENRY NASH. With numerous Illustrations by LANCELOT SPEED. Large crown 8vo., handsomely bound, gilt edges, 5s.

WAGNER'S HEROES. By CONSTANCE MAUD. Illustrated by H. GRANVILLE FELL. Crown 8vo., 5s.

WAGNER'S HEROINES. By CONSTANCE MAUD. Illustrated by T. W. MAUD. Crown 8vo., 5s.

THREE SHILLINGS AND SIXPENCE EACH.

TALES FROM HANS ANDERSEN. With nearly 40 Original Illustrations by E. A. LEMANN. Small 4to., handsomely bound in cloth, 3s. 6d.

THE SNOW QUEEN, and other Tales. By HANS CHRISTIAN ANDERSEN. Beautifully illustrated by Miss E. A. LEMANN. Small 4to., handsomely bound, 3s. 6d.

HUNTERS THREE. By THOMAS W. KNOX, Author of 'The Boy Travellers,' etc. With numerous Illustrations. Crown 8vo., cloth, 3s. 6d.

THE SECRET OF THE DESERT. By E. D. FAWCETT. With numerous full-page Illustrations. Crown 8vo., cloth, 3s. 6d.

JOEL: A BOY OF GALILEE. By ANNIE FELLOWS JOHNSTON. With ten full-page Illustrations. Crown 8vo., cloth, 3s. 6d.

THE MUSHROOM CAVE. By EVELYN RAYMOND. With Illustrations. Crown 8vo., cloth, 3s. 6d.

THE DOUBLE EMPEROR. By W. LAIRD CLOWES, Author of 'The Great Peril,' etc. Illustrated. Crown 8vo., 3s. 6d.

SWALLOWED BY AN EARTHQUAKE. By E. D. FAWCETT. Illustrated. Crown 8vo., 3s. 6d.

HARTMANN THE ANARCHIST; or, The Doom of the Great City. By E. DOUGLAS FAWCETT. With sixteen full-page and numerous smaller Illustrations by F. T. JANE. Crown 8vo., cloth, 3s. 6d.

ANIMAL SKETCHES: a Popular Book of Natural History. By Professor C. LLOYD MORGAN, F.G.S. Crown 8vo., cloth, 3s. 6d.

THREE SHILLINGS EACH.

THE LOCAL SERIES. Full gilt sides, gilt edges.

The Story of Lancashire.	The Story of Wales.
The Story of Yorkshire.	The Story of Scotland.
The Story of the Midlands.	The Story of the West Country.
The Story of London. [In prep.	[In prep.

TWO SHILLINGS AND SIXPENCE EACH.

THE LOCAL SERIES. Handsomely bound, gilt top.

TWO SHILLINGS EACH.

THE CHILDREN'S FAVOURITE SERIES. A Charming Series of Juvenile Books, each plentifully Illustrated, and written in simple language to please young readers. Price 2s. each; or, gilt edges, 2s. 6d.

My Book of Wonders.	My Book of Perils.
My Book of Travel Stories.	My Book of Fairy Tales.
My Book of Adventures.	My Book of History Tales.
My Book of the Sea.	My Story Book of Animals.
My Book of Fables.	Rhymes for You and Me.
Deeds of Gold.	My Book of Inventions.
My Book of Heroism.	

ONE SHILLING AND SIXPENCE EACH.

THE CHILDREN'S HOUR SERIES.

All with Full-page Illustrations.

THE PALACE ON THE MOOR. By E. DAVENPORT ADAMS. 1s. 6d.

TOBY'S PROMISE. By A. M. HOPKINSON. 1s. 6d.

MASTER MAGNUS. By Mrs. E. M. Field. 1s. 6d.

MY DOG PLATO. By M. H. CORNWALL LEGH. 1s. 6d.

FRIENDS OF THE OLDEN TIME. By ALICE GARDNER, Lecturer in History at Newnham College. Cambridge. Second Edition. Illustrated. Square 8vo., 2s. 6d.

THE INTERNATIONAL EDUCATION SERIES.

THE INTELLECTUAL AND MORAL DEVELOPMENT OF THE CHILD. By GABRIEL CAMPAYRE. 6s.

TEACHING THE LANGUAGE-ARTS. Speech, Reading, Composition. By B. A. HINSDALE, Ph.D., LL.D., University of Michigan. 4s. 6d.

THE PSYCHOLOGY OF THE NUMBER, AND ITS APPLICATION TO METHODS OF TEACHING ARITHMETIC. By JAMES A. McLELLAN, A.M., and JOHN DEWEY, Ph.D. 6s.

THE SONGS AND MUSIC OF FROEBEL'S MOTHER PLAY. By SUSAN E. BLOW. 6s.

THE MOTTOES AND COMMENTARIES OF FROEBEL'S MOTHER PLAY. By SUSAN E. BLOW and H. R. ELIOT. 6s.

HOW TO STUDY AND TEACH HISTORY. By B. A. HINSDALE, Ph.D., LL.D. 6s.

FROEBEL'S PEDAGOGICS OF THE KINDERGARTEN; or, His Ideas concerning the Play and Playthings of the Child. Translated by J. JARVIS. Crown 8vo., cloth, 6s.

THE EDUCATION OF THE GREEK PEOPLE, AND ITS INFLUENCE ON CIVILIZATION. By THOMAS DAVIDSON. Crown 8vo., cloth, 6s.

SYSTEMATIC SCIENCE TEACHING. By EDWARD G. HOWE. Crown 8vo., cloth, 6s.

EVOLUTION OF THE PUBLIC SCHOOL SYSTEM IN MASSACHUSETTS. By GEORGE H. MARTIN. Crown 8vo., cloth, 6s.

THE INFANT MIND; or, Mental Development in the Child. Translated from the German of W. PREYER, Professor of Physiology in the University of Jena. Crown 8vo., cloth, 4s. 6d.

ENGLISH EDUCATION IN THE ELEMENTARY AND SECONDARY SCHOOLS. By ISAAC SHARPLESS, LL.D., President of Haverford College, U.S.A. Crown 8vo., cloth, 4s. 6d.

EMILE; or, A Treatise on Education. By JEAN JACQUES ROUSSEAU. Translated and Edited by W. H. PAYNE, Ph.D., LL.D., President of the Peabody Normal College, U.S.A. Crown 8vo., cloth, 6s.

EDUCATION FROM A NATIONAL STANDPOINT. Translated from the French of ALFRED FOUILLÉE by W. J. GREENSTREET, M.A., Head Master of the Marling School, Stroud. Crown 8vo., cloth, 7s. 6d.

THE MORAL INSTRUCTION OF CHILDREN. By FELIX ADLER, President of the Ethical Society of New York. Crown 8vo., cloth, 6s.

THE PHILOSOPHY OF EDUCATION. By JOHANN KARL ROSENKRANZ, Doctor of Theology and Professor of Philosophy at Königsberg. (Translated.) Crown 8vo., cloth, 6s.

A HISTORY OF EDUCATION. By Professor F. V. N. PAINTER. 6s.

THE VENTILATION AND WARMING OF SCHOOL BUILDINGS. With Plans and Diagrams. By GILBERT B. MORRISON. Crown 8vo., 4s. 6d.

FROEBEL'S 'EDUCATION OF MAN.' Translated by W. N. HAILMAN. Crown 8vo., 6s.

ELEMENTARY PSYCHOLOGY AND EDUCATION. By Dr. J. BALDWIN. Illustrated, crown 8vo., 6s.

THE SENSES AND THE WILL. Forming Part I. of 'The Mind of the Child.' By W. PREYER, Professor of Physiology in the University of Jena. (Translated.) Crown 8vo., 6s.

THE DEVELOPMENT OF THE INTELLECT. Forming Part II. of 'The Mind of the Child.' By Professor W. PREYER. (Translated.) Crown 8vo., 6s.

HOW TO STUDY GEOGRAPHY. By FRANCIS W. PARKER. 6s.

A HISTORY OF EDUCATION IN THE UNITED STATES. By RICHARD A. BOONE, Professor of Pedagogy in Indiana University. Crown 8vo., 6s.

EUROPEAN SCHOOLS; or, What I Saw in the Schools of Germany, France, Austria, and Switzerland. By L. R. KLEMM, Ph.D. With numerous Illustrations. Crown 8vo., 8s. 6d.

PRACTICAL HINTS FOR TEACHERS. By GEORGE HOWLAND, Superintendent of the Chicago Schools. Crown 8vo., 4s. 6d.

SCHOOL SUPERVISION. By J. L. PICKARD. 4s. 6d.

HIGHER EDUCATION OF WOMEN IN EUROPE. By HELENE LANGE. 4s. 6d.

HERBART'S TEXT-BOOK IN PSYCHOLOGY. By M. K. SMITH. 4s. 6d.

PSYCHOLOGY APPLIED TO THE ART OF TEACHING. By Dr. J. BALDWIN. 6s.

THE SCHOOL SYSTEM OF ONTARIO. By the Hon. GEORGE W. ROSS, LL.D. 4s. 6d.

FROEBEL'S EDUCATIONAL LAWS FOR ALL TEACHERS. By JAMES L. HUGHES. 6s.

SCHOOL MANAGEMENT AND SCHOOL METHODS. By Dr. J. BALDWIN. 6s.

THE NATIONAL REVIEW.

Edited by L. J. MAXSE.

Price Half-a-crown Monthly.

The 'National Review' is the leading Unionist and Conservative Review in Great Britain. Since it passed into the control and editorship of Mr. Leo Maxse, most of the leaders of the Unionist Party have contributed to its pages, including the Marquis of Salisbury, Mr. Arthur Balfour, Mr. J. Chamberlain, and Lord George Hamilton. The episodes of the month, which give a masterly review of the important events of the preceding month, form a valuable feature of the Review, which now occupies a unique position among monthly periodicals.

PUBLICATIONS OF THE INDIA OFFICE AND OF THE GOVERNMENT OF INDIA.

Mr. EDWARD ARNOLD, having been appointed Publisher to the Secretary of State for India in Council, has now on sale the above publications at 37 Bedford Street, Strand and is prepared to supply full information concerning them on application.

INDIAN GOVERNMENT MAPS.

Any of the Maps in this magnificent series can now be obtained at the shortest notice from Mr. EDWARD ARNOLD, Publisher to the India Office.

SYMBOLIC EDUCATION. By SUSAN E. BLOW. 6s.

HERBART'S A B C OF SENSE-PERCEPTION AND INTRODUCTORY WORKS. By W. J. ECKOFF, Ph.D., Pd.D. 6s.

PSYCHOLOGIC FOUNDATIONS OF EDUCATION. By W. T. HARRIS, M.A., United States Commissioner of Education. 6s.

THE PRINCIPLES AND PRACTICE OF TEACHING. By J. JOHONNOT. 6s.

BIBLIOGRAPHY OF EDUCATION. By W. S. MUNROE. 8s. 6d.

THE STUDY OF THE CHILD. By A. R. TAYLOR. 6s.

The following Catalogues of Mr. Edward Arnold's Publications will be sent post free on application:

CATALOGUE OF WORKS OF GENERAL LITERATURE.

GENERAL CATALOGUE OF EDUCATIONAL WORKS, including the principal publications of Messrs. Ginn and Company, Educational Publishers, of Boston and New York.

CATALOGUE OF WORKS FOR USE IN ELEMENTARY SCHOOLS.

ILLUSTRATED LIST OF BOOKS FOR PRESENTS AND PRIZES.

Index to Authors.

Index to Authors—*continued.*

Classified Index.